MARYLAND
A History

MARYLAND

A History

SECOND EDITION

Suzanne Ellery Chapelle
Professor Emerita of History
Morgan State University

Jean B. Russo
Maryland State Archives

Jean H. Baker
Dean R. Esslinger
Edward C. Papenfuse
Constance B. Schulz
Gregory A. Stiverson

JOHNS HOPKINS UNIVERSITY PRESS
Baltimore

© 1986, 2018 Johns Hopkins University Press
All rights reserved. Published 2018
Printed in Canada on acid-free paper
9 8 7 6 5 4 3 2 1

This book was first published in 1986 as *Maryland: A History of Its People*

Johns Hopkins University Press
2715 North Charles Street
Baltimore, Maryland 21218-4363
www.press.jhu.edu

Library of Congress Cataloging-in-Publication Data
Names: Chapelle, Suzanne Ellery, 1942– | Russo, Jean Burrell
Title: Maryland : a history / Suzanne Ellery Chapelle, Jean B. Russo, et al.
Description: Second edition. | Baltimore : Johns Hopkins University Press, 2018. | Includes bibliographical references and index.
Identifiers: LCCN 2017056667 | ISBN 9781421426228 (pbk. : alk. paper) | ISBN 9781421426235 (electronic) | ISBN 1421426226 (pbk. : alk. paper) | ISBN 1421426234 (electronic)
Subjects: LCSH: Maryland—History.
Classification: LCC F181 .M265 2018 | DDC 975.2—dc23
LC record available at https://lccn.loc.gov/2017056667

A catalog record for this book is available from the British Library.

All maps were created by Bill Nelson.

Special discounts are available for bulk purchases of this book. For more information, please contact Special Sales at 410-516-6936 or specialsales@press.jhu.edu.

Johns Hopkins University Press uses environmentally friendly book materials, including recycled text paper that is composed of at least 30 percent post-consumer waste, whenever possible.

Contents

List of Maps, Graphs, and Tables   *vii*

A Word to Readers   *ix*

one   Maryland's Formative Years, 1634–1763   *3*

two   The Revolutionary War Era, 1763–1789   *43*

three   Maryland in the New Nation, 1789–1850   *85*

four   Maryland in Peace and War, 1850–1870   *127*

five   A New Century, 1870–1917   *169*

six   Prosperity, Depression, and War, 1917–1945   *215*

seven   Maryland after World War II, 1945–1985   *259*

eight   Maryland, 1985–2015   *301*

Appendix A: Supplementary Maps   *343*

Appendix B: Governors of Maryland   *348*

Glossary   *351*

Further Reading   *355*

Index   *361*

Maps, Graphs, and Tables

■ Maps

Major Native American Groups in Maryland, 1500–1650   *9*
Major Land Battles of the American Revolution involving Maryland Troops,
     1775–1781   *63*
The War of 1812 in the Chesapeake Region, 1813–1814   *92*
The Battle of Baltimore, September 12–14, 1814   *95*
Agriculture and Industry in Maryland, 1840   *100*
Maryland Transportation in 1840: Railroads, Canals, and Rivers   *109*
Support for Pro-Union Gubernatorial Candidate Augustus Bradford,
     1861   *153*
Civil War: Major Battles and Skirmishes and Raids in the Maryland Region,
     1861–1865   *157*
Maryland Transportation in 1890: Railroads, Canals, and Rivers   *172*
Major Coal Deposits in Maryland   *197*
State Primary Highway System, 1978   *272*
Major Drainage Basins of the Chesapeake Bay System   *293*
Political Map of Maryland, 2015   *344*
Geographic Regions of Maryland   *345*
Progress of Settlement in Maryland, 1631–1800   *346*
Evolution of Maryland Counties, 1755, 1860, and 2015   *347*

■ Graphs

Structure of Maryland Society, 1755   *35*
Percentage of the Total Value of Maryland Industrial Production
     in Baltimore, 1860–1910   *170*

Maryland Oyster Harvest, 1840–1980   *199*

Age-Sex Pyramid of the Maryland Population, 1980   *261*

Types of Employment in Maryland as a Percentage of the Total Labor Force, 1950 and 1980   *277*

■ Tables

3.1. Maryland's Population by Region, 1790 and 1850   *98*

4.1. Leading Free Black Occupations in Baltimore, 1850 and 1860   *136*

4.2. Maryland Population by Color and Condition, 1860   *141*

5.1. Maryland Population Growth, 1870–1920   *174*

5.2. Population of Selected Maryland Towns, 1870, 1890, and 1910   *174*

5.3. Place of Origin of Foreign-born Maryland Residents   *176*

8.1. Maryland Population Growth, 1980–2010   *301*

8.2. Income Inequality in Maryland by Household, 1980–2010   *316*

8.3. Racial and Ethnic Origins of Maryland Residents, 1990–2010   *318*

8.4. Population of Maryland's Largest Cities, 1990–2010   *326*

A Word to Readers

Native Americans inhabited the land in the Chesapeake Bay region for many centuries before the first Europeans and Africans arrived in the early 1600s. Today's Marylanders have roots all over the world: in North America, Europe, Africa, the Caribbean, Asia, Central America, South America, and the Pacific. Over the years, the early Marylanders and those who followed worked in agriculture, industry, and later technology. This book is a history of what these people accomplished on the fertile land and precious water that Marylanders call home and of the ways in which people worked together to build modern Maryland. It is a history of the important ideas that shaped the state and its cultural heritage. The book recounts the many struggles as well as both achievements and failures throughout the centuries.

This history of Maryland was written for use by the general public, students, and scholars at the request of Johns Hopkins University Press, incorporating the newest research and resources. The book covers the years from the 1600s to Governor Lawrence J. Hogan Jr.'s inauguration in 2015. The authors are all recognized scholars with PhDs from leading universities with experience in research, writing, and teaching. They are experts in Maryland history and the periods about which they have written.

At the end of the book, you will find resources for further reading in both general Maryland history and specific time periods. The book is extensively illustrated with photographs and maps. We commissioned additional material to make statistics and other factual information clear and easy to follow.

We owe a great debt of thanks to the Maryland Historical Society and the Maryland State Archives for maintaining extensive resources and for their help in providing materials for this history. Their collections of written and visual material are essential to the work of historians of Maryland. We thank many members of the staff of Johns Hopkins University Press for their thoroughgoing work on this book.

Suzanne Ellery Chapelle
Jean B. Russo

MARYLAND
A History

Maryland		The Nation and the World
Spanish visit the Chesapeake Bay	1524	
	1587–1604	War between Spain and England
	1607	Virginia settled
John Smith explores the Bay	1608	
	1612	New York settled
	1619	First Africans sold in Virginia
	1620	Plymouth Colony settled
	1630	Massachusetts Bay Colony settled
Trading post established at Kent Island	1631	
George Calvert dies Charter granted to Cecilius Calvert	1632	
Ark and *Dove* arrive at St. Clement's Island	1634	
	1642	English Civil War begins
Ingle's Rebellion	1645–1646	
Act Concerning Religion	1649	Charles I executed
	1660	English monarchy restored
	1676	Bacon's rebellion in Virginia
	1681	Pennsylvania granted to William Penn
	1688	Glorious Revolution in England
Proprietor overthrown	1689	
	1689–1697	King William's War
Maryland becomes a royal colony	1691	
Anglican Church established	1692	
	1693	College of William and Mary founded
Capital moves to Annapolis	1695	
King William's School founded	1696	
	1702–1713	Queen Anne's War
Proprietorship restored	1715	
First issue of *Maryland Gazette* published	1727	
Baltimore Town founded	1729	
Paper money legislation enacted	1733	
Continuous publication of *Maryland Gazette* begins	1745	
Tobacco Inspection Act	1747	
Maryland census taken	1755	
	1756–1763	Seven Years' War (French and Indian War)

chapter one

Maryland's Formative Years

1634–1763

In 1634, two ships carrying a small group of mostly male settlers dropped anchor off the shores of the new colony of Maryland. The passengers had spent three months crossing the wide and sometimes turbulent Atlantic Ocean before sailing into the Chesapeake Bay looking for a suitable place to settle.

The landscape confronting the pioneers bore no resemblance to that of their native country. They saw no houses, only Native American dwellings. They found no stores or markets, craftsmen's shops, churches, schools, or courts. They had no newspapers, books, music, inns, or theaters. Before any of these could be created, basic necessities of food and shelter had to be acquired.

Explorer John Smith had written of the area in 1608, "Heaven and earth never agreed better to frame a place for man's habitation." The wealth of woodlands and fields, fertile soil and plentiful wildlife, and water's bounty held great promise for these adventurers in their new life in the American wilderness. Some would achieve notable success but others would not long survive their arrival in the new colony.

Many of these and later immigrants died soon after their arrival. Others were held in bondage with no chance to work for themselves. The search for greater opportunity led many people to move on, so that by the end of the colonial period settlement had spread across the colony.

Maryland's early history tells the story of how colonists adapted English society and government to their new environment. They built and nurtured institutions to provide a framework of stability and order. As other men and women joined the early settlers and their descendants, together these people built a new society in the Maryland colony.

The Founding of Maryland

The founding of the Maryland colony was not an isolated or unique event. It took place during a period when many European countries spent much effort and money to establish New World colonies.

European Exploration and Colonization

The 1400s and 1500s were an age of European exploration, overseas trade, and colonial settlement. Portuguese sailors ventured along the African coast and on to India. Dutch and English traders formed companies to follow the Portuguese lead. Christopher Columbus, an Italian, explored for the Spanish Crown. After Columbus made landfall in the Americas in 1492, Spaniards sailed to the New World to conquer its inhabitants and settle there. Frenchmen and Englishmen fished the waters off Newfoundland in the sixteenth century, while French fur traders built trading posts in North America. In the late 1500s, Englishmen failed in several attempts to settle colonies in Newfoundland and at Roanoke.

War between Spain and England interrupted colonization efforts but, after 1604, overseas trade and colonies again commanded attention. Englishmen formed groups to promote settlement in Ireland, Newfoundland, Virginia, New England, and elsewhere. Investors included court officials, merchants, and gentlemen, among them George Calvert. As a secretary of state in the court of King James I, Calvert had many opportunities to engage in colonization efforts, including one in Newfoundland, where he began a settlement in 1621.

Calvert resigned his offices in 1625 over issues of foreign policy, but James I rewarded his years of service with the title Baron of Baltimore in the Irish nobility. Calvert now had a title and would be known as Lord Baltimore, but he had lost an important source of income, so he looked to North America for new opportunities. Calvert traveled to Newfoundland in 1627 but, finding its climate too harsh, decided to look farther south for the site of a permanent colony.

■ Queen Henrietta Maria, wife of King Charles I of England, in whose honor George Calvert selected "Terra Mariae" (Mary land) as the name of his new colony. Collection of the Maryland State Archives, MSA SC 1545-1100.

A Charter for Maryland

George Calvert arrived in Virginia in October 1629, but he was not well received there. He returned to England, where he obtained land north of Virginia from King Charles I. A formal charter, or grant, would define his powers as the territory's proprietor, or owner. The chartering process begun by Calvert did not become final until shortly after his death, making his son Cecilius, now Lord Baltimore, Maryland's first proprietor. The king's grant gave Lord Baltimore and his heirs power in Maryland equal to the king's own power in England.

The proprietor could defend his province by raising an army and waging war against his enemies. He could encourage trade and economic growth by founding towns, building forts, establishing ports, and imposing customs duties. He could establish courts; appoint a governor, justices, and other officials; and enact laws with the agreement of the colony's freemen. He could grant land to settlers, who would hold it as his subjects. He could give the title of lord to those holding large grants, or manors, and authorize them to hold courts to govern their tenants. The charter gave Lord Baltimore a vast territory and broad powers. In return, he owed the king only two Native American arrows each year and one-fifth of all precious metals found in Maryland.

Terms of Settlement

Cecilius Calvert promised every settler who joined his colony 100 acres of land for himself and 50 or 100 more for every person he brought with him. Anyone transporting 5 or more men received at least 1,000 acres of land for every 5 persons of working age. Large investors also received 10 acres of land in the city being planned as the colony's capital. This system of "head rights" governed land distribution until 1683; after that date, prospective owners had to buy land. Calvert also offered settlers shares in a company to control fur trading with Native American groups. Profits from furs, he hoped, would provide income for the investors, including himself, while the colony's land was being developed.

■ Cecilius Calvert, the second Lord Baltimore, portrayed here with his grandson and a liveried African page, completed the chartering of the Maryland colony after his father's death. Calvert holds Augustine Herrman's map of Maryland that he commissioned, c. 1660. Courtesy of the Enoch Pratt Free Library.

The inducements to encourage settlers had two purposes. First, they would provide Lord Baltimore with steady income from rents collected on land granted to investors and from duties on exports of furs and agricultural products. Second, they would form a basis for political leadership and organization. Because large investors depended on Lord Baltimore for their grants of land, offices, and titles, he expected their loyalty in return. Cecilius Calvert also expected ordinary settlers to follow the leadership of these wealthy men. In this way, an orderly and obedient colony would grow and prosper for the benefit of both settlers and proprietor.

Religious Toleration

The Maryland settlement was also intended as a refuge for Roman Catholics. George Calvert, who had been raised as a Roman Catholic, and his heir Cecilius did not seek to establish Maryland as a Roman Catholic colony. Rather, they

The Founding of Maryland

The Voyage of the *Ark*

The first colonists traveled to Maryland on the *Ark*. Their fifteen-week voyage was cramped and uncomfortable, like all seventeenth-century ocean travel. Only the gentlemen might have shared cabins. Servants spent most of the voyage confined to the lower deck, where they slept, ate, and lived together without any privacy. Each day they faced water-soaked bedding, monotonous food, fear of pirates, and seasickness.

Early in the voyage, two storms broke the routine. During the second, colonists feared "imminent death all . . . night." Ships traveling to the Chesapeake Bay sailed south to Africa before turning west across the Atlantic. Calm weather during the long ocean trip could also be fatal, as food and water ran out if a ship remained becalmed too long.

Passengers on the *Ark*, instead, suffered from excess drink when they celebrated Christmas Day. Some consumed too much wine and thirty fell ill with a fever that killed twelve.

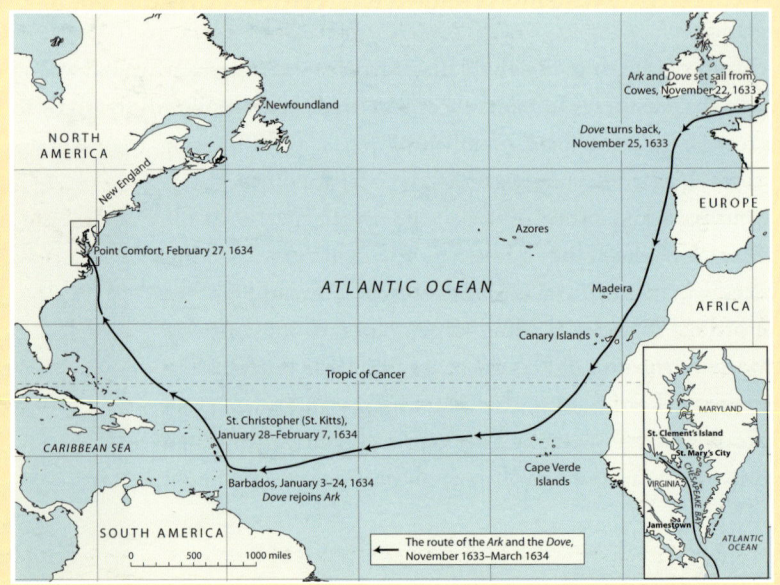

The *Ark* and the smaller *Dove* carried provisions for the voyage and also supplies settlers needed once they arrived. Colonists were advised to bring food such as coarsely ground grain, peas, oil, vinegar, salt, sugar, and spices; clothing and bedding; muskets, powder, and shot; hoes, axes, and other tools; iron cooking pots; and seeds for their crops. They carried cloth, clothing, wine, sugar, raisins, and honey to trade for cows, pigs, and horses in Virginia. Whatever they did not bring or trade for, they would do without until the next ship arrived from England.

■ A depiction of the *Ark* and the *Dove*, the two ships that carried the first settlers to Maryland in the winter of 1633–1634. Courtesy of the Maryland Historical Society, MS 1955.44.1.

wanted to enable persons of all Christian denominations to practice their religion in private, without persecution, discrimination, or exclusion from political life. Catholics as well as Protestants could vote and hold office, something Catholics could not do in England. The Calverts hoped that in Maryland Catholics could worship without suffering any penalties.

George Calvert did not live to see his plans carried out. He died in April 1632, leaving his eldest son Cecilius to complete the chartering of the Maryland colony that June. The charter gave Cecilius Calvert the land between the Potomac and Delaware Rivers, as far north as the fortieth parallel and as far west as the Potomac's headwaters. The grant included only "parts of America not yet cultivated or planted," thus excluding the lower Eastern Shore, already settled by Virginians. A trading post at Kent Island in the Chesapeake Bay remained within Maryland's boundaries, to be a source of dispute for many years.

The First Settlers

Once Cecilius Calvert had his charter, he needed to find men to settle his colony. He succeeded in attracting a group of seventeen gentlemen, mostly younger sons of wealthy Roman Catholic families, as investors. The Jesuits, an order of Catholic priests, also made a major investment in the first voyage. In all, nearly 150 colonists set sail from England in November 1633 on 2 small sailing ships, the *Ark* and the *Dove*. Most of the passengers were indentured servants, nearly all of them young, male, and Protestant. The few women on board and any children would also have been indentured servants. These passengers signed a contract, or indenture, agreeing to work for an investor for a set term of years in return for free passage. Once the individual completed the term of servitude, he or she would be free, with the right to acquire land.

The two ships made stops in the West Indies and Virginia, where they bought needed supplies, including livestock, and then, in early March, after a voyage of more than three months, sailed up the Chesapeake Bay to the Potomac River. Here the passengers hoped to locate a suitable site for their settlement.

Two Passengers on the *Ark*

Mathias de Sousa arrived in Maryland on the *Ark* in 1634. Of mixed African and European descent, he came as a servant indentured to one of the Jesuit priests. Like other indentured servants, de Sousa later became a freeman, after which he captained a vessel engaged in trade with Native Americans and exercised his political right to attend the General Assembly in 1642.

At age 54, **Father Andrew White**, an English-born Jesuit priest, was probably the *Ark*'s oldest passenger. His "Brief Relation of the Voyage unto Maryland" is the most vivid extant account of the journey and of the colony's founding. White conducted missionary work among local Native Americans, learning their language, compiling a dictionary and a grammar, and writing a catechism for instructing Native American converts. In 1645, a Protestant rebel captured White and took him back to England in chains.

■ The New World

When the colonists on the *Ark* and the *Dove* sailed through the mouth of the Bay at Capes Henry and Charles, they encountered one of the most distinctive features of Maryland's geography. The Chesapeake Bay, the submerged mouth of the Susquehanna River, is the largest inlet on the East Coast. Maryland's portion of the Bay stretches 195 miles in length and includes an area of nearly 2,000 square miles. By comparison, the colony contained about 10,000 square miles (or 7 million acres) of land.

The Geography of Maryland

Numerous rivers drain into the Bay on both shores, forming large necks of land on the Western Shore and many smaller fingers of land on the eastern side. More than 150 rivers, creeks, and branches give Maryland a tidal shoreline of about 3,000 miles, roughly equal to the distance between Maryland and England. Rivers and creeks served as roads for early settlers, allowing them to trade from their own wharves, or landings, directly with England.

Maryland has three major geographic regions. The land on both sides of the Bay forms the coastal plain, or Tidewater region, a low, flat area with light, sandy soils, swamps, and tidal marshes. West of the coastal plain lies the Piedmont plateau, extending from the fall line, or first series of rapids on the rivers, to the Blue Ridge. Rolling hills and fertile soil mark this area. Finally, the Appalachian region is a forested, mountainous area covering the western portion of the state from the Piedmont plateau to Garrett County.

The land supported a variety of plants and animals. Virgin forests of oak, walnut, pine, cedar, poplar, hickory, maple, black gum, elm, ash, and chestnut trees covered the colony. Strawberries and raspberries, sorrel and other herbs, grape vines and fruit trees, grew in abundance. Bears, elk, deer, wolves, and wildcats roamed the woods. Squirrels, rabbits, wild turkeys, foxes, and other small game animals were plentiful. Flocks of geese, ducks, cranes, and wild pigeons filled the sky. Terrapin, crabs, and oysters were there for the taking; shad, herring, bass, and many other species of fish swam in the waters of the Bay and its tributaries.

Native Americans in Maryland

Long before the colonists arrived, Native Americans had been living around the Chesapeake Bay and enjoying the region's natural abundance. The first Native Americans reached Maryland at least 12,000 years ago, during the glacial period. These semi-nomadic people, known as Paleo-Indians, moved through the area hunting large game animals like mammoths, great bison, and caribou that could survive the cold climate.

When the climate warmed and the glaciers melted, about ten thousand years ago, big game animals died out. Forests replaced grasslands, and smaller game like deer became the main sources of food and clothing. During this period, known as the Archaic, Native Americans gathered into more permanent villages and depended more heavily on fish and wild plants for their food.

About 1000 BCE, the Woodland period began. Agriculture now played a major role in the Native American food supply, with corn becoming the most important crop. Native American groups also raised beans, peas, squash, sun-

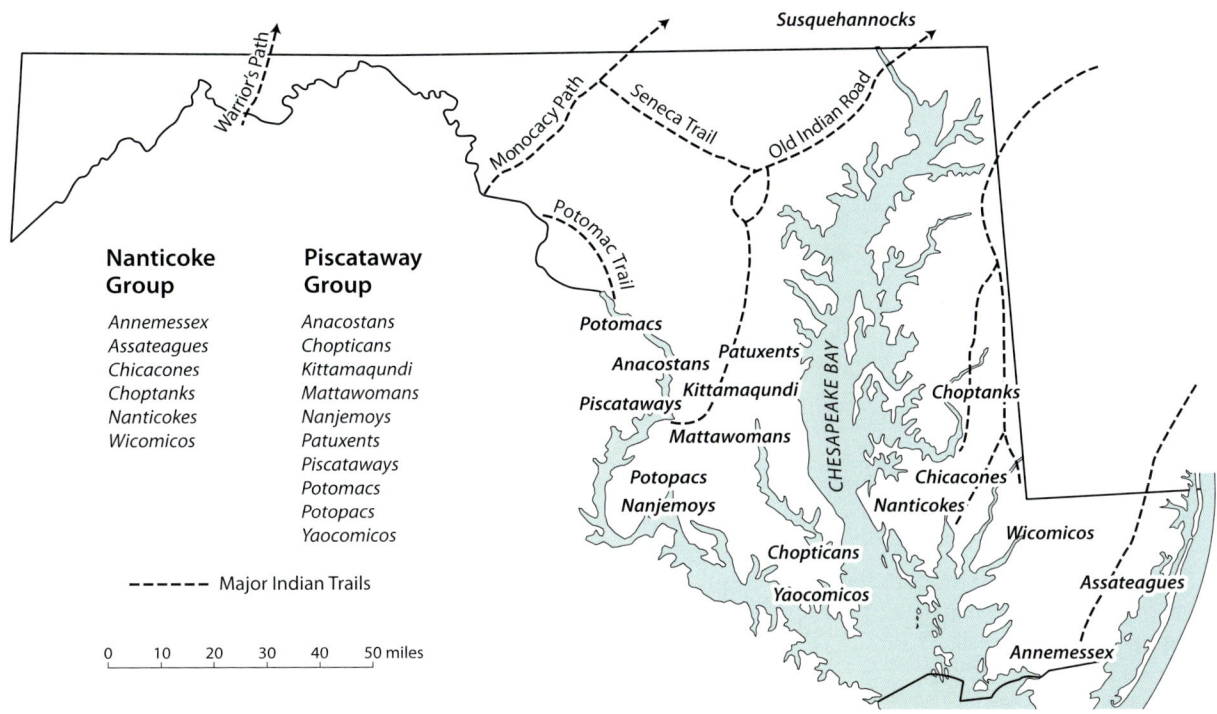

■ Major Native American Groups in Maryland, 1500–1650

Woodland Native American Life

Native American women and children raised crops of tobacco, corn, and other vegetables. Women loosened the soil with a crude hoe to plant seeds, while children did the weeding. Young boys were also "living scarecrows," sitting on sheltered platforms, ready to scare away birds that might eat the crops. Women wove mats and baskets and made clay pottery for cooking and holding water. Men hunted and fished to supply meat and skins.

Native Americans constructed their homes, known as witchotts, of sapling frames covered with bark shingles or mats. Several families usually shared one large room. The arched spaces were generally about 20 feet long, 15 feet wide, and 10 feet high. In winter, fires on the dirt floor provided warmth and cooked food; smoke escaped through a hole in the roof. Low benches, lining the wall and covered with mats, served as beds.

Native American clothing, made of deerskins, consisted of an apron-like garment worn by both men and women. Long cloaks and leggings added warmth in colder weather. Native Americans also wore ornaments made of beads, shells, animal teeth and bones, and copper. In addition, they sometimes decorated their bodies with tattoos or painted designs. Both men and women wore their hair long, but men usually had more elaborate hairstyles and dressed more colorfully.

Native Americans believed that water, stone, fire, and animals possessed a spirit. They made sacrifices to these spirits to bring themselves good fortune. Religious ceremonies included special songs and dances as well as prayers.

The New World

■ The Woodland Native American hamlet at Historic St. Mary's City with a corn field, cooking site, and reconstructed witchott, or longhouse, the traditional home of the Yaocomaco. Courtesy Historic St. Mary's City.

■ Artifacts from the earlier Native American occupation of the land settled by Europeans in 1634. Recovered objects shown here include an effigy-etched pipe bowl, fragments of Yaocomaco pottery and tobacco pipes, and projectile points. Courtesy Historic St. Mary's City.

flowers, and tobacco. Women and children foraged for wild plants, berries, and nuts; men hunted wild birds and game and fished the Bay and rivers for crabs, shrimp, oysters, eels, and fish.

By the seventeenth century, about forty Native American groups lived in the area that formed Lord Baltimore's province. Nearly all were part of the Algonquian-speaking people who lived on land that extended from the Carolinas to Hudson's Bay in Canada. Lower Western Shore groups, such as the Choptico, the Mattawoman, and the Patuxent, belonged to a loose federation, with the Piscataway as the dominant group. The Piscataway chief acted as the federation's tayac, or head. On the Eastern Shore, the Nanticoke, numbering about 1,500, provided leadership for smaller groups such as the Choptank, the Pocomoke, and the Wicomico. At the head of the Bay lived the powerful Susquehannock, members of the Iroquois nation. In all, Native Americans numbered about eight thousand to ten thousand people when the first Europeans arrived.

Chesapeake Indians traded goods with one another in networks reaching as far as the Ohio River Valley, using a form of money known as wampum, from the Algonquin word meaning "white strings." Peak, the more valuable type, used polished dark purple or white shells. Roanoke, made of broken pieces of unpolished shells, was worth only one-half to one-third as much. Bark canoes and log dugouts carried Native Americans along the region's rivers to trade furs and other goods. A network of foot trails, mostly running north and south, connected hunting lands and villages and also served as trade routes.

European Exploration

Europeans visited the Chesapeake region as early as the sixteenth century. Spanish explorers described the Bay as the best and largest port in the world. The first lengthy exploration occurred in 1608, when Captain John Smith led two expeditions from Jamestown, Virginia, that probed rivers on both shores. Smith used knowledge gained on these trips to draw the Bay's first detailed map, which he decorated with a drawing of a Susquehannock warrior.

After Smith's visit, Maryland's Native American peoples continued to have occasional contact with Europeans who came to trade or to explore. In 1631, William Claiborne set up a trading post on Kent Island; as many as one hundred people lived there by 1634. There were also unfriendly encounters. Native American uprisings in Virginia in 1622 set off raids against the Piscataway and other groups. A more serious source of trouble for the Algonquian peoples, however, came from raids by the warlike Susquehannock.

These experiences with white settlers and Native American groups in Virginia and on the Eastern Shore affected the way Western Shore Native Americans received the first colonists. Although suspicious of these newcomers, the Native Americans also viewed them as potential allies against the Susquehannock and thus allowed the English to settle peacefully.

■ Early Years of Settlement

The *Ark* and the *Dove* landed at St. Clement's Island in the Potomac River about March 5, 1634. Leonard Calvert, Lord Baltimore's younger brother and the colony's governor, led a small party up river to meet with the Piscataway federation tayac. The tayac did not invite the English colonists to stay in his territory but, mindful of the Susquehannock, neither did he ask them to leave. Instead, he granted them permission to settle where they wished. Calvert and the others then rejoined the ships anchored off St. Clement's Island, where, on March 25, the Jesuits offered a Mass of thanksgiving, a day still celebrated annually as Maryland Day.

St. Mary's City

Calvert and his men set off again to look for a place to settle. They struck a bargain with the nearby Yaocomaco, a peaceful farming and hunting group, for their village land. The settlers gave the Native Americans cloth, hatchets, and hoes; in exchange, the Yaocomaco agreed to turn half the village over immediately and the remainder the following year. They would stay for one year to help the colonists grow their first crops and to teach them skills needed for their new life.

Three days later, the remaining colonists arrived at the site, which they named St. Mary's City, and immediately built a fort to augment its natural defenses. Over the next few years, they added about ten houses, a storehouse, a mill, a Catholic chapel, and a blacksmith's forge. The settlers never built the planned town, however. The fur trade proved to be a failure and they found no veins of precious metals. Instead, Maryland settlers quickly turned to agriculture and made tobacco their cash crop. To grow tobacco (too bulky and fragile to be car-

■ In 1612, Captain John Smith used this image of a Susquehannock brave carrying his bow, his club, and the animal he killed during a hunt as an illustration for his map of the Chesapeake Bay. Courtesy of the Library of Congress, G3880 1624. S541.

St. Mary's City in 1685 with a butterfly-shaped baroque town plan, radiating from the town center and anchored by the brick chapel, the State House, and other principal buildings. Courtesy Historic St. Mary's City.

ried far over land) profitably, planters needed easy access to waterfront landings. Reliance on tobacco led to scattered settlement, not the growth of towns.

Settlement Patterns

Large investors laid out their manors along the main bodies of water: the Bay and the St. Mary's, Potomac, and Patuxent Rivers and their branches. Ordinary freemen located their plantations near the manors. As these riverbanks filled up, settlers repeated the same process along new rivers. Colonists did not begin claiming an area's interior until waterfront lands had been taken.

Population grew slowly at first and depended on immigration for that growth. By 1642, there were probably between 340 and 390 Europeans in Maryland, survivors of the 500 or more who had arrived since 1634. Nearly all new arrivals underwent a period of sickness, known as seasoning, and many died, most likely from malaria and dysentery. Others were left too weak to survive later illnesses. More than one of every five persons who came to Maryland seeking opportunity instead suffered an early death.

By 1642, settlers had claimed only 37,000 acres of the 7 million in the colony, with land ownership unevenly divided. Sixteen manors accounted for 31,000 acres, while many smaller freemen claimed the other 6,000 in holdings that averaged only 125 acres each. Yet even of this land, little had been cleared for crops. Much remained as it had been before the colonial grant, marked only by the villages and trails of the Native American groups who lived there.

The Government of the Colony

Although colonists had barely made a mark on the vast wilderness, they were not isolated from European civilization. Ships that came to Maryland to collect tobacco brought new settlers and news from home. They carried supplies of tools, cloth, salt, and other essentials that were not made in the colony. Marylanders also maintained ties with England by establishing a familiar pattern of government.

Leonard Calvert served as Maryland's governor and three gentlemen appointed by Lord Baltimore, the colony's proprietor, made up his council of advisors. A secretary kept the colony's records and oversaw distribution of land. Together these five men served as the executive branch. The governor and his council, meeting as the Provincial Court, formed the judicial branch. Englishmen who came to Maryland brought with them English common law and a long legal tradition. The Provincial Court settled disputes over land and collection of debts, quarrels between neighbors or husband and wife, questions of inheritance, and many other matters.

The charter had given Lord Baltimore the power to make laws with the agreement of the freemen, and it was also practical to consult with the colonists to encourage their acceptance of the government and its actions. Thus, a legislature, called the General Assembly, was established. By 1650, the Assembly had assumed the form it would keep for the duration of colonial rule. The governor and council made up the Upper House and voters in each county elected delegates to the Lower House. In the earliest years of settlement, all freemen could

■ The reconstructed State House, built in 1934. St. Mary's City served as the seat of government from 1634 to 1695. Courtesy Historic St. Mary's City.

Early Years of Settlement

vote for delegates. Eventually, however, restrictions concerning religion and ownership of land or other property limited the right to vote.

Daily Life

Whether living in a household of their own or as servants in someone else's home, most early settlers enjoyed few comforts, although Maryland never experienced the "starving time" of the first settlements in Virginia and New England. Colonists grew corn as their main source of food, and also cultivated vegetables like beans, peas, and squash. Before long, colonists raised enough livestock, primarily cows and hogs descended from the animals bought in Virginia or imported in later years, to feed both residents and newcomers. Tobacco provided a small income for buying goods that had to be imported from England.

In addition to tending crops and livestock, settlers needed to build homes for themselves. The earliest dwellings were usually small, one-story wood-framed buildings covered with split boards or a mixture of clay and twigs. These houses had only one or two rooms and few furnishings: a straw or cattail mattress (but no bed frame), a chest or two for storage, perhaps a crudely made table and some benches, a few iron pots, and wooden bowls and utensils.

Because servants' most important tasks were to clear land and raise crops and livestock, most laborers brought into the colony were young men. Until well into the seventeenth century, the population of Maryland consisted mostly of young, single men. Masters did not usually allow servants to marry, but with so few women not even all freemen could find wives.

As indentured servants became free, newly arrived indentured servants took their places. Former servants, however, did not easily join the ranks of landowners. Often they continued to work for and live with former masters while trying to save money. They needed cash or credit to pay the costs of surveying and patenting, or obtaining title to, land. They needed money to build a house and stock a plantation with tools, livestock, and other necessities.

The task of creating a society out of a wilderness proved to be a difficult one. Many of those who attempted to make a new life for themselves died before achieving any success, while few of those who survived a normal life span became wealthy. Nonetheless, the first settlers, both rich and poor, established a toehold on which later generations could build.

■ The Godiah Spray plantation in St. Mary's City re-creates the small house and kitchen garden in which early settlers of middling means lived and worked. Women tended the vegetable and herb garden while men toiled in the fields to produce tobacco and corn. Courtesy Historic St. Mary's City.

A "Time of Troubles"

Cecilius Calvert, Lord Baltimore, originally planned to sail with the first expedition. Attempts in the early 1630s to block his charter convinced him, however, that it would be unwise to leave England. Similar concerns prevented later visits, so that Calvert died in 1675 without ever visiting his colony. But, by staying in England, the proprietor outlasted his enemies and protected his charter.

Challenges to Lord Baltimore

Initial opposition to Lord Baltimore's grant came from the "Virginia interests," a group of English merchants and Chesapeake planters. They challenged the grant because it included land they considered part of Virginia. These men also feared that a colony in Maryland would slow Virginia's growth and threaten their control of the Chesapeake economy. While they did not stop Lord Baltimore from getting his charter, they did keep the lower Eastern Shore in Virginia.

Kent Island provided another source of conflict. William Claiborne argued that his trading post was a cultivated settlement and, because the charter granted only "uncultivated" land, should thus be exempt from proprietary rule. A combination of force and rewards gave the St. Mary's government control over the Kent Island settlers. By 1638, Kent sent delegates to the Assembly and formally became a second county in 1642, but Claiborne and his supporters resisted the proprietor's authority for many years, occasionally rebelling in hopes of regaining control.

Maryland's harmony suffered further when civil war broke out in England in the 1640s over religious and political issues. Anglicans, Catholics, Puritans, Presbyterians, and other Protestants had many deep-seated disagreements. Politically, Parliament vied with the king for power and fighting between the two sides broke out in 1642. Seven years later, Parliament executed King Charles I and, led by Oliver Cromwell, took control of the English government. When Cromwell died in 1658 with no clear successor, Parliament eventually restored royal authority under King Charles II in 1660.

Fighting among different groups in England inevitably spilled over into Maryland. With a Catholic proprietor and governing elite, and a mostly Protestant population, Maryland could not avoid being drawn into the fight. A Puritan ship captain, Richard Ingle, and his men attacked the colony in 1645, driving Governor Leonard Calvert and other settlers to seek refuge in Virginia. In 1646, with the aid of soldiers recruited in that colony, Calvert recaptured the province. Those who lived through the nearly two years of Ingle's Rebellion called the period the "time of troubles" or the "plundering time."

Puritan Settlement

After Leonard Calvert died in 1647, proprietor Cecilius Calvert tried to ease the colony's religious tensions by naming a Protestant governor to replace his brother and adding several Protestants to the council. Calvert offered new encouragement for Protestant settlers, including more generous head rights and broad toleration of dissenters. Non-conformists being harassed in Anglican Virginia, and others took up land in a new county, Anne Arundel, north of the St. Mary's City area. The Assembly in 1649 passed an "Act Concerning Religion" that granted toleration to all Christian denominations, the first such legislation in the English-speaking world.

Toleration of religious beliefs other than their own, however, was not a Puritan trait. The Puritan dissenters took control of the colony in 1654, defeated the governor and his soldiers in a 1655 skirmish known as the Battle of the Severn, and held power until November 1657, during which time they repealed the act granting toleration. When Lord Baltimore regained control of Maryland, he agreed to grant amnesty for his opponents and to restore the Act Concerning Religion.

Causes of Instability

As a new settlement, Maryland was not yet a society linked by ties that encouraged cooperation and concern for common welfare. For a long time it lacked men whom other settlers accepted as worthy leaders. While men with leadership skills did immigrate to Maryland, they did not always settle there permanently. Furthermore, potential leaders often pursued their own search for wealth, power, or office at the expense of general stability.

Nevertheless, the colony did not fall into a state of lawlessness. Many of the people who filled the offices of delegate, justice, sheriff, and lesser posts carried out their duties responsibly and helped to hold society together through the early contentious years.

Expansion of Settlement

As population grew and settlement expanded into new territory, government institutions also evolved and adapted to serve a more widely dispersed population. During the earliest years, provincial government and county government were virtually the same. St. Mary's County was the province. Kent became a separate county by 1642, and settlers on and near the Severn formed Anne Arundel County in 1650. By the end of the 1660s, the Assembly had created Calvert, Charles, and Baltimore Counties.

A 1652 treaty with the Susquehannock allowed colonists to begin claiming land on the Eastern Shore without fear of Native American attacks. Within a decade, Kent was carved up into four counties, with the addition of Talbot, Somerset, and Dorchester. Each new county assumed a role in the colony's government by sending delegates to the Assembly who served on an equal basis with those from older counties.

Maryland Counties during the Colonial Period

Year	County
1637	St. Mary's
1642	Kent
1650	Anne Arundel
1654	Calvert
1658	Charles
1660	Baltimore
1662	Talbot
1666	Somerset
1669	Dorchester
1674	Cecil
1695	Prince George's
1706	Queen Anne's
1742	Worcester
1748	Frederick
1773	Caroline
1773	Harford

Sources of Stability

The Assembly soon established its right to initiate legislation. Delegates could act with firsthand knowledge to address issues vital to the colony's welfare. Laws regulated ownership and inheritance of land, payment of debts, administration of justice, fees for public officials, and other matters of concern. The Assembly could not end conflicts between the proprietor and Virginians or repel raids by English Puritans, but it could establish a framework for a stable society.

In each county, justices of the peace sat as a court to hear criminal and civil cases. They also served as the local administration. Justices appointed constables and highway overseers to keep order and maintain roads. They named and supervised guardians for orphans, and provided poor relief. Justices paid bounties for killing wild animals that preyed on livestock; licensed inns; and set rates for food, drink, and lodging. They arranged for construction of courthouses, jails, and bridges, and levied taxes to pay county expenses.

In the seventeenth century, most freemen participated in local government. The governor appointed justices and a sheriff from among each county's wealthiest and most capable men. Less prominent men filled minor county offices, such as constable and highway overseer, and sat on juries. Service in these positions provided these men with an important social role and gave them a voice in shaping their society.

Seventeenth-century Maryland lacked many elements that normally bind a society together. Kinship ties, family groups, and long-term friendships rarely existed in a population welcoming a steady influx of immigrants and suffering a high death rate. The colony had no villages and towns or markets and fairs, and few churches, to bring people together. Postal service, newspapers, social clubs, and other channels for exchanging views and concerns did not yet exist.

Meetings of the Assembly and county courts therefore served social as well as political purposes. Freemen gathered together not only to attend sessions but also to conduct business, exchange news, and socialize. The General Assembly in St. Mary's City and the county courts provided two strands that helped hold the colony together during the early upheavals.

■ Building the Colony

The political turmoil of the seventeenth century engaged the attention of Lord Baltimore and many Marylanders and the two years of Ingle's Rebellion had a profound impact on the colony. In 1648, Maryland's population was smaller than it had been in 1642. Furthermore, the fighting destroyed homes, livestock, outbuildings, and crops that colonists had worked long hours to accumulate.

Nevertheless, new counties were created throughout the period, so that growth, as well as turmoil, formed part of seventeenth-century life. The small planter living in Charles County or Somerset County was not likely to be concerned with challenges to Lord Baltimore's rule. He was occupied with clearing a new field for his tobacco crop or building a tobacco house for curing it; he worried about the weather and the price of tobacco.

The Tobacco Economy

By the time Maryland's settlement began, Virginians had already established tobacco as the Chesapeake region's cash crop. The Tidewater region enjoyed a suitable climate and soil, while European customers provided a growing market for the "sotweed," as it was known. Colonists around the Bay concentrated on producing tobacco, using income earned from its sale to buy manufactured goods from Europe. In time, larger planters began to buy additional cloth, tools, and other items for resale to less wealthy neighbors. In return, they took the small household's tobacco in payment or extended credit.

The ordinary planter could tend up to 3 acres of tobacco each year. In addition, he grew corn to feed himself and his household and raised hogs and cattle for meat and for leather to make shoes and clothing. As time allowed, colonists planted apple orchards for cider. But to move beyond subsistence, or the ability to satisfy basic needs, a planter needed more than just his own labor. If he married, he also had the help of his wife and of their children when they were old enough. And a household with women meant labor to milk cows, make butter and cheese, and tend kitchen gardens.

Bound Labor

To obtain greater profits from agriculture, planters needed bound, or unfree, labor. Initially, most bound male and female workers were indentured servants; almost all came from the British Isles but a few were of African or Euro-African descent and some households included Native Americans as indentured servants.

Tobacco

Tobacco required more effort to grow than other Maryland crops. Tending the crop kept workers busy in the fields from early spring to late fall, and tobacco-related tasks also filled their winter days.

Planters cleared land for their crops by cutting a groove around tree trunks to kill them, a process called girdling, which prevents nourishment from traveling above the cut. The dead trees remained standing, but produced no leaves to keep sunlight from reaching the tobacco plants. In early spring, planters sowed seeds, saved from the previous year's crop, in special beds, to be moved by June to the cleared fields. Workers planted seedlings 4 feet apart among the leafless trees. Every day, workers hoed the fields to kill weeds and picked tobacco worms off the plants. When enough leaves had formed, workers pinched off the tops to prevent flowering.

In the fall, when the tobacco had fully ripened, the entire plant was cut, carried to the tobacco house, and hung to dry for about six weeks. When the leaves had dried enough to prevent rotting but not enough to crumble, they were stripped from the stalk and packed for shipment to England in large barrels known as hogsheads. During the winter, workers cleared new fields and prepared new hogsheads for the next year's crop.

After completing their terms, servants received freedom dues from their master—clothing, corn, and a few tools—and the right to claim 50 acres of land. Many servants eventually did become landowners, after paying ownership fees. The most successful brought the process full circle by acquiring servants of their own.

Merchant-Planters

Men with enough wealth to import a large number of servants held more land and harvested larger crops. Their greater income allowed them to buy extra imported goods for sale to neighbors. They also speculated in land, buying large tracts to subdivide and sell when population increase spurred demand. As merchant-planters, these men organized the colony's commercial agriculture and trade. Because of their wealth, they held prominent social positions in their neighborhoods and counties and took part in the colony's government. As these men lived long enough to marry and have children, their families became part of the native-born elite that governed the colony in the eighteenth century.

Merchant-planters were also least hurt by the downturn in the tobacco market that began in the 1680s. As the growth in demand for tobacco slackened and prices began to fall, small planters increasingly lacked cash or credit to buy bound labor. At the same time, the supply of indentured servants dwindled. By the 1690s, enslaved workers became an increasingly important part of Maryland's bound labor force. But only wealthy planters could afford to buy these more expensive workers who served for life as did their children.

Enslaved and Free Africans

Although indentured servants dominated the labor force before the 1690s, a demand for enslaved workers existed from the colony's earliest days. In 1637, for example, Lord Baltimore asked that the secretary of the Virginia colony buy on his behalf ten slaves as well as some livestock for his personal plantation. Men with trading connections to the Caribbean bought Africans there for themselves or for resale to neighbors. Some immigrants who came from islands like Barbados brought enslaved people with them. Most Africans, then and later, came involuntarily, but their legal status was not clearly defined in the earliest years. Records are few, but there are examples of Africans, like Mathias de Sousa, who came as indentured servants. When these individuals completed their servitude and became free, some acquired land of their own.

The legislature enacted the key laws that defined enslaved status in the 1660s, well before slaves became a significant part of the labor force. Maryland adopted one of the harshest aspects of the American system of slavery in 1663. Legislation decreed that all blacks brought into the colony should be held as slaves for life and that their children would inherit that status. Enslavement thus became a perpetual condition. Colonial courts had often decided that a slave baptized as a Christian could be freed. To prevent the further loss of enslaved property by this means, the Assembly passed a law in 1671 declaring that baptism did not alter a slave's status. At the time, these laws affected relatively few individuals, for large-scale arrivals of African slaves did not begin until the late 1690s. But the enslaved workers in Maryland in the 1660s and 1670s belonged to the colony's political leaders, who enacted these laws to protect their investments.

Ethnic and Religious Groups

During the seventeenth century, the lure of tobacco-based wealth drew thousands of immigrants to Maryland. These new arrivals differed considerably in status—from wealthy landowners to men of modest means to bound workers. The people who came to Maryland also had different ethnic backgrounds. Most enslaved workers came from regions along the west coast of Africa, and some had lived for a time in the West Indies. Almost all of the others came from Europe, mostly from the British Isles. A few Dutch, French, German, and Italian settlers arrived during the century and Scottish immigrants began to settle on the Eastern Shore in the 1680s.

The colony's inhabitants had varied religious beliefs as well as ethnic and national diversity. During the early years, most settlers of English origin belonged to the Anglican and Roman Catholic faiths. Migration from Virginia brought

From Captive to Capitalist

When Charles Willson Peale painted the portrait of Yarrow Mamout (c. 1736–1823) in 1819, Mamout was a free man, living in Georgetown, DC. Believed to be from Guinea, Mamout was a Muslim and literate in Arabic, indicating that he came from an elite family. But Mamout arrived in Maryland, at the age of about 16, in shackles, sold to Colonel Samuel Beall Jr. of Montgomery County by the captain of the ship that brought him from Africa. Brooke Beall, who lived in Georgetown, DC, inherited Mamout from his father, employed him in brickmaking, and hired his labor out to others. After Upton Beall became Mamout's owner upon his father's death, he manumitted the now 60-year-old man. As a free man, Mamout earned enough from burning charcoal, loading ships, weaving baskets, and other odd jobs to buy a house and lot in 1800, to have shares in the Columbia Bank of Georgetown, and to lend money at interest. One hundred years earlier, Mamout's story would have been almost unique, but in the post-Revolutionary period, as manumissions and successful freedom suits became more common and as the economy grew and diversified, new opportunities arose for free blacks, although never with the full range of civil liberties that whites enjoyed.

■ *Portrait of Yarrow Mamout*, by Charles Willson Peale, oil on canvas, 1819, Philadelphia Museum of Art, purchased with the gifts (by exchange) of R. Wistar Harvey, Mrs. T. Charlton Henry, Mr. and Mrs. J. Stogdell Stokes, Elise Robinson Paumgarten from the Sallie Crozer Hilprecht Collection, Lucie Washington Mitcheson in memory of Robert Stockton Johnson Mitcheson for the Robert Stockton Johnson Mitcheson Collection, R. Nelson Buckley, the estate of Rictavia Schiff, and the McNeil Acquisition Fund for American Art and Material Culture, 2011-87-1.

dissenting Protestants in the early 1650s. Although they experienced persecution in most other colonies, members of the Society of Friends, or Quakers, found asylum in Lord Baltimore's colony in the 1660s. In particular, Quakers formed an influential part of the community in Anne Arundel County and on the Eastern Shore. When the Scots arrived, they added Presbyterianism to the religious mix. Native Americans and most Africans had belief systems that were not part of the Judeo-Christian tradition. Some of the Africans brought to the colony came from regions where Islam was the religious faith. Simon Overzee's household, for example, included John Baptista, "a moore of Barbary."

A predominantly native-born white population also developed in the seventeenth century. By the end of the century, the majority of inhabitants of European descent were Maryland natives, and white population growth now resulted primarily from children being born in the colony rather than from immigration. The native-born African American community followed the same pattern of development, reaching a majority of the black population by the second quarter of the eighteenth century.

Effects on the Environment

Growing population, spreading settlement, continued clearing of land for crops, and the introduction of livestock changed the natural environment. The light soils of the bayside coastal plain washed away easily in heavy rains, particularly after they had been broken up for planting, and the runoff caused silting in streams and creeks. Silt killed marine life and blocked passage for larger ships. Tobacco cultivation led to depletion of important soil nutrients of lime and potash. After a few years of tobacco and several more of corn, planters had to abandon fields for a period of fifteen to twenty years to restore fertility. In the meantime, new fields had to be cleared and planted. To rest worn-out fields, a planter needed 20 acres of tobacco land for each worker.

As settlers claimed more and more of the colony's land, they made it harder for Native Americans to follow their traditional practice of combining hunting and agriculture. Settlers slaughtered fur-bearing animals (either for their skins or because they threatened livestock), constantly cleared woodland, and destroyed plants and animals on which Native Americans relied, so that they became increasingly dependent on Europeans for food, clothing, utensils, and other goods. In addition, Europeans brought two destructive imports: smallpox and alcohol.

Faced with these challenges, many smaller Native American groups simply moved away or disappeared as other groups absorbed their remaining members. A few, such as the Piscataway, managed to coexist with settlers during the seventeenth century. The Nanticoke and the Choptank, in contrast, asked for and received land in Dorchester County to use as reservations. Settling on reservations bought time for the two groups, but did not provide a permanent solution to the problems caused by European settlement.

The Royal Period, 1689–1715

In 1689, a group of Maryland colonists succeeded in wresting control of the province from Charles Calvert, the third Lord Baltimore. For twenty-five years, the Crown administered Maryland directly as royal colony. The Calvert family regained the province's government only after Benedict Leonard Calvert, who had earlier converted to the Anglican faith, inherited the title Lord Baltimore from his father in 1715. The Calverts continued to own the colony's land and to collect revenue from it throughout the royal period.

The Revolution of 1689

Two main sources of tension lay behind the Revolution of 1689. As was true of earlier conflicts, these issues had mixed religious and political origins. First, many Protestants, whether Anglicans, Presbyterians, Quakers, or others, re-

■ The Calverts

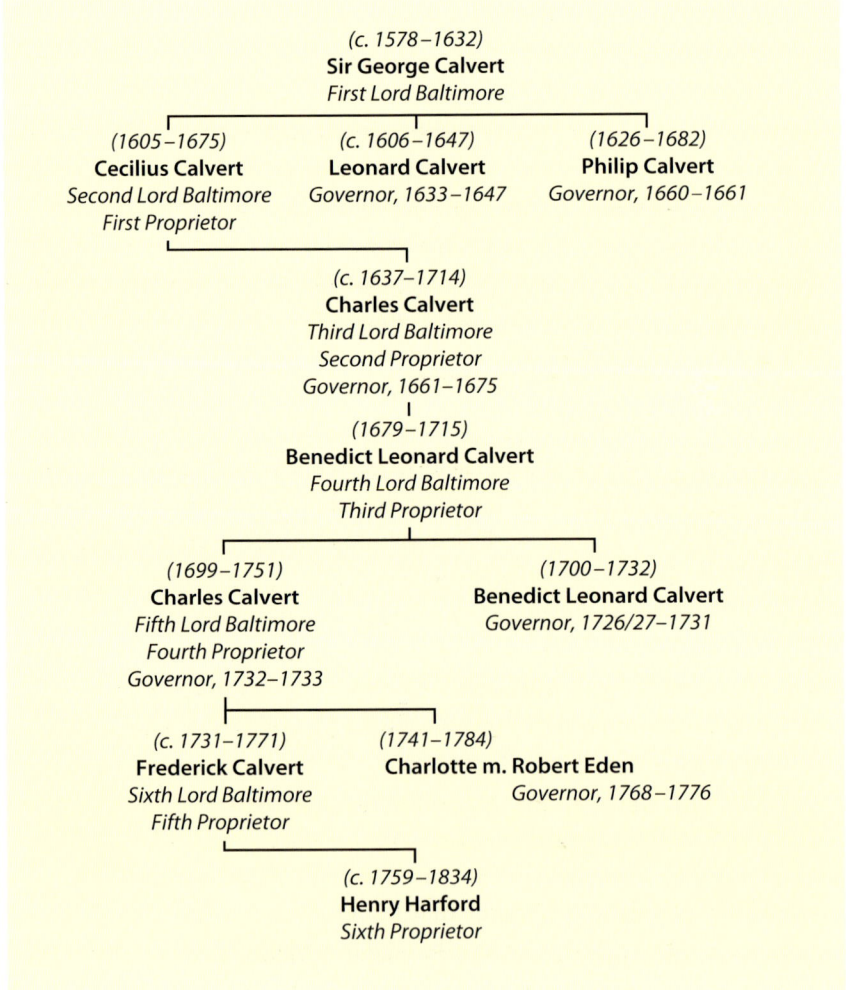

sented Lord Baltimore's practice of giving provincial offices to his kin and to Catholics. Second, his policy of toleration aided Catholics and non-Anglican Protestants, like Presbyterians and Quakers, more than it did the official Church of England, or Anglican Church. Because it lacked government support, the Anglican Church in Maryland had few ministers and places of worship.

Discontented Protestant colonists seized the opportunity given them by events in England. In 1689, Parliament replaced the Catholic king, James II, with his Protestant daughter Mary and her husband William of Orange. The change, known as the Glorious Revolution, gave those opposed to Lord Baltimore their chance. Using the lack of an immediate declaration of Maryland's loyalty to the new rulers and fear of a French-Indian-Maryland Catholic conspiracy as their pretext, in July 1689, John Coode and other Protestant leaders on the lower Western Shore recruited a growing force of men and by the first of August had taken control of the government at St. Mary's.

The colony's new leaders, known as the Protestant Association, asked the Crown to establish a Protestant government for Maryland. A new Assembly named civil and military officials for all counties and ruled the colony peacefully for two years in a bloodless change of authority. When royal Governor Lionel Copley arrived in 1692, Protestant voters chose a new Assembly. Use of standing committees made this legislature a smaller, colonial version of Parliament. A key factor behind successful revolt from England in the next century was the long experience of self-government that colonists gained through their own legislatures. Marylanders began that learning process in earnest with their 1689 "revolution in government."

Francis Nicholson, Royal Governor

Copley's death in 1693 brought Francis Nicholson to Maryland as the second royal governor. Nicholson's tenure strongly influenced future development in several ways. One of his first actions proposed moving the capital from St. Mary's, now on the periphery of Maryland's settled area, to the more centrally located "Arundell Town." Nicholson renamed the new capital Annapolis in 1695 to honor Princess Anne, England's future queen.

Nicholson also aided the colony by encouraging local education. Responding to his interest, the Assembly in 1696 passed an act founding King William's School in Annapolis as Maryland's first school supported by public money. The male students studied Greek, Latin, writing, and other subjects to prepare them to enter Virginia's newly established College of William and Mary. Nicholson supported the Annapolis school with gifts of money and land.

The Establishment of the Anglican Church

Nicholson's efforts also benefited the Anglican Church. An act passed by the Association Assembly made the Anglican faith Maryland's official religion, but

■ Old Trinity Church, located on Church Creek in Dorchester County and built between 1693 and 1698, is the state's oldest brick church in continuous use. Surviving seventeenth-century buildings are rare in Maryland, but religious groups have preserved two over more than three centuries. The frame Third Haven Meeting House in Easton, built between 1682 and 1684, still stands but is no longer used for Sunday meetings. Private collection.

no steps were taken to put the law into effect until Nicholson became governor. At the time, there were only three qualified Anglican ministers; in contrast, Quakers met in one of seventeen weekly meetings, or congregations, and eight priests cared for Catholic colonists.

Nicholson took several steps to strengthen the Anglican Church. He offered money to each parish that built a house and provided land for a minister, and worked effectively with the bishop of London to find ministers for all parishes. Passage of a poll tax authorized sheriffs to collect 40 pounds of tobacco for each taxable person to pay the ministers' salaries. Catholics, Quakers, and other dissenters now paid taxes to support the Anglican Church, but still had to raise funds among themselves for their own meetings or churches. Furthermore, Quakers lost their right to sit in the Assembly. Catholics experienced the strongest discrimination, as they successively lost the right to hold any public office, vote, and celebrate Mass in public.

War and the Tobacco Market

The years of royal rule were also years of international warfare. England fought against France in King William's War (1689–1697) and then Queen Anne's War (1702–1713). Attacks on tobacco ships by French privateers disrupted the tobacco trade. Convoys of British warships sailed with the tobacco fleets, but the convoys' organization favored Virginia's trade over Maryland's. Tobacco exports fell, and the supply of European imports dried up. Shortages forced many settlers to make their own cloth, shoes, and other items, or do without. The colony experienced a short economic boom during the brief period between the two wars, when the European tobacco market opened up again.

These years also witnessed the beginning of large shipments of African captives. Enslaved workers, who accounted for only three thousand of the colony's people in 1697, totaled nearly eight thousand, roughly 18 percent of Maryland's population, by 1710. The greater number of enslaved people overall marked the development of a new group of planters. Men who owned dozens of workers and vast tracts of land began to emerge as a distinct population segment.

Maryland in Transition

Maryland society at the end of the royal period reflected changes that took place over the preceding century. Instead of an immigrant population of young single men, the colony had a predominantly native-born population composed of family groups. Instead of a society with a few wealthy men and a large number of small landowners or tenants, there was a broader variety of small, middling, and large planters. A labor force of permanently enslaved blacks began to replace short-term white servants. Large planters and the wealthiest of the middling sort now formed an elite group that took the leading role in local and provincial government.

Even though the late seventeenth century was a time of political and economic difficulties, life improved in many ways. Families began to benefit from the labor of their fathers and grandfathers who had settled the colony. Colonists could now devote some income to expanding or rebuilding the family home and filling it with better furnishings. The bare existence of the early years began to give way to a standard of living with more comforts.

The Planter's Wife

For most of the seventeenth century, planters' wives were immigrants who had survived seasoning and completed their terms as servants. Most of these women, therefore, married in their mid-twenties. Because of high mortality in the region, only one in three marriages lasted even ten years. Most marriages produced three or four children; of these children, one probably died as an infant and one or two might die before reaching adulthood. Thus, the planter's wife might see only one child reach maturity, if she herself lived that long.

Exposure to malaria made childbearing riskier for Chesapeake wives, as pregnant women were particularly vulnerable to the disease. Those who survived childbearing were likely to outlive their husbands, for wives were often much younger. Generally, widows with small children to feed and a tobacco crop to grow soon remarried.

In addition to raising children, the planter's wife prepared the family food, a time-consuming task. Corn, for example, had to be ground into flour in a mortar or handmill before being baked as bread. She also washed the household's clothing and linens. In a large household, these jobs probably consumed much of her time, but planters' wives also raised vegetables in a kitchen garden, milked cows, and made butter and cheese. In households without any laborers, wives undoubtedly also provided valuable help in the fields.

The royal period thus marked a pivotal era in the colony's history. In these years, the province went through a transformation from an experiment in colony building to an Anglo-American society firmly planted in the New World.

■ Colonial Politics

Throughout the royal period, members of the Calvert family worked in England for restoration of their proprietorship. When the Calvert heirs converted to the Anglican faith, King George I was persuaded to return Maryland to their authority. In 1715, Benedict Calvert, the fourth Lord Baltimore, became proprietor of Maryland. With his death just eight weeks later, the proprietorship passed to his young son Charles, the fifth Lord Baltimore.

Changes during the royal period meant that the Calverts and their appointed governors were confronted with a political situation greatly altered from circumstances their predecessors had faced two decades earlier. Religious discrimination was written into law. The enlarged population now formed distinct social groups. Local leaders had grown in both wealth and political experience. They had effectively challenged the power of the later royal governors and were prepared to stand up to the proprietor for their own interests.

Leaders of the emerging Country Party represented the colonists' views. The men opposing the Country Party consisted mainly of a small group of proprietary appointees, including the governor, councilors, and major provincial officeholders. Because these men owed their posts to Calvert, they were known as the Court Party. Disputes between Court and Country Parties did not take place continuously, but they occurred often during the remainder of the colonial period.

Political Controversies

The proprietor and the Country Party delegates contested a number of issues in the 1720s and early 1730s. One focused on the colonists' claim to enjoy all the protections of English law—an assertion that they had the same rights as people living in England. Marylanders saw English law as protection against the broad powers given to Lord Baltimore and his officials by the charter.

A second dispute developed over fees paid to colonial officials. The colonists who paid the fees wanted to keep them as low as possible by having their elected representatives in the Lower House set the fee schedule. This authority would also increase the power of elected representatives over the appointed proprietary officials.

The third disagreement centered on an economic issue. Tobacco served as money in colonial Maryland, but was awkward to use because of its bulk and fragility. Colonists wanted their government to authorize the printing and use of paper money, but the proprietor had refused this request.

Disagreements between the two sides brought some legislative sessions to an early end. In other years, the governor avoided quarrelsome meetings by not calling delegates into session. The Country Party often turned to the printing press to aid its fight. In 1728, a pamphlet entitled "The Right of the Inhabitants of Maryland to the Benefit of English Laws" set forth the party's views on this issue. In it, Daniel Dulany the Elder presented one of the earliest arguments on a theme that reappeared later in the struggle for independence. He strongly asserted the claim that American colonists had the same rights as those living in the mother country.

Lord Baltimore's Visit

The contest between the two parties reached a settlement of sorts when Charles Calvert visited Maryland in 1732. Annapolitans greeted him with a royal salute, bonfires, dancing, and toasts of rum. A glittering social season did not distract the proprietor from the main goals of his visit, however. First, Calvert silenced his most able opponent by naming Dulany to three provincial offices. Second, he agreed to passage of a bill authorizing the use of paper money.

Lord Baltimore then resolved the remaining issues on his own terms. One of these involved his own finances. Since 1717, the proprietor had collected a duty on tobacco in place of the rents, known as quitrents, that landowners owed, but in 1733, Calvert changed the policy and again began collecting quitrents through local agents. Rent revenue totaled far more than the tobacco duty ever had. In later years, the proprietor always rejected Lower House proposals to return to a version of the old system.

Calvert also settled the dispute over payment of colonial officials. By decreeing that the governor would receive a salary that did not depend on an Assembly vote, the proprietor eliminated a strong weapon—control of the governor's salary—that other colonial legislatures used effectively in quarrels with their governors. Finally, Calvert settled the question of officers' fees by issuing a new table of fees by proclamation. Early in the summer of 1733, having resolved the disputes to his satisfaction, Lord Baltimore sailed for England.

The proprietor's settlement left the Country Party without strong leaders and without major issues. For a time, the Court Party directed the colony's affairs. Lord Baltimore's English staff and advisors issued instructions, drew up positions, appointed men to patronage offices, and examined laws for threats to proprietary powers. They and Lord Baltimore enjoyed the income from the proprietor's revenues and a share of the fees paid to provincial officials.

Not until 1738 did the Country Party enjoy a rebirth of leadership and assertiveness. Dr. Charles Carroll, a leading Anglican landowner and merchant, and a group of similar men were elected to the Assembly, prepared to challenge Lord Baltimore. Brief and stormy sessions characterized the legislature in the 1740s as delegates again took up the issue of officials' fees. Governor Samuel Ogle, his

■ Eighteen-year-old Daniel Dulany the Elder arrived in Maryland from Ireland in 1703 with his two older brothers. Colonel George Plater purchased his contract as an indentured servant and employed Dulany as a law clerk. By the 1730s, Dulany had become one of the wealthiest and most powerful men in the colony. Collection of the Maryland State Archives, MSA SC 4680-10-0057.

Colonial Politics

> **Dr. Charles Carroll: Colonial Merchant**
>
> Dr. Charles Carroll was born in Ireland around 1691 and immigrated to Maryland sometime after 1715. Carroll, a convert to the Anglican faith, settled in Annapolis and established his medical practice. As of 1738, he served as a delegate to the General Assembly from Anne Arundel County and as one of the "country" party leaders.
>
> Carroll practiced medicine until the final decade of his life. But soon after arriving in Maryland, he began investing profits from his medical practice in land and trade. Carroll shipped his and his neighbors' tobacco to merchants in London and Bristol. He sent cargoes of lumber, barrel staves, grain, and other food items to the West Indies, southern Europe, and the Wine Islands. In return, Carroll received either cargoes of sugar, molasses, and wine, which he then sold, or a form of payment called bills of exchange, which he could use to buy goods in England.
>
> Carroll invested in the ships that carried his cargoes and the land that produced them. In addition, he was one of five men who began the Baltimore Iron Works. While Carroll's land purchases included working plantations, his major holdings were more than 28,000 acres of undeveloped western land. As new settlers moved west, Carroll subdivided and sold this property at a profit. When he died in 1755, Carroll left his son, Charles Carroll, Barrister, of Baltimore, a "handsome estate," built up over the years through the success of his diverse economic activities.

successor Thomas Bladen, and Ogle in a second term all failed to calm the protests. With a century of settlement behind them, colonists no longer willingly accepted the subordinate role assigned to them by the Maryland charter.

The Tobacco Inspection Act

Because officials were paid in tobacco, the dispute over fees became mixed up with an effort to increase the price paid for Maryland tobacco. In 1730, Virginia passed a tobacco inspection act that raised the price of Virginia tobacco by guaranteeing its quality. A similar system in Maryland would allow officials to inspect all tobacco and burn any of inferior quality. The superior-quality tobacco would then command a higher price in England. Although fewer pounds of tobacco would be sold, total income would be greater.

Because a given amount of tobacco would now be worth more, Maryland's Assembly insisted on a provision to lower the amount of tobacco paid as fees to colonial officials and to Anglican clergymen. For a time the proprietor would not accept a law that adjusted fees for the increased value of tobacco, but repeated letters from Dulany finally convinced Calvert to accept the compromise.

A Period of Expansion

Tobacco was still the major export and source of revenue for Maryland during the eighteenth century, but in these years the colony began to develop a significantly more diversified economy. Wheat brought new prosperity to both growers and shippers, a greater variety of craftsmen offered wares and services, merchants opened year-round stores to sell goods imported from England, and new towns became centers of trade and culture.

Changes in the Tobacco Trade

The return of normal trade following European peace in 1713 accounted in part for the tobacco economy's improvement. In addition, buyers from countries other than England, particularly France, became increasingly important customers for Chesapeake tobacco.

New marketing systems also aided middling and small planters. Agents of English and Scottish merchants began setting up permanent colonial stores in the 1730s. They bought the smaller planters' crops and sold imported goods in return, usually on long-term credit. In addition to giving planters steadier prices, the credit provided by these new merchants enabled planters to expand tobacco production.

Because a planter profited more from unpaid, rather than paid, workers, as tobacco production increased and credit became available, more and more planters bought slaves. In 1720, only about one-quarter of all planters owned enslaved workers, but by 1760, nearly one-half held slaves. Most owners had no more than five, but even five enslaved workers could produce four times as much tobacco as could a single planter. Because planters spent only a minimal amount to feed, clothe, and house their slaves, they profited by keeping for their own use most of the income earned by the crops and products that enslaved workers produced.

Agricultural Diversification

A decisive expansion of enslaved labor was one of the changes that took place in the eighteenth century. Another change was the greater diversity of economic life. Although tobacco continued to be the primary cash crop for the whole colony, cereal crops grew in importance, and the value of the corn crop exceeded the value of tobacco on many estates. Planters used corn to feed their households and fatten livestock, and they traded it to the West Indies, where sugar planters imported corn to feed their enslaved laborers.

During the first half of the century, wheat began to replace tobacco as the main cash crop in some areas, particularly near Pennsylvania. By mid-century, southern European demand for wheat stimulated growth of the Philadelphia area's flour-milling industry, and the mills' agents looked to Maryland for additional supplies of wheat. As settlers moved into the Piedmont region, wheat also became the major cash crop there.

Planters could also diversify by producing barrel staves and headings, planks, and other timber products. In the lower Eastern Shore counties of Dorchester, Somerset, and Worcester, which had larger areas of poor soil, marshland, and swamps than the other Tidewater counties, settlers had long emphasized lumber products as an export valued in the West Indies and in the wine-producing areas of southern Europe. Planters in every region also enlarged their herds of livestock to sell salted beef and pork to the West Indies.

Nonagricultural Activity

Colonists also moved into nonagricultural activities. As early as 1719, investors built a profitable ironworks at Principio Creek, in Cecil County. They took advantage of easily mined high-grade ore, forests to supply the charcoal used to process the ore, and water routes for shipping the iron to markets. In 1731, five wealthy colonists set up the Baltimore Iron Works on the Patapsco River in Baltimore County. This was the most successful Maryland ironworks, returning a handsome profit to its owners for many years.

Shipbuilding also made use of Maryland's natural resources. Somerset County was an early center of production and ships were built there throughout the century. As settlement and population grew more rapidly on the Western Shore, shipyards prospered on that side of the Bay, particularly in Anne Arundel County.

Craftsmen became more numerous in the colony, although there was never the variety found in more urban colonies to the north or in England. Carpenters and other woodworkers, shoemakers and tanners, tailors, and blacksmiths provided needed goods for neighbors. Other men followed careers as members of the professions, chiefly as lawyers, physicians, and clergymen, and many were merchants.

■ The furnace of the Principio Iron Works, established in 1719 in Cecil County by the Principio Company with funds from British investors. The Chesapeake colonies accounted for one-seventh of British Empire iron production by the end of the colonial period. Courtesy of the Library of Congress, Historic American Buildings Survey, HABS MD, 9-PRINF, 1-1.

Wealthy colonists also invested in vacant land. As settlement spread to frontier areas, landowners sold property to newcomers. During the eighteenth century, with areas around the Bay becoming more populated, settlers began to develop the Piedmont region. Colonists moving outward from Prince George's, Anne Arundel, and Baltimore Counties joined large numbers of German immigrants moving south from Pennsylvania.

The Development of Towns

The growth of a more diversified and prosperous economy led to the development of the region's first towns. Initially, Maryland was too thinly settled to encourage town growth. Annapolis, the new capital, grew only because it was the seat of government, providing services and homes for members of the provincial bureaucracy and for colonists drawn there by legislative sessions or government-related business.

The Maryland Assembly frequently tried to "create" towns: Oxford in 1706, Chestertown in 1707, Joppa in 1724, and Port Tobacco and Baltimore Town in 1729, among them. Town growth, however, depended on more than legislative acts. Oxford, for example, became a thriv-

This painting of the Spencer shipyard on Gray's Inn Creek is the earliest known view of a Chesapeake shipyard. On shore, sawyers use whipsaws to cut timber while carpenters work on construction of two vessels. A variety of local vessels travel the waters of the creek. Courtesy of the Maryland Historical Society, 1900.5.1.

ing port for about forty years, but never drew many residents or craftsmen. Joppa and Port Tobacco also languished. Chestertown prospered when the upper Bay became a wheat-producing area. Baltimore Town grew only slowly for several decades but then, like Chestertown, it developed rapidly when its economy became linked with the grain trade.

Western Towns

Maryland's western frontier offered soil well-suited to the grain and cattle agriculture tradition of German, Scottish, and Irish immigrants, who arrived in the colonies at Philadelphia but soon moved west and south through the backcountry. Population in the area grew rapidly once the Assembly bought rights to land between the Potomac and Susquehanna Rivers from Native Americans in 1744. Wheat stimulated town development more than did tobacco. For crops of equal value, wheat was bulkier and required more processing before export. Wheat farmers needed wagons to move their grain, mills to grind it into flour, and barrels for shipping it overseas. Landlocked western settlers also needed stores where they could buy supplies.

Daniel Dulany the Elder became the chief developer of the Piedmont area. He arranged the survey of a town site near the Monocacy River in Frederick County in 1747. By offering good terms to artisans and tradesmen, he drew craftsmen and professional men to Frederick Town, which quickly became the center of western settlement. The proprietor granted the right to establish weekly markets and two annual fairs. German Lutheran and Reformed congregations built churches on lots donated by Dulany. By 1750, Frederick Town had become the largest town in Maryland. Thirty miles farther west, another center grew up around the property of Jonathan Hager, who bought his first tract in 1739; by the 1760s, he owned 2,500 acres. In 1762, perhaps inspired by Frederick Town's success, he laid out a town he named after his wife Elizabeth but that local people called Hager's Town, the name it retains today as Hagerstown.

In 1754, Carolina and Virginia troops built a trading outpost farther west, on high land along the Potomac River. Maryland militia troops constructed a

A Period of Expansion

Colonial Baltimore

In the 1660s, settlers first claimed land in the area that is now Baltimore. By the 1720s, the population had grown enough to spur creation of a town. In 1729, the Assembly chose 60 acres of land inherited by brothers Charles Carroll of Annapolis and Daniel Carroll of Duddington from their father Charles Carroll the Settler as the site of Baltimore Town. The location had a good harbor, rapid streams to provide waterpower for mills, a fertile backcountry, and forests to supply wood for fuel and buildings.

An earlier settlement, at nearby Fells Point, had three homes, several tobacco houses, an orchard, and a mill. A third settlement, Jones Town, grew up at the mouth of the Jones Falls, linked to Baltimore Town by a bridge over the stream. In 1745, Jones Town became part of Baltimore Town, but Fells Point was not added until 1773.

In the 1750s, Baltimore began to grow as a center for processing and exporting wheat. Wheat moved into town on a network of roads that extended into central and Western Maryland and into Pennsylvania. Wagons brought grain to mills along the Jones and Gwynns Falls, and ships carried flour from the mills, as well as wheat and baked ship's bread, to overseas markets. Baltimore also served as the port through which the area's ironworks shipped iron to Britain.

By this time German immigrants began to enter Maryland through Baltimore rather than Philadelphia. Refugees fleeing western settlements during the French and Indian War also swelled the town's population. The 1750s saw construction of several new churches and a public wharf; by 1764, the town had grown to about two hundred houses. In 1768, the Assembly recognized Baltimore's growth by making it the county seat for Baltimore County.

■ In 1752, Baltimore was a tiny town on the Patapsco River. Its two hundred residents supported a church, a hotel, two taverns, a barbershop, a tobacco inspection house, and a brewery. Courtesy of the Maryland Historical Society, Hambleton Print Collection, H16.

Maryland's Formative Years, 1634–1763

■ Elias Brunner, son of a German immigrant family, built a new stone house on his Schifferstadt property in Frederick County in 1758. The rebuilding of the family home in stone reflected the prosperity achieved by the second generation of settlers in the fertile Monocacy Valley. Courtesy of the Maryland Historical Trust.

crude frontier fort across the river at its confluence with Wills Creek. As conflict between French and British interests in the Ohio Valley developed into the French and Indian War, the reinforced outpost became Fort Cumberland in 1755. Little effort was made to develop towns in this area, however. Native American raids during the French and Indian War and British opposition to

■ Fort Cumberland, built at the junction of Wills Creek and the North Fork of the Potomac River, is depicted here in 1755. Because of British restrictions on western settlement, the town of Cumberland was not laid out until after the Revolution. Courtesy of the Maryland Historical Society, McCauley.V56.

A Period of Expansion

> ### The French and Indian War
>
> While Englishmen settled colonies along the Atlantic Coast, Frenchmen built forts, missions, and trading posts in Canada and down the Mississippi River. French and English settlers competed for furs, fish, and control of the region between the Appalachian Mountains and the Mississippi. The French began building a series of forts in the Ohio River Valley to control the route from Canada to Louisiana. Pennsylvania fur traders and Virginia land speculators with claims in the area opposed their plans, and fighting erupted in 1754 over a French fort at the head of the Ohio River.
>
> Maryland formed a company of riflemen to protect settlements from Frederick Town to Hager's Town. In February 1755, General Edward Braddock arrived from England to lead two thousand men (British regulars and colonial volunteers) against the French. George Washington accompanied him as an aide, while Maryland Governor Horatio Sharpe and Benjamin Franklin of Philadelphia organized the supply effort.
>
> Braddock's defeat in July at Fort Duquesne left Maryland's western settlements open to attacks by France's Native American allies. Refugees from these settlements fled as far east as Baltimore. The Maryland legislature, afraid the colony would be attacked, voted money for the war effort in 1754 and 1756. As British troops captured French forts and then Quebec in 1759, they relieved pressure on Western Maryland and shifted fighting away from the colony. When the war ended in 1763, France ceded to Britain all of its territory in North America except New Orleans, which went to Spain.

land grants west of the Appalachians held back settlement of the Appalachian region during the colonial period.

Town Life

In the mid-eighteenth century, most Marylanders still lived on plantations. By 1755, as many as one thousand people might have lived in Annapolis, but the total town-dwelling population in the rest of Maryland did not exceed two thousand. No more than two out of every one hundred people lived in a town, and of these only Annapolis offered some of the amenities available to residents of colonial cities like Philadelphia and Boston.

A "golden age" for Annapolis began in the 1750s. For several decades the city was the colony's social and cultural center, attracting lawyers and merchants, who made Annapolis their home, and members of the elite, who came to town for legislative sessions. Craftsmen who were seldom, if ever, found elsewhere in the colony settled in Annapolis to serve the wealthy clientele. They included watchmakers, hatters, wigmakers, saddlers, and silversmiths, as well as the most skilled cabinetmakers and a few women who worked as quilters and seamstresses.

The colony's only newspaper, the *Maryland Gazette*, began regular publication in Annapolis in 1745. It printed news from abroad and from other colonies, provided a forum for debating public issues, ran notices of runaway servants and slaves, and advertised the sale of land and merchandise. Traveling English and colonial theater groups visited regularly, performing material from Shakespeare to farces. Social groups like the Tuesday Club brought together members of the elite, while horse races attracted enthusiasts from all social levels.

Outside Annapolis, there were no newspapers or theaters and few clubs. Horse races in country towns, however, attracted eager horsemen and enthusiastic crowds, just as they did in Annapolis. Neighborhood taverns, Sunday church services, and county court sessions all provided places for social gathering. A network of roads and paths, as well as the many rivers and creeks, connected plantations to churches, stores, taverns, and the county courthouse. Well-traveled main roads linked the colony's towns and also extended north and south to Pennsylvania, Virginia, and beyond.

■ Maryland Society at Mid-Century

In 1764, *Gentleman's Magazine* of London printed a Maryland census from 1755, when nearly 153,000 people lived in the colony's 15 counties. The interiors of older counties were not yet densely settled, and Frederick, Baltimore, and western Anne Arundel Counties still held large stretches of vacant land.

Demographics of colonists included gender, age, race, wealth, nativity, and status, and their rights, privileges, and ways of life varied with all these factors. Only free white adult males (15 percent of the population) enjoyed full legal rights. An even smaller group of property holders had the right to vote and hold office.

Enslaved People

In 1755, blacks comprised 28 percent of Maryland's population, while mulattoes (people of both black and white parentage) made up 2 percent, but the proportion of blacks to whites varied from region to region. In prime tobacco-producing areas on the Western Shore, blacks made up 40 to 50 percent of the population. Tobacco's need for year-round cultivation made enslaved workers the most economical labor option for those who inherited or could buy workers. Wheat

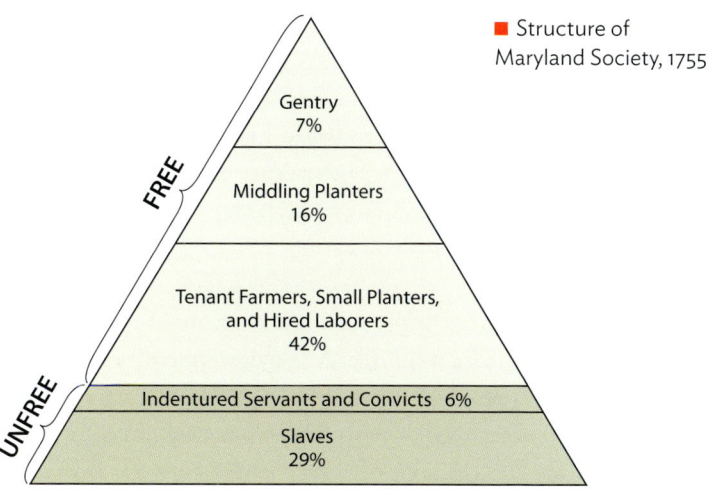

■ Structure of Maryland Society, 1755

> ### Slave Family Life
>
> Enslaved women usually married in their late teens and formed a new household with their children. Mothers took their newborn children with them to the fields, where the infants lay on the ground while their mothers worked. Young children stayed at home, playing, while women too old for field work looked after them.
>
> Children began to work in the fields between the ages of 7 and 10, picking up stones or pulling worms off tobacco plants. Most children older than 10 years were trained as field workers. A few boys might be taught carpentry, smithing, or other skills, and some girls trained as cooks or in the tasks of other household servants.
>
> Slavery both fragmented and extended black family life. Planters kept women and their small children together, but frequently separated husbands and older children from the rest of the family. Planters often bequeathed a slave or two to their widows and bequeathed others to their children. Enslaved property could also be mortgaged or sold to cover debts. These actions frequently divided slave families. If the distances involved were small, at night and on Sundays and holidays, enslaved men and women could visit with family and kin living on nearby plantations. But for most, their status as property made enslaved people vulnerable to permanent separation from loved ones.

farmers, however, needed extra help only for one or two weeks at harvest time and could hire temporary labor for that brief period. Thus, in northern and western wheat-producing counties, such as Frederick and Cecil, enslaved workers made up just 13 or 14 percent of the population.

Enslaved people formed the broad group at the bottom of colonial society, and much of the wealth and privilege of those at the top derived from enslaved labor. Those held as slaves enjoyed few legal rights. Although protected by law from extreme abuse, they could not bring suit in court or testify on their own behalf except in petitions for freedom. Slaves could marry with their owners' permission, but could not sue to prevent the breakup of a marriage or family. They were legally unable to own property, but in practice did have the right to tend a patch of ground and raise poultry. Slaves could sell chickens, eggs, and any produce they raised and use the proceeds as they wished.

On larger plantations, enslaved laborers lived in small cabins furnished with mattresses and blankets for sleeping, perhaps a crude homemade table and some stools, and a few utensils for cooking. On small plantations, the few slaves might live in an outbuilding or the kitchen loft. By mid-century, the enslaved population had begun to develop broad kinship networks within local neighborhoods. Those on plantations with twenty or more slaves generally lived with groups of kinfolk, while slaves on small plantations often had relatives nearby.

Free Blacks

Not all people of African origin were enslaved: about 1 percent of all blacks and 40 percent of mulattoes were free. A few descended from the earliest Africans brought to Maryland and Virginia before the laws of slavery defined their status. Others had been freed or descended from slaves freed by will or manumission. Most were the children of relationships between free women (whether black or white) and enslaved men. The county courts sold these children as servants until the age of 31, but they then became free. Free blacks generally worked as field hands or servants in the homes of wealthy whites. Others were craftsmen, and a few became independent planters, owning land and raising crops in the same manner as white planters.

Servants and Hired Laborers

Servants made up 12 percent of the total white population in 1755. They might have been hired laborers, indentured servants, or transported British convicts. In 1717, Parliament had passed a law allowing courts to send convicted criminals to the colonies for sale as servants. Convicts—adults and children—accounted for one of every five servants.

Hired laborers became an increasingly important source of workers during the eighteenth century. Greater numbers of young men reached their teens and early twenties without inheriting land or the money to buy, or even rent, land of their own. By working for a neighboring planter or by doing odd jobs while helping with the family's crops, these young men could try to save enough money to become landowners themselves or to finance a move to a frontier area.

Tenant Farmers and Small Planters

Tenant farmers and small landowners made up the next level of society. Together they accounted for more than one-half of free householders. Although tenant farmers had the extra expense of rent, there were few differences in terms of living standards between the two groups. The average head of household was married and had several children. Most owned one or two horses, and nearly as many raised some cattle and a small herd of hogs. Nearly all grew tobacco, earning between £5 and £10 a year. In addition, most raised crops of corn and many cultivated wheat. Families lived in simple one- or two-room houses, often with a loft for sleeping and storage and a separate kitchen. The plantations had tobacco houses and perhaps a corn house, but no barns to shelter animals. Dwellings were sparsely furnished, but these families lived more comfortably than had previous generations.

Shoemaker David Prichard was a typical member of this group. He was a servant in 1725, but by 1733, headed his own household and had at least three children. Prichard rented property on which he kept horses, cows, and hogs, and he grew tobacco and corn. The home's furnishings included two beds, a pine table, a chest, a chest of drawers, and one armchair and four side chairs. Mary Prichard prepared meals in a kitchen equipped with iron and tin utensils, pewter dishes, and a small amount of earthenware. She also had tubs for washing clothes and linens, a box iron for pressing them, and a woolen wheel for spinning yarn. In addition to his shoe-making equipment, Prichard owned two plows, some basic carpentry tools, and a supply of leather and hides.

The Middling Group

A group known to colonists as "middling" planters occupied the next level and comprised about one-quarter of the colony's freemen. Within this group, 70 percent owned land, with the average owner holding nearly 200 acres. The same percentage of middling planters owned enslaved laborers, usually between one and five. Nearly all of the middling planters raised cattle, horses, sheep, and hogs, and cultivated tobacco, corn, and wheat. Middling planters annually earned about twice as much as small planters and enjoyed greater comforts in their homes. They were likely to have rebuilt or enlarged the family home so that it was now a full two stories with at least two rooms on each floor. In addition to a separate kitchen and tobacco and corn houses, there might be a smokehouse or henhouse or barn.

Noah Corner, a native-born carpenter and planter, belonged to this middling group. The Corners lived on a 250-acre plantation, planted with tobacco, corn, wheat, and oats. Cattle, horses, sheep, and pigs foraged on the land. Corner did not own a slave, but bought at least one servant during his career. Household furnishings included four beds with feather mattresses (the best mattresses available), a cot, three tables, three chests, eight chairs, and a walnut desk. An hour glass and silver watch measured time, candlesticks held candles to provide light for reading or needlework, and a looking glass allowed Corner to adjust his brown wig. Rachel Corner prepared the family meals in a kitchen equipped with brass skillets and skimmers, two dozen glass bottles, flasks, iron and tinware, pewter dishes and serving pieces, and a tea kettle.

■ The LeCompte House in Dorchester County, the oldest surviving colonial house that retains its original style, is a typical middling home of eighteenth-century Maryland. Courtesy of the Maryland Historical Society, SVF, D-Dorchester-Houses-Hooper's Island.

The Gentry

The gentry stood at the top of the social pyramid, owning the greatest share of the colony's wealth, organizing its trade and other commercial activities, and filling its political and judicial offices. Elite men accounted for no more than 10 percent of the colony's householders, yet they owned nearly one-half of all patented land, almost two-thirds of total moveable wealth, and close to two-thirds of the colony's enslaved laborers. The group included a scattering of craftsmen but most members were merchants, planters, lawyers, and government officials.

The gulf between the gentry and the middling planters was far wider than that between the middling and small planters. Small planters voted and occasionally served as jurors; middling planters were constables and jurors; the gentry served as justices and delegates to the assembly. Small and middling planters earned a living from their crops, livestock, and perhaps a craft. The gentry combined planting (the work being done by their enslaved workforce) with a profession, business, investments, office holding, and land speculation. They built large brick Georgian homes that have come to symbolize Tidewater society and furnished them with many marks of wealth, such as imported mahogany furniture, silver tea and coffee services, portraits of themselves and their families, and large collections of books.

■ Somerset County's Almodington, Georgian in style and dating to c. 1750, was the home of the Elzey family. Considered one of the Eastern Shore's most elaborate homes of the period, it appears modest when compared with the houses built across the Tidewater region in the decade before the Revolutionary War period. Courtesy of the Library of Congress, MD0813.

Jeremiah Nicolls, a typical member of this group, was a merchant and planter in Talbot County who married into one of the county's oldest and richest families. Nicolls served as a justice and sheriff and acted as the Talbot agent for a London tobacco firm. Twenty-three slaves worked Nicolls's 500 acres, cared for his livestock, and ran his Choptank River ferry. Nicolls's mahogany tea table, violin, large library, wine cellar, gold jewelry, silver tea and coffee services, and small carriage all marked him as a member of the colony's wealthy elite.

Despite differences in wealth and power, numerous strands wove together these three groups of planters. Kinship ties or a relationship of employer and employee, or landlord and tenant, linked some. Small and middling planters gave the elite their votes, and in turn, the gentry used their power to hold down the costs of government, enforce contracts and payment of debts, prosecute those who stole from or assaulted members of the community, and settle disputes over ownership of land. Members of the elite also helped middling and small planters by marketing their crops, extending them credit, or hiring out a slave when an extra hand was needed. In these ways, the groups generally worked together to foster economic and social stability for white society.

Men, Women, and Children

In the colony as a whole, there were as many free white women as free white men, but here again with regional variations. In Frederick County, men made up 56 percent of the free white population (the highest percentage of any county), reflecting its frontier nature, which drew young men who could not afford land in older counties.

Because planters continued to prefer adult males when buying workers, 70 percent of servants were men. Planters could also choose to buy men when purchasing imported Africans, but by mid-century most blacks, like most whites, were native born. Blacks too were evenly divided between men and women.

Children (younger than 16) made up 52 percent of both the free white and the black populations. This represented a major change from the seventeenth century, when most immigrants and imported slaves were adults and the colony had few children.

The Original Marylanders

One final group composed part of the total population of the state, but the census figures did not include these people. Nanticoke and Choptank Native Americans continued to live on reserved land. A 1756 estimate placed the number of "domestic Indians" at about 140, the remnants of various groups whose members had totaled at least 8,000 when colonization began.

As early as the 1740s, Nanticoke Indians began moving north to join groups in Pennsylvania, New York, and Canada; by the 1760s, the colony sought to buy back the reservation land. A small group of Choptank Indians continued to live on their reservation, but by the end of the century they, too, had gone. Most of the Native Americans left in Maryland were scattered families living in remote marshes and swamps on the Eastern Shore.

■ The Colony Matures

In the course of 130 years of settlement, the men and women who crossed the Atlantic and their descendants cleared land; planted crops; raised livestock; built houses and churches; cultivated orchards; erected fences; laid out roads; and operated stores, taverns, and ferries. In a landscape initially described as an endless forest, they had created a new society. Three thousand miles from Europe, they nevertheless remained firmly linked to that continent through a vast trade network stretching across the Atlantic and beyond. Although colonists came from widely varied backgrounds, shared institutions of government and political ideas bound them to Great Britain.

In the 1760s, British imperial needs clashed with colonial interests, just as proprietary and colonial interests had clashed in earlier decades. Their English heritage and their colonial experience of self-government and economic development powerfully shaped the ways in which colonists responded to the challenges of the 1760s. These same colonists shaped the nation's future in the American War of Independence in the 1770s.

Maryland		The Nation and the World
	1763	Treaty of Paris signed, ending French and Indian War
Mason and Dixon survey Maryland boundary line with Pennsylvania and Delaware	1763–1767	
Zachariah Hood, Maryland stamp collector, burned in effigy	1765	Stamp Act
	1767	Townshend Acts
Proprietor names Robert Eden governor of Maryland	1769	
Governor Eden issues Fee Proclamation	1770	Boston Massacre
Frederick Calvert, sixth Lord Baltimore, dies; son Henry Harford becomes proprietor of Maryland	1771	
Cornerstone laid for new State House in Annapolis	1772	
Caroline and Harford Counties formed	1773	Tea Act Boston Tea Party
First convention meets in Annapolis *Peggy Stewart* burned in Annapolis harbor	1774	First Continental Congress meets
	1775	Battles of Lexington and Concord George Washington becomes commander-in-chief of American army
Governor Eden leaves Maryland Montgomery and Washington Counties formed First Maryland constitution adopted Continental Congress meets in Baltimore	1776	Declaration of Independence signed
First General Assembly elected under new constitution meets in Annapolis Thomas Johnson takes office as first state governor	1777	
Maryland signs Articles of Confederation	1781	Articles of Confederation adopted British surrender at Yorktown, Virginia
Washington College established at Chestertown	1782	
Importation of slaves into Maryland for sale from foreign countries prohibited	1783	George Washington resigns his military commission
Congress of the Confederation meets at State House in Annapolis	1783-1784	
St. John's College established at Annapolis	1784	Congress ratifies Treaty of Paris, affirming independence
Annapolis Convention calls for a convention in Philadelphia	1786	
	1787	Constitutional Convention meets in Philadelphia
Maryland Convention ratifies US Constitution	1788	US Constitution ratified by the nine states necessary for adoption
	1789	George Washington takes oath of office as first president of US French Revolution begins

chapter two

The Revolutionary War Era

1763–1789

Peace at last! In early February 1763, Maryland's Governor Horatio Sharpe announced that Britain had won the nearly decade-long war against its historic foe, France, and Maryland's western settlements were again safe from attack. Marylanders joined other American colonists in celebrating the victory, rejoicing in being part of the powerful and successful British Empire. Yet just thirteen years later, Britain and its colonists would be at war with each other in a bloody and prolonged battle for American independence.

The transformation of the loyal colonists of 1763 into the rebels in arms of 1776 was a wrenching experience in every colony. Independence posed a particular challenge for Marylanders, however, because it meant they would have to reject not only the authority of Britain but also of Maryland's colonial proprietary government. Marylanders in effect had to declare independence twice—first from the proprietary authority established by the Maryland charter of 1632 and then from the Crown and Parliament.

While the political crises of the 1760s and 1770s convulsed Maryland and transformed it and the other British colonies into the United States, daily life for most seemed far removed from the fray. Most Marylanders—black and white, bound and free, male and female—spent their days scratching out a subsistence living on small farms and plantations with little hope of improving their lot. Annapolis was different. In the years after 1763, Maryland's capital city entered its golden age. Rich men built substantial mansions in town and furnished them with fashionable goods imported from England; skilled local craftsmen flourished; the annual fall races showcased prized Arabian horses; and men who disagreed violently on the political issues of the day met companionably at exclusive gentlemen's clubs in the evening.

Independence ended Annapolis's golden age. Maryland's new political leaders no longer had time for frivolous entertainment. Declaring independence was the easy part, it turned out. Winning the war and shaping a new government for the state and the nation would be much harder, demanding the best that Maryland's citizens could give. Despite the challenges, by 1789, the thirteen colonies had become the United States and the former colonists of Britain had become Americans.

■ New British Policies

Britain's victory in the French and Indian War came at a high cost. British national debt doubled and keeping troops posted in the western frontier won from France would be a continuing expense. Britain expected the Americans to pay at least part of the costs for protecting this new territory. Parliament's efforts to raise this revenue from the colonies led to protests in Maryland and elsewhere that became increasingly vocal and violent, ultimately ending in the War of Independence.

The Sugar Act

The Sugar Act of 1764 represented Britain's first attempt to raise more money from its colonies, imposing a tax on molasses imported into the colonies from the West Indies. The act had little effect on Maryland because few Marylanders participated in the West Indian molasses trade. New Englanders, on the other hand, were outraged and protested that the Sugar Act violated the principle of "no taxation without representation." Parliament soon concluded that the Sugar Act was a bad idea and repealed it.

The Stamp Act

In 1765, Parliament passed the Stamp Act, which required colonists to purchase tax stamps for all legal and commercial documents, newspapers, playing cards, dice, and licenses. This revenue bill affected every colony and most segments of the population; Marylanders joined colonists elsewhere in protesting vigorously against the act.

In Maryland, anger against the Stamp Act focused on Zachariah Hood, an Annapolis merchant. He accepted the position of stamp collector for Maryland while on a business trip to England. The *Maryland Gazette* quoted Hood as saying that if the colonists had to be taxed, it would best be done by a native son. Most Marylanders thought Parliament should not tax the colonies at all without their approval. In Annapolis on August 26, 1765, an angry crowd hanged and burned an effigy of Hood. A few days later, a mob of more than three hundred people tore down his Annapolis warehouse. The terrified Hood fled to New York.

Opponents of the Stamp Act asked Governor Horatio Sharpe to call a special session of the General Assembly to discuss the act. When the governor called the Assembly on September 23, 1765, it chose three people to attend the Stamp Act Congress, to be held in New York that October. The Assembly or-

dered its delegates to support the principle that the colonists could not be taxed without representation in Parliament.

Dulany's "Considerations"

The next chapter in the protest against the Stamp Act came from Daniel Dulany the Younger, a wealthy member of the proprietary establishment. He wrote a stinging attack on the Stamp Act entitled "Considerations on the Propriety of Imposing Taxes in the British Colonies." Dulany's reputation as a brilliant lawyer and his compelling argument against the Stamp Act helped to rally opposition to it.

■ American colonists strongly resisted the use of tax stamps such as these. This image shows the only known proof sheet for the stamps, from which the proof number has been cropped. Courtesy of *Wikimedia*.

New British Policies

■ The *Maryland Gazette* denounced the Stamp Act. The skull and crossbones, symbol of mortal danger, appeared in the October 10, 1765, issue. Collection of the Maryland State Archives, MSA SC 2731-1-13.

■ Archaeologists recovered the paper's lead skull and crossbones type during excavation of the Green family print shop. Archaeology in Annapolis, University of Maryland.

Governor Sharpe realized that the people of Maryland would not stand for stamps in the colony. When the first shipment of stamps arrived in the Annapolis harbor in late October 1765, he asked the ship's captain to keep them on board his vessel. Because there were no stamps and no stamp collector, most legal and government business in Maryland stopped on November 1, 1765, the date the Stamp

Act went into effect. Jonas Green, the editor of the *Maryland Gazette*, called this date "Dooms-Day" and promptly stopped publishing his newspaper.

The nearly complete shutdown of the colony did not continue for long. Court justices in Frederick County soon resumed business, even though the legal papers they processed had no tax stamps. Other county courts followed Frederick's example and by spring even offices in Annapolis conducted business without stamped paper.

The Stamp Act Repealed

On April 10, 1766, the *Maryland Gazette* resumed publication with the announcement that Parliament had repealed the Stamp Act. Marylanders rejoiced that the colonists had forced Parliament to back down once again from levying new taxes on them.

The fight against the Stamp Act had given some younger men, such as Samuel Chase and William Paca, who organized the Annapolis Sons of Liberty, an opportunity to become leaders. The Baltimore Sons of Liberty included not only wealthy merchants like William Lux, but also ordinary tradesmen. The protest had given them all experience in organizing resistance to authority. This experience would be valuable sooner than they expected in struggles against both the proprietor and Parliament.

■ Anne Catharine Green. *Anne Catherine Hoof Green*, by Charles Willson Peale, oil on canvas, 1769, National Portrait Gallery, Smithsonian Institution.

■ Religion and Taxes

With the Stamp Act threat behind them, Maryland political leaders turned their attention to matters at home. Throughout most of the colonial period, the proprietor was of more concern to Marylanders than the king and Parliament. A loosely organized group known as the "country" or Popular Party fought what it considered unreasonable acts by the proprietor and his officials.

The Popular Party's power centered in the elected Lower House of the General Assembly. The proprietor appointed and richly rewarded the governor and his council (which also made up the Upper House of the General Assembly), so they and their associates defended his interests as the "court" or Proprietary Party. Popular Party and Proprietary Party disagreement led to stalemate on many important political issues during the final decades of the colonial period.

The Proprietor's Churchmen

Under the charter, Lord Baltimore had the authority to appoint clergymen to parishes of the Anglican Church, Maryland's official tax-supported religion since 1692. Members of the Popular Party

> ### Anne Catharine Green and Mary Katherine Goddard: Printers
>
> Politics in colonial Maryland was a male affair. When a man wanted to express his views in the pages of the local newspaper, however, he often had dealings with women. From 1767 until her death in 1775, Anne Catharine Green published the *Maryland Gazette* in Annapolis. In 1774, William Goddard started a rival newspaper in Baltimore, the *Maryland Journal and the Baltimore Advertiser*, and one year later his sister Mary Katherine Goddard took over the paper. She published it all through the War of Independence.
>
> Anne Catharine Green began printing the *Maryland Gazette* after her husband Jonas Green died in 1767. Jonas Green had been the public printer, meaning that he did all of the printing work required by the Maryland government. The mother of fourteen, six of whom were still alive, Green finished the printing work her husband had under way at the time of his death. The General Assembly then appointed her public printer for the colony.
>
> Mary Katherine Goddard gained her experience in the printing business because her brother would never stay in one place long enough to finish what he had started. After her physician father died, Goddard and her mother helped her brother start printing businesses in Providence, Rhode Island, and Philadelphia. In 1773, William settled in Baltimore and began publishing a newspaper there. As usual, however, he soon became interested in other projects and left the business. After settling the family's affairs in Philadelphia, his sister took over operation of the Baltimore press.
>
> Anne Catharine Green and Mary Katherine Goddard kept Marylanders informed in the important years before and during the War of Independence. The hundreds of pages of newsprint they filled, and the dozens of books and pamphlets they published and sold, show that both women did their jobs well.

objected to the high cost of supporting these clergymen, especially since the people of the parish had no say in who became their clergyman or how long he could hold his position. When the Reverend Bennet Allen arrived in Maryland in late 1766, the colony's Popular leaders found a focus for their disgust.

The Reverend Allen bragged about his close connections with the proprietor, Frederick, the sixth Lord Baltimore. He claimed that Lord Baltimore had promised him the richest parish in the province. When he found that the richest parish already had a clergyman, he demanded that the governor give him two parishes and two salaries. Allen's struggle to get two parishes to satisfy his greed caused nearly everyone to turn against him. Allen also drank to excess, fought in public, and behaved in a cowardly way by backing out of a duel he had arranged.

Allen's scandalous behavior offended nearly everyone in Annapolis. Governor Horatio Sharpe must have been relieved when All Saints' Parish in Frederick Town, the richest parish in the colony, became available. He promptly appointed the Reverend Allen to All Saints'. The people of Frederick knew all about the Reverend Allen's bad behavior in Annapolis, however, and they were determined to keep him out of their church.

During services the first Sunday Allen was in Frederick, members of the congregation tried to pull him out of the pulpit. Allen drew a pistol on the ringleader of the group and made his way warily out of the church. Convinced he could never serve in a Maryland parish again, Allen made his way to Philadelphia and then back home to England.

Reverend Bennet Allen's brief stay in the colony forcefully reminded the Popular Party that Lord Baltimore was as much of a problem for Marylanders as the British government. The proprietor's power to appoint despicable people like Allen to highly paid positions could be just as dangerous a threat to the colonists' liberties as the actions of the Crown and Parliament.

The Townshend Revenue Act

While Marylanders were busy with the Reverend Bennet Allen affair, the British Parliament passed another measure to raise money from the colonies. Named for Charles Townshend, Chancellor of the Exchequer, Britain's treasury department, this act placed an import duty on lead, painters' colors, several types of glass, and large sheets of paper, none of which were used widely by the colonists. The bill also included tea, however, which was consumed throughout the colonies.

Tea was a product of the Far East—India and China—and was costly because it had to be shipped halfway around the world. It was also heavily taxed by the British government, which added dramatically to its selling price in the colonies. Colonists, especially the women, nevertheless loved it, and for many it was the one indulgence they allowed themselves. Peter Kalm, a Swedish traveler in America, reported seeing "hardly a farmer's wife or a poor woman, who does not drink tea in the morning." Another visitor snorted, "The women are such slaves to it, that they would rather go without their dinners than without a *dish of tea*."

The drafters of the Townshend Revenue Act counted on tea's popularity with women to help gain acceptance for the bill in the colonies, hoping that pressure from wives would keep husbands from embracing tea boycotts as a protest against the bill. To make the tax even more palatable in the colonies, the Townshend Revenue Act actually reduced the tax on tea exported to the colonies, making tea in America much cheaper than it was in Britain. How could anyone complain about such a small tax on tea or on the other items covered by the Townshend Revenue Act, they reasoned.

■ The 1648 Maryland seal used during the colonial period, with a motto meaning "grow and multiply." The image of the seal, impressed into wax attached to a document, confirmed the document's authenticity. Collection of the Maryland State Archives, MSA SC 1551-3-1.

Opposition to the Townshend Revenue Act

Colonists understood what Parliament was trying to do with the Townshend Revenue Act. By taxing only a few things that most people did not need or use and by dramatically lowering the tax on tea, Parliament hoped that colonists would at last accept a tax bill. That would establish a precedent for Parliament imposing additional taxes on the colonies. But the colonists were having none of it. Protests against the Townshend Revenue Act began in New York and Massachusetts and within a few months had spread south to Maryland.

The controversy in Maryland was sparked by a letter from the Massachusetts House of Representatives, which asked for support in fighting the Townshend Revenue Act. Governor Sharpe ordered the Lower House of the Assembly to ignore the letter. Delegates responded that as the elected representatives of the people they had every right to express their concerns. Sharpe tried to thwart the delegates by adjourning the General Assembly. Before leaving for home, however, members of the Lower House sent a letter to the king declaring that the Townshend Act violated their rights as Englishmen as well as the principle of "no taxation without representation."

Nonimportation

In August 1768, Boston merchants agreed to stop importing goods from England. They hoped this new form of protest, called nonimportation, would cripple British commerce and force a repeal of the Townshend Revenue Act. By March 1769, Baltimore merchants had also signed an agreement to stop importing British goods, and Annapolis merchants followed in May. By June, almost all Maryland counties had formed nonimportation associations to ensure that no ships entered Maryland ports with banned items on board.

In April 1770, the brigantine *Good Intent* entered the Annapolis harbor with banned goods imported from England in its hold. The largest part of the cargo was consigned to an Annapolis merchant, Anthony Stewart, and his business partner and father-in-law James Dick. Despite Stewart's argument that the goods had been ordered before nonimportation went into effect, the local merchants' association ordered the *Good Intent* to sail back to England without unloading its cargo, reaffirming Maryland's support of nonimportation.

Parliament repealed most of the duties listed in the Townshend Revenue Act in April 1770, but retained the tax on tea as a way to preserve the right of

■ This cartouche (decorative emblem) from a 1751 map of Maryland and Virginia shows enslaved men loading hogsheads of tobacco for shipment to England as merchants and planters enjoy a refreshing drink. The Tobacco Inspection Act was designed to maintain the quality—and thus the price—of Maryland's major export. Courtesy of the Library of Congress, G3880 1755.F72.

Parliament to tax the colonies. Most colonists were willing by then to overlook the tax on tea, however, and to celebrate instead their victory in once more forcing Parliament to repeal taxes on the colonies.

■ Tobacco and Fees

Even before Parliament repealed the Townshend Revenue Act, members of Maryland's Popular Party were involved in another issue that pitted them against the proprietor. The Tobacco Inspection Act of 1747, which ensured that only good-quality Maryland tobacco reached European markets, was due to expire in October 1770. Everyone agreed that a new inspection act had to be passed. If not, the incomes of everyone would drop—planters who grew tobacco as their cash crop, proprietary officials and Anglican clergymen whose salaries were paid in tobacco, and the proprietor himself, whose handsome annual income depended on the price of tobacco.

The Popular Party, which controlled the Lower House of the Assembly, decided to test the new proprietary governor, Robert Eden, by renewing its long-standing demand that fees paid to proprietary officials be reduced in exchange for passage of a new act to require tobacco inspection. Eden refused and both the 1747 Tobacco Inspection Act and the schedule of fees for proprietary officials expired on October 20, 1770.

The Lower House of the Assembly warned public officials and clergymen not to accept or collect any more fees. William Stewart, clerk of the Land Office, ignored the warning and the Lower House ordered his arrest. Governor Eden dismissed the General Assembly, freed Stewart from jail, and then, on November 26, 1770, issued his controversial Fee Proclamation.

The Fee Proclamation

Eden's Fee Proclamation bypassed the Lower House of the General Assembly entirely. Exercising the king-like authority the Maryland charter granted to the proprietor, Eden in his proclamation provided that until the General Assembly acted on a new fee schedule all proprietary officers and Anglican clergymen would continue to collect the same fees as they had before the fee schedule expired. After Eden issued his proclamation, the lines of battle were drawn. The Lower House demanded its repeal. The governor and the Council adamantly refused, blaming the Lower House for refusing to pass a new tobacco inspection law.

Arguments over the Fee Proclamation raged on for three years. During 1773, Daniel Dulany the Younger and Charles Car-

■ Robert Eden, the last colonial governor of Maryland, faced protests during his entire administration. Collection of the Maryland State Archives, MSA SC 1545-1108.

roll of Carrollton engaged in an important newspaper debate on the question. Dulany signed his writings "Antilon." Carroll wrote under the pen name "First Citizen." Dulany defended the governor's Fee Proclamation; Carroll argued that fees established by proclamation were, like the Stamp Act and the Townshend Revenue Act, nothing more than taxation without representation. His reasoning won him many accolades and made him one of the leaders of the Popular Party.

People made their opposition to the Fee Proclamation known through carefully planned street demonstrations that brought together ordinary citizens and Popular Party leaders. After the election for new General Assembly delegates in May 1773, voters walked in solemn procession to bury Governor Eden's hated Fee Proclamation under the public gallows. William Paca and Matthias Hammond, two Popular Party leaders who had just won election as Annapolis delegates to the Lower House, led the protest.

The Fee Proclamation controversy ended later in 1773, when the Assembly passed a new Tobacco Inspection Act that had no fee schedule. It seemed that the governor and the Council had won this long-running fight with the Lower House because Eden's Fee Proclamation remained in effect. The Lower House had, however, won wide public support and honed its ability to argue effectively against the proprietor and his officials in the colony. The Fee Proclamation controversy also nurtured new leaders like Charles Carroll of Carrollton, who because he was a Roman Catholic could not otherwise participate in the public life of the colony.

Complicating matters for the proprietary side, the proprietor, Frederick, the sixth Lord Baltimore, died in 1771 while the colony was convulsed in debate over the Fee Proclamation. Ownership of Maryland passed to his son Henry Harford, a 13-year-old who was too young to provide any support for his governor, proprietary officeholders, and clergymen in Maryland. Because Harford was born out of wedlock, he was not eligible to inherit the title of Lord Baltimore.

The Tea Act

No sooner had the problem of tobacco inspection been solved than the colony's attention was again directed to the wider world. This time tea became the symbol of British oppression. In May 1773, Parliament passed the Tea Act, which gave the East India Company a virtual monopoly on the sale of tea in the American colonies. Parliament eliminated the duties the East India Company formerly paid, expecting colonists to welcome a historically low price for tea without objecting to the means by which the price had been lowered, which resulted in tea being cheaper in America than ever.

The colonists liked cheap tea, but they objected to Parliament giving a monopoly to a favored British company. They were afraid that Parliament would grant monopolies to other British companies that marketed products in America, crippling colonial trade and local businesses. Massachusetts was first to react against the Tea Act. In that colony's most famous act of protest, the Boston Tea Party of December 1773, the local Sons of Liberty boarded three British ships and dumped 342 chests of tea into the harbor.

Parliament punished Boston for dumping the East India Company's tea by passing the Boston Port Act, closing the port of Boston until the city paid for the tea that had been destroyed. Boston, whose economic livelihood depended on its port, sent letters to all the other colonies asking for help. In response merchants in Baltimore and Annapolis joined with merchants elsewhere in adopting nonimportation and nonexportation measures, pledging neither to receive goods from nor to send goods to Britain.

Revolutionary Governments

Organized opposition to British policies reached new heights in the wake of the Boston Port Act. Citizens in towns throughout the colonies destroyed tea in protests like the Boston Tea Party. Maryland's Popular Party took advantage of the outrage over the Boston Port Act to take control of the colony's government. Benjamin Franklin had called earlier, in 1773, for a meeting of representatives from all the colonies to coordinate protests against the actions of Parliament. This idea bore fruit when delegates to the First Continental Congress met in Philadelphia to discuss coordinating actions.

Opposition to the Boston Port Act quickly spread throughout Maryland. Popular Party leaders proposed a general meeting and within days men from all the counties met in Annapolis on June 22, 1774, to discuss the plight of Boston. This meeting was extralegal, or outside the law, but Governor Eden did not try to stop it. The ninety-two delegates to this extralegal Convention condemned the Boston Port Act and voted to send aid to Boston's citizens. The Convention also appointed delegates to the Continental Congress, scheduled to meet in Philadelphia in September.

First Continental Congress

Delegates from twelve of the thirteen colonies met in Philadelphia in September 1774 to discuss coordinating opposition to the Boston Port Act. Maryland's delegation to this meeting consisted of Robert Goldsborough, Thomas Johnson, Matthew Tilghman, William Paca, and Samuel Chase, all leaders of the Popular Party. The members of this First Continental Congress petitioned the king for repeal of the Boston Port Act and voted to stop all trade to and from England. They also voted to hold another Congress if the king and Parliament did not grant their petition. The formation of the Continental Congress was an important step toward independence because it provided a forum where representatives from all the colonies could coordinate their protests against Britain.

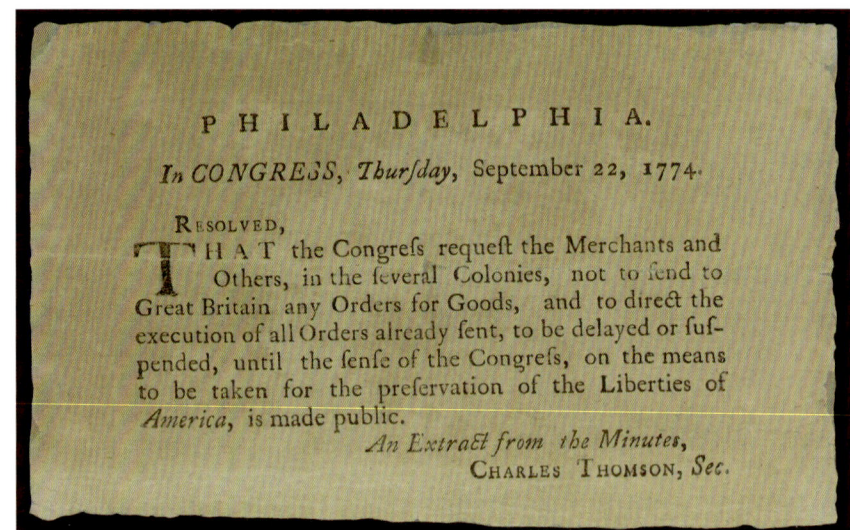

■ Congressional Congress Document 1, Congress's first resolution, which in September 1774 called for nonimportation—a boycott of British goods by "Merchants and Others." Courtesy of the Library of Congress, bdsdcc.00101.

A New Government Emerges

Encouraged by the success of the first extralegal Convention held in June 1774, Maryland's Popular Party leaders called for other Conventions in November and December. By the fourth Convention, held in April 1775, these meetings had taken over all law-making power in Maryland. The actions of the Convention were called "resolves" instead of laws, but they had the force of law. Local political organizations established in all of the counties and towns, called committees of observation and committees of correspondence, publicized and enforced the Convention's resolves.

By August 1775, the extralegal Convention government had assumed all executive and legislative powers in Maryland. Governor Eden remained in the colony and retained his title but no longer had any real power. The Popular Party had, in effect, overthrown the proprietary establishment.

The Burning of the *Peggy Stewart*

The powerlessness of Governor Eden and other proprietary officials to stand in the way of the Popular Party was demonstrated by an event that happened shortly after the first Convention met. On October 15, 1774, the brig *Peggy Stewart* arrived at the port of Annapolis. Anthony Stewart, the same Annapolis merchant who had been involved in the *Good Intent* controversy in 1770, owned the ship, which he had named after his daughter. The ship's cargo included more than 2,300 pounds of tea consigned to an Annapolis merchant firm.

Before Stewart could land the ship's cargo, word about the tea began to circulate in town. Stewart published a public apology, but that did nothing to stop the growing public anger. On October 19, a large crowd of people gathered in Annapolis to decide the fate of the *Peggy Stewart* and the tea. Stewart offered to burn all the tea, and some in the crowd thought that would be enough punishment. But others demanded destruction of the ship as well. Afraid for his family's safety, Stewart ran the ship aground in full sight of Annapolis and set it afire. The blazing ship convinced many that the established order was crumbling and that the governor and his officials in the colony were powerless to preserve public order.

The Association of Freemen

In July 1775, the fifth Maryland Convention issued a proclamation supporting the raising of an army to "repel force by force" and signed it as the Association of

■ The burning of the *Peggy Stewart* marked the climax of Maryland's protest over tea. The ship's owner, Anthony Stewart, who feared for the safety of his home and family, burned the vessel in the Annapolis harbor. Collection of the Maryland State Archives, MSA SC 1545-1111.

the Freemen of Maryland. All freemen in the colony were required to sign copies of the Association document, pledging their loyalty to the extralegal Convention. The names of those who refused to sign were to be reported to the Convention. The Association of Freemen document thus provided a loyalty oath to the new extralegal government as well as a means of identifying men of military age throughout the colony.

Recognizing the need for an administrative body for more effective governance, the Convention delegated executive authority to a Council of Safety; it also assigned quasi-judicial powers to the various county committees of observation. The delegates charged the Council of Safety with establishing an armed and trained militia, consisting of all able-bodied freemen between the ages of 16 and 50. The Association exempted Quakers from military service as well as German immigrants in Western Maryland who were Dunkards, Mennonites, or members of other sects that prohibited bearing arms.

With adoption of the Association of Freemen pledge and the delegation of executive and judicial powers, the Popular Party formalized its struggle to win the right to govern Maryland without interference from the proprietor and his officials. Most Popular Party leaders thought this victory was enough political revolution for Maryland. Few saw much to be gained by going further and declaring independence from Britain.

Opposition to Independence

As other colonies moved ever closer to a declaration of independence, Maryland's extralegal government continued to resist. As late as May 1776, the Maryland Convention voted unanimously to prohibit its delegates in the Continental Congress from supporting independence. Maryland's resolute opposition to independence frustrated and annoyed many members of the Continental Congress. John Adams of Massachusetts wrote a friend that nearly every state except Maryland was ready to support independence. Maryland, Adams continued, "is so eccentric a Colony—sometimes so hot, sometimes so cold; now so high, then so low—that I know not what to say about it or to expect from it."

War Approaches

Maryland's opposition to independence became increasingly tenuous as the other colonies moved ever closer to separation from Britain. The American colonies were already at war with England, although neither side had declared hostilities. Pitched battles between colonists and British troops had already occurred. The number of British troops in America increased monthly. British warships had entered Maryland waters in January 1776. In response, the Maryland Convention had taken steps to create its own navy, launching its first warship, named *Defence*, in March. In June 1776, Maryland agreed for the first time to raise more than two thousand men to send to the Continental army.

In June 1776, Governor Robert Eden finally left Maryland. Both Eden and the Council of Safety decided that he could no longer serve a useful purpose in the colony. The Convention's letter to Eden asking him to leave ended by expressing the wish that he would return to govern the colony when peace returned.

The Virginia Resolution

On June 7, 1776, Richard Henry Lee, a Virginia delegate to the Continental Congress, introduced a resolution that stated: "These United Colonies are, and of right ought to be, free and independent States, that they are absolved from all allegiance to the British Crown, and that all political connection between them and the State of Great Britain is and ought to be totally dissolved." This was the call for independence that many Marylanders had dreaded. The Maryland Convention asked Congress to put off consideration of the Virginia Resolution until Maryland could consult with its delegates in Philadelphia. Congress flatly refused.

At the same time, Samuel Chase, Charles Carroll of Carrollton, Matthew Tilghman, Thomas Johnson, and others concluded that Maryland had no choice but to join the other colonies in declaring independence. They urged political leaders all over Maryland to support separation from Britain. The result, on the surface at least, was a remarkable change of heart. On June 28, the Maryland Convention unanimously adopted a resolution freeing its delegates in Congress to support independence.

In truth, Maryland's beliefs had not changed overnight. Most Maryland politicians simply recognized that the struggle for compromise had failed and that Maryland could not afford to stand alone against the other colonies. It was clear that the delegations of most colonies would vote for independence. Maryland, for better or worse, must succeed or fail with the rest.

■ Independence

The new instructions from the Maryland Convention arrived in Philadelphia on July 1, 1776. The delegates to the Continental Congress were just entering the great debate over independence. Only three members of the Maryland delegation were present in Congress: William Paca, Thomas Stone, and John Rogers. These three Marylanders joined the other members of Congress on July 2 in declaring the colonies free and independent states. Two days later, these same three Marylanders approved the language of the Declaration of Independence, which explained to the world why the colonists had declared themselves independent of Britain.

Congress decided that an official copy of the Declaration should be prepared and signed by all the delegates. The parchment copy of the Declaration of Independence was ready for signing on August 2, 1776. The Maryland men present in Congress who signed for the state were Charles Carroll of Carrollton, Sam-

Maryland's Signers of the Declaration of Independence

Charles Carroll of Carrollton. Courtesy of the Yale Center for British Art, B1981.25.521.

William Paca. Collection of the Maryland State Archives, MSA SC 1545-1117.

Charles Carroll of Carrollton was the wealthiest of Maryland's four signers. Born in Anne Arundel County in 1737, Carroll was the only child of one of Maryland's richest landowners and slaveholders, Charles Carroll of Annapolis. He received a fine education in France and studied law in England before returning to Maryland at the time of the Stamp Act. Just one thing stood in the way of a brilliant career for Carroll: he was a Roman Catholic. At the time Catholics could not vote, hold public office, or worship openly in Maryland.

The young Carroll nevertheless took an active part in protests against the policies of the proprietor and Parliament. He gained fame in 1773 writing as "First Citizen" in a newspaper debate with Daniel Dulany over Governor Eden's Fee Proclamation. When the Maryland Convention assumed control of the colony's government, it set aside the rule against the election of Catholics. Carroll attended the convention, which in 1776 elected him as a delegate to the Continental Congress.

Carroll had a long and honorable career, serving in the Maryland Senate from 1776 to 1800 and as a US senator from 1789 to 1792. He made a large fortune through planting, leasing land, and investing in iron manufacturing and other projects. He is best remembered today, however, for two things over which he had no control: he was the only Catholic signer of the Declaration and he lived longer than any other signer. Carroll died on November 14, 1832, at age 95.

William Paca was born on October 31, 1740, in the area of Baltimore County that later became Harford County. The second son of a well-to-do and politically active planter, Paca received an excellent education at the College of Philadelphia and studied law in Annapolis so that he could make his fortune by practicing law. But Paca found a surer way to wealth, influence, and power. Shortly after finishing his legal studies, Paca married Mary Chew, one of the most eligible young women in the colony, and used her inheritance to build a suitably elegant mansion in Annapolis.

Paca soon developed a successful legal practice but pursued a second career in politics as well. He quickly became a leader of the Popular Party in the Lower House and represented Maryland in the Continental Congress longer than any other delegate. After independence, he served in both houses of the General Assembly and three terms as governor. For the final ten years of his life, Paca was a federal judge for the district of Maryland. He died at his estate on Wye Island in Queen Anne's County on October 13, 1799.

Samuel Chase. Courtesy of the Maryland Historical Society, MS 1892.2.1

Thomas Stone. Collection of the Maryland State Archives, MSA SC 1545-1116.

Samuel Chase has been called the "stormy patriot." He was a gifted speaker who could raise a mob in the streets as quickly as he could sway a jury in the courtroom. Chase was born near Princess Anne in Somerset County on April 17, 1741. His father, an Anglican minister, was not well-to-do, but he gave his son a fine education and sent him to Annapolis to study law. Chase spent much of his life trying to gain the wealth and status denied him by his humble birth but was often in or near bankruptcy.

His appointment to the US Supreme Court in 1796 crowned Chase's long and distinguished public career. A strong Federalist, Chase was accused of using his position to make political remarks, in violation of his role as judge, and was impeached by the US House of Representatives in 1804. After a dramatic trial, the Senate found Chase innocent on March 1, 1805. He remained on the Supreme Court until his death on June 19, 1811.

Chase was a man who had intense friends and violent enemies. Even they, however, agreed that he made many valuable contributions to his state and the nation.

Thomas Stone was born in 1743 in Charles County. He was well educated and, like his fellow signers, he trained as a lawyer. Unlike them, he decided to pursue his career in far-off Frederick Town in Frederick County. He was, therefore, away from the center of politics during the 1760s, but in 1771 he moved back to Charles County, where his political career began in 1774 with his election to the first Maryland Convention. After independence, Stone served in both houses of the General Assembly and as a delegate to the Constitutional Convention.

Stone's life ended tragically. His wife Margaret's health began to fail in 1776, after she received a smallpox inoculation. She suffered from rheumatism for the next eleven years, and then died suddenly on June 1, 1787. Stone, crushed by the loss of his wife, resigned from public office and on the advice of his doctor planned a sea voyage to recover from his grief. But he died in Alexandria, Virginia, on October 5, 1787, while waiting for the ship that was to take him on the voyage.

uel Chase, Thomas Stone, and William Paca. Of the four, only Stone and Paca had actually voted for independence a month earlier.

Maryland's four signers of the Declaration of Independence were all leaders of the Popular Party. William Paca, of Baltimore (now Harford) County, and Samuel Chase, of Somerset County, were successful Annapolis lawyers who had worked together on every political controversy since the Stamp Act. Thomas Stone, a Charles County native whose early law career had been in Frederick Town, returned to Charles County and represented it in the extralegal Convention governments. Charles Carroll of Carrollton, an Annapolis native, was the wealthiest of the four Maryland signers and the oldest at age 38. Carroll was also the only Roman Catholic among the fifty-six men who signed the Declaration of Independence.

And what of John Rogers, the Marylander who voted for independence on July 2 and approved the Declaration of Independence on July 4? He was from Prince George's County, a lawyer and landowner, and a firm supporter of the Popular Party. He served in every extralegal Convention and was elected as one of Maryland's delegates to the Continental Congress in December 1775. Rogers was reelected to Congress in May 1776 but for some reason he was not returned to Congress as a delegate when the Maryland Convention selected a new delegation in July. Therefore, Rogers was not in Philadelphia on August 2 to sign the engrossed copy of the Declaration of Independence—the only member of Congress who voted for independence who did not sign the engrossed copy. Rogers is therefore largely lost to history, even though he as much as any of those men we call "the Signers" risked his life and fortune to support independence from Great Britain.

A "Declaration of the Delegates of Maryland"

On July 6, two days before news of the Declaration of Independence reached Annapolis from Philadelphia, the Maryland Convention adopted "A Declaration of the Delegates of Maryland." This Declaration explained why the Convention had allowed its delegates in Congress to vote for independence. The Declaration was almost apologetic. It said that "no ambitious views, no desire of independence induced the people of Maryland to form a union with the other colonies." All Marylanders had asked for was freedom from taxation by Parliament and the right to govern the colony through its own General Assembly.

Maryland's Reasons for Caution

The members of Maryland's Convention government had good reason to be cautious about supporting independence. It was hard to imagine how the thirteen separate and poorly organized states could win the war for independence. After all, Britain had the greatest land and sea force in the world. The "United States" were not really united at all. The thirteen states had no navy and few trained and experienced military officers. The colonial economy depended on trade with Britain and Europe, which would be endangered by war. The former colonies had no uniform currency and little credit in the financial capitals of Europe to help finance a war. Under the circumstances, it was reasonable for Marylanders to be cautious and to seek a compromise that would avoid war.

■ Maryland and the War of Independence

Once Maryland joined the struggle for independence, no one could question its loyalty or the energy of its leaders. Problems were plentiful, as they were in other states. Supplies of all types were scarce. Many of Maryland's men left their homes and work to join the fighting, while others concentrated their energies on producing food and other supplies for the American army.

Maryland's Wartime Contributions

No Revolutionary War battles took place on Maryland soil, but there was always the threat of enemy invasion. British ships entered the Chesapeake Bay on several occasions and both British and American forces marched through the state, earning Maryland the nickname "crossroads of the Revolution." Both British and American troops caused local suffering as they looted farms, stole fence rails for firewood, and made dinners of farm animals.

The war gave more people than ever an opportunity to participate in public life. Many did this by serving in the Continental army, in a local militia unit, or on one of the state's warships. Men and women, black and white, enslaved and free, joined together to build local defenses wherever a British invasion threatened. Farmers everywhere grew additional bushels of wheat or raised an extra hog or cow to help feed the troops. Thousands of citizens came forward with what they could spare for the war effort. Maryland became such a valuable and reliable source of supplies for the American army that it became known as the "breadbasket of the Revolution."

Another nickname bestowed on Maryland—the "Old Line State"—refers to the outstanding contributions of Maryland soldiers in the Continental Line, the American army commanded by General George Washington. Maryland soldiers were heroes at the Battle of Long Island in September 1776. In this first major battle after independence, Baltimore native Major Mordecai Gist with a force of between perhaps three hundred to four hundred untested Maryland soldiers suffered substantial losses as they held back a far larger British attack long enough for nine thousand American soldiers to escape across the East River to safety in Manhattan, thus saving the American army to fight another day. At the Battle of Harlem Heights a month later, Maryland troops forced British soldiers to retreat from the field of battle for the first time, boosting the sagging morale of Washington's beleaguered army.

■ At the Battle of Long Island in August 1776, Maryland soldiers charged the British line repeatedly and held the enemy long enough to allow the rest of the American army to reach safety. Courtesy of the Brooklyn Historical Society, M1986.29.1

Some of the first Marylanders to enlist in the War of Independence were members of the German Battalion. Outraged by Britain's use of German mercenaries, the Continental Congress in May 1776 authorized formation of this battalion, which was to consist of officers and men of German descent from Pennsylvania and Maryland. Maryland raised four companies of ninety men each from Baltimore and Frederick Counties, with Colonel George Stricker of Frederick County as the ranking Maryland officer. The German Battalion fought bravely in the early battles in New York and New Jersey and continued to serve with distinction until the end of the war.

War on the Water

Maryland's shipping industry also helped support the American cause, supplying ships for both trade and battle. Baltimore shipyards equipped the *Wasp* and the *Hornet*, two of the first ships in the American navy. Many Maryland mariners became privateers, ship captains licensed by the government to capture enemy ships and the cargoes they carried. A risky adventure, privateering brought wealth and glory to some men, like Joshua Barney, and ruin or death to others. Locally, Maryland ship pilots, both black and white, patrolled the state's rivers and the Chesapeake Bay. Their great knowledge of Maryland's waterways served the nation well during the Revolution.

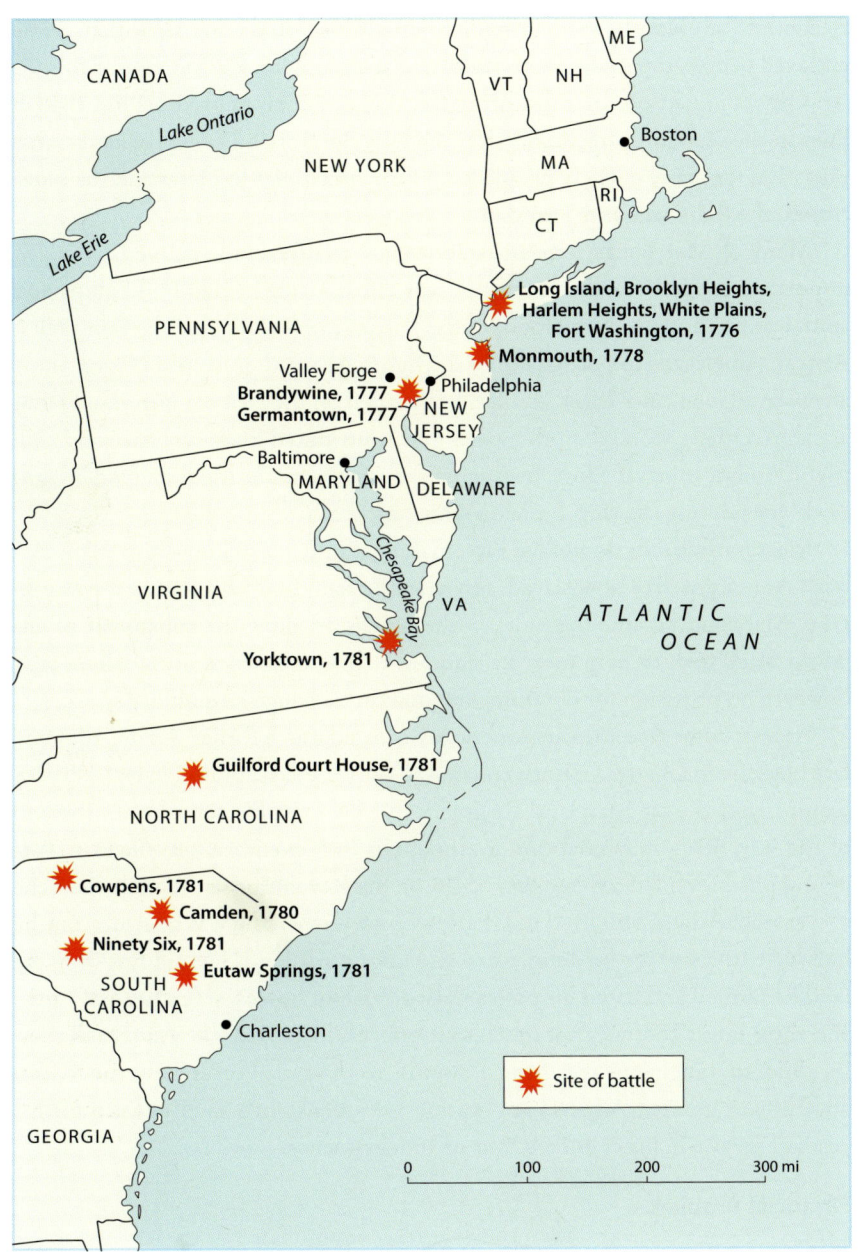

■ Major Land Battles of the American Revolution involving Maryland Troops, 1775–1781

Maryland African Americans and the War Effort

There was a clear discrepancy between the revolutionary ideals of freedom and rights for all and the existence of slavery. This was not lost on African Americans, both enslaved and free, or on the British who understood the value of blacks as potential fighters and as producers of food and other needed military supplies. In 1775, John Murray, Lord Dunmore, governor of Virginia, offered freedom to any slaves or indentured servants who would join the British. Some enslaved people, especially from Southern Maryland, took advantage of this offer. Others joined the British during the war or simply moved behind British lines in the search for freedom. After the war, the British Navy provided transportation for many of these people from former colonies to places such as Nova Scotia, the Bahamas, and Trinidad.

Many of Maryland's African Americans, both free and enslaved, provided important support for the American war effort. They helped build ships and land defenses and produced food for the Patriot army and navy. Maryland's first African Americans to participate in the fighting served on ships. "Negro Tom," an enslaved man, and "Black Yankee" both sailed on the *Defence*, Maryland's first warship. Others worked on the water and contributed both expertise and skill to the American naval effort. In August 1777, for example, the state paid "Negro Dick" for piloting the ship *Lydia* on state business.

Most muster rolls do not list race, making it difficult to know how many African Americans, free or enslaved, served in the army and navy during the war. In 1780, Maryland became the only southern state to allow the enlistment of enslaved black men to help meet its quota for the Continental army. There was, however, no provision for obtaining freedom in exchange for military service.

At least some free African Americans enlisted much earlier. Adam Adams, a free black from Charles County, enlisted as a private in Captain Henry Gaither's Company of the 1st Maryland Regiment in May 1777. He served until the end of the war, being mustered out at Annapolis in November 1783. In 1820, Adams applied for a federal pension based on his Revolutionary War service. The 57-year-old Adams still lived in Charles County, where he was a farmer, but he had little to show for his long years of working the land. He did not own the land he farmed and listed his assets as two draught horses, seven head of cattle, and three hogs. That was not much to support himself, his wife Anne, and their six children, ranging in ages from 3 months to 14 years. Fortunately, the federal government granted Adams's application for a pension, a small reward for his years of service in his country's War of Independence.

Financial Problems

The cost of financing the war forced the Maryland government to print paper money. Because it was not backed by gold or silver, the currency quickly lost its value. The result was price inflation, which increased throughout the years of fighting, hurting many Marylanders. Many goods were hard to find at any price during the war. The food, clothing, shoes, and other supplies needed by the army meant that civilians often could not find what they needed for themselves and their families. Most of the items imported from England before the war, such as furniture, tools, clothing, and even sewing needles, were no longer available. With so much being spent on the war effort, many peacetime projects had to be put on hold. Baltimore, for example, had to wait to pave its streets, with its citizens enduring dusty roads in summer and deep mud in winter until the war was over. In Annapolis, work on the new State House took years longer than expected due to a shortage of money and building supplies.

Wartime Economic Expansion

Although the war caused many hardships, it also brought growth to Maryland's economy. Wheat replaced tobacco as Maryland's main cash crop and the state became a reliable supplier of flour and bread for the American army. Maryland iron foundries produced cannon and shot for the war effort. Early in the war, saltworks along Maryland's Atlantic coast eased the shortage of salt, an important item that had been imported prior to the war. Merchants and shippers in ports like Baltimore and Annapolis prospered, especially from the grain trade, and the shipbuilding industry boomed in Baltimore. Shipbuilding, trade, and manufacturing helped make Baltimore the largest city in Maryland by war's end.

Loyalists

Not everyone supported independence. Marylanders who believed that the colonies should remain a part of Britain were called Loyalists. People had different reasons for becoming Loyalists. Men who worked for the proprietor or for the established Anglican Church had their jobs and incomes at stake. Recent arrivals from Great Britain often felt greater loyalty to their mother country than to their new home. Other people did not like the way Maryland's extralegal revolutionary government tried to force everyone to join the protest. And the promise of freedom enticed some enslaved African Americans to flee to the British. Many people on Maryland's lower Eastern Shore felt that the new state government did not address their needs and interests. Some wanted to trade with the British ships in Chesapeake Bay, which would pay well for foodstuffs and locally made pitch and tar. On several occasions Maryland troops had to be dispatched to subdue Eastern Shore Loyalists who rebelled against the authority of the new government.

■ The New State Government

Independence formally ended the authority of Maryland's proprietary government. After July 1776, Maryland, like all the former colonies, had to form a new government. Eleven of the states wrote constitutions to spell out how their new governments would function and what roles and rights citizens would have. Members of the ninth Convention met in Annapolis in August 1776 to write Maryland's first constitution. By the time they finished their work in November, Maryland had adopted the most extensive bill of rights of any of the new states and one of the most conservative constitutions.

> ### William Paca: How Did *He* Pronounce His Name?
>
> A Baltimore native will pronounce William Paca's name with a short *a* (*pack-uh*) as surely as he will call his own town "Bawlmer." But in Annapolis, where Paca built a handsome brick mansion, residents insist his name should be pronounced *pay-kuh*, with a long *a*. Which pronunciation is correct? How did Paca pronounce his own name? This is one puzzle the historian can solve.
>
> During the winter of 1770, a new social club, called the Hominy Club, formed in Annapolis. Members included leading citizens in the community, and William Paca was invited to join. Part of the fun of the club was putting all communications to and from club members in the form of verse.
>
> On March 21, 1771, two non-members asked to attend a meeting. In response to the request, club members responded in rhyme. John Clapham, secretary of the club, wrote,
>
>> If any man gainsay, on his Pate I will rap him,
>> By virtue of my commission, Secretary John Clapham.
>
> Clapham was followed by William Eddis, who wrote,
>
>> I fully assent to what above said is,
>> And am your most obedient Will. Eddis
>
> If Paca had pronounced the first syllable of his name with a short *a*, the way Paca Street is pronounced today in Baltimore, he might have written:
>
>> And so do I, tho' I fear we may lack a
>> Spare glass of wine, but no more from Will Paca.
>
> Instead, Paca selected a word with a long *a* to rhyme with his name:
>
>> And so do I, tho' I cannot but think we take a
>> Rash Step in so doing, but no more from Will Paca.

Despite the Revolution raging about them, Maryland's political leaders felt strongly that politics in Maryland should not become revolutionary. They wanted to ensure that they, not the "lower sort," would continue to govern. The ninth Convention chose prominent leaders of the Popular Party—Samuel Chase, William Paca, Matthew Tilghman, George Plater, Charles Carroll of Carrollton, Robert Goldsborough, and Charles Carroll, Barrister—to draft a bill of rights and a constitution for the new state. As wealthy landowners and slaveholders, they worked hard to keep the reins of government in their own hands with as little change in society as possible.

Maryland's Conservative Constitution of 1776

Maryland's first constitution was written to reduce the possibility of an abuse of power, either by the government or by the people. Fearing the consequences if an evil man got control of the government, the authors made the office of governor weak. Fearing a misuse of power if voters directly elected both houses of the General Assembly, they created a Senate that was elected indirectly to lessen the chances of abuse. Fearing the consequences if poor and middling men got power, the writers of Maryland's first constitution kept government in the hands of men with property.

The Maryland constitution limited the role of ordinary people in the government in several ways. In order to vote for delegates to the General Assembly, a person had to be male, at least 21 years of age, and owner of at least 50 acres of land or property worth £30 current money, an amount that was about one-third less than had been required during the colonial period. Interestingly, race was not a factor in determining suffrage; free African Americans who met the property requirements were eligible to vote. Still, most small farmers, laborers, watermen, and recent immigrants, regardless of race, could not meet those requirements and therefore could not vote.

Officeholders had to meet even higher qualifications. The more important an office, the higher the requirements in terms of property qualifications, age, and length of time a person had lived in the state. These thresholds guaranteed that no poor person or recent immigrant—no matter how wealthy—could hold an important office.

Fear of the Abuse of Power

The framers saw to it that most people could not vote or hold office because they thought democracy would lead to irrational mob rule. They also sought to achieve a balance of power between the two houses of the General Assembly—the Lower House, now called the House of Delegates, and the Senate, the former Upper House. The House of Delegates, the more numerous branch of the legislature, was intended to represent the concerns of ordinary people. Each county had four delegates while Annapolis and Baltimore had two each. All voters directly elected members of the House of Delegates to one-year terms. Because each county sent the same number of delegates to Annapolis, the smallest county had as much power in the legislature as the largest. The rapidly expanding population in the vast western portion of the state would get a larger voice in the General Assembly only with the creation of new counties.

The Senate was a much smaller body, consisting of just fifteen members, nine from the Western Shore and six from the Eastern Shore. Voters chose Senate electors; the electors chose senators for five-year terms. The constitution's framers hoped that this indirect system of electing senators and their long terms of office would help give them the independence necessary to check any democratic or radical excesses that might emerge in the popularly elected House of Delegates. Maryland's first constitution also provided that the state's chief executive would be free of direct public influence. Both houses of the General Assembly, not the voters, annually elected the governor and the governor's council.

The Convention writing Maryland's first constitution recognized the growing importance of Western Maryland by creating two new counties, Washington and

■ With independence, the Maryland government needed a new seal to authenticate its acts. This seal, designed by Charles Willson Peale, became the state seal in 1794. Collection of the Maryland State Archives, MSA SC 1551-5-1.

Montgomery. New delegates from these two Western Maryland counties would make the Lower House of the General Assembly more geographically representative. But any additional Western Maryland counties would have to be approved by the General Assembly, where delegates from the existing counties would be reluctant to see their power diluted by adding delegates from new counties.

Liberties Guaranteed to the People

While Maryland's first constitution sought to preserve the status quo and to thwart democratic tendencies, it did guarantee the state's citizens an extensive list of individual liberties. The forty-two-article Declaration of Rights, which was adopted along with the constitution, asserted that the state government existed "solely for the good of the whole" and that the people "have the sole and exclusive right of regulating the internal government and police thereof." The Declaration guaranteed citizens freedom of speech and press and the right to petition the legislature for redress of grievances. The Declaration outlawed general search warrants and guaranteed citizens a speedy trial by an impartial jury and freedom from cruel and unusual punishments. It deemed monopolies—that danger to liberty raised by the Tea Act of 1773—"odious" and "contrary to the spirit of a free government."

The Declaration eliminated the poll tax, which had supported the established Anglican Church and its clergymen, and guaranteed freedom of religion for all Christians. This provision had special importance for Maryland Catholics, who for decades had not been allowed to worship openly, vote, or hold public office. Now Catholics could once again participate in all aspects of public life, as could Quakers and members of German religious sects who refused to take oaths. The Declaration of Rights allowed them to affirm rather than to swear when an oath was required. The state's small Jewish community was able to worship without government interference, but Jews were not permitted to vote or hold public office in Maryland until 1826.

Prior to independence, only people born in Maryland or Great Britain and its colonies were natural-born citizens. People born in other countries had to be naturalized to enjoy the rights of citizenship. With independence, all free white persons living in Maryland became citizens of the new state. White servants enjoyed full citizenship rights when they completed their term of service. Free African Americans enjoyed citizenship rights as well, but enslaved blacks did not.

Conferring citizenship on all freemen resident in Maryland at the time of independence meant that many people who would have needed to be naturalized during the colonial period now automatically became citizens. This most benefited the large number of Germans who had settled in Western Maryland during the fifty years prior to independence. Citizenship, however, did not confer suffrage rights. Only those free men who met the requirements of land or property could vote.

Under Maryland's first state constitution, the pool of eligible voters did expand a bit because the amount of property a man had to own in order to vote was reduced slightly and because Catholics, Quakers, foreign-born Germans, and a few free African Americans became newly enfranchised. Still, this was far from the demands, made by some, that all men who served in the army should have a right to vote. It was even further from the ideal of others, that all white men should be able to vote. In the end, the first Maryland constitution was a carefully written and conservative document intended to ensure continued control by those who had authority in the counties and in the Lower House of the General Assembly before independence.

Regionalism

The new state constitution recognized that the Chesapeake Bay divides the state into two major regions, the Western Shore and the Eastern Shore. Because Eastern Shore residents often found it difficult and expensive to travel across the Bay to Annapolis for state business, the constitution established two sets of state offices. The offices serving the Western Shore were in Annapolis; the offices for the Eastern Shore were located in Easton.

The General Assembly's creation of institutions of higher education for the state also shows the new state government's concern with regionalism. Before independence, Maryland had no colleges. Native sons had to travel to another colony or to Europe for a college education. The state legislature was determined to change that. Even before the war officially ended, the General Assembly in 1782 established a college in Chestertown on the Eastern Shore, named Washington College in honor of the commander-in-chief of the American army. In 1784, the legislature established St. John's College in Annapolis as an institution of higher learning for the Western Shore. The same act that created St. John's formally associated it with Washington College, naming the two colleges the University of Maryland.

The End of the War of Independence

Victory in the War of Independence took years to achieve. Washington and his ragtag army suffered terribly, more because of poor clothing, lack of shoes, and disease than because of defeat in battle. In 1778, France joined the war on the side of the Americans. France's large fleet of ships and well-trained soldiers and sailors greatly improved the Americans' chances of winning the war, as did loans from the French government and other European countries.

Victory at Yorktown

Finally, in October 1781, good luck and bad weather combined to trap the main part of the British army at Yorktown, Virginia. Continental soldiers commanded by General Washington and French troops led by their commander, the Comte de Rochambeau, raced from the north through Maryland to reinforce the American army. The British under Lord Cornwallis had heavily fortified the town, but the Americans slowly encircled it. French warships under the command of Admiral Françoise Joseph Paul de Grasse defeated the British fleet dispatched to the Chesapeake Bay to rescue Cornwallis and his soldiers. In des-

■ Charles Willson Peale painted this portrait of George Washington with two of his closest aides, the Marquis de Lafayette and Tench Tilghman. Lafayette's French troops camped for a short period in Annapolis on their way to join the French fleet for the attack on the British at Yorktown. Tench Tilghman, of Talbot County, served as Washington's aide-de-camp and secretary throughout the war. Following the victory at Yorktown, Tilghman carried the Articles of Capitulation to the Continental Congress in Philadelphia. Collection of the Maryland State Archives, MSA SC 1545-1120.

peration, Cornwallis ordered his troops to evacuate Yorktown by water, but a severe storm scattered his vessels and left his army stranded. Lord Cornwallis, having no choice but to surrender, asked for terms on October 17. Two days later, while British fifes and drums played a "melancholy tune," British soldiers marched out of Yorktown and stacked their weapons as the victorious Americans and French looked on.

Congress Comes to Annapolis

Lord Cornwallis's defeat at Yorktown effectively ended the War of Independence. Serious peace negotiations began in France in the spring of 1782, but drafting an acceptable treaty proved time-consuming. While awaiting a peace treaty, Congress began considering a location for the permanent capital city for the new United States. Philadelphia had served as the home for Congress since 1774, except when that city was threatened or occupied by the British, but it was just one of many places Congress considered for its permanent home.

Nearly every state wanted the honor of having the capital city and offered land for it. The discussion became especially heated in the summer of 1783, when Congress was again forced to leave Philadelphia, this time because it was threatened by a mob of unpaid soldiers. Once more forced to select a place to meet, members of Congress struck a compromise: until a permanent site could be selected, Congress would alternate every six months between Trenton, New Jersey, and Annapolis, Maryland. These two cities were centrally located and neither was considered a serious candidate as a site for the permanent capital.

Congress had met in Maryland at the beginning of the war, from December 20, 1776, to February 27, 1777, at Henry Fite's house on Market (now Baltimore) Street in Baltimore. Now, in 1783, Congress accepted an invitation from Maryland officials to meet in the state again, this time in the nearly completed State House in Annapolis. The first congressional session in the State House was scheduled for November 26, 1783.

The weeks before Congress arrived were frantic ones for the state's officials. Construction of the State House had begun eleven years earlier, when Governor Robert Eden laid the cornerstone. But work had been slow during the war and much remained to be done to get the building ready for Congress. Governor William Paca gathered workmen to complete and furnish rooms for Congress's use. He also commissioned Annapolis cabinetmaker John Shaw to make two huge American flags. The completed flags measured nearly 10 feet wide by 23 feet long. The first of these so-called Shaw flags was hoisted in honor of the president of Congress, Thomas Mifflin, who arrived in Annapolis on December 3, 1783.

Other congressional delegates arrived more slowly, and not until December 13 were enough states represented to hold the first session. Under the Articles of

■ The Congress of the United States met in the State House in Annapolis from December 1783 to June 1784. Delegates ratified the Treaty of Paris, which formally ended the Revolutionary War, in the Senate chamber in the State House. Collection of the Maryland State Archives, MSA SC 194-1-3.

Confederation, which governed the actions of Congress, each state had only one vote, and for a state to be able to cast its vote, two delegates from that state had to be present. Congress could meet with a majority (seven) of the states represented, but votes on treaties required the presence of nine states.

The most important business before Congress that December was approving the treaty to end the war, known as the Treaty of Paris because British and American negotiators had drafted the document in a town outside Paris, France. A copy had been delivered to Thomas Mifflin, the president of Congress, on November 22. Time was of the essence because the treaty had to be ratified and returned to Paris by March 3, 1784. Travel by ship between America and Europe was slow, especially during winter, so Congress could not afford to delay ratification. But the members could not legally act until nine states were present.

Washington Resigns

On December 20, Congress received a letter from General George Washington in which he asked to come before Congress to resign his military commission. He had been commander-in-chief of the American army since June 1775. His steady command during the long war years had won him the respect of everyone, and some people even talked of making him king of the new United States. But Congress and Washington opposed such schemes, for they were determined to have elected legislative bodies, not the military, govern the new United

> ### Who Was the First President of the United States?
>
> Some say that George Washington was not the first president of the United States. They say that honor belongs to a Marylander, John Hanson, a Charles County native who later lived in Frederick County.
>
> The story of how Hanson became the first president of the United States reveals something about an often forgotten period of American history. Shortly after independence was declared, the Continental Congress drafted a formal plan to bind the thirteen states together. No one wanted a strong central government. Instead, Congress decided that each state would govern itself but would also cooperate with the other states, a form of government known as a confederation.
>
> Congress worked nearly two years on a plan of government. Finally, in November 1777, it sent the Articles of Confederation to the states for approval. Maryland refused. Before it would approve the plan, Maryland demanded that every state give up its claim to western lands. Virginia, which claimed lands as far west as the Mississippi River, did not want to yield that land, but Maryland would not budge. Finally, in January 1781, Virginia ceded its land claims. Maryland signed the Articles of Confederation on February 27 of that year. Congress finally approved the Articles at noon on March 1, 1781.
>
> John Hanson was elected first president of the United States in Congress Assembled, the official name of the confederation government, on November 5, 1781. Hanson suffered from poor health and complained of the "irksome" nature of the "form and ceremonies" required as president. He served his full one-year term, however, and then he returned to Maryland, where he died the following year.
>
>
>
> ■ John Hanson. Collection of the Maryland State Archives, MSA SC 1545-1033.

States. Congress and General Washington planned the details of his resignation ceremony to emphasize this idea.

General Washington arrived at the State House at midday on December 23, 1783. Spectators packed the gallery at the back of the chamber and the balcony above. When Washington entered the room, he faced the seated members of Congress and bowed, removing his hat as a gesture of respect. The members of Congress removed their hats briefly to recognize the general's presence, but they remained seated and did not return his bow. In this way they symbolically showed their superiority, as representatives of an elected government, over the military.

In a brief but moving speech, Washington thanked Congress for the confidence it had shown in him during the long years of warfare. He then handed his military commission to President Mifflin, who thanked Washington for his services to the country and accepted his resignation. After greeting the members of Congress and the spectators who had attended the ceremony, Washington departed for his home at Mount Vernon in Virginia. For the first time in eight years, Washington would spend Christmas Day with his wife and family in his own home.

The Ratification of the Treaty of Paris

On January 14, 1784, Congress finally had the nine states in attendance needed to address the most pressing business before it: ratification of the Treaty of Paris. The ratification vote was taken immediately, with the delegates unani-

■ General George Washington came before Congress to resign his commission as commander-in-chief on December 23, 1783, in a ceremony that emphasized the authority of the civilian government over the military. Collection of the Maryland State Archives, MSA SC 1545-1112.

mously approving the Treaty of Paris ending the war and officially recognizing the independence of the United States.

With peace came an even more formidable challenge. Maryland and the other states now had to figure out how to shape a viable and lasting nation out of the thirteen former colonies. Each of the new states faced the challenge of independence differently, but it soon became clear that they would have to work together as never before if the United States was to succeed.

■ The War's Effects on Maryland

In Maryland the conservative nature of the political leaders and the state's constitution ensured a measure of stability, but the long and costly war brought changes in the political landscape. Nowhere were the changes more pronounced than in Baltimore, which grew rapidly during the war. Unlike Philadelphia, New York, or Charleston, the port of Baltimore was never occupied by the British during the War of Independence. Baltimore had been an important shipping point for grain, flour, bread, pickled beef, and other goods in the ten years before the Revolution, and during the war it became even more important. When independence was declared in 1776, Baltimore's population was about 5,600. By war's end, 12,000 people lived there and Baltimore had become the largest and most active town in Maryland. As its fortunes increased, so did those of the state as a whole.

> ### Mary Ogle Ridout: Eyewitness to History
>
> Mary Ogle Ridout knew when she saw history in the making. She was the daughter of Governor Samuel Ogle and wife of John Ridout, secretary to Governor Horatio Sharpe. Ridout knew well the people who took part in the historic events that occurred in the Maryland State House in the winter of 1783–1784. She also knew that getting mail to England during the War of Independence was difficult. So, she took the opportunity offered by the ship carrying the ratified Treaty of Paris to France to tell her mother in England about George Washington's resignation of his commission on December 23, 1783. Her letter read, in part:
>
> Annapolis 16th Jan 84
>
> I went with several others to see Genl. Washington resign his Commission. The Congress were assembled in the State House. Both Houses of Assembly were present as Spectators; the Gallery full of Ladies. The General seem'd so much affected himself that every body felt for him. He addressed Congress in a short speech, but very affecting. Many Tears was shed. He has retir'd from all public business & designs to spend the rest of his Days at his own Seat. I think the World never produced a greater man & very few so good. . . .
>
> I am my Dr Madam your dutiful affectionate Daughter
> M. Ridout

New Opportunities

The war brought about important changes and opened up new opportunities for people in Maryland. Some merchants who supplied and transported goods for the army made a fortune. Other people enjoyed new opportunities to buy land. The state confiscated property belonging to those who remained loyal to Britain and sold it to raise funds to support its war effort. The largest of these estates belonged to Henry Harford, the proprietor of Maryland at the time of independence, who owned nearly 245,000 acres of land. Most people who bought Loyalist land already had large estates, but some people became landowners for the first time by purchasing property at the sales.

American victory in the war also removed British restrictions on settling west of the Appalachians. The whole country was opened up for the taking. As a result, the years after the war saw a great migration of Marylanders, especially poor tenant farmers and their families, who moved west in the hope of improving their fortunes.

Black Marylanders

Opposition to slavery grew during the war. In 1783, the General Assembly abolished the importation of enslaved persons from anywhere outside the United States effective January 1, 1784, and placed restrictions on the intrastate trade in

> ### Education of the Revolutionary Generation
>
> Nowhere was the difference among groups in colonial Maryland more evident than in their education. Poor Maryland children did not go to school at all. If the mother or father knew how to read, write, and do arithmetic, they taught their children during the off-season, when work in the fields was impossible. Many poor people only learned how to sign their names, however, and others not even that. Some children of middling parents learned their lessons at home, while others had the opportunity to study with a schoolmaster if they lived near enough to attend. Reading, writing, and basic arithmetic formed the core of their education in addition to learning a trade or planting.
>
> Education for the sons and daughters of the wealthy was a different matter. Whether they attended a neighborhood school or were privately tutored at home, boys received an English education. This meant that Latin and religion were important. Boys began their study with a simple ABC book, or hornbook, with the letters of the alphabet and the Lord's Prayer printed on it. As soon as he had learned the letters, a boy received a Latin grammar. For hours each day, several months of the year, he worked on his Latin lessons. Once a boy had learned Latin, he also was expected to learn at least a little Greek. Arithmetic, geography, and frequent study of Scriptures rounded out the curriculum.
>
> Girls from well-to-do families were not expected to study foreign languages as part of their schooling. After learning to read, write, and do simple arithmetic, girls spent most of their time learning useful arts and the social graces. Music, dancing, and fancy needlework were required parts of a girl's education.
>
> Some girls felt that they should learn the same things as boys. Eliza Custis, stepgranddaughter of George Washington and great-granddaughter of Charles Calvert, the fifth Lord Baltimore, complained that her stepfather had told her tutor that she was "an extraordinary child & would if a *Boy*, make a Brilliant figure." Eliza did not see that her gender made a difference. "I told them to teach me what they pleased, & observed to them I thought it hard [unfortunate] they could not teach me Greek & Latin because I was a girl. They laughed & said women ought not to know those things, & mending, writing, Arithmetic, & Music was all I could be permitted to acquire. I thought of this often, with deep regret."

slaves. Far more important in the long run for Maryland's population of African descent, however, was the increase in the number of manumissions during and after the war. A manumission was a legal document in which a master voluntarily freed an enslaved person. Religion provided the main motivation for the increase in manumissions, as Quakers prohibited slaveholding in 1777 and Methodists, both during and after the war, condemned slavery. In Maryland, hundreds of slaves received their freedom because Quaker or Methodist owners became convinced that slaveholding was wrong. Individuals freed during and after the Revolutionary War formed the basis of a significant free black community that continued to grow and develop in the nineteenth century.

The Perils and Promise of Independence

Too much can be made of the changes that occurred in Maryland because of the Revolution. When independence was finally achieved after years of struggle, most Maryland blacks were still enslaved and political and economic opportunity still lay beyond the grasp of most poor whites. Women, regardless of their status, enjoyed few legal rights, and no women could vote. Men who opposed making Maryland more democratic still firmly controlled the government.

Liberty for All?

The Declaration of Independence said that "all men are created equal" and promised "liberty and justice for all." American victory in the War of Independence encouraged the growing number of Americans who opposed slavery to hope that the new United States would give "liberty and justice" to the enslaved.

"Vox Africanorum," the "Voice of Africans," listed the reasons that slavery should be ended in the *Maryland Gazette* on May 15, 1783. The writer pointed out that Britain's "unjust and wicked attempts to forge chains to enslave America" had led Americans to respond "WE WILL BE FREE." Now that victory had been won, the author asked how Americans could tolerate "fellow creatures groaning under the chains of slavery and oppression."

Everyone desires freedom and has a right to it, "Vox Africanorum" argued. To deny freedom to blacks because of the color of their skin made no sense. Greed alone enabled whites to keep blacks in slavery. "Vox Africanorum" concluded: "Ye fathers of your country; friends of liberty and of mankind, behold our chains! Lend an ear to the voice of oppression. To you we look up for justice—deny it not—it is our right."

Eighty-one years would pass before slavery was finally abolished in Maryland. Slavery was continued only by denying the promises of the Declaration of Independence to a large and growing number of black Marylanders. Whites said that blacks were not able to exercise the rights of free men and women. "Vox Africanorum," and countless Maryland blacks, knew that was wrong.

But revolution leaves little unchanged or unchallenged. Never again can things be exactly as they had been before. The Declaration of Independence said, whether Maryland political leaders liked it or not, that everyone was created equal. Although greater political participation and freedom for all Marylanders remained in the future, when the War of Independence ended, few could deny that changes in that direction had already begun.

■ While manumissions increased dramatically after the Revolution, enslaved labor remained the primary workforce for tobacco planters. In 1800, only 15 percent of the state's population of African birth or descent enjoyed the benefits and privileges of citizenship. Courtesy of the Maryland Historical Society, 1960.108.1.3.21.

Postwar Debts

Like most states, Maryland went deeply into debt during the war years. A postwar economic recession made matters worse, hurting trade and depressing tax revenue. Accumulated debt and the bad economy affected the people of Maryland as well as the government. Even people who had been rich before the war often had trouble paying their bills.

Other problems made the shortage of money much worse. Europe produced large crops of grain in the mid-1780s, which drove down the price paid for American wheat. Also, the winter of 1784–1785 was so cold that ice blocked Baltimore's harbor until March, so merchants could not trade. The spring thaw brought heavy floods that destroyed farms and killed farm animals. There seemed to be no end to the economic hardship.

The Search for Relief

Many people who owed money thought the problems could be solved if the state issued new paper money. Having more money in circulation would help both the state and private citizens to pay their bills. Creditors objected, however, because debts owed to them would be worth less if new paper money flooded into the economy. Leaders like Samuel Chase of Annapolis and Charles Ridgely of Baltimore County supported the paper money bill, claiming it would make Maryland prosperous again. Both Chase and Ridgely, however, would also benefit from the bill because each needed to pay large debts for land purchased during the war.

The popularly elected House of Delegates supported bills to issue paper currency to help people who owed money. The more conservative Senate, however, rejected all these bills. By the summer of 1786, the problem had become so great that debtors rioted in Charles and Harford Counties. Still the House and the Senate could not agree on legislation to ease the financial plight of the state's debtors. The crisis began to ease by 1787, when good prices for tobacco brought new money into the economy. The political effects, however, remained. Debtors blamed conservatives, who held power in the government, for their suffering. Conservatives saw the violent protests and the storming of courthouses during the crisis as signs of what could happen if they lost control of Maryland's government.

Toward a New National Government

What kind of national government would be best for the new country? This question became more urgent in the years following the Revolution. Shortly after independence, the Continental Congress adopted a central government under a constitution called the Articles of Confederation. This constitution provided for a weak central government with the states retaining the right to govern their citizens much like independent sovereign nations.

This weak central government never functioned effectively, but the states did work together to win the war against Britain. Once there was peace, however, the shortcomings of the central government under the Articles of Confederation quickly became apparent. Political leaders increasingly realized that something had to be done to create a central government that could hold the now independent states together. Otherwise, all the pain and sacrifice of the War of Independence could be lost forever.

The Mount Vernon Conference

One problem with the Articles of Confederation was that every state could levy its own taxes on trade and commerce, even if those taxes hurt neighboring states or the country as a whole. In early 1785, Virginia proposed a tax on goods imported into Chesapeake Bay. The effect of this law, if it had been passed by the Virginia legislature, would have been to impose a tax on most of the maritime trade destined for Maryland ports. Maryland responded to this threat to its trade by citing the provision in its colonial charter that defined Maryland's southern boundary as the Virginia shore of the Potomac River. If Virginia taxed goods imported into the Chesapeake Bay destined for Maryland, Maryland threatened to close Virginia's trade on the Potomac, that state's most important river.

This controversy between Maryland and Virginia prompted leaders from both states to call for a meeting to discuss how to handle trade and commerce on shared waterways like the Chesapeake Bay and Potomac River. The meeting, held at General George Washington's Mount Vernon estate in March 1785, marked the first time two states had gotten together to discuss mutual problems of trade and commerce. The meeting was a success, adopting the Mount Vernon Compact that guaranteed free trade on shared waterways.

The Annapolis Convention

The success of the Mount Vernon Conference gave hope to those looking for a way to strengthen the central government under the Articles of Confederation. Governor Patrick Henry of Virginia called for a meeting of all the states to discuss mutual problems of trade and commerce. This meeting took place in Annapolis over four days in September 1786. Only twelve men from five states attended the Annapolis Convention. Even though the meeting was held in its capital city, Maryland refused to attend. The conservative members of the state Senate said that Congress should handle the issue of trade and commerce between the states.

Despite the poor attendance, the men who attended the Annapolis Convention were unanimous in their belief that the central government under the Ar-

■ This c. 1800 watercolor of Church Circle in Annapolis, depicting St. Anne's Church, the State House, and the Maryland Inn, portrays townspeople traveling the city's unpaved streets as they go about their daily chores. Courtesy of the New York Public Library, 54288.

ticles was too weak and that something had to be done quickly to save the country from collapse. The delegates to the Annapolis Convention called for a new Convention of all the states to be held in Philadelphia in May 1787. They declared that this new Convention should not be limited to looking only at problems of trade and commerce. Instead, the Philadelphia Convention should be authorized to do whatever was necessary "to render the Constitution of the federal government adequate to the exigencies of the Union."

The Philadelphia Convention and the Constitution

When this new Convention met in Philadelphia between May and September 1787, Maryland sent five delegates: Luther Martin, John Francis Mercer, Daniel Carroll, James McHenry, and Daniel of St. Thomas Jenifer. Instead of revising the Articles of Confederation, the men who met in Philadelphia drafted a completely new framework that created a new central government with the power to levy taxes, declare war, regulate trade, and much more. The proposed new Constitution took away many of the powers that states enjoyed under the Articles of Confederation and gave them to the central government. The Constitution and laws of this new national government would be the "supreme law of the land." This radical new approach to government, devised by the delegates to the

Philadelphia Convention meeting in secret, was made available for the first time to the public on September 17, 1787.

The debate over the Constitution divided people into two groups. Federalists favored ratification. Maryland's Federalists, led by Charles Carroll of Carrollton, George Plater, Thomas Johnson, James McHenry, and others, believed that the nation needed a strong central government to ensure prosperity and guarantee law and order. The Antifederalists opposed the proposed Constitution, arguing that the new government took too much sovereignty away from the states and provided insufficient protections for individual rights. Led by William Paca, Samuel Chase, and Luther Martin, they wanted to defeat the Constitution or to change it by adding a bill of rights.

Despite the concerns of the Antifederalists, Maryland's ratification convention overwhelmingly approved the new Constitution on April 28, 1788, the seventh state to ratify the document. Men like Paca and Chase continued to work for amendments to the Constitution that would protect the rights of the states and individuals. Their efforts succeeded in 1791 when the states ratified the first ten amendments to the Constitution, known as the Bill of Rights.

■ The New Federal City

Ratification of the Constitution brought renewed interest in a capital for the national government. Some politicians, including Virginian George Washington, the first president elected under the new Constitution, favored a site on the Potomac River. The Potomac was the gateway to the Ohio River Valley, and there were plans to build a canal to improve navigation on the river. A Potomac River site would also be more centrally located between north and south than other cities that had been proposed. Convinced by these arguments, Congress decided in 1790 to locate the federal district along the Potomac.

Washington, DC

The new federal city was built on land donated by Maryland, located south of Georgetown, Maryland, and across the Potomac River from Alexandria, Virginia. President Washington appointed Andrew Ellicott of Maryland to survey the city. Benjamin Banneker, a free black man from Baltimore County, assisted Ellicott in the survey. Largely self-educated, Banneker became an accomplished scientist, astronomer, and almanac publisher, who in the 1790s corresponded with Thomas Jefferson on the subject of slavery and racial equality. For the survey of the federal city, Banneker made the astronomical observations that determined the starting point of the survey and maintained a clock that played a key role in determining survey points on the ground.

The capital today is very different from the one in which Congress first met in 1800. Then the grand avenues were but broad dirt streets, the buildings inad-

■ Surveyor Andrew Ellicott, a Pennsylvania Quaker, came to Maryland when his father and uncles bought land on the Patapsco River in the early 1770s and established Ellicott's Mills. In 1791–1792, at the request of Secretary of State Thomas Jefferson, Ellicott worked under the commissioners for the new federal city to survey its boundaries. Ellicott also surveyed the future city of Washington, which occupied a small portion of the 100-square-mile Territory of Columbia, working initially with Pierre L'Enfant using L'Enfant's plan. After L'Enfant's dismissal from the project, Ellicott completed the survey using his revision of the original plan. Andrew Ellicott (1754–1820), by Jacob Eichholtz, 1809, oil on wood panel, 9 x 7 inches, 1916.3, New-York Historical Society.

equate, and the social life dull. Improvements came so slowly that when the British burned the capital during the War of 1812, some felt it ought to be abandoned rather than rebuilt. It would take many years for Washington to become a grand capital city for the nation.

■ The End of an Era

The time from 1763 to 1789 was a period of conflict and great change. Maryland successfully replaced the proprietary establishment with a government of its own making and then, at the last moment, joined with the other colonies in declaring independence from Britain. Maryland generously supported the war effort, with outstanding soldiers and bountiful supplies for the American army. The War of Independence formally ended in the State House in Annapolis, where Congress ratified the Treaty of Paris, acknowledging the United States as an independent nation.

Independence brought with it new problems and new political relationships. The state and its citizens wrestled with the effects of wartime debt and postwar

Benjamin Banneker

Benjamin Banneker (1731–1806) was an astronomer, a maker of scientific instruments, and an author who published an annual *Almanac* for a number of years. Banneker worked with Major Andrew Ellicott in surveying the land for the new national capital in Washington, DC, principally to make astronomical observations in Alexandria, Virginia, to determine the starting point for the boundary survey. When illness ended his service with the survey, Banneker returned home to begin the work that led to his almanacs.

Banneker's accomplishments were all the more remarkable because he was a free black in a slave society. He was born on the family farm in the Patapsco River Valley near Ellicott's Mills and received the help of local Quakers, including the Ellicotts, in obtaining his early education. The quality and originality of his mind led him to continue to learn through independent study and scientific experimentation during his productive life.

■ Benjamin Banneker. Courtesy of the Maryland Historical Society, MS 2700.

recession, as the central government under the Articles of Confederation proved too weak to hold the states together. Maryland helped forge a new political order built around the strong, truly national government that was formed by the adoption of the Constitution of the United States.

Maryland and the nation faced many challenges and dangers during these years. Independence had been won on the battlefield but independence was an experiment that had not been tried before. The experiment succeeded because Marylanders and all Americans believed that independence, and the new nation, were too precious to lose.

Maryland		The Nation and the World
Allegany County formed	1789	US Constitution ratified by all 13 states
	1793–1815	War between Britain and France
	1794	Whiskey Rebellion
	1800	Congress meets in Washington, DC Thomas Jefferson elected president
Construction of Basilica of the Assumption begins in Baltimore, first Roman Catholic cathedral in United States	1806	
College of Medicine of Maryland established	1807	*Chesapeake* Affair Embargo on foreign trade Congress outlaws the importation of slaves, effective January 1, 1808
All property requirements for voting abolished All free black men disenfranchised	1810	
Anti-Federalist violence in Baltimore College of Medicine chartered as University of Maryland	1812	War of 1812 begins
Defense of Baltimore "Star-Spangled Banner" written	1814	British troops burn Washington, DC Treaty of Ghent signed to end War of 1812
Bethel African Methodist Episcopal Church formed in Baltimore	1816	
	1817	American Colonization Society founded Construction of Erie Canal begins
Religious test for voting and office holding removed	1826	
Construction of C&O Canal and B&O Railroad begins	1828	Andrew Jackson elected president
Chesapeake and Delaware Canal opens	1829	
	1831	Nat Turner rebellion
	1833	Bank of United States crisis
Eight Million Dollar Act	1836	Roger B. Taney appointed chief justice of the US Supreme Court
Reform Act Carroll County formed	1837	
US Naval Academy founded at Annapolis	1845	
C&O Canal reaches Cumberland	1850	Compromise of 1850
New Maryland constitution adopted	1851	

chapter three

Maryland in the New Nation

1789–1850

The years immediately following the ratification of the US Constitution were a time of testing between the needs of the states and the policies of the nation, fostering both the growth of political parties and a series of congressional stalemates in search of compromise. In the 1790s, a new political party, the Republicans (later known as the Democratic-Republicans and predecessors of today's Democratic Party) rose to challenge the Federalists, who had successfully argued for the new federal Constitution. The two parties contested one another nationally and in Maryland on an array of issues, including foreign policy, trade and taxes, internal improvements, and sectional interests. Slavery, as both a political and a moral issue, strongly divided people in Maryland.

A principal goal of the Constitution was to stabilize the national economy through absorption of the national debt created by the Revolution and its repayment through national taxes, primarily duties on trade. Under the Constitution, all the states of the Union surrendered their ability to tax foreign trade and interstate commerce, but it required a number of federal court decisions to fully resolve trade and border conflicts between states. Pressures grew to expand the nation geographically and commercially by acquiring more land for producing exports, such as cotton and other agricultural products, and by creating more markets for American goods. Baltimore merchants supported these goals by financing privateers operating on behalf of independence movements in South America during the 1810s and 1820s and again during war against Mexico in the 1840s. Beginning in 1812, the nation once again fought the British, but not everyone thought this was a wise war. Further divisions stemmed from disagreements among the country's three major geographical sections, as East, South, and West all sought federal policies that would benefit their people.

Slavery was a major issue facing Maryland and the nation. Although all blacks and many white Marylanders opposed slavery, the institution lasted in the divided state until November 1864, when the new state constitution at last abolished slavery. Marylanders struggled with slavery in waves of resistance and acceptance. The 1790s offered hope that abolition might be possible, the 1830s were a time when colonization seemed plausible, but in the 1840s the institution became so entrenched under the tightening of federal legislation, culminating in the Fugitive Slave Law of 1850, that only bloodshed could uproot it.

Dramatic changes had taken place by 1850. Cities were flourishing, growing large, and industrializing. Baltimore, the second largest city in the United States with a population one-third the size of New York City, contained 30 percent of the state's total population. Immigrants from abroad swelled urban populations and increased their ethnic, racial, and religious diversity. More than one-quarter of the population of Baltimore City was foreign-born and two-thirds of Maryland's foreign-born population lived in the city. German and Irish immigrants predominated, filling factory jobs, building ships, and working as domestics. Ordinary working people demanded and gradually won a more democratic society. Slavery stood out as the nation's and Maryland's least democratic feature. More than any other single issue, it divided all Americans and kept them from finding common ground.

■ The Political System Matures

The new national administration, inaugurated in New York City in 1789 and led by President George Washington, wanted to create a strong central government, as the authors of the Constitution had intended. The president also wanted his administration to be nonpartisan, without parties that opposed each other as representatives of different interest groups. Washington hoped that all Americans would unite in a common program for the good of the country.

The nation still faced many economic problems that had developed during the Revolution. In the 1790s, Secretary of the Treasury Alexander Hamilton put together a program that he hoped would establish a strong national economy. He wanted the federal government to assume responsibility for all the debts of the individual states. He proposed creating a federal Bank of the United States to act as an agent for the Treasury in collecting and depositing funds and to circulate banknotes as the nation's common currency. He also believed that the United States should rebuild good relations with Great Britain so that trade could be resumed. Not everyone agreed with these Federalist policies. Men like Thomas Jefferson believed that Hamilton's proposals gave the federal government too much power and that, under Hamilton's system, the rich would gain and ordinary people would be neglected. The opponents of Hamilton's policies came to be known as the Republican, or Democratic-Republican, Party.

Early Parties in Maryland

Although men of wealth continued to dominate the state's political leadership, more Marylanders became politically active in the 1780s and 1790s, requiring leaders to pay more attention to voters. Politicians sought out groups of potential voters at gatherings like militia musters, Methodist meetings, civic events, and barbecues, and they used party newspapers to attract and organize active support.

Politics also became less of a local affair. The new federal election system, which often placed more than one county in a congressional election district, encouraged politicians to look beyond county boundaries for support and alliances. State leaders visited all the counties to make appeals for support at the local level.

As the Federalist and Republican Parties became organized, Marylanders chose sides. The Eastern Shore and Southern Maryland emerged as early strongholds of Federalism. Baltimore City, which had supported the Constitution,

---

The Whiskey Rebellion

The Whiskey Rebellion occurred in the western parts of Pennsylvania and the adjacent areas of Maryland during the summer of 1794. Most of the disturbances took place in Pennsylvania. But "Whiskey Boys" (farmers protesting the federal government's collection of an excise tax on whiskey) were also active in both Hagerstown and Westminster.

The farmers considered the tax unfair. They distilled whiskey from grain because it was easier to transport to market than bulk grain and brought a nice profit. In addition, like tobacco during the colonial period, whiskey was a medium of exchange in frontier areas where money was scarce.

President George Washington and Alexander Hamilton, who believed the rebellion ought to be subdued forcefully to demonstrate the strength of the federal government, mobilized militia units from the surrounding states. General Samuel Smith led a Maryland unit in a march to protect the federal arsenal in Frederick and then into Pennsylvania to help defeat the rebels there.

The Whiskey Rebellion was put down. The ringleaders were arrested and order was restored. Many people, including the farmers of Western Maryland and Pennsylvania, continued to object to Hamilton's economic policies and turned to political activity to bring about change.

■ On August 7, 1794, Washington called out about 13,000 militiamen from 4 states, including Maryland. Accompanied by Generals Daniel Morgan and Henry Lee, the president led the troops over the Allegheny Mountains, whereupon the insurgents dispersed and the rebellion ended. Courtesy of the Metropolitan Museum of Art, 63.201.2.

threw its support increasingly to the Republican Party. Western Maryland was divided by the early rivalries, but tended to support the Republicans.

The Federalists

A vital two-party competition existed in Maryland between 1790 and 1820. Federalists portrayed themselves as heroes of the Revolution and as the saviors of the nation in 1788. They claimed to be protectors of an ordered and religious society. As men of property and standing, they saw themselves as society's natural leaders, much like President Washington himself. Federalists drew leaders from Maryland's elite, men of great wealth and influence like Charles Carroll of Carrollton and Colonel John Eager Howard. Others who had achieved recognition in the war effort, such as General Otho H. Williams and James McHenry, also played prominent roles in the party. When Robert Goodloe Harper moved to Baltimore from South Carolina and married into the Carroll family, Federalists readily accepted him as a political leader.

The Republicans

Republicans were far less radical than the Federalists portrayed them. They, too, supported the Revolution and the Constitution, but they had reservations about the administration's domestic and foreign policies. They were suspicious about British policies and friendlier toward the French. Republicans had a stronger belief in democratic government. Maryland Republicans saw the state's underlying social and religious diversity as a source of strength, and therefore wanted to allow more people to take part in government. Republican leaders, like their Federalist counterparts, were also men of wealth, experience, and wide social connections. Many, like Samuel Smith of Baltimore, were former Federalists who left the party in the 1790s in protest against Alexander Hamilton's policies. Other leaders emerged from the broader community. Members of the Shriver family, for example, which had extensive connections with Maryland Germans, led the party in Frederick County.

The Election of 1800

Thomas Jefferson's election as the first Republican president in 1800 devastated the Federalists. The party in power for twelve years under the leadership of George Washington and John Adams now had to turn the presidency over to the leader of the opposition. Federalists feared that Republicans would put the government into the hands of the masses, whom they called a "mob." They feared that people like the debtors who closed courts in the 1780s would lead dissatisfied citizens in attacks on private property. While Republicans gloated and conservatives cursed their fate, Federalist James McHenry noted: "Public men, you will observe, are changed and changing. Whether there will be a total revolution in measures also, time must disclose."

Republican Reform

The national Republican victory was repeated in Maryland. For the next several years Maryland Republicans worked in the General Assembly on an ambitious reform program. They wanted to do away with property requirements for voting and office holding; abolish religious qualifications; and have direct elections for governor, the Senate, and certain local offices. But continued Federalist control of the state Senate limited their success. In 1802, Republicans succeeded in abolishing property requirements for voting and replacing viva-voce (oral) voting with the paper ballot. They also reformed the court system and generally succeeded in lowering property requirements for office holding. But their efforts to replace indirect elections with direct elections failed, and the restriction that only Christians could vote or hold public office remained in effect until finally ended by legislation passed in 1826. At the same time, free African American men who met the property qualification had been able to vote under the constitution of 1776, but legislation passed in 1802 and 1810 barred further voting by free blacks.

Republicans hoped to achieve more, but their hopes were dashed as Presidents Thomas Jefferson and James Madison became increasingly embroiled in foreign policy problems. Many of the Republican-backed reforms would not be addressed until the Jacksonian era. For now, the War of 1812 was on the horizon.

The War of 1812

The origins of the War of 1812 lay in America's need for foreign commerce. After independence, treaties regulated American relations with the British Empire, but many Americans believed that these treaties were biased against the United States. Problems worsened when war erupted between Britain and France, causing American trade to become a victim of European politics. Americans claimed the right of neutrals to trade with all sides, especially European colonies in the Americas where US produce brought high prices. The warring nations felt differently. The British tried to blockade European ports to prevent goods from reaching France, while France argued that anyone trading with Britain was its enemy. America was caught in the middle.

British actions also insulted American pride. Because they had difficulty manning their fleet, the British followed a policy called impressment. Ships of the

■ General Samuel Smith, a Baltimore Republican, led the state in war and peace. He served as a colonel in the Continental army during the Revolution and as a major general organized the defense of Baltimore during the War of 1812. He represented Maryland as a US congressman and a US senator, and, later, was elected mayor of Baltimore. Courtesy of the Maryland Historical Society, Baltimore City Life Museum Collection, CA681.

Royal Navy stopped American ships at sea, removed sailors, and pressed them into service with the British fleet. They claimed that these men were British citizens, but often that was not true. Americans were outraged at this practice. One Baltimore newspaper called Britain the "merciless marauder of the seas."

An Early Skirmish and the Embargoes

In 1807, the British ship *Leopard* attacked the American naval frigate *Chesapeake* at the mouth of the Chesapeake Bay, just off the Virginia coast. After a short battle, in which three of the American vessel's crew were killed and eighteen injured, the British forced the *Chesapeake* to surrender, boarded the defeated vessel, and impressed four sailors. The federal government now faced a dilemma. If diplomacy failed to protect American rights, the United States could either stop trading with Europe or go to war to defend those rights.

The government had tried the first alternative by declaring an embargo on trade in 1794 and now again in 1807. The embargoes kept American ships safe from attack, but they also stopped all commerce. Merchants lost money and mariners lost their jobs. Because trade was the primary source of federal revenue, the embargoes also dried up the Treasury as America prepared to defend itself.

The United States Declares War

This state of affairs plagued three presidential administrations. John Adams, Thomas Jefferson, and James Madison each tried to steer clear of war. The Federalist Party favored Britain and argued that Jefferson and Madison were puppets of the French. The Republican Party argued that British policies were unfair and that America should follow a neutral course. In the end, a neutral position became

---

The Baltimore Riot of 1812

When the United States declared war on England in 1812, Alexander C. Hanson, the young editor of the Baltimore *Federal Republican*, editorialized that the war was "unnecessary, inexpedient, and entered into from . . . motives . . . mark[ed] of undisguised foreign influence."

Hanson's editorial outraged Baltimore Republicans, who saw it as an insult to the Madison administration. A mob marched to the paper's office, destroyed the press, and pulled down the building. City officials, who were Republicans, refused to intervene. Crowds roamed the streets looking for the editor for days and lawlessness continued for several weeks.

Hanson fled to his residence in Rockville, where he decided on a dangerous plan. He secretly rented another house in Baltimore and organized a group of more than thirty Federalists to defend it with guns. He then printed a second issue of the paper, with an even sharper criticism of the Republicans.

Another mob formed after the paper hit the streets, determined to punish the Federalists. City authorities again reacted slowly, calling out the militia only after violence had erupted. Because the militia was mostly Republican, many refused to answer the call. Finally, the mayor negotiated an agreement whereby the Federalists would march to the city jail for their own safety.

The mob broke into the jail and took its revenge on the Federalists. Several men were killed; most escaped with their lives, but only after being severely beaten. Hanson survived and published the paper again, this time from Georgetown. That fall, Montgomery County voters elected him to Congress as a Federalist martyr.

impossible because the British pushed the Americans too far. President Madison issued the formal declaration of war in June 1812. For many Americans, this war was a second War of Independence. Many also saw the War of 1812 in terms of opportunity. Some hoped to liberate Canada from British rule and wanted to remove British troops from the West, where they had remained illegally after the Revolution. Some Americans believed these aims could be achieved because Britain was involved in a prolonged European war. Others worried that America could not win a war that had such far-reaching goals.

The Bitterness of Party Spirit

Maryland partisans took strong positions. The Republicans, under the leadership of the popular US Senator Samuel Smith of Baltimore, stood firmly behind Madison and the decision to fight. Republican suspicion of Federalists included the belief that some, known as "Blue Lights," were using signal lamps to send information to the Royal Navy. Federalists, the dominant party in state government, divided in their response to the declaration. Moderate Federalists, led by Frederick lawyer Roger B. Taney, represented the views of many merchants. They initially opposed Madison's foreign policy, but stood with the nation after the declaration of war. Robert G. Harper and Alexander C. Hanson headed a more radical group of Federalists. These men persisted in their outspoken criticism of Madison even after the war began. Such bitter party spirit led angry mobs to clash in Baltimore in 1812.

America's Private Navy

Much of the significant action of the War of 1812 took place at sea. Because America maintained only a small navy, the national government licensed privateers, as it had during the War of Independence. Baltimore merchants, frustrated by the British blockade, saw privateering as a way to regain lost profits. They outfitted fast ships and instructed their captains to capture British merchant ships. Prize ships and their cargoes were returned to port, condemned by special courts, and sold, producing quick profits for the owners and crews of privateering vessels. Through its "privateer navy," Maryland made a major contribution to the naval war. The slim and light Baltimore clippers, used by the daring and dashing privateers, were the fastest ships on the sea and easy to handle. Baltimore sent out more privateers than any other American port, so many that England called Baltimore a "nest of pirates." Captain Thomas Boyle was an especially heroic figure, cap-

■ A privateer, on the left, perhaps having mistaken an armed British navy vessel for a vulnerable merchant ship, has turned to escape a battering by her opponent's cannon, defiantly flying the banner "Catch Me Who Can" from her mast as she flees. Courtesy of the Maryland Historical Society, M1957-4-1.

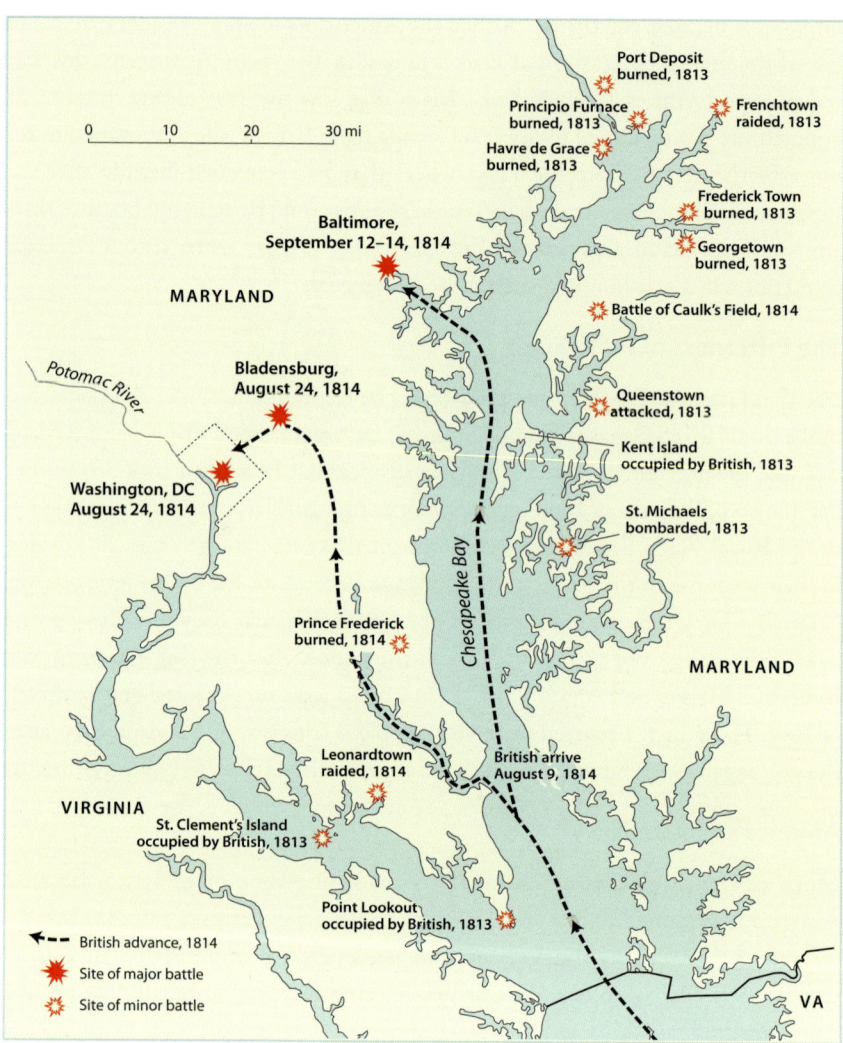

■ The War of 1812 in the Chesapeake Region, 1813–1814

turing between thirty and sixty ships. In addition, while commanding the sleek *Chasseur* in the English Channel in 1814, he had the effrontery to declare a blockade of the British coast. Try as it might, the British navy could not capture the elusive Captain Boyle.

Changing Tides

The tide of war shifted against America by 1813. Canadians resisted invasion by the American army and treated the Americans more like enemies than liberators. Despite occasional successes, defeats outnumbered victories on land and on sea. By 1813, a British blockade all but closed the Chesapeake Bay, and ships of the British fleet roamed the Bay at will. The British burned and looted Havre de Grace and Frenchtown, and attacked St. Michaels as well as isolated farms around the Bay. In 1814, the British decided to attack the American capital. Rather than approach Washington, DC, up the Potomac River, in August they chose to follow the Patuxent River and send the army overland from Upper Marlboro in Prince George's County. Their purpose was to humiliate the national government and to loot warehouses in Georgetown and Alexandria for prize money.

The Bladensburg Races

The American defense of Washington was as confused as it was ineffective. Under the command of Brigadier General William Winder, nephew of Maryland Governor Levin Winder, a ragtag army assembled at Bladensburg to block the British approach. Although it outnumbered the British force, the poorly equipped and poorly trained militia proved to be no match for British regulars. When the British attacked, some American units stood their ground, but most fled as the disciplined British veterans advanced. So many Americans ran away that newspapers called the encounter the "Bladensburg Races." The British victory at Bladensburg opened the gates to the national capital and threatened Baltimore as well. The pride of Baltimore's militia straggled back toward the city in confusion. Commodore Joshua Barney, whose naval gunners had stood their ground against the British attack, lay severely wounded on the battlefield. General Winder was in disgrace.

■ In the spring of 1813, a British fleet sailed up the Chesapeake Bay, stopping along the way to burn and loot several towns, including Havre de Grace on June 1, 1813. Courtesy of the Maryland Historical Society, Hambleton Print Collection, H151.

As British troops occupied and burned Washington, optimists hoped that the fleet would depart without doing further damage. Baltimore City leaders, who knew that the British had a grudge to settle with their city, believed otherwise. Baltimore's reputation as a Republican stronghold, a friend of the French, and a haven for privateers irritated the British sorely. As a London paper put it: "There is not a spot in the whole United States where an infliction of British vengeance will be more entitled to our applause than . . . Baltimore."

The Defense of Baltimore

The defense of Baltimore, one of the few bright moments in the War of 1812, was immortalized in the poem written by Francis Scott Key, a lawyer from Frederick, soon after he witnessed the bombardment of Fort McHenry. The words in his poem, set to music, gained instant popularity, eventually becoming the national anthem as "The Star-Spangled Banner" by an act of Congress in 1931.

Baltimore's defense was better planned and executed than was the defense of the national capital. All Baltimoreans worked together under Samuel Smith, the ranking militia general from the city, in a frantic effort to meet the British attack. Militiamen, free blacks, enslaved men, boys, and old men dug fortifica-

Commodore Joshua Barney: Naval Hero

Commodore Joshua Barney had a distinguished career as an American naval officer during the War of Independence, as a French officer during France's war with Britain, as captain of the privateer *Rossie*, and as commander of the naval flotilla defending Washington, DC, during the War of 1812.

Barney's abilities as a sea captain were recognized while he was still a young man. He received his first command in 1774, at age 15, when his captain died and he led the successful completion of the voyage. During the Revolutionary War, he distinguished himself as captain of the *Hyder-Ally* in combat with the British ship *General Monk* off Cape May. Between 1796 and 1802, he commanded ships for the French Republic.

During the War of 1812, Commodore Barney commanded a flotilla of armed barges and other ships on the Chesapeake Bay. Superior British forces drove these vessels up the Patuxent River, where their crews escaped with their guns after burning their boats.

Barney's force formed the core of the artillery at Bladensburg. As the militia units scattered, Barney's sailors and marines held fast until the superior British forces overran their position. Gravely wounded, Barney fell into British hands. The British treated Commodore Barney with great respect and consideration. General Ross and Admiral Cockburn paroled him immediately and saw that he received medical attention.

Barney received a commemorative sword from the citizens of Washington, DC, and was later appointed naval officer of Baltimore. He died in Pittsburgh in 1818.

■ Commodore Joshua Barney. Collection of the Maryland State Archives, MSA SC 1545-1038.

tions. Women and girls prepared food and rolled bandages. Mary Young Pickersgill and members of her household sewed a huge American flag, which flew from Fort McHenry to greet the British. The defenders correctly anticipated the British strategy of attacking the city by water and overland. Fort McHenry, which had been built in 1798 but never before tested in battle, blocked access to the city by water. North Point, where the Patapsco River enters the Bay, was the most probable landing site for the British army. Defenders therefore constructed an elaborate defensive works at Hampstead Hill, now the site of Patterson Park in Baltimore, on the outskirts of the city. They planned to meet the British attack farther out on North Point.

The British forces planned a coordinated assault on Baltimore. Under the command of Major General Robert Ross, the able and aggressive victor at Washington, the army landed at North Point on September 12, 1814. After offloading the soldiers, the fleet moved up the Patapsco River to take up positions to bombard Fort McHenry. When the British and the Americans clashed at North Point, both sides suffered losses, before the defenders fell back to their fortified positions. The American positions proved to be stronger than the British had expected when fighting resumed on the 13th.

Meanwhile, the bombardment of Fort McHenry, which began on the morning of the 13th, had not led to the fort's surrender, convincing the British naval commander that he could not conquer the fort, and therefore attack the city directly, without sustaining significant losses. Among the British commanders, General Ross was the most willing to take risks but after he was killed by a sniper on September 12, the British command fell to a less daring colonel. This new commander believed that an attack on Hampstead Hill would be too costly. Under the cloak of the night bombardment so vividly remembered by Francis Scott Key, the British army withdrew. They re-boarded their ships on September 14, and the fleet sailed away.

Victory and Peace

The successful defense of Baltimore was one of several victories that restored American pride by the end of the war. In September 1814, American forces in upstate New York stopped the British invasion from Canada. The British attack on New Orleans, in which the British used many of the ships and men who had attacked Baltimore, was thrown back in January 1815. The Battle of New Or-

■ The Battle of Baltimore, September 12–14, 1814

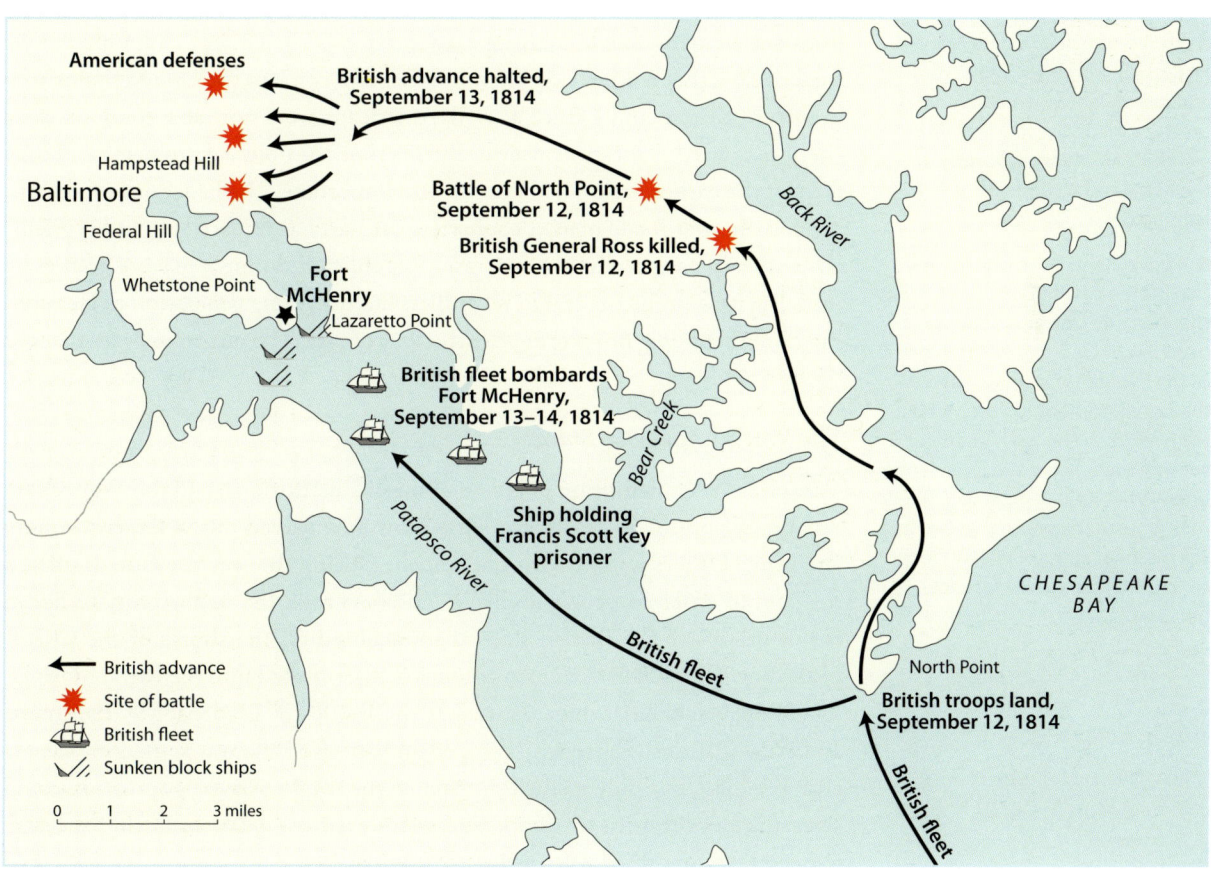

The War of 1812

95

■ Above, left: Seamstress Mary Pickersgill, working with her mother and her daughter in a Baltimore brewery, made the flag that flew over Fort McHenry. Courtesy of the Maryland Historical Society, 1976.80.61.

■ Above, right: Francis Scott Key, born in the part of Frederick County that became Carroll County, practiced law in Georgetown at the time of the War of 1812. He witnessed the bombardment of Fort McHenry from a British ship he had boarded seeking the release of a civilian prisoner. What Key witnessed inspired him to write the poem that became the national anthem in 1931. Courtesy of the Maryland Historical Society, Z24.1255.

leans was actually fought after a peace treaty was signed, but communications were so slow that neither side knew it. Peace had come to the United States and, in 1815, to Britain and France as well. Americans were now able to direct their energies toward domestic concerns. By this time the political problems and conflicts of the earlier period had become less important. The Federalists' failure to support the war made many people view the party as unpatriotic, and it gradually withered away so that Democratic-Republicans dominated state politics by 1820. But new problems and new conflicts faced a young generation of Republican leaders coming into power after the War of 1812. The return of peace marked the end of an era.

The War's Impact on Slavery

War often has a significant effect on domestic institutions, and the War of 1812 was no exception. Some African American men served in the American navy and army. Others fought with the British. During the war the British offered freedom to enslaved people and large numbers took the opportunity to flee in family groups to the British ships that anchored off the shores of the Chesapeake Bay. The able-bodied men among them, recruited into the Royal Marines, fought against their former masters at the Battles of Bladensburg, Baltimore, and New Orleans. Those who escaped and survived the war settled in Canada and Trinidad, but only a small portion of the total enslaved population could seize the opportunity to escape successfully. In the years following the war, many slaves continued to run away from their home plantations, as evidenced by increasing numbers of newspaper advertisements offering a reward for their

An artist observed the British bombardment of Fort McHenry from Federal Hill, as General Samuel Smith coordinated the successful defense of Baltimore. Courtesy of the Maryland Historical Society, Hambleton Print Collection, H89.

return. Most went off in search of families or to hide in a city like Baltimore, although some did attempt the journey to states farther north or to Canada. In Maryland that journey often led fugitives up the Chesapeake Bay or along the roads, canals, and railroads that were the internal improvements funded with tax dollars, both federal and state, in the years following the War of 1812.

The end of the war meant a significant shift in the future of slavery as an institution within and without Maryland. With national borders secured and a widespread belief in the Manifest Destiny of the nation to spread westward to the Pacific and southward into Mexican territory, the institution of slavery took hold in the "New South" as the plantation-based economy of cotton production rapidly expanded westward. Baltimore became a center of the slave export trade, collecting and sending thousands of enslaved workers south to their fate in the New Orleans slave market. At the same time that slavery became increasingly supported and reinforced by state laws, the demand for enslaved labor within the state and particularly the city of Baltimore declined. Marylanders began either manumitting (freeing) their slaves or selling or moving their enslaved people south. By 1850, enslaved people and "free colored" (the term used by the US

The War of 1812

Census Bureau) together accounted for 28 percent of Maryland's total population of 583,034.

■ The Regions of Maryland

During the years following the War of 1812, the nation turned inward to focus on economic growth and expansion. Marylanders, and most Americans, concentrated on American problems and on building their new nation. Across the country, this was a period of movement and expansion. Explorers, then pioneers, then settlers moved westward, developing more and more of the nation's open spaces. Cities grew in the East and along the river valleys of the Middle West. Immigrants crossed the Atlantic in great numbers and added their labor to the efforts of the native-born. Maryland's population grew from 319,728 at the first federal census, in 1790, to 583,034 in 1850. Some of this growth came from natural increase, some through migration from other states, and some by European immigration. New people brought changes in the social structure and Marylanders pressed for political change as well, especially for a more democratic government than the one provided by the state constitution of 1776. More people and new technology also brought major economic changes. Each of Maryland's vastly different regions experienced these changes in its own way.

The Eastern Shore

The Eastern Shore remained overwhelmingly rural and agricultural. Because many navigable rivers reached far inland to serve the region, goods continued to be transported easily by water. No extensive road system developed here in the first half of the nineteenth century. Even before the Revolution, many Eastern Shore planters had become farmers, abandoning the area's poor-quality tobacco

Table 3.1. Maryland's Population by Region, 1790 and 1850

	Eastern Shore[a]		Southern Maryland[b]		Western Maryland[c]		Baltimore City	
	1790	1850	1790	1850	1790	1850	1790	1850
Total population	107,639	128,504	106,754	109,308	91,832	176,168	13,503	169,054
Total white population	65,141	77,737	55,893	50,396	75,685	149,144	11,925	140,666
Total slave population	38,591	25,997	48,711	47,785	14,479	13,640	1,255	2,946
Total free black population	3,907	24,770	2,150	11,127	1,668	13,384	323	25,442

[a]Eastern Shore counties: Cecil, Dorchester, Kent, Queen Anne's, Somerset, Talbot, Worcester.
[b]Southern Maryland counties: Anne Arundel, Calvert, Charles, Montgomery, Prince George's, St. Mary's.
[c]Western Maryland counties: Allegany, Baltimore, Carroll, Frederick, Harford, Washington.

in favor of wheat. The decline of the old tobacco economy, with the loss of its guaranteed market for the crop in Britain, accelerated that shift. In the early part of the nineteenth century, some Eastern Shore farmers abandoned the region entirely, leaving their old homes for the new and fertile soil of Western Shore counties like Harford, Baltimore, and Frederick. As tobacco, with its year-round demand for labor, became less important, fewer farmers relied on enslaved workers. Some landowners, needing less labor to grow wheat, freed their slaves or sold them through the Baltimore and Alexandria slave markets. Others experimented with renting their slaves to the New South, or migrated there themselves with their enslaved property.

Slavery also came into conflict with religion on the Eastern Shore and in other regions of Maryland. Methodists and Quakers in particular pricked the consciences of their members, resulting in a significant movement to manumit enslaved men, women, and children and to abolish slavery altogether, witnessed by the significant rise in manumissions on the Eastern Shore. Out of the Eastern Shore came one of the best-known leaders of the resistance to slavery, Harriet Tubman. Tubman's exploits in helping her family and others escape to freedom became legendary. A large free black community grew up on the Eastern Shore in the years prior to 1850. In 1790, only 9 percent of the area's blacks were free; by 1850, 49 percent of the black population had become free. On the Eastern Shore, which did not attract large numbers of European immigrants, a continuous demand for free black labor meant less pressure for outmigration of freed people.

Eastern Shore towns had to adjust to Baltimore City's increasing commercial dominance. Former tobacco towns, such as Oxford, fell into decline as the tobacco trade withered away, while other towns benefited from increased commerce in wheat and other agricultural products. St. Michaels expanded its boatbuilding and boat repair activities. Prosperity, however, depended on many factors. As trees were cut and not replaced, and other shipbuilding centers emerged on the Western Shore, hard times returned. New pressures affected existing towns differently. Those that had developed around courthouses, for example, continued to be vital in county affairs. Easton, in Talbot County, prospered as Maryland's unofficial second capital. As the administrative center for the state's Eastern Shore offices, Easton developed newspapers, banks, and stores, making it an important commercial town.

Eastern Shore watermen participated actively in Chesapeake commerce, carrying agricultural goods and oysters to Baltimore markets. In Philadelphia the demand for Chesapeake oysters increased after 1829, with the opening of the Chesapeake and Delaware Canal across the Delmarva Peninsula. Eastern Shore farmers, if they wished, could now send their produce by boat up the Chesapeake Bay, over to the Delaware River, and on to Philadelphia.

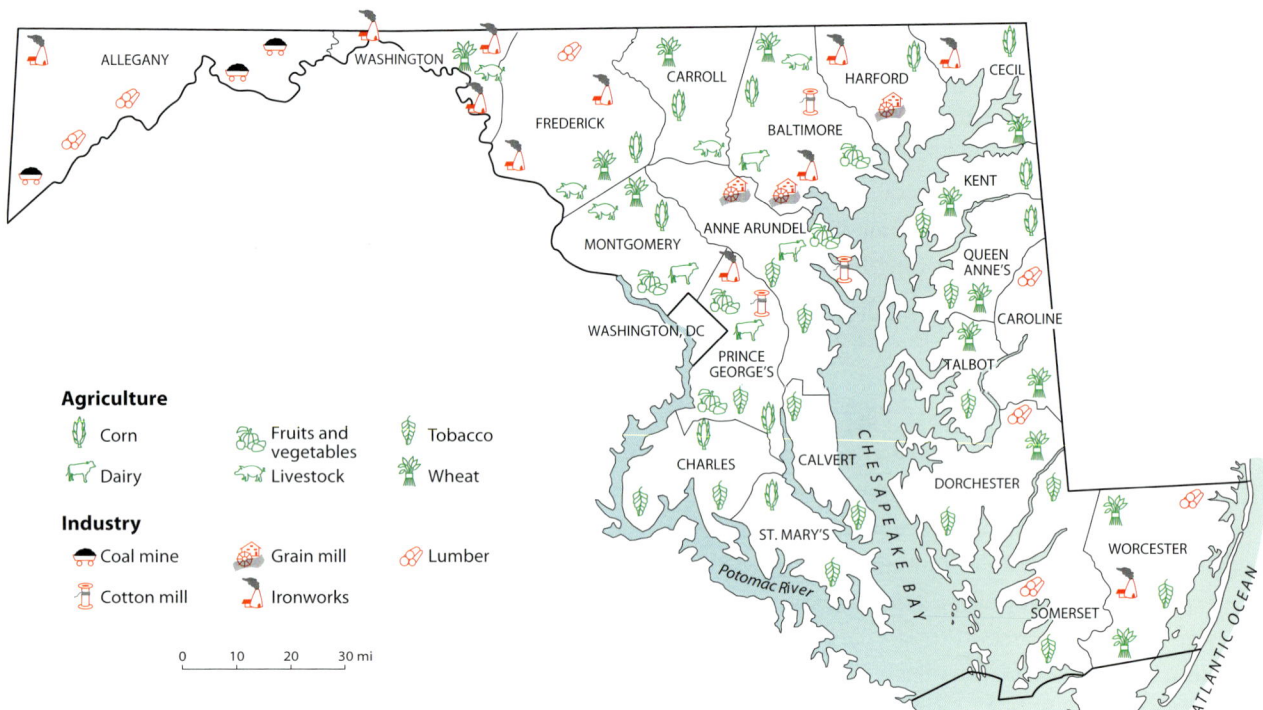

Agriculture and Industry in Maryland, 1840

Southern Maryland

Southern Maryland, like the Eastern Shore, remained a predominantly agricultural area. Composed of Anne Arundel, Calvert, Charles, Prince George's, and St. Mary's Counties, this region remained the center of Maryland's tobacco production and continued to rely on enslaved workers to cultivate the soil. Population changes in Southern Maryland illustrate the problems of tobacco cultivation in the nineteenth century. The area attracted few European immigrants, and its white population actually declined between 1790 and 1850, as the region's planters also moved west seeking better land and prospects.

The lower Western Shore's black population grew but, in contrast with the Eastern Shore, the free black component remained relatively small. Free blacks made up 4 percent of the total black population in 1790 and 19 percent in 1850. While the enslaved population generally shrank between 1790 and 1850 in other regions of Maryland, it remained constant in Southern Maryland. Slavery and tobacco continued to be important to a region with soil better suited to tobacco cultivation. Farmers on the Eastern Shore feared that tobacco depleted the soil and that slavery was a dying institution, but Southern Maryland agriculturists believed that their livelihood and prosperity were tied to both tobacco and slavery. Some branched out to produce market goods for sale in Washington, DC, or in Baltimore, but most followed the traditional pattern of tobacco growing, rotating their tobacco fields to conserve the soil, while population pressure on the land was relieved by migration westward or to the cities of Baltimore and Washington.

Like the Eastern Shore, Southern Maryland had few roads and few large towns. The abundance of navigable rivers met most of the region's transportation needs. Agricultural commodities continued to be exchanged for commercial goods arriving by ships, leaving little need for urban places to develop as centers for commerce. People in Southern Maryland did recognize the advantages of having the new federal city on the Potomac River, however. Not only did the capital's location generate demand for market produce, it also stimulated interest in improving the navigation of the Potomac into the Ohio River Valley. Such improvement would benefit the region as a whole.

Western Maryland

The rural upper and far western portions of the Western Shore absorbed much of the population growth that took place in Western Maryland. This growth, based on migration from other sections of Maryland and from other states as well as continued European immigration, resulted in a near doubling of the white population. Slavery existed in Western Maryland, but the number of enslaved people declined while the free black population grew.

In the 1790s, much of far Western Maryland was part of the American frontier, a wild, unsettled area whose inhabitants still expressed concern about the threat of raids by Native Americans. The rich land produced a wealth of crops, however, and as settlement pushed westward, the threat of Native American raids subsided and population increased. In response, the legislature divided several larger counties to create new ones: Allegany County in 1789, Carroll County in 1837, and Howard County in 1851. The new counties gave people in the developing region more convenient local government and greater representation in the state legislature.

Compared to other regions of the state, Western Maryland was a complex cultural mixture. The white population of the Eastern Shore and Southern Maryland

Oella and Other Factory Towns

Oella was a factory town on the outskirts of Ellicott City. The Union Manufacturing Company built a cotton mill there in 1810 to take advantage of the abundant waterpower provided by the Patapsco River. By 1825, the town had more than seventy stone and brick buildings—mostly houses, as well as a company store, a schoolhouse, and a church—and a population of seven hundred. W. J. Dickey & Sons bought the property in 1887 and operated a woolen factory there until 1972.

Other factory towns developed along fast-moving waterways during the early nineteenth century. On the outskirts of Baltimore, Dickeyville grew along Gwynns Falls, Hampden-Woodberry developed as an industrial site along the Jones Falls, and Avalon grew as a factory town on the Patapsco River. In Howard County, Savage developed along the Little Patuxent River.

These mill villages and factory towns reflected the economic and social changes taking place during the Industrial Revolution. The factory system required new types of organization and work discipline. The towns also showed the continuing importance of waterpower in an age when steam power dominated many industries.

■ *Gruber's German Almanac*, published in Hagerstown, circulated widely among the German population of Frederick and Washington Counties. This 1814 cover was identical to the cover of the first issue, published in 1797. Courtesy of John H. Hershey Jr. and the Research Library, Washington County Free Library.

was primarily of British stock, with strong Catholic, Anglican, Quaker, and Methodist religious roots. Western Marylanders, with British, Scots-Irish, and German roots, represented a richer religious and cultural variety, especially in Carroll, Frederick, and Washington Counties. In the early part of this period, many Germans preferred to retain their German language, religious ties, and cultural traditions. They maintained strong connections with German areas in Western Pennsylvania and many resisted absorption into Anglo-American culture. Indeed, the back pages of newspapers published in Frederick and Hagerstown reported the news in German. Official state documents were also available in the German language.

Farmers in Western Maryland grew cereal crops, particularly wheat, for which there existed a strong demand. The region's rich soil, combined with the new use of deep plowing and crop rotation, produced abundant yields, but there was a problem. Unlike the Eastern Shore or Southern Maryland, areas laced with navigable rivers, Western Maryland was mostly landlocked. Unless farmers lived close to the Potomac or Susquehanna Rivers, they needed a system of roads to get their grain to mills and markets economically. Because roads and turnpikes could be built in any direction, Western Marylanders supported all efforts to improve the transportation system.

The prosperous farms and their growing population supported regional towns. Frederick quickly became a booming place where young men went to make their fortunes. Roger B. Taney, a young lawyer from Calvert County and future chief justice of the US Supreme Court, moved there in 1801. He found a busy manufacturing center of three thousand people. Iron and glass works, wagon makers, breweries, and potteries turned out goods for local farmers and for people passing through on their way west. Shoe, hat, and textile factories made clothing for the area's residents. Merchants and bankers serving the community welcomed the young lawyer who had left Southern Maryland, and his practice grew rapidly. In 1817, Taney successfully defended a white Methodist minister, Jacob Gruber, for having given a supposedly incendiary sermon—in which he condemned slavery and quoted the Declaration of Independence—to slaves at a camp meeting in Washington County.

■ Baltimore City

The development of Baltimore as a major commercial and urban center represented a significant departure from Maryland's colonial past. Until the Revolutionary era, Annapolis had been the colony's most important town, the center of government, and the administrative center of much of the import-export trade of the upper Chesapeake Bay. Although Baltimore had been laid out as a city in 1729, it grew slowly until the Revolution, when commerce centered there began to flourish and the city to prosper.

Tobacco versus Wheat

Baltimore's original city planners wanted the town to serve as a tobacco- and iron-exporting port, but it never became a major center for the tobacco trade during the colonial period. With a relaxation in the British Navigation Acts—which had formerly required all colonial exports to go first to London—in the 1750s, Baltimore merchants began to ship grain grown on the Eastern Shore and in the west in increasing quantities to Europe, taking advantage of the town's ideal location for collecting, milling, and shipping grain and flour from the surrounding counties. Baltimore had an excellent harbor and a location on the fall line that provided an abundance of waterpower for milling flour. It also attracted the wheat trade from the Susquehanna River Valley. Other towns near the mouth of the river, such as Havre de Grace in Harford County and Charlestown in Cecil County, competed for this trade, but Baltimore prevailed.

Baltimore's success as a grain center concerned residents of other cities. Philadelphia merchants, for example, wanted to monopolize the rich wheat-growing region in the interior counties of Pennsylvania and Maryland. These merchants complained about Baltimore's competitive advantages as early as the 1760s. As treacherous as the Susquehanna River could be, it was still less expensive to float produce by water, down the Susquehanna to the Bay, than it was to haul it by wagon to Philadelphia. Baltimore would maintain its advantage until construction of the Chesapeake and Delaware Canal across the Delmarva Peninsula connected the Chesapeake Bay with the Delaware River in 1829. Trade could then flow easily across the Delmarva Peninsula and up the Delaware to Philadelphia.

The Influence of the Revolutionary Era

The Revolutionary era transformed Baltimore into a thriving commercial city. Shipbuilding became a major moneymaking industry. The city enjoyed the natural advantage of its location and was a relatively ice-free port in the winter. The British occupation of other American ports, notably Philadelphia and New York City, enhanced Baltimore's trade during the war years. The destruction of Norfolk, Virginia, Baltimore's chief Chesapeake Bay rival, also strengthened the city's position. Baltimore merchants made the most of these advantages during the war,

■ By 1847, Baltimore had grown into a large and successful commercial city, as depicted in this view from Federal Hill. Courtesy of the Maryland Historical Society, McCauley. V9.

both as privateers and as traders. They supplied the American army and, when France joined the American cause, they supplied the French army and navy as well. These mercantile relationships established a strong affinity between the city and the French nation. The most important development of the period, however, was Baltimore's involvement with the West Indies trade.

The West Indies

The islands in the Caribbean, known collectively if mistakenly as the West Indies, had been colonized by various European countries and quickly specialized in sugar production. Businessmen and farmers found it profitable to grow only sugar, while importing foodstuffs and other necessary supplies. As a result, the islands quickly became dependent on trade with other regions. During peacetime, European powers jealously regulated trade with their islands to ensure the home countries' advantage. War, however, disrupted normal trade patterns, creating great opportunities for profit by enterprising merchants. During the American War of Independence and the conflict between the British and the French in the 1790s, Baltimore merchants aggressively expanded their trade into the West Indies. This stimulated Baltimore's commercial development even more, and enhanced its domination of the Chesapeake grain trade.

The New Urban Society

Compared to the rural sections of Maryland, Baltimore's commercial society appeared to be new and radically inclined. The rest of Maryland had been reluctant to endorse President Madison's war in 1812, but a Baltimore mob took a different stand. They attacked the antiwar newspaper's building and then stormed the jail (where antiwar demonstrators had been taken for their protection) and killed General James Lingan, a Revolutionary War hero who opposed this new war. In fact, the activities of the Baltimore populace during the War of 1812 earned the city the nickname of "Mob Town."

In rural society, family ties and the status acquired by ownership of property, both land and, in many cases, enslaved workers, determined an individual's place. The city, on the other hand, seemed to be inhabited by strangers, and unruly ones at that, with status often determined by hard work and the accumulation of wealth. Baltimore's elite actually drew on a combination of the old and the new, however. Members of old and established families, like the Howards and the Carrolls, owned property in the city and influenced its affairs.

Many of the affluent merchants, however, came from modest means and undistinguished social backgrounds. Some were connected to German settlements or to Scots-Irish Presbyterian families in Western Maryland. Others were from Quaker families who had come to Baltimore from Philadelphia or other northern cities. Still other businessmen had emigrated from Europe. These merchants often built trade networks linking Baltimore with the rural areas and with other cities, frequently building on family relationships. Merchants like the Scots-Irish immigrant Alexander Brown believed that ties of blood forged a stronger bond than did a common economic interest between people who were not related. The family thus remained a strong institution in early nineteenth-century business, as it had been during the colonial period. Merchants, actively involved in Baltimore's political and civic culture during the Revolution, remained important political, civic, and religious leaders in the early national period.

Artisans and Workers

Baltimore commerce drew men with varied skills. There were mariners and shipbuilders, who lived primarily in Fells Point. The city also needed artisans to build houses and warehouses, make and repair wagons, craft barrels and furniture, fashion clothing and shoes, print newspapers, and butcher animals for food. The artisanal system of production, in workshops run by masters who

---

The Artisan System

In the artisan system, parents apprenticed their children to work in the shops of a master craftsman, such as a blacksmith, shoemaker, or cabinetmaker, to learn a skilled trade. Apprentices lived and worked in the artisan's household until they completed their training, at which time they became journeymen and worked for wages. Journeymen hoped eventually to become master artisans with their own shops.

The artisan system was an essential component of preindustrial society, as well as a source of stability and pride. Success would reward ability and hard work in the gradual movement from apprentice to journeyman to master artisan. Artisans following the same craft often lived in the same neighborhood and marched together in civic celebrations.

In the nineteenth century, the artisan system declined as emphasis centered on increased production rather than on quality workmanship. Manufacturers cut costs through greater use of unskilled workers and by introducing machines into more and more crafts to increase production. Machine-made goods cost less to manufacture, and thus could be bought by more people.

trained apprentices and journeymen in the "mysteries" of their trade, remained the core of the new urban society. There was also a great demand for unskilled workers in the city. These men loaded and unloaded ships, hauled goods from the docks to warehouses, and did general manual labor. Because of Baltimore's rapid growth, the city provided employment for many men willing to do unskilled work.

Although most women were expected to stay at home, caring for the house and raising children, some women joined the workforce. Both black and Irish women worked as domestics, doing cleaning, washing, cooking, and other household chores. Some women earned a living as seamstresses, milliners, and laundresses. On occasion, widows took over the business of their husbands and did what was generally considered "men's work." Around 1800, approximately 5 percent of white women worked to earn an income.

Frederick Douglass: Abolitionist

Frederick Douglass was a prominent abolitionist spokesman in the 1840s and 1850s and a notable defender of black rights during Reconstruction. Born into slavery in 1818, Douglass spent his early years working in the fields of Talbot County on the plantation of Edward Lloyd V. At age 9 he was sent to Baltimore City to be a companion to the son of relatives of the Lloyd family.

Douglass lived in Baltimore twice, the first time between 1826 and 1833. During the first two years he was primarily a companion to a boy his own age in the Auld household. The boy's mother taught Douglass the alphabet contrary to the custom of keeping slaves ignorant. When the son went to school, Douglass went to work doing odd jobs in a shipyard, where he eventually became a caulker.

Young Douglass learned firsthand of the increasing racial tension after the Nat Turner rebellion in Virginia in 1831. He saw at the shipyard that white workers went out of their way to abuse free black laborers. He learned of the abolitionists during this time.

Douglass was returned to St. Michaels in Talbot County in 1833, where he spent the next three years working as a field hand. Because Douglass was identified as being too independent, his owner sent him to Edward Covey in 1834 to be "broken." Although Covey did not succeed in breaking Douglass's spirit, he did cause him great pain.

Douglass returned to Fells Point in Baltimore in 1836 and worked again as a caulker, subjected to beatings by white workers who resented competition from enslaved men. He lived on his own and enjoyed more independence than he had in earlier years, but by now he wanted his freedom. In 1838, he escaped from slavery by disguising himself as a sailor and taking the train to Philadelphia. Douglass's bold plan worked. As a free man, he became a leading abolitionist during the pre–Civil War years. He gave antislavery lectures and published an abolitionist newspaper named the *North Star*. He also

■ *Frederick Douglass*, by unidentified artist, oil on canvas, c. 1844, National Portrait Gallery, Smithsonian Institution.

took the controversial position of supporting women's suffrage. After the Civil War, Douglass continued to work vigorously for civil rights. He died in 1895.

Maryland in the New Nation, 1789–1850

Black Workers

African Americans played an important role in the economic life of Baltimore. Although slavery did not prosper in Baltimore, some enslaved men and women did work in the city. One famous example is Frederick Douglass, who as a young man was sent from Talbot County to work in the Fells Point shipyards. Douglass, like many slaves who were "hired out," earned a salary, which he then had to give to his owner. In some cases, owners would return a portion of the money to the enslaved workers, who might be responsible for their own maintenance, paying for housing, food, and other necessities. In these cases, the line between slavery and freedom became blurred, but final control always remained with the owner, and the threat of being "sold South" never disappeared.

For the most part, Baltimore sought free labor, with the result that free blacks gravitated there. By 1850, one-third of the free black population in Maryland resided in Baltimore. Free blacks, even if working mostly as unskilled laborers, hoped that the city would provide greater economic opportunity. In addition, the relative anonymity of individuals in the large urban population made it easier for escaping slaves to remain unrecognized and to live a life of freedom. Their work contributed to economic expansion in the city and the state.

Poverty and Philanthropy

As the urban population grew, so did urban poverty. In an urban setting, the poor did not have access to land to produce food or the ability to gather wood for heat and cooking fuel. With employment opportunities limited for women, both white and black families of women and children without a working male head of household often faced severe challenges. Local men and women of means organized institutions to benefit those in need of help. A benevolent society to aid homeless girls; an organization to teach women and girls reading, writing, and a skill; and groups that provided meals to the destitute all played a role in alleviating poverty in Baltimore. While men generally provided the financial support, women often took the lead in developing and staffing programs.

The Commercial Economy

Baltimore's commercial success stimulated other developments. During the 1790s, the legislature chartered new banks and insurance companies to handle the complexity of increased trade, and Baltimore became the state's financial center. When the federal government created the first Bank of the United States in 1791, it located one branch office in Baltimore. The myriad business and commercial activities continued to attract new people to the city. In 1790, Baltimore contained 4 percent of the state's population, but by 1850, that figure had grown to 29 percent.

The Urban-Rural Conflict

Baltimore's rapid and unprecedented expansion as an economic and population center created tensions within the state. Areas of the Eastern Shore and Southern Maryland, which were losing population or saw themselves in decline, viewed Baltimore's growth as a threat. Those who feared losing influence in the state legislature fought to keep the power they had. Even areas that were growing, such as Western Maryland, shared a concern that Baltimore might become too powerful. Baltimore boosters, on the other hand, worried that the city might lose its competitive advantage. They argued that commerce alone was not enough to assure prosperity, that new forms of transportation were needed to connect the city with Western Maryland. These projects required legislation and money from the General Assembly, but rural interests dominated that body. Some boosters feared that Baltimore's prominence might be short lived; as rapidly as the city prospered, so it might also fall into decline. In addition, other Maryland cities and the new federal city of Washington sought transportation legislation in order to push into Western Maryland to reap the grain trade's profits for themselves. And there was always Philadelphia to challenge Baltimore's prominence in trade.

■ The Promise of the Future: Internal Improvements

Marylanders hoped they could improve both the regional and the statewide economies by building internal improvements like roads and canals. The best natural route from the Atlantic seaboard to the Ohio River Valley cut across Maryland. Entrepreneurs made ambitious plans for road and canal building, and even to experiment with the new technology of railroads, to exploit that route. To pay for such ventures, the legislature often authorized lotteries. The proceeds helped build not only transportation links but also monuments, public buildings, and other projects. But the difficulties and costs of constructing internal improvements proved far greater than anyone imagined. Furthermore, when the Erie Canal, which connected the Great Lakes with the Hudson River, opened in 1825, it seemed to steal away Maryland's geographic advantage to the benefit of New York City.

Roads and Turnpikes

The public road system was notoriously bad, with many roads plagued by ruts and holes several feet deep. But few people wanted to pay higher taxes to build and maintain an adequate road system. Because legislators did not want to support bills that would improve roads by raising taxes, the state chartered private turnpike companies that promised to build all-weather, hard-surfaced roads if they could charge tolls. Private toll roads radiated out from Baltimore into Western Maryland and Pennsylvania in the early nineteenth century. The federal government was also building the National Road from Cumberland, Maryland, to Wheeling, Virginia. This encouraged private companies to build roads to Cumberland and to continue the National Road east to Baltimore. The project also stimulated developers to think of ways to attract federal sponsorship for inter-

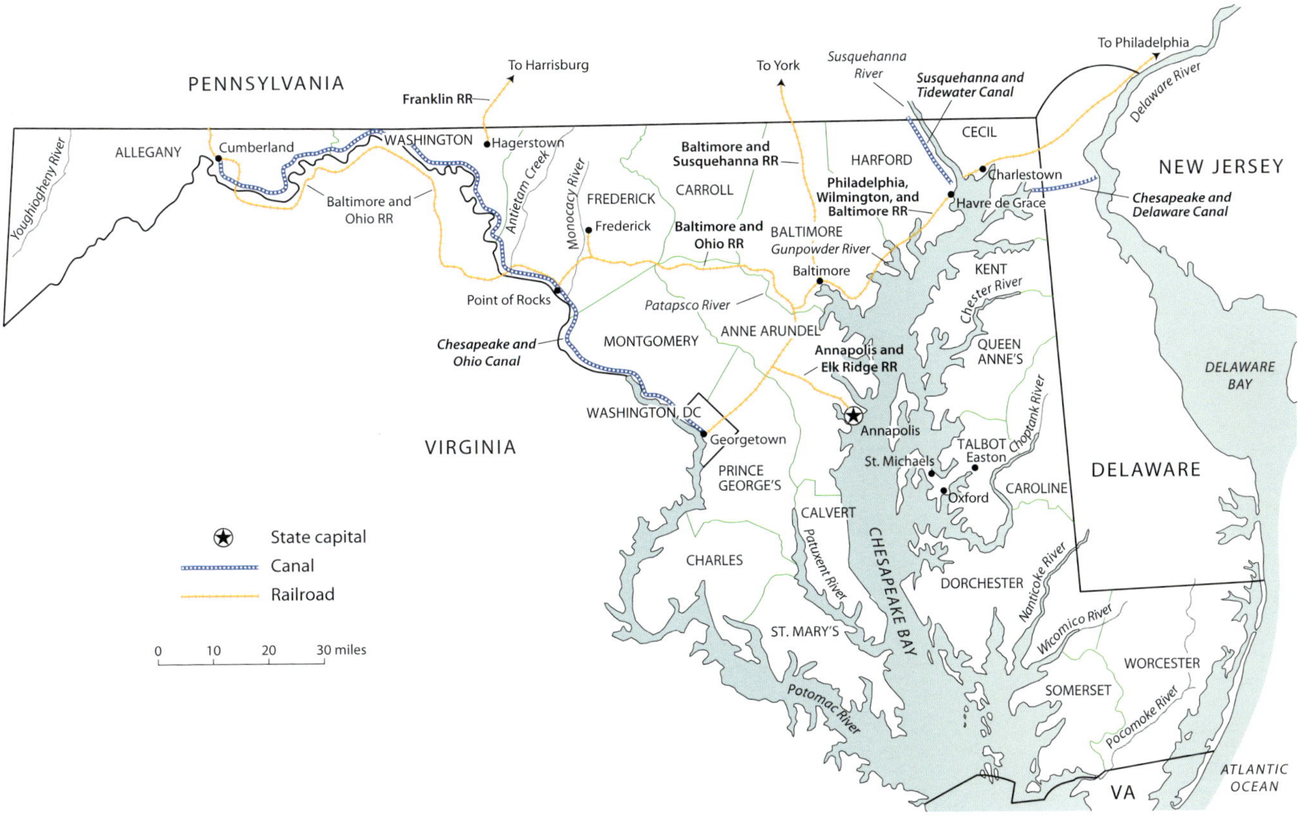

■ Maryland Transportation in 1840: Railroads, Canals, and Rivers

■ The Waterloo Inn, the first stop on the stagecoach route from Washington to Baltimore, was located in Howard County on what is today US Route 1. Courtesy of the Maryland Historical Society, Hambleton Print Collection, H121.

The Promise of the Future: Internal Improvements

nal improvement projects. Even at their best, roads and turnpikes still had disadvantages. Using them to haul agricultural produce by wagon was expensive and slow, no matter how well constructed the roadways were. Turnpike travel from Cumberland to Baltimore took seven days. Good roads were necessary, but the nation needed a more economical transportation system.

Canals

Maryland developers recognized the potential of improving navigation along the Potomac and Susquehanna Rivers. During the 1780s, Virginia and Maryland interests chartered the Potomac Company, and a group of Baltimore merchants formed the Susquehanna Canal Company, but both projects ran into construction and cost difficulties. In addition, the Pennsylvania legislature refused to improve transportation on the Susquehanna above the Mason-Dixon line unless Maryland agreed to allow a canal across the Delmarva Peninsula to improve access to the port of Philadelphia from the Chesapeake Bay.

The effectiveness of the British blockade during the War of 1812 stimulated renewed interest in canals. The Potomac Canal Company reorganized as the Chesapeake and Ohio Canal Company in 1827. Backed with federal, state, and local stock subscriptions, the company began work on July 4, 1828, on an ambitious project to build the canal to the Ohio River Valley. Planners again underestimated the difficulty and expense of their project. Plagued by construction, labor, and financial problems, the C&O Canal finally reached Cumberland twenty-two years later in 1850. Despite the failure to reach its intended terminus, the C&O Canal saw heavy use for more than seventy years to transport

■ In 1830, Ellicott's Mills became the first terminus of the Baltimore and Ohio Railroad outside Baltimore. That August, Baltimore foundry-owner Peter Cooper's iron steam engine, *Tom Thumb*, and a horse-drawn rail carriage raced from Ellicott's Mills toward Baltimore. A broken drive belt on the engine resulted in victory for the horse, but the speed of the engine before the breakdown clearly demonstrated that the iron horse's day had come. Carl Rakeman, 1830, Bureau of Public Roads, Federal Highway Administration, United States Department of Transportation.

■ Industries grew up along the route of the B&O Railroad, including the Avalon Nail and Iron Works 10 miles west of Baltimore, shown here in 1857. The two-family homes in the foreground housed workers; cattle and livestock grazed on the "common area." Steam from the railroad's engines mirrors steam from the factory furnaces. Courtesy of the Maryland Historical Society, Hambleton Print Collection, H83.

produce and coal along the Potomac River. Canal building on the Susquehanna remained tied to construction of a canal through the Delmarva Peninsula. Regional rivalry, between Maryland and Pennsylvania interests and between sections within Maryland, delayed work on these projects for many years. The Cross-Cut Canal, as it was called, linking the Delaware and Chesapeake Bays, was completed in 1829, and the Susquehanna and Tidewater Canal, uniting that river with the Chesapeake Bay, opened in 1840.

Railroads

A group of enterprising Baltimore merchants recognized the potential of a new transportation technology being developed in Britain. Led by Philip E. Thomas and George Brown, these men petitioned the Maryland General Assembly in 1827 to charter the Baltimore and Ohio Railroad. Construction of the B&O began on the same day as the C&O Canal: July 4, 1828. Initial construction of the B&O went quickly, and by May 1830, the first section opened to Ellicott's Mills. In the summer of 1830, cynics applauded when a horse defeated the steam engine *Tom Thumb* in a race. Supporters of the railroad persisted, however, and by December 1831, the line extended as far as Frederick. By April 1832, it reached Point of Rocks on the Potomac River. A lengthy legal controversy with the C&O Canal Company over the right-of-way at Point of Rocks then delayed further construction. A national economic decline in the late 1830s also hurt the railroad's progress, but the B&O reached Cumberland in 1842 and Wheeling, Virginia, in 1853. The success of the B&O railroad assured that Baltimore City would continue to dominate Maryland commerce.

As the B&O was being built, other railroads were chartered to connect Baltimore with Port Deposit on the Susquehanna, with Washington, DC, and with Pennsylvania. Railroads opened up new possibilities for all areas of the

The Promise of the Future: Internal Improvements

state. For example, they carried coal to market from the mines around Cumberland and other parts of Western Maryland. The railroad also enabled Laurel to become a small manufacturing center serving Southern Maryland, especially Prince George's County. The town had a cotton mill large enough to employ five hundred persons, a woolen mill, and a machine shop.

Regionalism

The fight over internal improvements highlighted the persisting pressures of regionalism. Men interested in Baltimore's future did not want to use state money to benefit Potomac interests, and the Potomac and Eastern Shore groups saw no advantage in helping Baltimore. Ultimately, all of the improvement projects needed state support, and there arose, in the end, a spirit of compromise. In 1836, the state passed the Eight Million Dollar Act, which provided funding for the C&O Canal, the B&O Railroad, several Western Shore railroads, and construction of a railroad on the Eastern Shore.

■ African Americans in the Early Nineteenth Century

Both enslaved and free blacks played a major role in Maryland's economy during these years. African Americans, a large and important segment of the population, made up almost 35 percent of the state's people in 1790 and 28 percent in 1850. In the first decades of the nineteenth century, the number of people held in bondage in Maryland gradually declined for several reasons. Eastern Shore farmers produced less tobacco, so fewer of them had work for enslaved laborers. Grain, vegetable, and dairy farmers simply did not require year-round help,

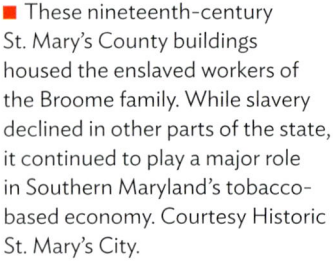

■ These nineteenth-century St. Mary's County buildings housed the enslaved workers of the Broome family. While slavery declined in other parts of the state, it continued to play a major role in Southern Maryland's tobacco-based economy. Courtesy Historic St. Mary's City.

making slavery an unprofitable labor system. At the same time that more and more enslaved people became free, the numbers sold to the New South also steadily increased. In the rapidly growing western section of the state, most farmers owned small farms, large enough to support a family but not large enough to yield money to buy slaves or to require their labor. Most of these farmers had never wanted to own slaves. Finally, as Baltimore concentrated on trade and crafts, slavery became less profitable there as well so that the city's free population grew steadily.

Slavery in Maryland thus declined as a major source of labor partly for economic reasons. At the same time, Quakers, Methodists, and other religious groups to which a growing number of Maryland families belonged increasingly condemned slavery as an institution. The most radical opponents of slavery in Maryland were the abolitionists, whose influence in Maryland politics peaked about 1850.

Abolitionists

On the question of slavery, Marylanders reflected the national division of opinion. In the early nineteenth century, most wealthy and influential men in Maryland owned enslaved workers. At the same time, vocal antislavery advocates worked to end the practice of human bondage. Following the Revolution, some Marylanders recognized the discrepancy between the institution of slavery and the words of the Declaration of Independence and the Bill of Rights. They believed that slavery went against the principles of liberty and equality they considered essentially American. In addition, most Quaker and many Methodist slave owners manumitted their slaves at this time because both religious groups adopted positions opposing the institution.

The late eighteenth century saw the establishment of the Maryland Society for Promoting the Abolition of Slavery. Quakers, including prominent Baltimore mill owner Elisha Tyson and other members of the extended Ellicott-Tyson family, made up a large part of the membership of this and similar local societies, but many prominent people who were not Quakers also joined. They tried unsuccessfully to get the General Assembly to abolish slavery, as legislatures in states farther north had done. During the 1820s, an abolitionist of national renown, Benjamin Lundy, published the nation's only exclusively antislavery newspaper, *The Genius of Universal Emancipation*, in Baltimore with William Lloyd Garrison, another prominent abolitionist, as co-editor. After Lundy wrote a series of articles exposing the practices of a local slave trader, the publisher was attacked and beaten on the street. The judge hearing the case set Lundy's attacker free because he believed that Lundy's articles had provoked the attack. Lundy moved his newspaper to Washington and Garrison went to Boston, where he soon published his own antislavery paper, *The Liberator*. After this time, overt abolitionism was a dangerous activity in many parts of Maryland.

Some whites who opposed slavery, some whites who feared the growing free black population, and a few blacks in the 1820s, 1830s, and 1840s proposed sending free blacks "back" to Africa. This "colonization" movement, part of a wider national effort, involved resettling African Americans in what is modern-day Liberia. People from Maryland founded a separate colony called Maryland in Liberia. Leaders in that settlement included Daniel Coker, a minister, and Daniel Warner, who served as Liberia's third president. Most African Americans opposed the deportation plan and chose instead to work for freedom in the land where they had been born.

The Free Black Community

Baltimore was home to the largest antebellum free black community in the nation. Annapolis and the Eastern Shore also had significant free black populations, while smaller numbers lived throughout the rest of the state. By 1810, one-third of all Maryland African Americans, more than 33,000 individuals, were free; three decades later, more than 62,000 free blacks called Maryland home. Although the vast majority worked at unskilled or semi-skilled jobs, some were successful craftsmen, such as blacksmiths, barbers, and seamstresses, as well as businessmen, farmers, and ministers. In Annapolis, William Bishop II, who operated a carting business and worked on the construction of the Naval Academy, was the twelfth wealthiest man in town. In Baltimore, Joshua Johnson painted portraits of some of the city's leading citizens and Thomas Green owned a barbershop that provided profits he used to buy other properties. At his death in 1859, he was worth $17,000, a large sum at the time. On the Eastern Shore, free blacks worked on ships and in the oystering business as well as on farms and at crafts. Free black Americans refuted one basic argument used by the defenders of slavery. They proved that African Americans could live independently, responsible for their own jobs and housing.

Free blacks joined together to build institutions to meet some of their needs and to provide community support. Of these, churches were of vital importance. Initially, many African Americans were drawn to the Methodist Church because its preachers and congregations reached out to them. Over the years, churches lowered the status of African Americans to the point where they often had to sit in balconies and take communion after the white worshipers. Black religious leaders began to form their own congregations; in 1816, they founded their own denomination, the African Methodist Episcopal (AME) Church. Other black congregations included Baptists, Methodists who stayed within the larger Methodist organization, Catholics, and Episcopalians. The Sharp Street Methodist Church and the Bethel AME Church, both in Baltimore, were large, important congregations. African American communities across the state built churches that generally served as the main community institutions and as places where free blacks and slaves often mingled. Many churches organized mutual

> ### Small African American Communities
>
> During the decades between the War of Independence and 1850, free blacks built many small communities across the state of Maryland. Here, people owned homes and, in some cases, farms or small businesses. People in these areas generally were not isolated but lived in close proximity to whites. Black community members, sometimes working jointly with enslaved men and women in the area, often built churches, a few of which held classes where reading, writing, and basic arithmetic were taught. Some of these communities came into existence when Quakers, Methodists, and others manumitted all their slaves, to whom they often granted land. Significant numbers of free blacks in Baltimore and Annapolis and smaller numbers in places like Easton and Sandy Spring illustrate the geographic spread of these settlements. Many of the free black communities were small places in which everyone knew everybody else and many people were related.
>
> One small community was Bare Hills along the Falls Road Turnpike in Baltimore County. According to family tradition, James Aquilla Scott, a free black man from St. Mary's County, settled in the area. Scott bought his land from Johnzee Hook, a white general store owner, built a home, and opened a blacksmith shop, next to Hook's store, to serve travelers going to and from Baltimore. In 1833, he was one of a group of local African Americans who built a church in nearby Ruxton where both free blacks and enslaved people worshiped. Scott served as preacher at this church, later named St. John's. His son James Aquilla Scott Jr. married an enslaved woman named Anar, or Honora, from a settlement called Cuba in northern Baltimore County. According to family tradition, Anar was the daughter of a slave owner, to whom Scott paid $50 for her freedom. Over the years, their children and grandchildren bought land and built other houses in this area, where family members still lived in the late twentieth century.
>
> Another small free black community grew up in the village of Berkley in Harford County. Many enslaved people in the area became free when they were manumitted by Quakers in the decades following the Revolution. Land records of Harford County show that an African American blacksmith, Moses Harris (or Harrison), bought a piece of land from a white landowner, Joseph Worthington, in 1812 and that he sold part of the land to another free black man, Cupid Paca, in 1816. Paca built a home along Castleton Road (then called Berkley Road), and purchased the freedom of his wife and their infant daughter. Over the years, he bought more land, farmed, and practiced cobbling and masonry. Moses Harris and Cupid Paca were principal builders of stone fences in the area. Paca, in his will, subdivided his land among his children. His son Robert gave land in Berkley on which community members built a house of worship, called the Hosanna Church, around 1835. Before the Civil War, local Quakers taught white and black children together in a small school in the community.

aid and burial societies and provided opportunities for members to learn and use leadership and financial skills.

Maryland never passed a law, common in states farther south, which forbade blacks from learning to read and write. Many churches and some schools, often run by free blacks or Quakers, offered education in day, evening, and weekend classes. Although most of these emphasized basic reading, writing, and arithmetic, at least one black school in Baltimore offered a higher curriculum, including French and Latin, during the early 1800s. The Oblate Sisters of Providence operated a school for young African American women attended by students from Washington, DC, as well as Maryland.

Maryland's free blacks played a major role in opposing slavery. Leaders such as Frederick Douglass and Henry Highland Garnet, both of whom were born into slavery but eventually escaped and made their way north, were prominent, nationally known figures. Many others provided hiding places and transportation for escaping slaves as they made their way north to freedom. The Underground Railroad was active throughout Maryland, with leadership by both black and white "conductors."

Although free blacks were not enslaved, they did not have rights equal to those of whites. Free blacks, like slaves, could not testify against whites in court or serve on juries. After 1810, none had the right to vote. Meetings in groups, except for church attendance, were limited. Free blacks had to be able to prove their freedom at the risk of being forced into slavery if they did not carry the right papers. Conditions for free blacks, as well as for the enslaved, were often harsh, and freedom did not mean equality.

The Nat Turner Insurrection

After 1832, the Maryland General Assembly passed a series of bills that imposed greater control over the state's free black residents. The Nat Turner rebellion in Virginia, in which the enslaved Turner led a bloody uprising in the summer of 1831, provided the stimulus for this legislation. Although no similar uprising took place in Maryland, the incident provoked a general debate over the future of slavery in the Upper South and led directly to the tightening of laws governing the movement and activities of both enslaved and free blacks. The legislation made manumissions more difficult and required anyone who freed slaves to pay for their transportation out of the state, although that provision was often not enforced. The legislature also appropriated money to pay the passage for all free blacks who agreed to "go back" to Africa, but most chose not to go. As the Civil War neared and tensions between North and South grew more strained, the debate on the status of free blacks in a slave society became more intense.

■ Toward a More Diverse Culture

In the early nineteenth century, Maryland occupied a prominent national position for a number of major religious denominations. During the same period, there were also important developments in education, literature, and the arts. Thousands of immigrants brought with them their native language as well as cultural and religious traditions, which also influenced the state's culture.

Religious Diversity

The democratic sentiments that followed the Revolution combined with the end of an officially established Anglican Church in Maryland to encourage religious diversity. Many denominations flourished and several brought about nationwide change. Severing the Church of England's ties with Great Britain brought the most dramatic change for Anglicans but at the same time offered new possibilities for growth and influence to other denominations.

With independence, Anglicans faced the challenge of creating a new governing framework for their church, a process that began in Maryland in May

1776 when the provincial convention resolved that the Book of Common Prayer's prayers and petitions to the king be omitted in all future church services. In November, the convention's Declaration of Rights confirmed denominational ownership of all church property but ended public taxation for support of the Church of England. Priests and laymen began the process of organizing a new diocese for Maryland in 1780 at a convention held in Chestertown, the first of its kind in the former colonies. They adopted the name Protestant Episcopal for the Maryland Church, a name accepted by all former Anglican churches in 1789. It was not until 1792, however, that an ordained bishop became the head of the Maryland Church. Elected by a diocesan convention in 1792, Thomas Claggett was consecrated as bishop at Trinity Church in New York City in September of that year by four American bishops who had themselves been consecrated in Great Britain, becoming the first American bishop of the Episcopal Church ordained in the United States.

For Maryland's Roman Catholics, under the leadership of men like Charles Carroll of Carrollton, the state constitution of 1776 restored their political equality with Protestants, removing the restrictions on voting and office holding that had been imposed on them earlier in the century. In 1790, Baltimorean John Carroll, a cousin of Charles Carroll of Carrollton, became the country's first consecrated Roman Catholic bishop. Maryland was also the location of the first Roman Catholic cathedral in the United States, the Basilica of the Assumption,

■ Thomas John Claggett, a native of Prince George's County, became the first bishop of the new Episcopal Church to be ordained in the United States. Two months later, Claggett visited Annapolis to consecrate the newly rebuilt St. Anne's Church in one of his first acts as bishop of the Diocese of Maryland. Courtesy of the Maryland Historical Society, Z9.863.PP8.

■ John Carroll, born in Prince George's County, strongly supported the movement for independence and the principles of freedom of conscience and separation of church and state. Ordained as the first American Roman Catholic bishop in 1790, Carroll served first as bishop and then as archbishop of Baltimore until his death in 1815. Gilbert Stuart, c. 1806, Georgetown University. Courtesy of Creative Commons.

begun in Baltimore in 1806. Determined to build a thoroughly American Catholic Church, Bishop Carroll worked with other religious leaders on a variety of educational and civic endeavors. This set an important precedent in interdenominational cooperation, now an accepted practice in the United States but not in many other countries.

Maryland was also a center of Methodism. American Methodists officially separated from the Church of England (to which British Methodists originally belonged) at a conference held in Baltimore during Christmas 1784. They chose Francis Asbury, who had come from England as a missionary in 1770, as their first American bishop. At the same conference, the delegates passed a resolution calling slavery "contrary to the golden Law of God . . . as well as every principle of the Revolution" and declared that all Methodists should free their slaves. Many, but not all, complied.

Despite the abolitionism of the Methodist Church, many congregations began to discriminate against African Americans, for example, by requiring black members to sit in an upstairs balcony separated from the rest of the congregation. Such practices led black Methodist leaders from Maryland and Pennsylvania to form the new African Methodist Episcopal Church in 1816.

Like blacks, and like Catholics before the Revolution, Jews also faced discrimination. Although they had served in the military and had contributed generously to the war effort during the Revolution and War of 1812, Jews still could not vote or hold public office in Maryland. Thomas Kennedy, a Scots-Irish, Presbyterian legislator from Washington County, recognized the injustice of this discrimination and from 1818 to 1826 pressed the General Assembly to change the law. Shortly after Jews were finally enfranchised in 1826, Baltimore voters elected two popular Jewish businessmen, Jacob Cohen and Solomon Etting, to the City

■ The cornerstone of Mt. Moriah Church in Annapolis inscribed "A.M.E. Connection Founded 1816" to commemorate the establishment by the Philadelphia Conference of a national African Methodist Episcopal Church. The original Mt. Moriah church building is now part of the Banneker-Douglass Museum. Private collection.

■ The Baltimore Hebrew Congregation built the Lloyd Street Synagogue, designed by noted Baltimore architect Robert Cary Long Jr., in 1845. This was the first synagogue constructed in Maryland and is the third-oldest surviving synagogue in the United States. The building, when enlarged in 1861, retained the original Greek revival style of Long's exterior. Today the synagogue is part of the Jewish Museum of Maryland. Courtesy of the Ross J. Kelbaugh Collection and the Jewish Museum of Maryland.

Council. Jews worshiped in private homes until 1845, when community leaders built the state's first synagogue on Lloyd Street in Baltimore.

Education

Before the Revolution some Marylanders had discussed the need for a system of public education, but the state did not act until 1826, when the General Assembly authorized a public school system. Even then the legislature voted little money to support the system. Furthermore, the law permitted all counties to hold a referendum to decide whether to participate. Most initially chose not to spend the money, but Baltimore City and Annapolis made early commitments to public schooling in 1829. In Baltimore, a school for girls, with 34 students, and

A Free Black Church and School

Free blacks in Baltimore established a vital community during the early nineteenth century. Placing emphases on religion and education, free blacks tried to improve their lives.

Because of discrimination, black members of several Methodist Episcopal congregations began meeting separately in the late 1700s. They incorporated as a separate church, the Bethel African Methodist Episcopal Church, in 1816, with Daniel Coker as the church's first ordained minister. In 1820, Coker immigrated to West Africa, where he became one of the spiritual leaders of the new settlement of Liberia and where he remained for twenty-six years actively challenging slavery and the slave trade.

In the late 1790s, the African School opened in conjunction with the Sharp Street Methodist Church, a black congregation within the regular Methodist Episcopal connection. Daniel Coker taught there from 1802 to 1816 before he joined Bethel. In this and a number of other day and Sunday schools, black and white teachers taught black pupils throughout the antebellum period, a time when other schools were closed to them.

■ Daniel Coker portrait, Sartain family papers [Coll. 1650], Historical Society of Pennsylvania.

2 schools for boys, with 235 enrolled, began offering instruction. The first public primary school in Annapolis for boys opened in a new one-story brick schoolhouse with almost 200 students. A school for girls opened in 1840 with classes in City Hall. A few other towns supported public schools, but no statewide system existed until after the Civil War, and none of the publicly funded schools educated free black children.

Other opportunities for an education existed for some children. Most counties had private academies for students who could pay the tuition. Furthermore, private donors and both black and white churches supported schools that students could attend free of charge or for a minimal fee. For example, in 1818, a group of Annapolis women opened free, nondenominational "Female Sunday Schools" for both white and African American girls, supported by contributions from local charities. Students who could read studied the Bible and learned hymns. Those who could not read were taught that skill before going on to Bible study. Although the students were divided by race, classes met in the same building under the same administrators. In the first year, perhaps thirty white students attended regularly; the twenty black students included both children and adults.

As a result of the opportunities that existed, more Marylanders were literate than people in states farther south, but not as many Marylanders could read and write as residents of northern states where free education was more readily available. Maryland had a somewhat better record in higher education. Washington College, founded in Chestertown in 1782, and St. John's College, an Annapolis institution chartered in 1784, offered a liberal arts curriculum. The Medical College of Maryland opened its doors in Baltimore in 1807. By 1850, people desiring education at all levels could obtain it more easily than in 1790, but many Marylanders still grew up without any formal schooling. More than half of Maryland's children went to work on farms or in factories at ages when they are now required to be in school.

Culture

Maryland, with Baltimore as its cultural center, made notable contributions to the nation's literature. Writers of national stature included not only Edgar Allan Poe, but also John Pendleton Kennedy. Kennedy published his best-known work, *Swallow Barn, or A Sojourn in the Old Dominion*, in 1832 and *Horse-Shoe Robinson* in 1835, winning a permanent place of respect in the history of American fiction. Also, in 1835, Kennedy helped introduce Poe to Thomas Willis White, editor of the *Southern Literary Messenger*. Poe, writer of fantastic tales and often called the father of the modern mystery, lived and wrote in Baltimore, where he is buried in the Westminster Presbyterian burial ground. In a different literary genre, one of the best-known document editors and historians of his day, Jared Sparks, preached and wrote for a time in Baltimore, before returning to New England to purchase and edit the *North American Review*.

■ Edgar Allan Poe lived in Baltimore at times in the 1830s and 1840s, dying in the city in 1849. Poe achieved his greatest praise as a literary critic, but was also noted for his short stories and development of the genres of detective and science fiction. Courtesy of the Library of Congress, LC-USZ62-10610.

Some women also participated in the literary renaissance of Baltimore that followed the War of 1812. Mary Chase Barney, wife of one of the War of 1812's heroes, William Bedford Barney, established a literary magazine. In a more practical vein, she was also the author of a scathing political pamphlet concerning President Andrew Jackson's treatment of her husband. African American Frances Ellen Watkins Harper was the niece of William Watkins, who ran a school for free black students. She published poetry, essays, and a novel, and traveled and lectured for several antislavery societies.

Baltimore was a national center of the printing industry, a role that it continued to play well into the twentieth century. Every sizable town published its own newspaper. Annapolis, Cambridge, Cumberland, Easton, Elkton, Frederick, and Hagerstown, for example, all had newspapers in the 1830s. Newspapers, journals, and almanacs generally enjoyed a wider circulation than did books. *Niles' Weekly Register*, published in Baltimore by Hezekiah Niles, won nationwide respect and continues to be an important historical source for the years of its publication.

Architects Robert Cary Long Sr., his son Robert Cary Long Jr., and Benjamin Henry Latrobe designed numerous buildings in Baltimore, some of which are still standing. Renowned portrait painter Rembrandt Peale, born in nearby Bucks County, Pennsylvania, moved to Baltimore, where he opened a museum and portrait gallery. Peale is particularly famous for his portraits of George Washington and Thomas Jefferson. Noted African American portrait painter Joshua Johnson lived and worked in Baltimore.

Newcomers from Abroad

Economic opportunity lured some people to travel across the Atlantic Ocean to Maryland. Hardship drove others from their European homes to the haven of a growing country that needed their labor. By 1850, more than fifty thousand of Maryland's residents had been born abroad. Almost all of these immigrants came from Great Britain, Ireland, or Germany and all brought with them a cultural heritage that added to Maryland's diversity.

Irish immigration grew gradually through the early nineteenth century, but increased dramatically when the potato famine in Ireland during the 1840s forced a massive emigration by people faced with starvation and disease. Most of those who came to Maryland were rural people who arrived with little or no money, and most of them settled in Baltimore, where they had to take the lowest-paying unskilled jobs. Many immigrant men signed on to work on major construction projects, helping build roads, canals, and railroads across the state. Although these Irish immigrants settled in a state with a long Catholic tradition, they met with discrimination in jobs and housing. Churches and the Hibernian Society, which was sponsored by earlier immigrants including some Scots-Irish Protestants, provided what help they could to the newcomers.

Many German immigrants enjoyed better prospects. Some came with savings, enabling them to buy a farm, while those who knew a craft could earn a decent wage. Large numbers of Germans remained in the port of Baltimore, but many journeyed farther west, toward Frederick. The Maryland German Society helped the newcomers find jobs in Baltimore, Frederick, and other parts of the state. German communities supported German-language newspapers and schools in which all instruction took place in German. German immigrants came from a variety of faiths: Catholic, Lutheran, German Reformed, and Jewish. All brought their traditions of worship with them and, for a while, conducted services in German before their children and grandchildren switched to English.

In 1850, 70 percent of the state's foreign-born population lived in Baltimore City. Many of the other immigrants settled in Western Maryland, where they,

■ Frances Ellen Watkins Harper, the daughter of free Baltimore parents, was orphaned at an early age. Raised by an aunt and uncle, she attended the private Watkins Academy for Negro Youth, run by her uncle William, until her early teens. Working as a housekeeper for a bookstore-owning family, she read widely and began writing poetry and essays. Watkins moved to Ohio in 1850, where she taught at Union Seminary, an AME Church school that became Wilberforce University and where she published her first book of prose and poetry, *Forest Leaves*. In addition to her literary career, she traveled and lectured widely on social causes, including women's suffrage. Courtesy of *Wikimedia Commons*.

like native-born migrants, found a growing economy. Few immigrants went to the Eastern Shore or Southern Maryland at the time.

Political Reform and Dissension

The growth of cities with their commerce and manufacturing, the immigration of new workers, and the decline of the tobacco economy and slavery had an impact on politics. Demands grew for more democratic institutions such as public education and wider suffrage, which would be achieved by ending property requirements to vote.

As the Republican Party of Jefferson and Madison continued in power after the War of 1812, its leaders moved increasingly toward cooperating with business leaders. Gradually some men, calling themselves Democratic-Republicans and later Democrats, split off from the old party. When they nominated Andrew Jackson for the presidency in 1824, they described themselves as the party of the common man, although they won the support of the last surviving signer of the Declaration of Independence, Charles Carroll of Carrollton, one of the wealthiest men and largest slaveholders in the state. Within ten years, the anti-Jacksonian forces formed a new party called the Whigs. By the early 1830s, Whigs and Democrats replaced the earlier Federalists and Republicans as the two major political parties. This new political rivalry would continue into the 1850s.

Democrats and Whigs

Although the Democrats called themselves the party of the common man, wealthy and less affluent men participated actively in both parties. The one real difference in party makeup was that most immigrants tended to support the Democrats.

After removal of the property requirement for voting in state and local elections in 1802, more and more men participated in politics. All white men could vote—but no Jews, no blacks, and no women—until 1826, when legislation allowing Jewish men to vote and hold public office finally passed. The parties adapted to the expanded franchise by making political activity both enjoyable and rewarding. They held barbecues and hired bands for political rallies. They repaid faithful supporters with government jobs, called patronage jobs. Responding to demands for greater popular participation in the nomination process, the parties began to hold conventions to choose both state and national candidates. Baltimore became a favorite site for national conventions because of its proximity to Washington, DC.

Jacksonian Economics

President Jackson's economic policies in the late 1820s made Whigs of many Marylanders. Two policies stand as examples. The first was Jackson's refusal to support internal improvements. At a time when most Marylanders expected to benefit from new roads, canals, and railroads, Jackson maintained that the federal government had no power to spend money for those purposes. Local Whig opposition to the Jacksonian Democrats also grew because Democrats opposed the Bank of the United States. Believing that the bank exercised too much power over the nation's finances, Jackson closed it down. This action triggered bank failures in Maryland and elsewhere in 1833 and 1834. Many people lost lifetime savings; business failures and wide unemployment followed. An angry group of citizens protested by destroying the homes of some Baltimore bank directors. Until 1835, as political debates centered on economic issues, Maryland voted predominantly against Jacksonians and for the Whigs through this period and into the early 1850s, although by narrower margins.

The Reform Act of 1837

After 1835, questions of reform also dominated Maryland politics. The pressure for greater democracy, which had begun during the Revolutionary era, increased. Members of both parties worked to end the longtime control of politics by the state's rural landed gentry. Throughout this period, however, political participation remained limited to adult white males.

Sweeping change came in the Reform Act of 1837, which restructured Maryland's political system and made it more democratic. Beginning in 1838, state senators, one from each county, were chosen by popular vote. For the first time, all eligible voters directly elected the governor, choosing William Grason, from Queen Anne's County. To give equal representation to the state's three regions, the governorship was to rotate among the Eastern Shore, Southern Maryland, and Western Maryland. All candidates in a given election had to have lived for at least three years in the district whose turn it was to provide the governor.

Overexpansion and Economic Problems

The state had chosen to invest heavily in internal improvements, but in doing so also edged itself toward bankruptcy. By the mid-1840s, the state owed more than $40 million that it could not pay. Had it not been for the willingness of banker George Peabody to hold the bonds issued to cover the debts, the government of Maryland would have fallen off the fiscal cliff. Through the prudent management and advocacy of Governor Thomas Pratt (1845–1848), and a temporary increase in taxes, the crisis was avoided. Peabody's investments led him to think so highly of Baltimore that he built and endowed the Peabody Institute on Mount Vernon Place. Governor Pratt's grave in St. Anne's cemetery, Annapolis, reads simply "he saved the credit and upheld the honor of his state."

■ Thomas Pratt was born and educated in Washington, DC, before establishing a law practice in Prince George's County. Pratt held a succession of elective state offices, culminating with his term as governor from 1845 to 1848. He served the state well by setting its finances on a firm foundation that averted the threat of repudiating its public debt. Collection of the Maryland State Archives, MSA SC 1545-1086.

The Constitution of 1851

Although bankruptcy had been averted, the economic crisis led to demand for a new state constitution. A debate raged between Whigs, who wanted to levy a tax to raise the necessary money, and Democrats, who offered two different proposals. Some Democrats suggested that the state simply renounce the debt, but many believed that course too irresponsible. Others proposed that the government cut back on its programs to save money that could then be used to pay off the debt. The slogan of these Democrats came to be "retrenchment and reform."

As the state's economic problems changed the minds of many early opponents of constitutional reforms, men began to talk seriously about holding a convention to write a new state constitution. Only four counties opposed the proposal: Charles, Dorchester, Prince George's, and St. Mary's. With a majority of counties in favor, the convention went forward, resulting in the Maryland constitution of 1851.

The new constitution specifically prohibited the state from incurring any indebtedness greater than $100,000. It also shifted yet more political power to Baltimore City and Western Maryland, providing for one senate seat for each county and for Baltimore City. It also specified that seats in the House of Delegates be allocated according to each county's population. Baltimore City could have up to four delegates more than the largest county. The governorship, with a term of four years, would still rotate among the state's three regions. This constitution further democratized the political process by allowing the popular election of local governments. It also provided for elected, rather than appointed, judges and gave Baltimore City its own judiciary separate from that of Baltimore County, whose court and courthouse were moved to Towson. The constitution of 1851 remained in effect until 1864. It established the form of state government that faced the problems that led to the outbreak of Civil War in 1861.

■ Beyond 1850

During the antebellum period, in a number of ways Maryland mirrored the country as a whole. Maryland's people included planters and small farmers, slave owners and strong opponents of slavery, native-born whites, native-born blacks, and immigrants. Although most counties were still devoted to agriculture, the cities, especially Baltimore, had grown in national importance. Industrialists, merchants, and workers had concerns similar to those of urbanites farther north but at the same time Baltimore became one of the leading financial centers for the slave-holding South. Because these different interest groups could not find a peaceful way to settle their disagreements, the decade that followed witnessed steady progress toward war.

Maryland		The Nation and the World
	1850	Compromise of 1850
New Maryland constitution adopted Gorsuch raid Howard County formed	**1851**	
Statewide convention of free blacks	**1852**	Harriet Beecher Stowe's *Uncle Tom's Cabin* published Democrat Franklin Pierce elected president
B&O Railroad reaches Wheeling, Virginia	**1853**	
	1854	Kansas-Nebraska Act
Know-Nothing Millard Fillmore carries Maryland	**1856**	Democrat James Buchanan elected president
Know-Nothing Thomas Hicks elected governor	**1857**	*Dred Scott* decision
John Brown's raid	**1859**	
Democrat John Breckinridge carries Maryland	**1860**	Republican Abraham Lincoln elected president South Carolina secedes from the Union
Baltimore mob attacks federal troops John Merryman case Unionist Augustus Bradford elected governor	**1861**	Confederate government forms Fort Sumter, South Carolina, fired on Lincoln calls for 75,000 volunteers
Battle of Antietam	**1862**	
First Maryland draft First black regiments organized	**1863**	Emancipation Proclamation First draft instituted Battle of Gettysburg
New Maryland constitution adopted Jubal Early's raid Slaves emancipated in Maryland	**1864**	
Democrat Thomas Swann elected governor	**1865**	Confederacy surrenders at Appomattox, Virginia Lincoln assassinated Andrew Johnson takes oath as president
	1866	Reconstruction begins
New Maryland constitution adopted Wicomico County formed	**1867**	
Black men vote for the first time since 1810	**1870**	Fifteenth Amendment ratified: enfranchisement of black males

chapter four

Maryland in Peace and War

1850–1870

The years from 1850 to 1870 were transformative ones in Maryland's history. Economic, political, and social changes, along with the tumultuous effects of a civil war fought on its soil, altered traditional arrangements in ways that demonstrated the impact of external events. The nation's history abruptly came to direct that of the state in ways never anticipated by earlier Marylanders whose lives had been barely brushed by the hand of the federal government, save for a visit to the local post office or when they cast their ballots for the men who would represent them in Congress. Given Maryland's location as a slaveholding border state, some Marylanders favored, and even fought for, the Confederacy, although the state was staunchly Unionist in its allegiance. Throughout four years of war, families were disrupted in this bloody struggle between brothers; relatives, like cousins of Carroll County's Shriver clan, faced each other across battle lines. With young men gone to war, Maryland women replaced men on farms, and in some instances, in factories and shops. Yet the greatest transformation took place in the lives of the state's 170,951 African Americans, who represented nearly one-quarter of the total population of 686,869 in 1860.

For 87,009 enslaved people the Civil War meant freedom when, in 1864, white male Marylanders accepted a new state constitution that prohibited slavery. A few years later, blacks found themselves protected by the US Constitution's Fourteenth Amendment, which gave those born in the United States citizenship and the right of due process and equal protection of the laws. Then the Fifteenth Amendment extended to black males the right to vote. In theory, by 1870, Maryland's male African American residents had obtained essential civic rights, but in practice they had not. Instead, the formerly enslaved people joined the state's free black population of 83,942 in a system characterized by white supremacy and an institutionalized, statutory separation of the races that survived into the 1960s.

Politics changed as well, as the state rewrote its constitution three times—in 1851, 1864, and 1867. Familiar parties such as the previously popular Whigs, who elected four governors after 1831 and nearly two-thirds of the state's congressional representatives during the 1840s, died out. As either cause or effect of the disruption of traditional parties, the new anti-Catholic, anti-immigrant Know-Nothings briefly reigned. Yet, by 1860, the Know-Nothings had ceased to exist and after the war two durable organizations, the Democrats and the Republicans, dominated state politics for the rest of the century.

Amid these changes in politics and society there was continuity, as Marylanders lived the paradox that in the midst of tumultuous transformations much survived. Like blacks, women continued in subordinate roles. Most Marylanders continued to farm for their livelihood, raising wheat, corn, and tobacco in the same ways as had their fathers and grandfathers. Industry and commerce were still concentrated in Baltimore, although the expanding coal mining and iron production in Western Maryland fostered the growth of small cities such as Hagerstown and Cumberland.

■ Politics during the 1850s

Political parties were popular organizations in the 1850s when the state's turnout on Election Day often reached more than 60 percent of eligible voters, though with large segments of the population disenfranchised only one-quarter of all adult Marylanders could vote. More so than today, political parties served as fraternal lodges promoting civic activities that engaged the white male electorate. Absorbing rituals such as parades, pole raisings, and conventions encouraged participation by Marylanders. Because elections were frequent and competition intense, especially after the constitution of 1851 increased the number of patronage positions and elective offices such as county commissioners, politics entered into everything Marylanders thought and did during this period.

A grand rally held in Baltimore's Monument Square in 1856 exemplified the political events of the period. According to the *Baltimore Sun*, fifty thousand Baltimoreans (of a total city population of more than two hundred thousand) crowded into the square for a pre-election rally. Some carried banners and sang martial songs adapted to their partisanship. Stimulated by such activities, in the presidential elections of 1856 and 1860, 72 percent of the white males over age 21 voted, having qualified by living in the state for a year and their county for six months.

The American, or Know-Nothing, Party

After the election of Andrew Jackson in 1828 and the development of a two-party system of Whigs and Democrats, Maryland enjoyed a period of stable, competitive electoral politics. In the 1850s, however, the Whig Party lost support. A new party called the Americans, or Know-Nothings, emerged as the state's most popular political organization. The uncomplimentary name Know-Nothings signaled the party's origins because, counterintuitively for an institution seeking public support, it began as a secret society, its members responding to questions from outsiders that they knew nothing.

In fact, these societies that sprang up around the state reflected changing conditions in both Maryland and Europe. The arrival of large numbers of Irish immigrants after the potato famine and of Germans fleeing political upheaval meant stiff competition with natives for jobs throughout the state—from the coal mines in Western Maryland to the shipbuilding firms in Baltimore. By 1850, one out of every seven residents in Baltimore was foreign-born; by 1860, the figure was one in four. In some areas of the city, such as the Second Ward in the southeastern section, there were more foreign-born residents than natives. These new Marylanders lost no time in organizing social clubs, newspapers, schools, taverns, and fire companies and in accepting jobs at lower wages than native-born workers.

The Know-Nothings attracted the support of Protestants who were convinced that Catholic immigrants gave their allegiance to the pope and that Catholics violated the separation of church and state by seeking public aid for their schools and insisting that their version of the Bible be used in public schools. When Martin Kerney, a Democratic Catholic state legislator, sponsored a bill to use public funds to support Catholic schools, the proposal brought a heated response from Protestants. Reacting to the visible signs of cultural difference between themselves and these newcomers, Know-Nothing banners proclaimed "America for the Americans" and "None but Americans must rule America." Know-Nothings were offended, for example, when Germans held festivals on Sundays and when Irish Catholics established new churches. The Know-Nothing newspaper *The Baltimore Clipper* grimly noted the construction of seven new Catholic churches in Baltimore between 1851 and 1858. According to one nativist, Irishmen and Catholics "come among us, remain a short time and announce themselves Dimecrats [sic]."

Additionally, there was a growing sense that politics was a corrupt, unresponsive enterprise undermining the health of the republic. Election violence became one of the central issues of this period. Although the Know-Nothings were usually held responsible, in fact Election Day violence was a bipartisan affair. Both parties encouraged the formation of political clubs, often associated with firehouses, whose names—Bloody Tubs, Butt Enders, Rip Raps, and Gladiators—conveyed their intentions. In the mayoral election of 1856, pitched battles that included cannon as well as less lethal stones and bricks raged near Mount Vernon Place. Four Baltimoreans were killed and 70 wounded. The presidential election, a month later, was even more violent as 10 Baltimoreans

■ Rivalry between Know-Nothing and Democratic clubs often resulted in violence. This 1856 cartoon pictures a gang of armed men known as Plug Uglies aboard a coach named after the Know-Nothing mayor of Baltimore. Courtesy of the Maryland Historical Society, 1967.30.1.

were killed and more than 250 wounded in fighting with participants using awls, knives, and axes as well as guns. Given its partisan, undermanned police force, the city was unable to control the violence.

Located between an increasingly antislavery North and a vehemently proslavery South, Marylanders turned to the Know-Nothings because that party avoided sectional issues. Henry Winter Davis, a congressional representative from Baltimore, summarized such positions when he noted that the way to settle controversies over slavery was to keep silent about it. Nationally these years were marked by increasing attention given to controversial congressional efforts to solve problems over slavery in the territories by means of the Compromise of 1850 and the Kansas-Nebraska Act of 1854. Residents of Maryland, on the other hand, were attracted to political solutions promoting reform in politics, an avoidance of sectional issues, and solutions to the immigrant problem, all advanced under the Know-Nothing Party banner.

Much to the surprise of political observers, in 1854, the Know-Nothings won Baltimore's mayoral race as well as control of the Maryland General Assembly. For the next six years, in one of those rare periods of party realignment when voters shift previously durable partisan attachments to a new party, the Know-Nothings controlled the state with the northern and western counties

> ### Thomas Hicks: Know-Nothing Governor
>
> Thomas Hicks was born in Dorchester County in 1798, the eldest boy in a large farm family. He attended a local subscription school. Early in his adult years, he combined farming and politics, serving as town constable and county sheriff. First a Democrat, then a Whig, he became Maryland's first, and only, Know-Nothing governor in 1858.
>
> As governor, Hicks witnessed the final stage of the conflict that led to the Civil War. He was in Baltimore when its citizens attacked the 6th Massachusetts Regiment as it passed through the city. Although Hicks did not oppose slavery, during the critical days of 1861 he supported the Union. Hicks moved the General Assembly to Frederick because he was afraid that pro-southern sentiment in Annapolis would affect decisions.
>
> When Hicks's term as governor ended in 1862, his successor, Augustus Bradford, appointed him to fill an unexpired term in the US Senate. He died in Washington, DC, in February 1865.

along with Baltimore strongly Know-Nothing, and the formerly Whig southern and eastern counties of the state shifting their allegiance to the Democrats. In 1856, Maryland was the only state in the Union to support the American (Know-Nothing) Party candidate Millard Fillmore in that year's presidential election. In 1857, Know-Nothings elected Thomas Hicks as governor along with four of the state's six congressional representatives. But once in power the party found it impossible to enact its program of a longer naturalization period (some party members promoted twenty-one years) and restrictions on the Catholic religion's public agendas. Lacking a national presence and the federal patronage that tied supporters to party ranks, the organization split over the issue of slavery. Thereafter, the Know-Nothings disappeared, in Maryland and elsewhere, as quickly as they had arrived.

The Democrats

More durable, even amid the partisan changes occurring between 1850 and 1870, were the Democrats, the state's other major party whose members perceived themselves as nationalists and who cast their opponents as particularists who appealed to only a segment of the population: aristocratic elites in the case of the overspending Whigs, intolerant mobs in the case of the Know-Nothings, and abolitionists in the case of the newly created Republican Party. In the 1850s, when the secretive Know-Nothings emerged as their principal opposition, Democrats saw their new political opponents as subverting national values of tolerance. While the state had virtually no Republican Party, Democrats joined the chorus that exaggerated that party into an abolitionist crusade intent on destroying slavery and thereby the Union. Unlike the Know-Nothings, the Democrats paid close attention to issues affecting slavery, especially the issue of fugitives. For example, Democrats from Southern Maryland introduced a resolution condemning Pennsylvania for its failure to return enslaved runaways to their owners. Democratic leaders also urged the federal government to compensate the owners of fugitive slaves.

During the 1850s, some Democrats, especially native-born workers in Baltimore, shifted their allegiance to the Know-Nothings. In turn, former Whigs became Democrats as Marylanders in the southern counties as well as on the Eastern Shore embraced the party as a bulwark for southern rights under supposed attack by northerners. While the Democratic Party revived after the Know-Nothings evaporated, the 1850s was still a period of lessening support. In statewide elections the Democratic vote declined to around 45 percent. In the hotly contested gubernatorial election of 1857, the Know-Nothing Thomas Hicks defeated the Democrat Jacob Groome, a former Whig from Cecil County, by a margin of 10 percentage points.

Repelled by the violent political environment, a group of business and professional men, along with some of Baltimore's temperance advocates, formed a nonpartisan third party, seeking to increase the number of polling places and to tighten registration procedures. In Baltimore's crucial mayoral election in 1860, George Brown, a prominent banker and member of the mercantile gentry, became mayor of a city known throughout the United States and England as "Mob Town."

■ Maryland's Economy: The Old and the New

A microcosm of the North and the South, Maryland's diverse economy reflected the growing modernization of the North—rapid urbanization, extensive industrialization, capital formation, and efficient transportation marked by continued dependence on farming. Yet throughout the period, the value of the state's agricultural production remained greater than its industrial production.

The Traditional Economy

Maryland's small farms persisted as the backbone of the traditional economy. These units ranged from an acre or so to 50 acres and were largely self-sufficient. Rather than sell crops to urban markets, small farmers traded or bartered any surplus they had. Existing throughout the state, usually on less fertile soil, their farms were often somewhat distant from the growing transportation system based on roads, railroads, and canals. The families who comprised the traditional economy raised corn, potatoes, wheat, and vegetables and sometimes kept a few cows and pigs. They could afford neither the iron plows nor the new steam harvesters used on larger agricultural units. Nor could they pay the dollar a day to rent a slave or hire a neighbor's son at harvest time. In fact, they sometimes served as day laborers themselves or hired out their sons to more prosperous farmers.

Often their challenges were as fundamental as trying to drain marshes or Tidewater lands, as they struggled against natural disasters of drought, flood, and, in 1853, the invasion of an especially malevolent, crop-destroying insect, the Hessian fly. From a modern perspective their lives seem tedious, routinized, and dull.

They lived in small, single-story, unscreened wooden or log houses that were no more than cabins. A table and a bedstead were prized possessions. One observer of Southern Maryland described a dreary area "of uncultivated wastes, a barren soil . . . lean and hungry stock, a puny race of horses and houses falling to decay."

The Modern Economy

By comparison, other Maryland farmers were tied into a burgeoning market economy. In this arrangement large farms produced surpluses of various grains, corn, fruits, and vegetables, and some tobacco, though the latter was no longer the featured crop of the state. Now able to export their produce into a national and international market, these farmers engaged in a commercial system that provided the cash they needed for provisions, seed, agricultural tools, and clothing. When the B&O Railroad reached Wheeling, Virginia, in 1853, markets in previously isolated areas became available. Smaller trunk lines stretched north and linked Maryland with Philadelphia and New York. Meanwhile the celebrated Chesapeake and Ohio Canal reached Cumberland in 1850, though railroads were making canals obsolete.

Wealthy Marylanders continued to use their profits to build brick and stone houses. By the 1850s, large country villas existed throughout the state, with the richest families depending on enslaved men and women to work in the fields and to do time-consuming domestic tasks. The money these families amassed provided the necessary capital for commercial ventures. Men like Charles Reeder and John Pendleton Kennedy, whose fathers had been prosperous farmers, moved to Baltimore and provided the capital for railroads, canals, and factories, enterprises that were also aided by subsidies from the state and national governments.

The large units owned by wealthy farmers, many of whom were members of the Maryland Agricultural Society, relied on new technology and an understanding of soil exhaustion. The crisis over the latter initiated efforts to protect the environment at a time when no one paid attention to the damage inflicted by a modernizing society on natural resources. Until the twentieth century, whether it was lumbering operations that removed forest cover from the shores of the Susquehanna River, water contamination from sewerage, or pollution from coal mines released into the state's rivers, natural resources were considered God's gift for man's unhampered use. Yet large farmers were aware of the benefits of protecting their soil. Edward Lloyd VI's 3,629-acre Wye plantation in Talbot County and Charles Calvert's 2,000 acres in Prince George's County used fertilizers and horse-pulled deep plows and reaping machines. Both Lloyd and Calvert had sufficient funds and information to try new methods, and in the late 1850s, Calvert was one of the leaders in setting up the Maryland Agricultural College intended to educate "ordinary" farmers in more scientific methods. Lloyd's and Calvert's properties, like those of cotton planters in the Deep

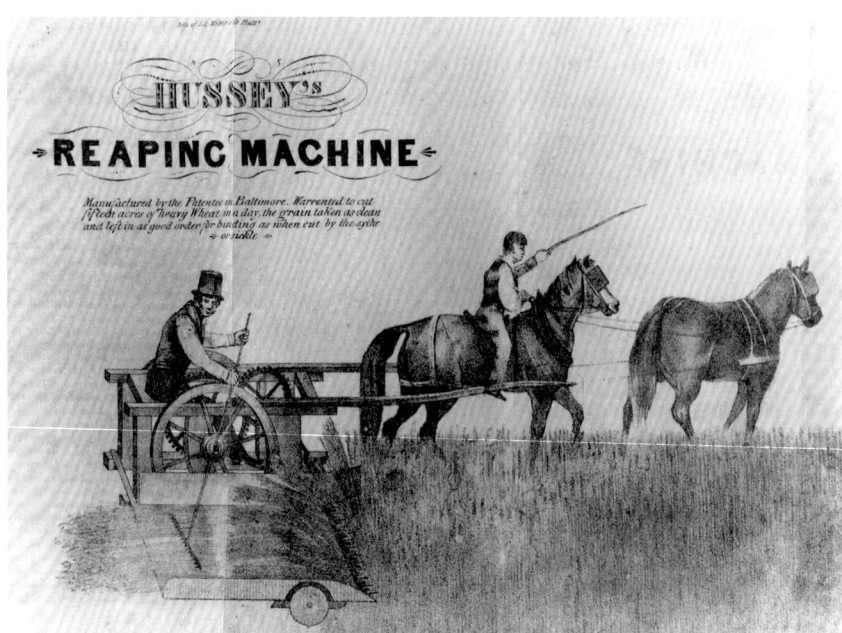

■ It took a farmer using a scythe two to three weeks to harvest a 40-acre field. With Hussey's reaping machine, pictured here, or McCormick's reaper, a farmer could harvest the same field in two and a half days. Courtesy of the Maryland Historical Society, McCauley.E23.

South, depended on the labor of enslaved workers. In 1850, Lloyd owned 210 slaves and Calvert more than 100.

On the smaller 400-acre Epsom Farm in Baltimore County near Towson, Henry Chew depended on a diverse labor force that, mirroring the state's population, included not just enslaved workers but also free blacks from the Towson area and German immigrants newly arrived in nearby Baltimore. Chew was one of many Maryland farmers who by the 1850s paid close attention to the quality of their soil. With the help of an overseer he planted various types of hay on 90 acres along with 50 acres of corn and vegetables on smaller units, most of which he sent to Baltimore on the horse-drawn wagons that were an essential part of his operation. Like many of the state's larger farmers, Chew employed crop rotation on a regular schedule, as well as the ashes from his lime kiln and the planting of clover hay to replenish nutrients in his fields.

Baltimore

Baltimore stood at the hub of this modernizing economic system. By 1860, nearly one out of every three Marylanders lived in the city, making Baltimore the third largest city in the United States. Thousands of German and Irish immigrants found work in the city's foundries, shipbuilding shops, mills, and railroad yards. As well, free blacks discovered opportunities for employment. Thus, while the population of Baltimore more than doubled from 1840 to 1860, the white population in Southern Maryland and the Eastern Shore remained stagnant. Meanwhile Baltimore's free and enslaved African American population increased by 30 percent.

Baltimore's port supported the city at a time when commerce was more important than industry. Coal from the Cumberland area of the state, flour from Baltimore County mills, and vegetables from the Eastern Shore arrived in the harbor and at Fells Point, to be transported throughout the world. The city had an especially brisk trade with South America, exchanging agricultural products such as high-grade flour as well as finished textiles from the city's factories along the Patapsco River Valley for coffee and guano, a natural fertilizer that was becoming important on the state's farms.

Besides its significance as an international depot, Baltimore stood at the center of an important national trade. Products such as coffee and copper ore were sent throughout the United States by means of railroads, canal barges, and improved macadamized roads. In a distribution network that soon had political implications, by the 1850s, most of these goods went north and west, rather than south. With capital from this trade Baltimore businessmen built leather and clothing factories that transformed natural products into finished goods. By 1860, Baltimore employed more than half of the state's industrial wage earners and produced more goods than any southern or border state city, including St. Louis. In a modernizing process occurring throughout the United States, the city's workplaces grew as companies consolidated manufacturing production into larger units. For example, the Mt. Clare B&O Railroad yards employed more than one thousand men.

On a lesser scale, the state's towns, especially in the west and north, also participated in this modernizing economy. By 1860, Frederick, the state's second largest city with nearly 7,000 residents, and Annapolis, with 4,500 people, served as regional trading centers. Factories replaced the small workshops of the past; artisans became workers, and shops were transformed into large units employing more than fifty workers.

Industrial Workers

The diverse labor force on which this production depended was a mixed and typically American one. Many of the unskilled workers who earned as little as 50¢ a day (equal to $15 in 2015 currency) were recent German and Irish immigrants, some of whom lived in boarding houses near the harbor. Others were recently freed African Americans. Still another labor source consisted of enslaved people hired out by their masters who then collected the wages. In his autobiography a frustrated Frederick Douglass described the process whereby each Saturday night he was compelled to turn over his wages to his "Master Hugh." In return, he received board, some clothing, and occasionally a few pennies.

For all these workers—and there were 17,000 industrial workers in Baltimore by the 1850s—the hours were long, sometimes more than 10 hours a day, 6 days a week. To protect themselves, skilled workers organized workingmen's associations such as the Association of Black Caulkers, the Society of Employ-

Table 4.1. Leading Free Black Occupations in Baltimore, 1850 and 1860

Occupation	1850	1860	Occupation	1850	1860
Barbers	91	96	Ostlers	11	9
Blacksmiths	31	27	Oystermen	24	50
Bricklayers	63	93	Porters, waiters, etc.	236	226
Butchers	16	9	Ropemakers	12	1
Carriage drivers	33	34	Sawyers	146	47
Carters, draymen, etc.	385	331	Seamen	94	107
Carpenters	26	13	Seamstresses	20	4
Caulkers	75	63	Shoemakers	24	11
Cooks	22	26	Shopkeepers	21	13
Grain measurers	27	17	Stevedores	35	34
Hod carriers	14	10	Washers	260	142
Hucksters	19	28	Whitewashers	70	62
Laborers	799	571			

Source: Matchett's *Baltimore Directory*, 1849–50 (Baltimore: R.[ichard] J. Matchett, 1849), 439–73; *Wood's Baltimore City Directory* (Baltimore: John W. Woods, [1860]), 427–59. Courtesy of the Maryland Historical Society.

ing Shipwrights, and the short-lived General Mechanics Association. Before the Civil War, Baltimore became well known for the strikes that usually focused on obtaining a ten-hour day and higher wages.

Wages remained stagnant during this period and subject to national economic conditions, especially during the devastating 1857 depression. In 1860, William Finley paid each of the 20 women who worked in his textile mill near the Jones Falls $5.05 a month (approximately $150 in purchasing power with each dollar worth $30 in 2015), while male workers in a cabinet shop nearby earned $16.00 each month. Few small businessmen, much less laborers, were able to move up the economic ladder into the middle class. Those who succeeded included Simeon Hecht, an immigrant goatherd from Hesse, Germany, who began by peddling goods on the Eastern Shore and saved enough capital to set up his own store. Soon he was employing others to distribute his wares. In time he was able to bring his family to Baltimore, and after the Civil War his descendants organized the Hecht Department Stores, patronized by Marylanders for a century.

■ Daily Life at Mid-Century

The lives of most Marylanders centered on their family and church. Larger than families today, a typical mid-century Maryland family consisted of parents and four children. The image of the nineteenth century as one in which grandparents, parents, and children all inhabited one household is incorrect.

In fact, nuclear families of just parents and children prevailed, although many Marylanders employed domestic servants—mostly enslaved blacks or Irish-born women—who lived with the family. But the growing population of the Almshouse in Baltimore, with its seven hundred residents, the new House of Refuge for delinquent youths, and the Home of the Friendless for orphan girls testified to the need for public-supported institutions for those whose families could not take care of them.

Fathers and husbands held extensive legal and economic powers under the common-law provisions inherited from England. Women could not vote, sit on juries, or, if married, sign contracts. Only by a special legislative bill could a woman end a marriage, even with an abusive husband. One Baltimore County woman, Madge Preston, wife of the prominent lawyer William Preston, described in a secret diary life with her unfaithful, wife-beating spouse. In practice, long-term separations took the place of legal divorce, but for Madge Preston and others like her there was no solution to life with a powerful abusive husband who wanted neither divorce nor separation.

The division between males and females, especially in the middle and upper classes, became far more pronounced than in earlier years. Women—or their servants—worked in the home, cleaning, laundering, cooking, and raising the children, while men became breadwinners in the public sphere. The lives of country and city women also diverged. Country women still tended the animals, churned the butter, kept a vegetable garden, and generally provided their household with goods that their city cousins increasingly bought in stores. Married women who worked outside the home did not control their wages. Nor did they control any inherited property until, in 1882, the Maryland legislature finally passed a Married Woman's Property Act.

The largest employers of young single women were the textile mills in Baltimore County near Phoenix and along the Jones Falls, where children as young as 10 toiled part-time. Women made up half the workforce in the mills along the Patapsco River, employed because of the dexterity of their fingers and their lower wages. In Baltimore in 1860, women were most likely to be employed as live-in servants, cigar wrappers, laundresses, and textile spinners.

Health

Death was more likely to disrupt families than today, as families were reformulated through remarriage. One of every four children died before the age of 16 from malaria, tuberculosis, diphtheria, typhoid, whooping cough, and a host of bacterial infections now treated by antibiotics. Average life expectancy in mid-century Maryland was less than 40 years. For those who resided in the malarial Tidewater region of Southern Maryland and the Eastern Shore as well as for enslaved people throughout the state, average rates of life expectancy dipped into the twenties.

> **Medical Therapies**
>
> Medical care in the nineteenth century differed in many ways from the medical care of today. Some of the treatments employed by doctors threatened life more than the home remedies did. One example involved bleeding a patient by using small knives, or lancets, and the blood-sucking worms called leeches. Bleeding supposedly restored the body to its proper balance.
>
> Doctors also used massive doses of drugs. Thus, the prescription for cholera included laudanum (an opium derivative), camphor, and calomel. One Maryland doctor advised taking a dose every five minutes "until vomiting ceases," at which time the patient was to be bled.
>
> Home remedies were based on herbal preparations. Mint was used as a remedy for nausea and vomiting. Rhubarb stalks boiled with saffron were thought to cure dysentery. Cooked cabbage leaves were rubbed on boils. Ergot, a rye fungus, was used to bring on labor. Some of these home cures were effective, and some of them were not. Generally, they were not as dangerous as techniques like bleeding.

Epidemics of cholera, yellow fever, and typhoid were terrifying and all-too-familiar. In 1855, when Baltimoreans heard rumors of a yellow fever epidemic in Norfolk, some stuffed rags dipped in vinegar around their faces; others attended public prayer meetings. The commonly held notion that germs were airborne led other city dwellers to stay inside and keep their windows shut. There were no hospitals, few trained doctors, and even fewer treatments, with women often delivering "invalid cookery" of homemade medications crafted from herbs and edibles.

Some advances occurred during the period in the critical matter of urban public health, with regular collection of garbage, street manure, and night soil by municipal employees. By 1850, Baltimore employed a city health officer, but gave him an insufficient budget to address collective health problems. Little was done to deal with a water supply that permitted privies to empty into the Jones Falls. Those who could not afford the cleaner water offered by private contractors depended on the city's eighty pumps, the latter contaminated by surface water and the city's limited and often defective sewers.

Religion

Like the home, religion defined the lives of mid-century Marylanders. With a history of religious toleration, the state had been an early haven for Roman Catholics. During the 1850s, largely as a result of immigration, Catholics increased their numbers as well as their institutional presence. So too did Protestants, as Methodists, Lutherans, and Episcopalians emerged as the largest denominations in the state. While the number of congregants is uncertain, Methodists maintained more than 400 churches, a number that far exceeded that of the Episcopalians' 133 and the Catholics' 65 structures. Jews and Quakers made up a small but important minority of Maryland's population.

Sunday, for most a day of respite from labor and an opportunity for socializing, also remained for many a special day marked by lengthy worship services, sometimes twice a day. Maryland's religious institutions had for years been the architects of social welfare outreach, such as schools and orphanages, with Quakers the special benefactors of schools for African Americans and the Methodists similarly attentive to education. By the 1840s, there were significant changes in worship among Protestant denominations. Places of worship celebrated more observances of the feasts of the church, such as Christmas. Weddings and funerals as well as the commemoration of national holidays now took place in houses of worship throughout the state. Chapels in the forest became churches in towns as generous congregations provided funds for building enduring stone and brick edifices.

Education

During this period before state-mandated schooling, Maryland had a variety of different institutions at all levels. In private all-male academies the sons of the wealthy continued to study Greek and Latin, along with theology, philosophy, and some science. A few of these boys went on to college, with Washington College in Chestertown and St. John's in Annapolis among the private institutions of higher learning in the state. Other young boys, such as Lutherans or more typically Catholics, completed their education in parochial schools. Although there was no public statewide system, some counties set aside property taxes in a school fund in order to educate the greatest number at the least expense. Throughout the state, one-room schoolhouses, sometimes with as many

■ This 1784 engraving, the earliest to feature a Maryland landmark, depicts the original building of Washington College, an institution chartered in 1782 to provide a "more extensive seminary of learning," beyond the grammar school, "for training up good, useful and accomplished men." In a time when most colleges had religious affiliations, the college was to be nondenominational in all aspects. Two years later, the legislature chartered a second school, St. John's College in Annapolis, to serve the Western Shore. Courtesy of the Maryland Historical Society, MLD 573.W22 S, frontispiece.

Daily Life at Mid-Century

as fifty students to each teacher, survived, and it was in such settings that most Maryland students of all ages and levels of ability learned their ABCs.

Typically, enrollment, even in publicly supported schools, varied according to the economic circumstances of parents. In some wards in Baltimore fewer than 10 percent of those between ages 6 and 16 attended, and in rural areas the agricultural calendar dictated an interrupted attendance. In the classrooms women were replacing men as teachers; neither spared the rod. Learning was based on the concept that the mind, like a muscle, strengthened with use. Thus most material had to be memorized and recited in a question-by-teacher, answer-by-student process. For a small number of older children in Baltimore learning continued in the public, single-sex high schools located in prominent stone buildings of permanence like that of the Western Female High School, completed in 1858.

These public institutions admitted no blacks, and accordingly, black children received far less schooling than did white children. Enslaved blacks, like Frederick Douglass, taught themselves, sometimes with the help of their masters, fellow workers, or friends. Among the most successful of the schools for blacks were the Wells Free School and the classrooms for black girls organized by the African American Oblate nuns. For years William Watkins ran a private school that numbered among its students his talented orphaned niece, future poet and lecturer Frances Ellen Watkins Harper. Most effective of all, in terms of numbers, were the night and Sabbath schools run by black churches, particularly those of the African American Methodist Episcopal Church. The success of these efforts is apparent in the 1860 census, which listed nearly 55 percent of Baltimore's 34,000 free blacks over the age of 12 as literate.

■ The Enslaved in the "Free State"

Just as their ancestors had for more than two hundred years, many white Marylanders continued to support slavery as a social, political, and racial institution, even as its economic advantages declined. In Maryland, unlike the version of the "peculiar institution" farther to the south, the number of those enslaved continued to drop. By the 1850s, only one of every six Maryland households owned enslaved workers; the overwhelming number of those families held under ten bondspeople. In fact, most owned only one enslaved worker. Following the state manumission laws that freedom could be granted only to slaves between ages 18 and 45 who could support themselves, some were emancipated by owners who no longer needed their labor on soil-exhausted tobacco fields. Others obtained their freedom through self-purchase or purchase by relatives. Many were sold to work in the cotton fields of the South, having been held before their departure in the slave pens along Pratt Street. A few escaped to the North or into the District of Columbia or Baltimore. The process of emancipation explains the substantial increase in the free black population, which grew from 62,000 in 1840 (or 40 percent of all Maryland African Americans) to 83,000 in 1860 (or nearly 50 percent of the state's black population). With the city a mecca for freedom, 90 percent of Baltimore's 34,000 blacks were legally free and formed the largest free black community in the nation.

Like other aspects of Maryland life, slavery was a regional institution, with wide variation in its distribution. The five southern counties, where only 10 percent of the state's whites lived, encompassed nearly 50 percent of the enslaved population. The Eastern Shore accounted for another 30 percent. In the northern and western parts of Maryland there were few blacks, enslaved or free. And in Baltimore City, by 1860, enslaved people accounted for only 3 percent of the total population.

Table 4.2. Maryland Population by Color and Condition, 1860

County	White	Free Black	Enslaved	Total County Population
Allegany	27,215	467	666	28,348
Anne Arundel	11,704	4,864	7,332	23,900
Baltimore*	231,242	29,911	5,400	266,553
Calvert	3,997	1,841	4,609	10,447
Caroline	7,604	2,786	739	11,129
Carroll	22,525	1,225	783	24,533
Cecil	19,994	2,918	950	23,862
Charles	5,796	1,068	9,653	16,571
Dorchester	11,654	4,684	4,123	20,461
Frederick	38,391	4,957	3,243	46,591
Harford	17,917	3,644	1,800	23,415
Howard	9,081	1,395	2,862	13,338
Kent	7,347	3,411	2,509	13,267
Montgomery	11,349	1,552	5,421	18,322
Prince George's	9,650	1,198	12,479	23,327
Queen Anne's	8,415	3,372	4,174	15,961
St. Mary's	6,798	1,866	6,549	15,213
Somerset	15,332	4,571	5,089	24,992
Talbot	8,106	2,964	3,725	14,795
Washington	28,305	1,677	1,435	31,417
Worcester	13,442	3,571	3,468	20,481
Total	515,918	83,942	87,009	686,869

Source: Eighth US Census, 1860.
*Includes city.

■ An enslaved woman sold to a prominent Baltimore family in 1853, Martha Atavis cared for the children of Dr. John Whitridge, including his daughter Alice. Atavis was one of the five thousand enslaved people in Baltimore in 1860, two-thirds of whom were women in domestic service. Courtesy of the Maryland Historical Society, Cased Photo Collection, CSPH 546.

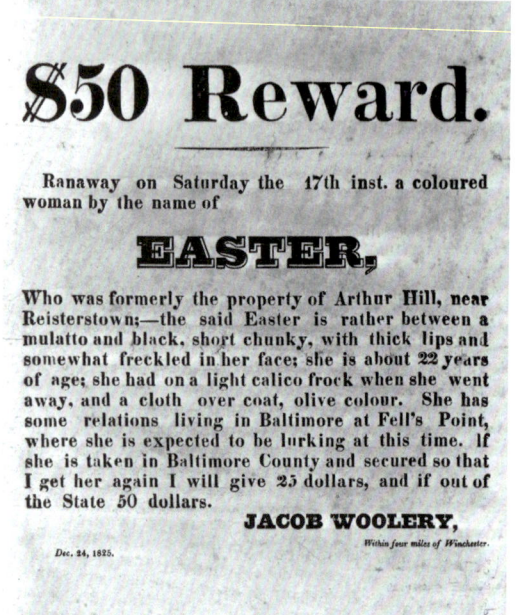

■ Many enslaved people ran away to escape their bondage. In this broadside, Easter's owner, Jacob Woolery, offered a reward for the capture of the 22-year-old runaway. Courtesy of the Maryland Historical Society, Z24.01744.

Because schooling was generally denied to the enslaved, there are few surviving records by which to reconstruct the daily lives of African Americans. Exceptions are the published diaries and accounts by Marylanders like Noah Davis, John Thompson, and Thomas Henry. Later oral histories given by descendants indicate the variation in where slaves lived and what they did. Some toiled on the tobacco fields of Calvert and St. Mary's Counties or the truck farms on the Eastern Shore; others held more skilled jobs as blacksmiths and bricklayers, cooks in the master's great house, or laundresses. But they all shared the devastating fact that they were property, subject to the whim of their masters. Even the simplest of activities, such as walking to town, required a pass.

As a border state Maryland became an avenue to freedom, and even today along its northern border with Pennsylvania there are country lanes used by fugitives that bear the name "Freedom Road." The famous Liberty Line, or Underground Railroad, aided runaways as they hastened northward across the Mason-Dixon line. "Conductors" directed the fugitives to safe houses or stations, such as a church, a barn, or to the home of a free black or Quaker where they could eat and rest along the way. Maryland's most famous "conductor" of the Underground Railroad was the intrepid Harriet Tubman of Dorchester County. After her

The Underground Railroad

Volunteers across the country helped men, women, and even some children escape from the horrors of slavery. "Conductors" offered directions and transportation to "safe houses" as "passengers" traveled northward. Many seeking freedom traveled through Maryland to Pennsylvania and destinations farther north. Some walked through the Appalachian region toward Pittsburgh. Others journeyed through Maryland's central counties to southern Pennsylvania towns like York, sometimes hidden in wagons under farm produce, straw, or blankets. A network of conductors and safe houses on the Eastern Shore helped people travel overland to Delaware on their way to Philadelphia. Members of Baltimore's large free black community as well as both black and white abolitionists, especially Quakers, offered hiding places and sustenance. African Americans and sympathetic whites who worked on the water carried escapees on ships sailing north on the Chesapeake Bay.

Harriet Tubman, from Dorchester County, escaped on foot and later returned more than once to lead men, women, and children through Delaware to Philadelphia. They walked through woods and waded through swamps, frequently at night when capture was less likely. Tubman often took people to the home of Thomas Garrett, a white Delaware Quaker, who then arranged for them to travel onward. William Still, a free black man in Philadelphia, received many fugitives from Maryland. Still kept records on the hundreds who passed through his home and published a book of their stories.

William Green, an enslaved man from Oxford Neck in Talbot County, escaped with a companion and journeyed northward with the help of the Underground Railroad. The two men traveled on foot for two days, and receiving help from a friend, reached the home of a Quaker man who gave them a meal and directions. They walked for several more days until they reached the home of "Aunt Sarah," whose husband put them on a boat for Philadelphia. From Philadelphia, Green traveled by boat to New York and then on to Springfield, Massachusetts, where he settled, married, and raised a family. Green published the story of his life in 1853.

Ann Maria Weems, an enslaved 15-year-old from Rockville in Montgomery County, was in danger of being "sold South" as her brothers had been. To prevent that, a lawyer and abolitionist, Jacob Bigelow, had Weems kidnapped and hid her in his home in Washington, DC, for several months until her "conductor," a medical school professor from Philadelphia, arrived in his coach to retrieve her. With Ann Maria dressed as a coach boy and traveling under the name "Joe Wright," the two made their way to Philadelphia and the home of William Still. Ann Maria then traveled to New York, where she stayed at the home of a Congregational minister before making her way to Canada.

After passage of the 1850 Fugitive Slave Act, which required residents of free states to catch and return runaways or face prosecution, many fugitives journeyed all the way to Canada in order to be safe. If captured during the perilous journey runaways could be beaten, put in jail, returned to their former owners, or "sold South," where conditions were harsher than they generally were in the border states. The men and women who helped runaways could also be arrested and punished. The Underground Railroad required courage and daring from all who participated.

■ Harriet Tubman, born a slave in Dorchester County, became Maryland's best-known conductor on the Underground Railroad. She lectured to abolitionist societies throughout the North between raids. Courtesy of the Library of Congress, USZ-7806.

The Enslaved in the "Free State"

own escape to the North in 1849, she returned many times to lead others to safety. Her most frequent route took her through Caroline County, into Delaware, and on to Philadelphia.

Emancipation Efforts

While antislavery societies flourished in New England, even by 1850 few white Marylanders were willing to say publicly that slavery should be abolished. One exception was William Gunnison, a Baltimore merchant who suffered for his principles. Among slavery supporters, the term "Old Gunny" became an epithet of ridicule. Soon Gunnison lost his business and was taunted and threatened. Nevertheless, he continued to speak out against slavery, as did some Maryland Quakers.

Earlier in the century some Marylanders had supported efforts to send blacks to Africa, where a community took hold in Liberia. But with free blacks making clear their opposition to colonization in resolutions passed in conventions held in Baltimore during the 1850s, few whites believed that colonization offered a practical solution to what some considered an impending race problem. As the numbers of free blacks, born and emancipated, rose everywhere in the state, racial fears intensified.

Meanwhile, free blacks in Baltimore served as liberators for their less fortunate enslaved brothers and sisters, even as they confronted their own marginal status. Maryland severely restricted the legal status of free blacks: they could not own guns, testify in court against whites, or vote. Free blacks were required to carry certificates of freedom and forbidden to receive abolition literature or meet in groups except for religious purposes. In this condition of limited liberty in a hostile environment, free blacks had to be aware of Baltimore's seventeen slave catchers. Despite these many disabilities, free blacks often worked and saved money for many years to buy freedom for enslaved family members.

As whites became increasingly opposed to the growing free black community, that group in turn formed its identity through churches. Free blacks established community centers in places of worship such as the Sharp Street Methodist Church in Baltimore. They created Sabbath and night schools for adults, sponsored benevolent societies such as the Ladies Sewing League, and organized petition drives under the leadership of men such as Noah Davis and William Watkins.

Challenges to Freedom

In 1850, Congress passed the Fugitive Slave Act requiring that all enslaved people who had escaped to "free soil" be returned to their former owners. Slave catchers could travel into Pennsylvania, New York, and other free states and legally recover their human "property." Most northerners and all abolitionists were appalled and angry. African Americans living in the North were now subject to seizure and return to former owners or to being sold in slave markets. Slave catchers, on occasion, even seized free blacks in terrifying kidnappings.

Contemporary newspapers, especially advertisements, tell the story of the efforts white owners made to retain their enslaved property. Some owners tracked down runaways themselves, but mostly they hired slave hunters who could be found on the streets of Baltimore. In 1851, Edward Gorsuch, a Baltimore County slave owner, tracked four people into Pennsylvania, even though his uncle had apparently freed them. A pitched battle took place at the home of William Parker, a runaway slave from Anne Arundel County, between blacks living near Christiana in Lancaster County, Pennsylvania, on one side, and on the other a group of Gorsuch's family and a federal posse. The exchange of gunfire killed Gorsuch. In the increasingly tense atmosphere of the 1850s, this incident and other skirmishes with slaves played a critical role in the response of those Marylanders who demanded security for property rights and wanted federal action to assist in recovering the people they considered their property.

The infamous *Dred Scott* decision written by US Supreme Court Chief Justice Roger B. Taney in 1857 took away additional rights from African Americans. When Dred Scott, who was held in slavery in Missouri, sued in court for his freedom based on his earlier residence in the free state of Illinois and in the free territory of Wisconsin, the Court held that since he had returned to the slave state of Missouri he was not free. Taney furthermore wrote that residence in free territory did not make Scott free because Congress had no power to bar slavery in any territory, essentially making the Missouri Compromise of 1820 void. He wrote further that Scott was not a citizen of either Missouri or of the United States and, therefore, did not have the rights held by citizens.

Although in other American states by the 1850s the central issue dividing the sections was the extension of slavery into the territories, in Maryland the fugitive slave issue became a critical concern. The number of slaves who actually fled was small—279 reported in 1849, a number that dropped to 145 by 1860. But the numbers were less significant than the perception that the growing numbers of free blacks and the violence associated with efforts to control the enslaved population threatened white society. To some extent Maryland's support for Union in 1861 was embedded in the conviction that the federal government provided the best security against the disorder associated with slave escapes.

John Brown's raid in Western Maryland intensified such feelings. With Maryland as his staging ground, Brown, a white abolitionist, and his small band of blacks and whites attacked a federal arms depot at Harpers Ferry in October 1859. They intended to arm slaves who could then fight for their own liberation. But the militia captured Brown, who believed that he acted as God's lieutenant in a struggle against the sin of slavery, and hanged him for treason. Before his death he uttered his grim prophecy: "I John Brown am now quite certain that this guilty land will never be purged away but with blood."

■ Escaping from slavery meant walking through woods and swamps in all kinds of weather, often under cover of darkness. This drawing of twenty-eight fugitives escaping from the Eastern Shore of Maryland indicates the discomfort but not the danger of an escape. William Still, *The Underground Railroad*; courtesy of the Maryland Historical Society, E540.S85, p68.

Slave Songs

Enslaved people used music to express feelings they could not express openly and to convey messages. Frederick Douglass wrote down the following song that expresses the slave's sense of unfair treatment by the master.

> We raise de wheat,
> Dey gib us de corn;
> We bake de bread,
> Dey gib us de cruss;
> We sif de meal,
> Dey gib us de huss;
> We peal de meat,
> Dey gib us de skin
> And dat's de way
> Dey takes us in.

Some spirituals told of an escape or were used to signal such an escape.

> Steal away, steal away,
> Steal away to Jesus;
> Steal away steal away home,
> I ain't got long to stay here.
>
> My Lord calls me
> He calls me by the thunder
> The trumpet sounds within my soul
> I ain't got long to stay here.
>
> Green trees abendin'
> Poor Sinner stands a tremblin'
> The trumpet sounds within my soul
> I ain't got long to stay here.
>
> Steal away, steal away,
> Steal away to Jesus;
> Steal away, steal away home,
> I ain't got long to stay here.

The reaction to the raid was swift. Conservative white Marylanders embarked on a plan to return to enslavement all Maryland blacks and to close the state's borders to any free blacks. Curtis Jacobs, a slave-owning delegate from Worcester County, introduced legislation to prohibit any future manumissions. Jacobs wrote: "Free-negroism is a blight. The natural state of blacks is slavery." Yet in 1860, even with concerns over fugitive slaves widespread, most Marylanders disagreed with such extremism. A weakened version of Jacobs's bill failed in a referendum, not because the state's voters supported freedom for the enslaved, but because they saw the institution as undermining the state's progress. Voters believed that the bill would create a permanent enslaved labor force, making it difficult for farms dependent on free labor to compete. With the moment coming when Maryland would decide where its sectional allegiance lay, Jacobs insisted, correctly, that his legislation was a test of whether Maryland was a northern or a southern state.

■ Politics during the 1860s

During the 1850s, Maryland had tried to avoid sectional issues, but by 1860, such avoidance was impossible as state voters faced a critical presidential election in which the future of slavery and, by extension, the Union was paramount. The differences between North and South emerged early in the year when the Democratic nominating convention in Charleston, South Carolina, could agree on neither platform nor candidate. Meeting again—this time in Baltimore— the party split into a northern wing led by Illinois Senator Stephen A. Douglas that supported the right of settlers to decide for themselves over slavery and a southern wing led by Kentuckian John Breckinridge that proposed federal protection of slavery in the territories. A new organization, the Constitutional Union Party, attractive to some Marylanders including Henry Winter Davis and John Pendleton Kennedy, promoted a vague platform of support for the Union and Constitution. Meanwhile the Republican Party, of recent origin, opposed the extension of slavery into the territories, while the Breckinridge Democrats, who professed a commitment to states' rights in most matters, dedicated themselves to a policy of nationalizing slavery: "it is the duty of the Federal Government, in all its Departments to protect when necessary the rights of persons and property in the Territories."

In the presidential election in November 1860, although Republican Abraham Lincoln won nationally, state voters overwhelmingly rejected the Republicans, whom they inaccurately, but in line with southern propaganda, associated with abolitionism. Throughout the campaign that party's meetings were disrupted, their speakers harassed. The Douglas Democrats fared little better, receiving only 6 percent of the state's vote. The real contest for Maryland's eight electoral votes was between Breckinridge and John Bell, the candidate of the Constitutional Union Party. Both men proclaimed their support of the Consti-

> ## Party Platforms in the Presidential Election of 1860
>
> Sections of the 1860 presidential party platforms addressed the issue of slavery in the territories, with the Constitutional Union platform particularly vague.
>
> *Constitutional Union Platform (Bell):* Resolved, that it is both the part of patriotism and of duty to recognize no political principle other than the Constitution of the Country, the Union of the States and the Enforcement of the Laws.
>
> *Democratic Platform of 1860 (Douglas):* Resolved: inasmuch as a difference of opinion exists in the Democratic party as to the nature and extent of the powers of a Territorial Legislature, and as to the powers and duties of Congress under the Constitution of the United States, over the institution of slavery within the Territories that the Democratic party will abide by the decision of the Supreme Court of the United States upon these questions of Constitutional Law.
>
> *Democratic Platform of 1860 (Breckinridge):* That is the duty of the Federal Government, in all its Departments, to protect when necessary the rights of persons and property in the Territories.
>
> *Republican Platform of 1860 (Lincoln):* That the new dogma that the Constitution of its own force carries slavery into any or all of the Territories of the United States is a dangerous political heresy at variance with the explicit provisions of that instrument.
>
>
> ■ Crowds throng the 1860 Republican Nominating Convention in Chicago. *Harper's Weekly*; courtesy of the Library of Congress, a10051.

tution, the Union, and enforcement of the laws. A vote for Breckinridge, however, was generally considered a vote for the extension of federally protected slavery in the territories. In Maryland Breckinridge narrowly defeated Bell by 522 votes out of 92,302 cast. In Baltimore, which Breckinridge carried by large margins, local issues dominated. Many Baltimoreans apparently identified the Democrats as a reform party and voted for that party's candidate because they wanted an end to corrupt elections, not because they were taking a stand on national politics.

In another interpretation the election can be seen as a pro-southern statement, though not necessarily a pro-Confederate one. While Breckinridge's supporters employed the slogan "Maryland Must and Will Be True to the South," the state's anti-Breckinridge vote represented a majority of 56 percent of the total. In a harbinger of the future, only a minority of Marylanders had voted for the southern rights position, if that is what Breckinridge represented. In the coming months critical events forced Marylanders to define their allegiances.

The Critical Days of 1861

Reversing the traditional American acceptance of majority rule, a few Marylanders now argued for secession on the basis that Abraham Lincoln intended to free the slaves. In part, theirs was a response to the departure of South Carolina immediately after Lincoln's victory, followed by six other states in the winter of 1861 and the formation of the Confederate government in February 1861. Recognizing the vital importance of the border slave states, the Confederacy sent agents to Maryland to lobby for their new "nation." Yet, as did others, a commissioner from Alabama found Governor Hicks and most Maryland leaders vigorously opposed to secession. And pro-southern sentiment was never synonymous with a desire to secede, just as professed Unionism was not, at this stage, a commitment to fight a war against the South.

Maryland Chooses the Union

A crucial debate now took place: Should Governor Thomas Hicks convene the state legislature, not scheduled to meet until 1862, in a special session to address the issue of secession? Would the Union better protect slavery and the existing social order? Was it possible for the state to join with other border states to effect some sort of reconciliation between the North and South, perhaps based on the Missouri Compromise? At spontaneous gatherings throughout the state Marylanders discussed these questions. In the winter of 1861, skilled workers in Baltimore signed a petition opposing secession. In nearby Reisterstown, a group of farmers adopted the southern symbol of a blue cockade and named their militia company the Confederate Minute Men. Palmetto flags, the symbol of South Carolina, waved over homes alongside the Stars and Stripes.

Most businessmen opposed secession, and a group of citizens from towns as far apart as Towson and Annapolis shouted their approval for resolutions supporting the Union and Constitution. A Baltimore correspondent to the *National Intelligencer* cautioned that if Maryland seceded, there would be a stampede of slaves, the loss of $50 million of property, and one hundred thousand "servile laborers." On the Eastern Shore there was considerable Union spirit. *The Kent Conservator* proclaimed, "This section of the country is almost unanimous against secession." But such was not always the case in Southern Maryland or Baltimore.

Fast-moving events created flexible loyalties. The immediate effect of the political disagreement in 1860 and 1861 was to depress economic activity, as businessmen refused to support financial ventures during such uncertain times. Maryland's trade with the South virtually ceased, highlighting the importance of its rail connections to the North. Banks suspended payments, stocks dropped in value, and employment suffered.

Meanwhile, Governor Hicks faced continued pressure to call the legislature into special session, but this slaveholding Know-Nothing from Dorchester County initially resisted, convinced that the pro-southern atmosphere in Annapolis would influence delegates. The governor understood the disproportionate voting power given to the slaveholding counties. The thirteen Maryland counties with an enslaved population of more than 10 percent held less than one-quarter of the white population but elected nearly half of the state's delegates. By the spring, Hicks refused to meet with Confederate commissioners who intended to emphasize the state's emotional and economic solidarity with the South. But leaders as diverse in their party politics as Congressman Henry Winter Davis, S. Teackle Wallis, and John Pendleton Kennedy opposed any coercion of the South because, in their view, allegiance to the Union must be voluntary, not forced. "Let them go in peace" became a popular slogan. No doubt Congressman George Hughes of Anne Arundel County was correct when he informed Congress that "the doctrine of secession has no more friends in Maryland than a corporal's guard," a reference to only a few.

Events in the early spring forced the hand of Hicks and those who supported his policy of "masterly inactivity." On April 12, 1861, the Confederacy initiated war by firing on the federal installation of Fort Sumter in Charleston Harbor. Two days later, President Lincoln called for 75,000 volunteers to suppress this insurrection. Marylanders who had hoped to avoid war and remain neutral now found themselves volunteering to save the Union. A few, attracted by recruiting stations in Baltimore, traveled south to serve in a Maryland regiment in the Confederate army. Other men joined local groups, as the sale of arms soared. With militias a familiar local institution but a national army a foreign, threatening idea, many opposed the passage of northern troops through the state, claiming that such passage violated states' rights.

The Baltimore Riot and Its Aftermath

Geography dictated that to protect the nation's capital, surrounded as it was on three sides, as Lincoln noted, "by the soil of Maryland," northern troops had to pass through the state. Some Marylanders encouraged their fellow citizens to prevent what they deemed a "Yankee invasion." At meetings throughout the state when leaders asked whether Lincoln's troops should travel through Maryland, sometimes the response came back "no, never." It was this kind of thinking as well as the city's penchant for unruly gangs uncontrolled by the local police that led to the Baltimore riot of 1861.

On April 19, 1861, a mob attacked the soldiers of the 6th Massachusetts Regiment and seven companies of Pennsylvania militia in city streets as they marched from the railroad station where they had arrived from the North to a different station for their train to Washington. A hostile crowd surrounded the soldiers. At first civilians hurled only curses, firecrackers, and rocks. Then a shot rang out and a soldier dropped. After the ensuing mayhem, both soldiers and civilians lay dead, with many others wounded. The first casualties of the Civil War had come in a Union state, even as public officials moved to restore order. The mayor of Baltimore, George Brown, had marched alongside the soldiers during the riot, and that night both mayor and governor made a bipartisan appeal to end the violence.

■ Baltimoreans rioted against the 6th Massachusetts Regiment as it traveled through town on its way to Washington, DC, at the beginning of the Civil War. Soldiers from out of state and local civilians were killed and injured in the fighting. Courtesy of the Maryland Historical Society, Hambleton Print Collection, H244.

Standing next to the state flag, Governor Hicks proclaimed his support of the Union: "I am a Marylander. I love my state and I love the Union." Hicks also announced his opposition to striking "a sister state," and he may have authorized the destruction of bridges leading into the city. Both he and Brown hastened to Washington to persuade federal authorities to stop sending troops through Baltimore. The president, who knew he must retain the allegiance of the slaveholding border states, none more important than Maryland, agreed. Soon Union troops were boarding steamers at Perryville on the Susquehanna River for their journey down the Chesapeake Bay to Annapolis, where they then traveled the brief distance by land to Washington.

Three days after the Baltimore riot, Hicks announced that the legislature would meet in Frederick. Under Lincoln's specific instructions no one interfered with the lawmakers at this crucial time in state history, a fact that contradicts persistent views that Maryland remained in the Union only because troops arrested the legislators. In fact, the legislature proved a paper tiger. While hostile to Lincoln and any suppression of liberty such as the president's suspension of the writ of habeas corpus, legislators agreed that they had no right to debate a

■ Less than a month after the Baltimore riot, Union General Benjamin Butler and the 8th Regiment occupied Federal Hill, overlooking the city's harbor, to make sure Union supplies passed safely through the city. Courtesy of the Maryland Historical Society, PPVF, Group Portraits, Civil War.

secession ordinance. Nor was there sentiment to call a convention as had occurred in southern states or to turn the authority of government over to a so-called Public Safety Commission. Gradually the tide of pro-southern sympathy and neutrality receded, suggesting the fluid nature of border state convictions in the face of Union troops stationed in key locations. The most violent proponents of secession went south to form the 1st Maryland Regiment of the Confederacy. In Baltimore shouts for Jefferson Davis gave way to those for the Union; Confederate flags and blue cockades disappeared, replaced by the Stars and Stripes. By November, in a free election, 68 percent of the electorate chose the pro-Unionist gubernatorial candidate Augustus Bradford over his States Rights Party challenger Benjamin Chew Howard.

■ Maryland and the Confederacy

Confederate Conspiracies

Even before the war started, a handful of Marylanders threatened Lincoln's life. Creditable threats forced the president-elect on his way to Washington and his inauguration to travel through Baltimore at night, much to his later embarrassment. Others engaged in sabotage. One Confederate partisan was Lincoln's future assassin, John Wilkes Booth of Harford County, who in October 1861 was listed as a suspected traitor, but was freed after he took a loyalty oath.

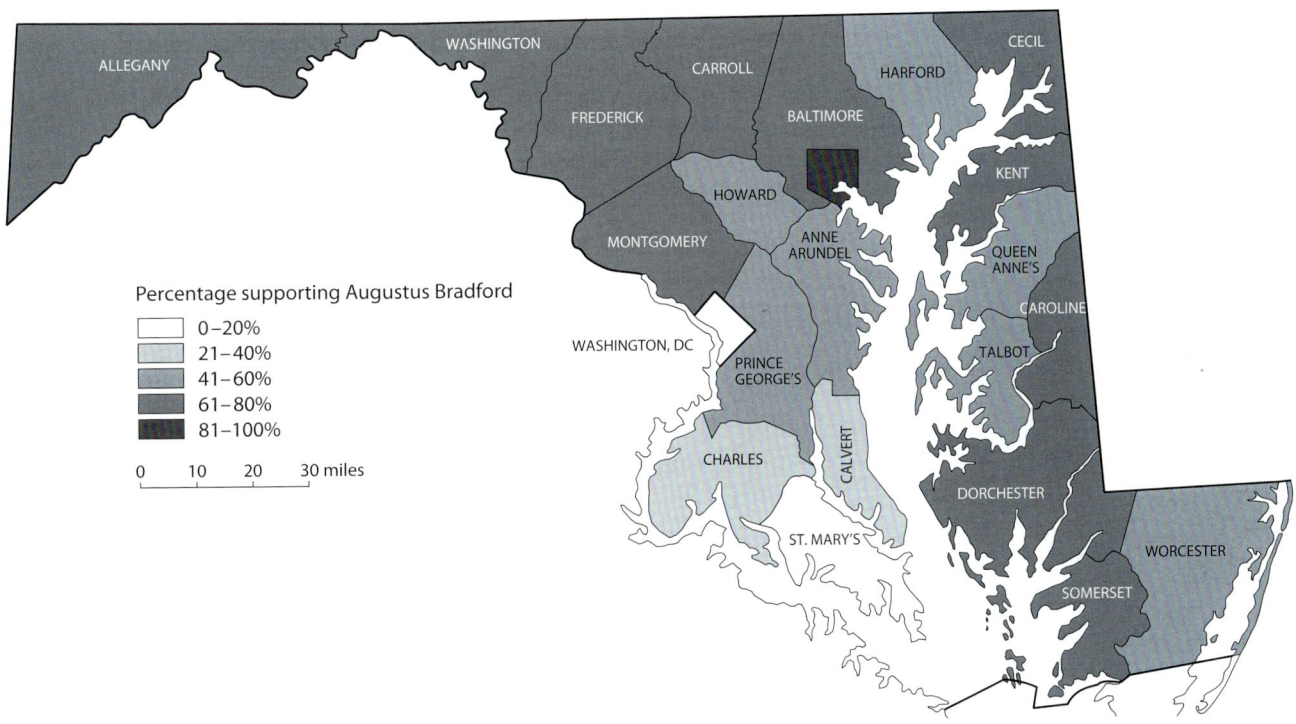

■ Support for Pro-Union Gubernatorial Candidate Augustus Bradford, 1861

Another southern sympathizer was John Merryman, a well-known Baltimore County farmer who destroyed railroad bridges in order to prevent Union troops from coming through Maryland. After Merryman's arrest in May, his case set off a controversy between military authorities and civilian officials. At first Merryman was held in Baltimore's Fort McHenry without being charged. Military officials argued that their authority for his imprisonment emanated from the wartime necessity of suspending the writ of habeas corpus, which requires that no prisoner be held without being charged with a specific crime. Eventually, still without a trial, Merryman was released, but not before the chief justice of the US Supreme Court, Marylander Roger B. Taney, had written a stinging brief disagreeing with the government's violation of a necessary protection for all free men. Without it, Taney asserted, even during a civil war, governments degenerated into tyrannies.

Persisting Differences of Opinion

The struggle between military and civilian authority—as well as that over Maryland's allegiance to the Union—continued throughout the Civil War. Union troops patrolled near some polling places on the Eastern Shore and in Southern Maryland, though nearly all of the state's wartime elections proceeded with no intimidation, as voters consistently chose Union Party candidates. In September 1861, Marylanders witnessed an unnecessary overreach of federal authority

> ### Judge Richard Bennett Carmichael: Southern Sympathizer
>
> In February 1861, as the nation teetered on the brink of war, Judge Richard Carmichael chaired the Resolutions Committee of the Southern Rights Convention held in Baltimore. The delegates, under Carmichael's leadership, unanimously adopted resolutions recommending that, if war came, Maryland should "cast her lot with Virginia and the South."
>
> The southern sympathies demonstrated in February soon led to an even more dramatic episode in Carmichael's career, one that further highlighted the mood in some parts of Maryland during the war's early years. As a circuit court judge on the Eastern Shore, Carmichael strongly objected to some arrests, which he considered arbitrary and wrongful, of southern sympathizers. When federal officials arrested three men charged with interfering with an election by heckling Unionists at a rally, Carmichael instructed the grand jury to indict the men who made the arrests rather than the hecklers. Lincoln's secretary of state, William Seward, then ordered Judge Carmichael's arrest. Federal troops entered Carmichael's courtroom in Easton in May 1862, dragged him from the bench during a court session, and pistol-whipped the judge when he resisted arrest. Taken first to Fort McHenry, Carmichael spent six months in Union prisons without a formal charge or trial before being released in December.
>
> Before the war, Carmichael served as a Democrat in both the House of Delegates and the US Congress. After leaving the bench in 1864, Carmichael was reelected to the House of Delegates in 1867 and served as president of the Constitutional Convention held that year. The 1867 constitution, with many amendments, remains to this day the document under which the state is governed.

in the arrest of twenty-seven members of the legislature considered disloyal. Briefly imprisoned, the legislators were released when they took the oath of allegiance to the United States. Southern sympathizers also expressed their opposition to the Union and Lincoln's policies in newspapers. The most radical was the short-lived *Baltimore South*, twice closed down for its open support of the Confederacy and its opposition to any limits on free speech and assembly even during wartime. But, by any standard, the violation of citizen rights during this civil war was minimal.

One Marylander expressed Confederate sentiments in an enduring way. James Ryder Randall, a Randallstown resident living in Louisiana when the war broke out, set hostile words to a well-known German tune:

> The despot's heel is on thy shore, Maryland.
> His torch is at the temple door, Maryland.
> Avenge the patriotic gore
> That flecked the streets of Baltimore,
> And be the battle queen of yore, Maryland, my Maryland.

The choice of this pro-Confederate song in 1939 as the official anthem for a state loyal to the Union remains offensive to many Marylanders to this day.

■ Maryland during Wartime

Small groups of men went south in the spring of 1861, in some cases taking their families with them, some of whom, as the war moved into Virginia, became refugees. By November 1863, 18,000 Marylanders served in the Confederate army, while approximately 3 times as many—some 53,000—were in the Union army. Most had volunteered, but with manpower needs soaring, in the spring of 1863, both the US Congress and the Confederate Congress had passed conscription (draft) laws that made all able-bodied male citizens between ages 20 and 45 liable for military service. But of the 29,319 Marylanders whose names were called, only 2,456 were actually drafted into the Union army, the rest being unfit for service, being exempt, commuting their service through a $300 fee, or hiring a substitute. For all Maryland soldiers, months of tedium were interspersed with periods of excitement and terror. In vital matters such as food and clothing, Confederate soldiers were never as well-supplied as soldiers in the Union army. Both armies suffered more casualties from disease, especially dysentery, than battle wounds.

The Civil War held special agonies for all of Maryland's soldiers, whether Confederate or Union. Fighting on the soil of their own state, they might, like the dashing Confederate commander Harry Gilmor, lead raids near their home and use their knowledge of the countryside to evade capture. Or, like William Goldsborough at the Battle of Front Royal, Virginia, they might find themselves shooting at a relative across the lines. In fact, Major Goldsborough captured his own brother. Or, on either side, they might end up as prisoners of war. The early expectation of being exchanged or paroled dimmed when the Confederate government refused to accept African Americans as legitimate soldiers and threatened to execute or enslave any captured black prisoners of war—an unacceptable provision for Lincoln, who promptly ended the exchanges.

A Soldier's Diary

The following is an excerpt from the diary of a Maryland Confederate soldier. It reveals the tedium of life at the front as well as the problem of disease, which both armies encountered.

- 7th to 21st Sick in camp with the measles.
- 27th Having nearly recovered I received my discharge from the Hospital and proceed to join my Regt.
- July 8th Second alarm in camp from pickets firing in the night all turned out in quick time ready for marching but quietness taking the place of noise and confusion, we return to our quarters and were soon again in the land of dreams.
- 12th Visited again by Brig. Genl. Bonham.
- 18th 19th 20th My regt laid these 3 days in the swamps of Bull Run, awaiting the enemy, half the time with half rations of hard bread and, muddy water, yet not a murmur is heard from one.
- 21st At night: A strange yet pleasing sight on a battlefield on returning from the pursuit of the routed enemy, we met a beautiful young lady in a buggy, and just a little farther on we are greeted by a sight of the cleanly shaven face of His Excellency President Davis, and give three cheers for both.
- 23rd to 31st My Brigade again take the advanced post.
- 1st to 15th August. My Company greatly reduced by sickness.
- 24th to 31st Make 3 forced marches from Centreville to near Fairfax Court House, in expectation of a battle each time but it was all a sham. During one of these marches I had the honour of seeing for the first time the renowned Stonewall Jackson, then in command of his Old Brigade.

■ In 1862, much of the land at Point Lookout in St. Mary's County became a busy port city with resident civilians and military personnel and several large installations, including a Union army hospital, a US army garrison at Fort Lincoln, and a Union prisoner of war camp for captured Confederate States army soldiers. Point Lookout was the largest such Union camp, housing 50,000 men between 1863 and 1865. Courtesy of the Maryland Historical Society, Hambleton Print Collection, H201.

Military Operations in Maryland

Marylanders had always known that a war between North and South would be fought on their soil, and this was one reason a policy of neutrality had been appealing. The state surrounded Washington at a moment in the history of warfare when there was no more important target than the enemy's capital. For four years—from April 1861 to April 1865—the state served as an epicenter of military action in the East. Vast armies marched across its territory; several major battles took place on its soil. Official records track thirty-one military engagements and hundreds of raids and skirmishes. Anne Schaeffer, a young resident of Frederick, noted after the Battle of Antietam: "a lovely Sabboth [sic] day but it does not feel like the Sabboth. Churches filled with the wounded and dying." Initially, Marylanders were swept up in calls to glory and patriotism, not the emancipation of slaves. And most, like leaders on both sides, believed the war would be short, a summer's adventure rather than the grim reality it became.

Antietam, Gettysburg, and Jubal Early's Raid

In the fall of 1862, a major battle took place in Western Maryland. After defeating the Union General John Pope at Manassas in Virginia, Confederate General

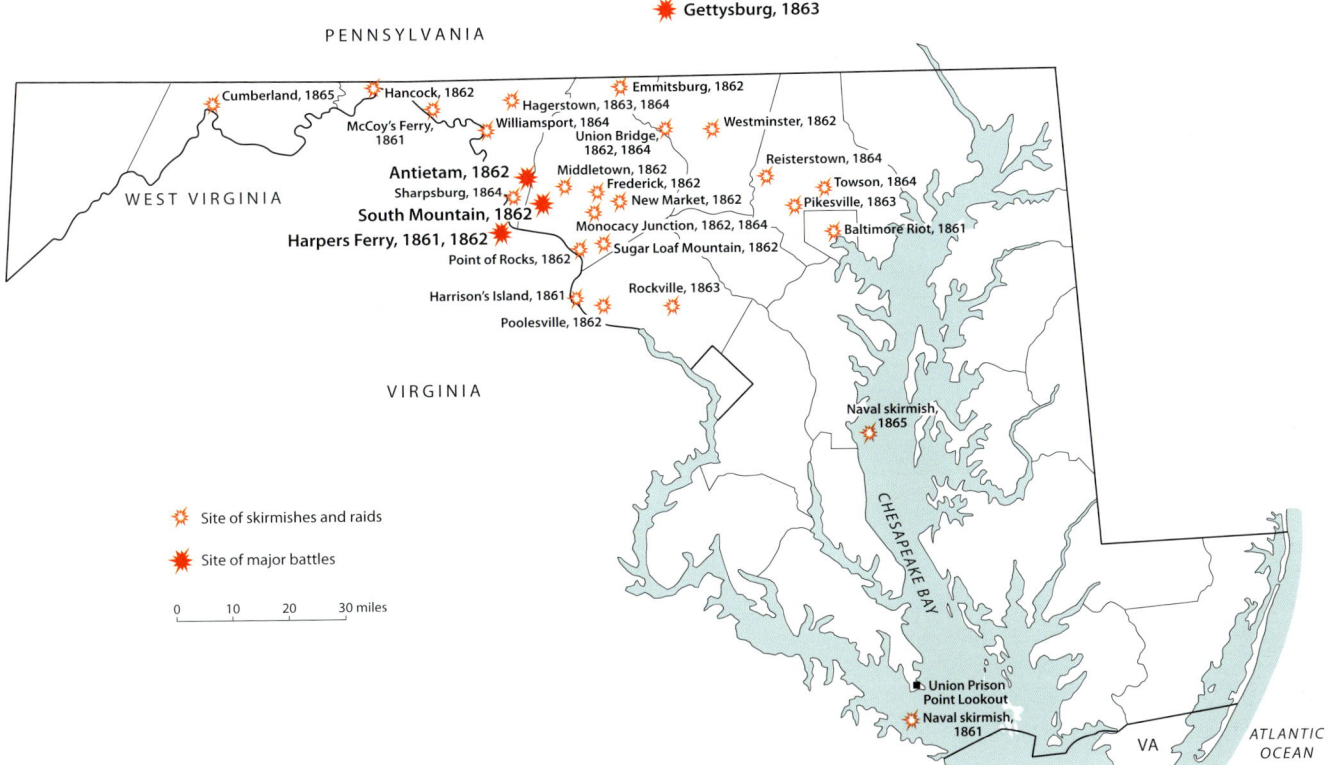

Civil War: Major Battles and Skirmishes and Raids in the Maryland Region, 1861–1865

Robert E. Lee and the 68,000-man Army of Northern Virginia crossed the Potomac River into Maryland. Lee intended to keep the better-supplied federal armies on the defensive by taking the offensive. He also expected to find provisions for his hungry army and, according to Lee, to free the state "from her foreign yoke." This was a miscalculation, for the Confederate army instead encountered a hostile civilian population in Western Maryland, some of whom remembered the earlier raids by Confederate units that had stolen their cattle and food.

On September 17, 1862, near the small town of Sharpsburg in Washington County, along Antietam Creek, the Confederate Army of Northern Virginia clashed with Union General George B. McClellan's Army of the Potomac. Lee had divided his army, sending one part to Hagerstown and the other to capture Harpers Ferry. Somehow Lee's orders, wrapped around three cigars, were dropped, and a Union soldier passed them on to his superiors who then planned their strategy with full knowledge of the Confederate plan.

On a gently rolling field crossed by a peaceful stream, the war's bloodiest single day of battle took place. By dusk, after a series of disjointed, uncoordinated attacks, 12,000 Union soldiers lay wounded or dying, along with 11,000 Confederates. McClellan claimed victory, but in fact this battle ended in stalemate for both armies, as Lee retreated to Virginia. Much to Lincoln's irritation, McClellan had missed an opportunity to destroy the southern army. Civilians

Maryland during Wartime

■ Burnside's Bridge across Antietam Creek was a focus of the September 17, 1862, battle that resulted in more than 23,000 casualties. Courtesy of the Maryland Historical Society, McCauley.E105.

who lived nearby never forgot the cries of the dying and wounded as churches, barns, and meeting halls were transformed into hospitals and shelters. "Oh this hellish war!" wrote Anne Schaeffer, "to maim and murder each other. Really I can scarcely believe I am living in Frederick—once so quiet and orderly and clean."

Less than a year later, after a series of victories at Fredericksburg and Chancellorsville in Virginia, Lee invaded Western Maryland. Again he gambled that the region would welcome his troops and that he could isolate Washington from the North. But his offensive ended catastrophically at Gettysburg, Pennsylvania, where a three-day engagement was the turning point of the war.

The final invasion of Maryland took place a year after Gettysburg when Confederate General Jubal Early, in order to divert pressure on Lee, crossed the Potomac River in the summer of 1864 and turned southeast toward Washington. He encountered a hastily improvised Union division whose defeat at the Monocacy River nevertheless allowed time to improve Washington's defenses. In this last desperate effort Early's forces destroyed bridges, cut telegraph wires, plundered stores and farms, and even burned Governor Bradford's home in Baltimore County. Jacob Engelbreck, a farmer who lived in Frederick, described the

President Lincoln visited Sharpsburg, near Antietam, on October 3, 1862. Courtesy of the Library of Congress, 98504543.

feelings of many civilians: "These are awful times. One day we are as usual and the next day in the hands of the enemy. But . . . I say come weal or woe, come life or death, we go for the union forever." By the fall of 1864, General Ulysses Grant's army had Lee's forces hemmed in, while General William T. Sherman slashed his way through Georgia. Finally, in April 1865, Lee surrendered at Appomattox in Northern Virginia, ending the war few Marylanders had wanted. The nation was saved on the battlefield. Now it had to be restored.

Life on the Home Front

For four years civilians in Maryland experienced armies of thousands trampling over closely tended fields, destroying fences, and confiscating animals. And while there were fewer marauders in Maryland than in Missouri, the state's strategic value made it a constant military theater. Communities in Western Maryland faced ransom demands from the rebel army, which if unmet would lead to their destruction. Families lost sons to the uncertainty of military service in a war in which as many as seven thousand Marylanders died and three times that number suffered war-related wounds. Even those who lived in relatively untouched areas on the Eastern Shore and in Southern Maryland suffered the

■ As casualties mounted in nearby Virginia, Baltimore became the location of several hospitals. The US army organized and ran this large facility on Camden Street, which cared for those suffering from battle wounds and disease. Other army hospitals in Maryland included two in Annapolis, where its two educational institutions became General Hospital No. 1 (the Naval Academy) and General Hospital No. 2 (St. John's College). Courtesy of the Maryland Historical Society, Hambleton Print Collection, H229.

political uncertainties of not knowing what kind of government the future would bring.

The war also led to shortages in goods and in food. Taxes increased when in 1861 Congress instituted the first income tax in American history—later a progressive 3 to 10 percent tax on income over $800. Although real wages rose, inflationary increases in the cost of living made survival difficult for those on fixed incomes. Wages increased in labor-short Baltimore for skilled workers like carpenters from a prewar $1.75 to $2.25 a day in 1864 and a clerk's salary rose from $30 a month to $50. But inflation ensured that groceries of $1.00 in 1860 cost $1.82 by 1864.

Party politics remained much the same, as a competitive two-party system between Democrats and the Unionist Party, home of many former Know-Nothings, emerged. One of the notable aspects of Maryland's wartime history is the commitment of state voters to the Unionists, who joined with the Republicans in seeking to preserve the federal union. Although Democrats exaggerated the interference by federal troops, there were only a few intrusions, the most significant in state elections occurring in Somerset County in 1863 when all voters were required to take a loyalty oath to the United States. In 1864, in the party's national convention in Baltimore the Republican Party nominated

Anna Ella Carroll: Military Strategist

Anna Ella Carroll was a political pamphleteer and military strategist during the Civil War. A member of the distinguished Carroll family of Maryland, she became a champion of the Know-Nothing Party. Her book *The Great American Battle* praised America and condemned Roman Catholicism as a foreign system.

Carroll's preoccupation with public affairs was unusual for a woman at the time. Always interested in politics, she wrote editorials supporting the Know-Nothings. During the Civil War she recommended that Union forces travel down the Tennessee River to launch an invasion that would split the Confederacy. In fact, she drew up a precise military plan and sent it to Lincoln.

After the war, Carroll supported black suffrage. She acted as a private lobbyist in expressing her strong views to senators and congressional representatives, many of whom she knew well, to influence them to support political rights for former slaves.

■ Courtesy of the Maryland Historical Society, 1961.101.1.

Lincoln for a second term and the president defeated his Democratic challenger General George B. McClellan in a close election. Lincoln, who had received less than 2 percent of the Maryland vote in 1860, received 54 percent in 1864.

Women and the War Effort

At home older men, young boys, and especially women took the places of husbands and brothers gone to war. Rural women planted crops, learned how to hook horses up to the plow, tilled fields, and harvested crops. Some women who had previously worked inside the home took paying jobs. A few traveled to Washington to work in the US Treasury Department, while others found employment in garment workshops that made army uniforms and blankets.

Middle-class urban women who had servants and more free time actively supported the war effort by organizing ladies' associations that provided clothing for soldiers. They also served as nurses in the informal soldiers' hospitals set up in churches and meeting halls. A wounded soldier in Western Maryland wrote admiringly of what he called the "Crinoline Brigade" that had raised his morale with their nurturing. In April 1864, Lincoln gave his blessings to the women when he traveled to Baltimore to attend a ladies fair where women sold their homemade soaps, knitted goods, and special foodstuffs, using the proceeds as their charitable contribution to the cause.

■ Successful civilian enterprises to support the war effort included fairs organized by the US Sanitary Association. Events such as this one held in Baltimore in 1864 helped raise funds to pay for food and clothing delivered to the battlefield. Courtesy of the Maryland Historical Society, Medium Print Collection, Section B.

■ Freedom for the Enslaved

In addition to saving the Union, the Civil War led to the emancipation of the state's 83,000 enslaved people, many of whom served in the Union army and navy. Many white Marylanders accepted liberation only grudgingly. Before their legal emancipation by the state's 1864 constitution, slaves freed themselves, running away on foot or sometimes fleeing by canoe during the confusion of the war to Baltimore, or the District of Columbia, where slavery was outlawed in 1862. The *Port Tobacco Times* complained that Washington had become "a free negro rendez-vous and slave hiding place."

National and State Policy

As early as 1861, some generals and political leaders in Washington urged Lincoln to approve the enlistment of blacks, free and enslaved, in the army. Certainly public opinion in Maryland did not initially support recruitment of those still considered private property covered by the Fugitive Slave Act of 1850. Initially cautious about offending a powerful slaveholding constituency, in 1862, Lincoln proposed that the federal government compensate owners for their enslaved workers, who would then become free, but Maryland's congressional delegation rejected the plan. Then on January 1, 1863, Lincoln freed the slaves in the Confederacy through his Emancipation Proclamation, but only those in bondage in states and areas in rebellion against the United States. Because Maryland remained in the Union, the proclamation did not include its slaves. Still the Emancipation Proclamation gave impetus to the state's Unconditional Unionists, who argued that slavery must end. The legislature, persuaded by arguments that slavery impeded the progress of the state, rewrote the state constitution. In a constitutional referendum in the fall of 1864, white male civilians and soldiers accepted, by the slim margin of 30,174 to 29,799, a Declaration of Rights that made slavery illegal and freed all persons held to service or labor as slaves. Eastern Shore and Southern Maryland voters overwhelmingly opposed the measure.

Congress had earlier passed legislation permitting blacks to join the Union army. By 1864, six black regiments from Maryland fought in engagements from the Siege of Petersburg to the Battle of Atlanta. Always commanded by white officers, black privates received $9 a month, compared to $13 a month for white privates. The state's slave owners challenged their slaves' enlistment, charging that they were "kidnapped" by the aggressive methods of Colonel William Birney, thus expressing, as one Marylander noted, the common delusion that the enslaved were so attached to their masters that they must be enticed into the army. In fact, they voted with their feet. Samuel Harrison observed a steamer leaving Oxford, former owners grim and silent on the shore, while the recently enslaved waved their hats and sang, rather than a patriotic hymn, a song of deliverance. Other African Americans found employment working on fortifica-

■ The 4th Regiment of the United States Colored Troops posed in front of its barracks in 1863. Among the six black Maryland regiments with nearly nine thousand men, this particular regiment guarded Confederate prisoners at the Point Lookout prison camp and later saw action at Fort Fisher in North Carolina. Collection of the Maryland State Archives, MSA SC 2431-1-12.

tions as day laborers, digging ditches and trenches that defended Washington and Baltimore. Unfortunately, the newly emancipated, whether in military camps or in Baltimore, faced harsh living conditions.

Maryland's Reconstruction

African Americans did not automatically become the social, political, and economic equals of whites, nor was their freedom uncontested. Racist beliefs in the inferiority of African Americans limited educational and economic opportunities for all blacks, regardless of whether they were free or enslaved at the beginning of the war. Blacks were frequently forced out of public facilities into segregated, inferior accommodations by laws upheld nationally by the US Supreme Court in *Plessy v. Ferguson* in 1896. Despite loyalty oaths intended to disenfranchise former Confederates, the postwar Maryland legislature controlled by Democrats passed laws empowering the Orphans Court to place black children in unpaid apprenticeships. Until Hugh Bond, a Baltimore judge, issued writs of habeas corpus challenging this system in 1867, more than three thousand black minors became victims of the practice. Meanwhile, adult blacks were forced to sign lifetime contracts that bound them to their former owners in sharecropping arrangements. Courts sold blacks convicted of petty crimes to local farmers for up to two years in what was emerging as a peonage system enforced by violence, as white planters maintained control of freed black labor.

For protection African Americans turned to the first federal agency in American history, the Freedmen's Bureau. Established by Congress in 1865 to oversee the transition from slavery to freedom, the Bureau provided for the destitute, including white refugees, and, most critically, administered land that had become government property through confiscation or military occupation. But Maryland had been a Union state, and whites insisted that they must be left to themselves to restore labor practices. The Bureau did open an office in Baltimore to aid blacks who came into a city whose African American population grew by 42 percent in ten years. Wherever possible, the Freedmen's Bureau insisted on contracts for black farm workers, and the Bureau briefly supported the efforts of a community of freed people living on "government farms" along the lower Patuxent River. Abandoned by Confederate Marylanders, this area of 3,000 acres in St. Mary's County constituted the only federally controlled land turned over to blacks in the state for purposes of relief. But with no protection from the courts, the land soon reverted to its original owners. While only a fraction of the formerly enslaved became landowners, several hundred did achieve that status. The number of blacks owning $100 of property or more in the 14 Tidewater counties rose from 1,467 in 1860 to 2,068 by 1870. Some succeeded in using their army wages and bounties to purchase property, but most former slaves and free blacks in the area rented or sharecropped.

Freed men and women also turned to the Bureau for food, shelter, medical care, protection from whites, and, in an area crucial for their future, education. The Freedmen's Bureau sent its agents into the field to start schools by buying land, building schoolhouses, and hiring teachers. Joseph Butler, a member of the free black community in Baltimore, was one of the Bureau's most successful field agents. Sent to Maryland's six southern counties on the Western Shore, Butler faced hostility and violence from the white community, but still managed to open eight schools in Calvert County, all dependent on Freedmen's Bureau funds and money from blacks. With local governments refusing to fund black schools, the Baltimore Association for the Moral and Educational Improvement of Colored People raised money to build and support approximately eighty schools in Baltimore and other parts of the state, along with a normal school that eventually became Bowie State University. Methodists sponsored a teachers' training program, later adding a liberal arts program at the college level to an institution that became Morgan State University. Yet for most African Americans who believed in the elevating possibilities of education, learning came in community schools, organized by blacks in churches and homes.

■ Sergeant John Murphy, the son of slaves, gained his freedom by volunteering to serve in Company G of the US Colored Troops, whose uniform he wore in this photograph. He fought in North Carolina with General Grant and at the end of the war with General Sherman. After the war Murphy worked in the US Postal Service, ran a feed store, and eventually became the president and publisher of the influential *Baltimore Afro-American* newspaper. Collection of the Maryland State Archives, MSA SC 2432.1.6.

■ Postwar Politics and Society

Postwar politics contained elements of change and continuity. Only white males over age 21 could vote until ratification in 1870 of the Fifteenth Amendment to the US Constitution enfranchising black men. In a signal of its future politics, Maryland was not one of the states approving this amendment and did not do so until 1973. A two-party system of Democrats and Republicans (the latter no longer using their wartime tag of Unionists) now competed for control of the state. Methods of voting remained the same, as did the disproportionate power of the rural counties.

One change in Maryland politics involved growing support for the Democratic Party. By 1868, Democrats controlled the state legislature, the congressional delegation, and the governor's house. Thomas Swann, who was elected as a member of the Unionist Party and took office as governor in 1866, exemplified the partisan shift when he denounced the Republican Party, political home of the former Unionists, and became a Democrat.

Swann explained that he was changing parties because he opposed the ironclad oath that became a central issue during Reconstruction. The oath required voters to swear that they had not aided the Confederacy, a requirement that had emerged as a wartime necessity based on the logical conclusion that Confederate supporters should not determine a government against which they had borne arms. After the war, the oath aided the Republicans but Swann believed that the requirement of past loyalty should be repealed. Democrats argued that Republicans were trying to replace the state's white voters with blacks.

Thomas Swann: Postwar Governor

Born in Virginia in 1806, a member of an old elite family of that state, Thomas Swann moved to Baltimore in his early twenties. He bought stock in the Baltimore and Ohio Railroad, and subsequently became a director and then the president of that company during the period of its westward expansion.

Swann experienced equal success in politics. As the Know-Nothing mayor of Baltimore in the late 1850s, he was responsible for many city improvements. During his administration, a professional municipal fire department replaced the inadequate volunteer fire department. He also established streetcar service in Baltimore. He is perhaps best remembered for acquiring Druid Hill Park, then on the outskirts of the city, to preserve some green space for the pleasure of the public.

Swann, elected governor of Maryland on the Unionist ticket, took office in January 1866. While governor he switched his allegiance to the Democratic Party, and he ended his political career as a four-term Democratic congressman.

■ Collection of the Maryland State Archives, MSA SC 1545-1044.

Swann now urged a constitutional convention, and the legislature obliged with a new constitution in 1867 that still stands as the state's basic charter. It repealed the ironclad oath and disenfranchised blacks, but gave black men the right to testify in court proceedings. Certainly the new constitution reflected the conservative views of new leaders like Oden Bowie, who took office as governor in 1869. Bowie had earlier argued for the removal of the clause "all men are created equally free." And until 1870, because the apportionment of state delegates included nonvoting blacks, the new constitution continued to favor the heavily Democratic Eastern Shore and Southern Maryland.

■ Change and Continuity in Postwar Society

Maryland life now settled into familiar economic and social patterns. With the transforming exception of the end of slavery, the war had done little to change landholding patterns, ways of making a living, racial attitudes, family structure, and church membership. The state's population had increased 13 percent during the decade, with Baltimore and the northwestern counties accounting for most of the gain. Baltimore in 1870 had 20 percent more people than in 1860, a growth

■ Baltimore between St. Paul and Calvert Streets. This lithograph indicates the increasing urbanization and growth of the city after the Civil War, when its location as a railroad center led to rapid expansion. Courtesy of the Maryland Historical Society, McCauley.V41.

Loudon Cemetery, c. 1866. A new cemetery opened in west Baltimore before the war, where the US government purchased several acres during the war. Eventually 2,300 Union soldiers were buried there and later a Confederate section was added. This romanticized lithograph suggests the human losses and their impact on families. Courtesy of the Maryland Historical Society, Hambleton Print Collection, H250.

that was largely the result of formerly enslaved people leaving farms for the city. Yet six of ten blacks still lived in Southern Maryland and on the Eastern Shore, while two of ten lived in Baltimore. Manufacturing, industry, and commerce continued to be centered in the city and northwestern Maryland. In 1870, more than 90 percent of the state's industrial production came from the region north of the Patuxent River, nearly 75 percent in Baltimore. The types of goods produced remained the same, as iron foundries, flour and sugar mills, clothing and cotton and shoe factories accounted for most of the state's annual production.

Most Marylanders still farmed the land, producing wheat, corn, tobacco, and dairy products. They worried about the weather and the soil, although by 1870 the Hessian fly had given way to a new pest, the potato bug. While the former slave owners could no longer depend on enslaved labor, they still relied on exploited black labor. If work remained much the same, so too did play. Costumed knights armed with lances competed in jousting tournaments that flourished in rural areas. Farmers from all over the state flocked to livestock and agricultural displays at the Maryland State Fair. In the city, German and Irish immigrants and their American-born children continued to enjoy the activities of their ethnic associations while gradually becoming more and more "American."

There was, however, one compelling sign of change. On April 8, 1870, Elijah Quigley, a black man from Towson, newly enfranchised by the Fifteenth Amendment, placed his ballot in a Baltimore County voting box. By the fall of 1870, 35,000 Maryland black men had registered to vote in the congressional election. The African American right to vote would be challenged in the future, but the war had brought a shining moment of liberation—and a continuing imperfect freedom—for former slaves.

Change and Continuity in Postwar Society

Maryland		The Nation and the World
Black men vote for the first time since 1810	1870	Fifteenth Amendment ratified; enfranchisement of black males
Garrett County formed	1872	
William H. Butler, Maryland's first black elected official, chosen as alderman in Annapolis	1873	
First hotel opens in Ocean City	1875	
The Johns Hopkins University opens	1876	
	1877	Radical Reconstruction ends in the South
Arthur Pue Gorman elected to US Senate	1880	
Charity Organization Society founded in Baltimore	1881	
Married Woman's Property Act	1882	
	1884	Democrat Grover Cleveland elected president
Reform League organized	1885	
Steel plant opens at Sparrows Point	1889	
	1893	Financial panic and depression
Reform Republican Lloyd Lowndes elected governor	1895	
	1896	*Plessy v. Ferguson* decision
	1898	Spanish-American War Annexation of Hawaii
	1900	Progressive Republican Theodore Roosevelt elected president
Maryland Woman Suffrage Association founded	1904	
Poe Amendment defeated	1905	
Reform Democrat Austin Crothers elected governor	1907	
	1908	Progressive Republican William Howard Taft elected president
Maryland urban population exceeds 50 percent of total population for first time Maryland enacts the nation's first workplace injury compensation law	1910	
Reform Republican Phillips Lee Goldsborough elected governor	1911	
	1912	Progressive Democrat Woodrow Wilson elected president
	1913	Sixteenth Amendment ratified: income tax Seventeenth Amendment ratified: direct election of US senators
	1914	World War I begins in Europe
Maryland National Guard begins training Baltimore Symphony Orchestra formed	1916	
	1917	United States declares war against Germany

chapter five

A New Century

1870–1917

The outcome of the Civil War meant the preservation of the United States as one nation and an end to a society based on legal bondage. Slavery had been eliminated and, after 1870, African American men were able to vote. Industrialization, which proceeded rapidly after 1870, became the predominant force for change and greatly altered both the state's economy and people's everyday lives.

As industries grew, people poured into Baltimore and other Maryland cities from the countryside, neighboring states, and overseas. Crowded cities faced problems of sanitation and safety. Some people experienced terrible poverty and discrimination while a few people acquired enormous wealth. Politicians disagreed on how to meet the new needs and challenges of industrialization. Early in the twentieth century, reformers called progressives sponsored programs that increased the government's responsibility for people's wellbeing. With industrialization, urbanization, African American voting rights, large-scale immigration, and political reform, Maryland and the nation changed forever.

■ The New Industrial Society

Once the turmoil of the Civil War subsided, the nation turned its attention to building industry. Industries that existed before the war expanded, and new ones were begun. As the years passed, more and more people moved into the cities and towns where the industrial jobs were located. In their daily lives, people used increasing numbers of factory-made products.

Maryland's Industries

Maryland's industries developed at a moderate rate compared with those of the nation as a whole. The wide variety of industries established in Maryland made

Sparrows Point: A Company Town

When the Pennsylvania Steel Company developed the Sparrows Point site, it also built a residential town for its workers. The 1,100 acres, located in Baltimore County, were laid out according to the company's ideas about the lives and relationships of these workers. Bethlehem Steel acquired the company and the community in 1916.

Sparrows Point was considered a good place to live. The town had sidewalks, electric lights, water pumped from deep wells, and underground sewers. The company planted trees and hedges. Progressive features included a free kindergarten, a clubhouse, and a manual training school. The company collected garbage and provided fire and police protection. The company owned the only store, however, and accepted payments only in cash. Residents were free to shop elsewhere if they chose to, something not always true when a company operated a store in its community.

The town provided several types of housing. Supervisors, technical and office staff, and teachers lived in detached houses with seven rooms, a bath, a furnace, and a cellar. All skilled workers qualified for houses with six rooms, stove heat, and cold water. Black and white skilled workers lived in segregated villages on opposite sides of Humphrey's Creek. Unskilled and unmarried workers, mostly immigrants or blacks, lived in barracks made of rough pine boards. Each 10- by 14-foot room contained two double bunk beds. Unskilled workers living there had to haul water from outside hydrants. Amenities varied as the years went by.

---

the economy more stable than one that depended on only one or two major products. The men's clothing industry employed significant numbers of workers in Maryland and earned large profits during these years. Other important industries included iron, steel, copper, and tin production. The steel plant at Sparrows Point in Baltimore County was Maryland's largest single manufacturing establishment. Its first giant blast furnace began operations in 1889; by 1892, the plant could produce 400,000 tons of steel annually and had begun to build ships. It made rails for the nation's rapidly expanding train system and for sale to foreign countries. The success of one industry often tends to stimulate others. In this case, the availability of steel and other metals led foundries and machine shops to open factories that made a wide range of metal products, some for sale to consumers and others as equipment for the rapidly expanding railroads and other industries.

Processed agricultural products also ranked high in Maryland's economy. Flour and grist mill products predominated until 1900, when canned seafood, vegetables, and fruit replaced them in importance. Chesapeake Bay oysters were canned during the winter months and sold throughout the country beginning in the 1840s. The rotation of oysters in the winter and fruits and vegetables in summer and fall provided steady work in the canneries as well as markets both

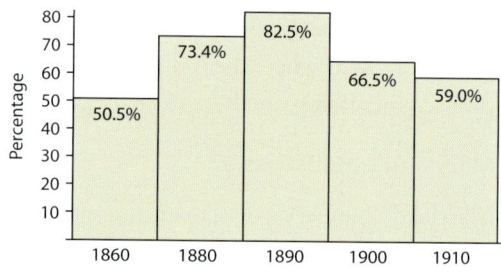

■ Percentage of the Total Value of Maryland Industrial Production in Baltimore, 1860–1910

1860: 50.5%
1880: 73.4%
1890: 82.5%
1900: 66.5%
1910: 59.0%

170   A New Century, 1870–1917

for produce from farms in nearby counties and for watermen working the Bay and its creeks. As canning techniques improved, fruits and vegetables surpassed seafood in total value. In the early twentieth century, slaughtering and meat packing also became major industries.

Baltimore's Leading Role

Baltimore's harbor played an important role in the national as well as the local economy. Domestic and foreign shipping produced vast revenues and many jobs. In 1870, Baltimore had $33 million worth of imports and exports; by 1900, the value of its foreign trade had risen to $130 million, making Baltimore the third largest of all US ports. Coal and grain were among the products that shippers sent out through the Baltimore harbor.

The Baltimore area dominated the state's industrial development until 1890, when towns in the rest of the state added new industries more rapidly than Baltimore, although a depression in 1893 and 1894 hurt industries across the state. As transportation and electrical power improved, a number of manufacturing establishments moved nearer to their sources of supply. By moving, the companies also benefited from reduced taxes, lower rents, and greater space available outside the city. These new industrial establishments provided job opportunities for residents of Maryland's smaller cities.

■ Chesapeake Marine Railway and Drydock Company. Isaac Myers, an African American man from Baltimore, purchased an extensive shipyard and marine railway in 1866 and within six months employed more than three hundred African American workers whom he paid $3 a day, an excellent wage for the time. Courtesy of the Maryland Historical Society, Peale Museum Collection, McCauley.L90.

■ Maryland Transportation in 1890: Railroads, Canals, and Rivers

Industrialization across Maryland

Until 1914, Cumberland was the second largest manufacturing center in Maryland. Its iron and steel industry benefited from nearby sources of iron and coal. Local timber provided the raw material for Cumberland's lumber industry. In 1914, Hagerstown surpassed Cumberland in the total value of its manufacturing, produced by a variety of industries, including machine shops; railroad repair shops; flour and grist mills; and manufacturers of furniture, organs, and knitted clothing.

Frederick, which ranked fourth in manufacturing, also had industries based on nearby resources. Because the city was located in the center of one of the state's major agricultural districts, flour mills and canning both flourished there. Numerous industries sprang up in Maryland's smaller cities. The lumber industry as well as flour and textile mills prospered in Salisbury; pulp mills, fertilizer plants, and canneries in Elkton; oyster packaging plants in Cambridge and Crisfield; and canneries and flour mills in Ellicott City.

Changes in Daily Life

In the long run industrialization strengthened the state's economy and led to higher living standards for most people. Food canning techniques freed the family shopper from the chore of daily grocery shopping. Mass production made

Old-fashioned washtubs and hand wringers, like these used by women in Allegany County c. 1900, were gradually replaced by indoor washtubs supplied with running water. Later, electric washing machines made washing clothes by hand a thing of the past. Courtesy of the Allegany County Historical Society, Slide 5861.

fashionable clothing available at affordable prices. A growing variety of consumer goods reached more and more buyers. Increasingly, complex machines like washing machines, typewriters, and telephones eased life in both the home and the workplace.

The rapid industrial growth came at an enormous cost, however. The population of cities grew so quickly that many new problems could not be handled within the existing governmental structure. Workers in industrial plants suffered from dangerous machines and an unhealthy environment. Industries filled the air with coal dust and the water with refuse and toxic substances. Cities grew ugly, but people still had to live in them. Natural resources were depleted and not replenished.

Cities and Immigrants

Industrial development drew people into cities and towns across America. The US census of 1920 revealed that, for the first time, more people lived in cities of 2,500 than lived in rural areas. Maryland and the nation were becoming more urban and also more diverse during the years between the end of the Civil War and the outbreak of World War I.

Urban versus Rural

Maryland's total population grew, but cities grew faster than did rural areas and small towns. Not only did more people live in cities, but there were also more

Table 5.1. Population Growth, 1870–1920

Year	Total State Population	Percentage Urban	Percentage Rural
1870	780,894	37.8	62.2
1880	934,943	40.2	59.8
1890	1,042,390	47.6	52.4
1900	1,188,044	49.8	50.2
1910	1,295,346	50.8	49.2
1920	1,449,661	60.0	40.0

Source: US Census, 1870–1920

Table 5.2. Population of Selected Maryland Towns, 1870, 1890, and 1910

City	1870	1890	1910
Baltimore City	267,354	434,439	558,485
Cumberland	8,056	12,729	21,839
Hagerstown	5,779	10,118	16,507
Frederick	8,526	8,193	10,411
Annapolis	5,744	7,604	8,609
Salisbury	2,064	2,905	6,690
Cambridge	1,642	4,192	6,407
Havre de Grace	2,281	3,244	4,212

Source: US Census, 1870, 1890, and 1910

cities in which to live. By 1910, fifteen incorporated cities and towns boasted a population of 2,500 or more, and more than half of all the people in Maryland lived in these places. Baltimore dominated both industrial development and population growth in the state. Because of the city's large population, urban changes were more accentuated there than they were in other towns.

People of Many Backgrounds

People of many different backgrounds contributed to all phases of urban growth. Demographic information from the census taken in 1870, for example, provides a picture of the people of Maryland in that year. The total population of the state was 780,894. Slightly more than one-third of Marylanders lived in urban areas, while the majority lived on farms or in small towns.

Of the state's total population, 22.5 percent were African American and more than 10 percent of all Marylanders had been born in another country. The black population was concentrated most heavily in agricultural Southern Mary-

■ After arriving by ship from Europe, newcomers had to wait for processing by immigration and health officials. This photograph shows an immigrant "pen" at a Locust Point pier in the Baltimore harbor. Courtesy of the Maryland Historical Society, MC 4733.4.

land and on the Eastern Shore, while few blacks lived in Western Maryland. Baltimore's African Americans belonged to a substantial community of whom 90 percent had been free before the Civil War.

The majority of foreign-born immigrants lived in urban areas. Of the major subdivisions, Baltimore City had the most foreign-born residents, while Baltimore County had the second highest number. Allegany County's mines, factories, and railroad construction had attracted the third largest number. More than half of the immigrant population in 1870 had come from Germany and the next largest group emigrated from Ireland. Germans, Irish, and others from northwestern Europe made up what is called the "old immigration."

Using 1870 as a base year, population changes can be traced easily. After 1870, more and more people came to work in urban industries and related services. Rural Marylanders, both black and white, migrated to cities seeking employment, and others came from neighboring states, especially Pennsylvania and Virginia. Immigrants from abroad swelled the urban population even further.

Immigrants

Immigration accounted for much of the United States' growth during the late nineteenth and early twentieth centuries. In some large cities in other states, immigrants and their children outnumbered the native-born population and rapidly gained influence. Maryland's foreign-born population lagged somewhat behind the national average during this period. Immigrants made up about 10 percent of the state's total population between 1870 and 1900. In Maryland, as in many parts of the nation, immigrants tended to settle in cities. Most, but by no means all, of these newcomers in Maryland lived in Baltimore City, where the immigrant population ranged from 21.1 percent in 1870 to 13.4 percent in 1900.

By the 1880s, a "new immigration" had begun. People from eastern, central, and southern Europe began to cross the Atlantic in greater numbers. Like the earlier immigrants, this group left their homes for a variety of reasons. Because of droughts, farm families in Italy faced starvation. Anti-Jewish pogroms in Russia threatened both lives and property. People from central Europe, like Poles and Czechs, left their homes for a variety of reasons: sometimes to avoid military service in the army of the Austrian Empire, sometimes because of religious persecution, and sometimes because discrimination kept them in poverty. Others made the choice more freely and came to seek the opportunities they had heard existed in America. Maryland's major groups of "new immigrants" came from Russia, central and eastern Europe, Italy, and Greece.

Many urban newcomers arrived with only meager provisions. Political refugees, victims of religious persecution, and disaster-stricken farmers all lacked the resources to make a new start easily. Many immigrants neither spoke nor read English when they arrived. Some immigrants were ridiculed because they dressed or worshiped differently. Often they were able to obtain only the lowest-level jobs. The newcomers faced discrimination, as did African Americans, in housing, education, employment, and other areas.

Table 5.3. Place of Origin of Foreign-born Maryland Residents

Place of Origin	1880	1900	1920
Germany	45,481	44,490	22,032
Ireland	21,865	13,874	6,580
England	5,231	5,299	5,113
Poland	642	3,681	12,061
Italy	477	2,449	9,543
Russia	213	11,301	24,791
West Indies	209	205	737
Africa	28	26	12
China	11	492	283
Greece	3	95	964
Central America	1	42	19

Source: US Census 1880, 1900, and 1920.
Note: The total given for Central America in 1920 includes South America as well.

Not all urban immigrants faced overwhelming problems, but many did. Their jobs were essential to the rapid industrial growth that was the basis for national prosperity, but often they did not share in that prosperity.

■ Problems of City Life

Living and working in American cities at the end of the nineteenth century challenged many newcomers. Working-class people of all racial and ethnic backgrounds earned low wages, resided in overcrowded dwellings, and endured generally unhealthy conditions. Epidemics, environmental hazards, inefficient fire protection, poor-quality roads, dangerous working conditions, unsafe water and milk, and the lack of governmental regulations and actions to deal with these and other problems made life precarious.

Working-Class Life

Poor wages and long working hours severely limited the lives of many urban residents. From 1885 to 1900, an unskilled worker, working 10 or 12 hours a day,

■ Women worked in crowded garment factories such as the Sonneborn Factory shown here, often earning less than a dollar a day. Courtesy of the Maryland Historical Society, Hughes Company Collection, Z9.703.PP8.

earned about $1.25 each day (approximately $35 in 2015), and a skilled worker could bring home between $1.75 and $3.00 a day, or the equivalent of about $50 to $80 in 2015. Those who found seasonal employment in industries like construction often spent several winter months with no income. From their earn-

---

The Comfortable and the Not So Comfortable

Financial standing determined the quality of life in Baltimore in the 1880s and 1890s. People who were financially comfortable described Baltimore differently than those who did not have even the barest necessities.

The Comfortable

Memories of a Baltimore Businessman of His Childhood (from *The Early Eighties*, 1924)

Baltimore of the eighties was a pleasant place. A charm of the old world pervaded the residential district; houses along St. Paul and Hamilton Streets, and elsewhere, had rose gardens. Piano music and snatches of song greeted passersby, for the study of music had a definite place in the upbringing of the young ladies of that day.

It cost less to live in those days! Posner's was one of the largest stores. M. Goldenberg was at 132 Lexington Street. I. Hamburger & Son, 104 W. Baltimore Street, offered "handsome Spring Overcoats $10.00," and Julius Gutman & Co., 120 W. Lexington Street, advertised "new summer silks, changeable effects, some very elegant designs in this lot, 50 cents." At 303 W. Fayette Street, table board [meals] was obtainable for $3.50 per week; a Help Wanted advertisement offered $10.00 a month for a "Girl, German Preferred, to do cooking, assist with washing and ironing," and Richard Walzl's Studio made "Elegant portraits $2.50 per dozen."

Memories of Journalist H. L. Mencken, Who Grew up in a Row House in a Middle-Class Neighborhood on Hollins Square (from *Happy Days*, 1940)

The city into which I was born in 1880 had a reputation all over for what the English, in their real-estate advertising, are fond of calling the amenities. So far as I have been able to discover by a labored search of contemporary travel-books, no literary tourist . . . ever gave Baltimore a bad notice. They all agreed . . . that its home-life was spacious, charming, full of creature comforts, and highly conducive to the facile and orderly propagation of the species. . . . There was some truth in all these articles, but not, I regret to have to add, too much. Perhaps the one that came closest to meeting scientific tests was [this]. Baltimore lay very near the immense protein factory of the Chesapeake Bay, and out of the bay it ate divinely.

The Not So Comfortable

Description of Early Immigrant Arrivals by Rabbi Isaac Fein (from *The Making of an American Jewish Community*, 1971)

There is a degree of suffering such as no pen can describe. Emigrants arrive every day almost from Europe in such numbers . . . and expect gold to be found in the streets. But when they have come, instead of gold, the picture is changed, and they find distress of every kind meeting them at every step. . . . [They] arrive without means, without a language, with new customs, often without a relative or even an acquaintance.

Description of the Immigrant Section of East Baltimore by a Local Reporter

A crowded place of tenement houses, saloons, filthy shops, foul odors, hideous noises. . . . Trees, flowers, lawns . . . gardens were sorely lacking . . . a saloon on this corner, a saloon on the opposite corner, a third saloon a few feet away . . . broken shutters and unsightly curtains.

They crowd into tenement houses, eat unwholesome food, breathe impure air, shun water and despise soap. Their children are covered with several layers of dirt. The women go unkempt, the men unwashed.

Memories of Hyman Blumberg, a Labor Union Organizer, of Life in the Sweatshops of His Youth

My father was a presser of pants making $8 a week when he worked. There were plenty of slack weeks. Unfortunately father's job was full of stoppages. I went to work at eleven to help support the family. My father was very religious . . . he believed that everything comes from God. . . . When I asked father whether he was satisfied with his boss's treatment, his answer was: "It is the will of God."

■ Children often had to work to help support their families. These boys worked in the J. S. Farrand Packing Company, an oyster cannery and a hazardous place to work as the machinery did not have safety guards. Because they worked all day, the boys could not go to school. Courtesy of the Library of Congress, LC-DIG-nclc-00725.

ings, the average family in 1885 paid $78.00 for rent per year. By 1900, this figure was closer to $100.00. Only 1 family in 10 could save any money, and 4 in 10 ended every year in debt.

Many women and children took jobs to help make ends meet. In Baltimore they worked most often in the clothing and canning industries. In 1880, more than 6,500 Maryland children worked in manufacturing and mechanical industries. Many African American and Irish women worked in domestic service. Women and children received as little as 40¢ a day for 10 to 15 hours of labor.

Poor working conditions resulted in health and safety hazards for all workers. In Baltimore's four hundred sweatshops, which made ready-to-wear clothes, employers crowded workers into second-story and attic rooms that lacked proper light and ventilation. Canneries and other industries used machines without safety guards. A worker who was seriously injured on the job generally was fired. There was no workers' compensation or unemployment insurance to help workers get through hard times.

The Unhealthy Environment

Overcrowded housing and lack of urban services further threatened people's health and safety. Baltimore had no underground sewer system or sewage treatment facility until 1909. Human waste was channeled into cesspools that often

The Baltimore Fire of 1904

On Sunday, February 7, 1904, a fire broke out in the Hurst Drygoods Company on Liberty Street. Inside the warehouse, smoldering cotton exploded, spewing burning debris over the neighborhood. High winds and freezing temperatures determined the magnitude of the catastrophe. Before the fire stopped, it destroyed 140 acres in the heart of Baltimore. One man was reported to have died. Several fire fighters and soldiers died of pneumonia acquired as they worked to put out the fire and keep the crowds out of harm's way. The 1,545 destroyed buildings took records, wealth, and jobs with them. Estimated damage stood at $125 million.

The city's fire chief had complained of the dangerous conditions for several decades. He noted that the city's closely built warehouses stored kerosene, cotton, fertilizer, chemicals, and grain side by side. In the downtown horse stables, hay was stored in the lofts. No regulations controlled storage or electric wiring.

After the fire, Mayor Robert McLane first appointed an emergency relief committee, then the Burnt District Commission, to plan long-term rehabilitation. Baltimore took advantage of the destruction to modernize the downtown. Streets were widened and smoothly paved. Sewer connections were installed under new streets. The fire department was enlarged and modernized. The fire helped win support for a new building code.

■ Little remained at Hopkins Place and Lombard Street after the great Baltimore fire of 1904. Courtesy of the Maryland Historical Society, VF Z24.53.

leaked into ground water that flowed into the city's drinking wells. Other waste flowed through the streets in open sewers, making its way slowly to local streams, rivers, and the Chesapeake Bay. Baltimore newspaperman H. L. Mencken wrote that in his childhood years the Back Basin sewage stench "radiated all over downtown Baltimore."

Disease spread rapidly because of the unsanitary water supply and overcrowded housing conditions. For example, Baltimore's smallpox epidemic of 1882–1883 killed 1,184 people, most of them in low-lying, densely populated areas like Fells Point, Canton, and South Baltimore. Other cities suffered similar outbreaks of disease. Until 1910, Cumberland drained its sewage into and drew its drinking water from the Potomac River. Thousands of cases of typhoid fever resulted every summer. Frederick in the 1880s lost more than fifty children each summer to diphtheria spread by impure drinking water. Towson, the county seat of Baltimore County and a summer resort for some city residents, experienced several typhoid outbreaks in the 1890s when sewage overflow contaminated its drinking water. Lack of medical knowledge about the transmission of diseases and lack of government regulation of water and sewage combined to permit these dreadful conditions.

Fires presented another major hazard in this period. An 1871 fire in Hagerstown leveled a prominent church and the county courthouse, and a fire that started in a grocery store burned a section of Annapolis in 1883. The largest of several fires in Pocomoke burned in 1888, and fires wiped out large areas of Cumberland and Frostburg during the late 1800s. The largest fire in the state, Baltimore's great fire of 1904, demolished 140 acres in the downtown business district. Because municipal fire companies often lacked the equipment to put out fires, large areas could be destroyed once a fire broke out. Many cities did take advantage of the destruction to modernize the burned-out areas with improvements such as widened, paved streets and sewer systems.

Discrimination

Discrimination based on race and religion increased the difficulties of numerous groups within the population. African Americans faced the most severe problems. Many employers refused to hire blacks for skilled or professional jobs. Health care suffered because Maryland's few black doctors could not admit patients to some Maryland hospitals. Black patients often were treated in segregated wards within predominantly white hospitals. The lack of medical care and widespread poverty contributed to a black mortality rate twice that of whites in Baltimore City. Tuberculosis posed an especially strong threat in African American neighborhoods because of overcrowding and poor sanitary conditions.

Segregation, although not as all encompassing as it was farther south, limited access of African Americans to stores, theaters, restaurants, and educational institutions. The state required segregated public schools throughout Maryland. Several times the Baltimore City Council voted to require that housing be segregated by block, but the US Supreme Court disallowed all such laws nationwide in 1917. It was, however, legal for neighborhood associations to keep out unwanted racial or religious groups, and many did.

Other groups faced similar discrimination. "Help wanted. No Irish need apply." was an advertisement that appeared frequently in newspapers and signs. Many employers refused to hire immigrants from southern and eastern Europe. Some neighborhood associations forbade the sale of houses to Jews, and some colleges set quotas that limited the number of Jewish students who could enroll. Many people used ethnic stereotyping to justify the rampant discrimination.

In this period many educated men and women espoused the philosophy of Social Darwinism. They believed that the best or "fittest" people rose to the top and inferior people fell to the bottom. Social Darwinists used the poverty of the poor to support the idea that they were inferior. They did not take into account how factors such as the heritage of slavery, discriminatory practices, lack of education, and lack of knowledge of the English language affected a person's position on the economic scale.

Life could be harsh in Maryland and America at the turn of the century: the workers who kept the nation's industries going suffered physically and emotionally. But many people believed that these conditions should be changed, and they set out to do so.

■ Fighting Back

The initial response to poverty and prejudice arose quickly, but help came first from private organizations and individuals rather than from public institutions. The government had not yet assumed responsibility for the economic and social conditions of its citizens. Only later in this period would it begin to do so. Until then, religious, ethnic, social, charitable, and labor groups filled the gap. Immigrant communities often formed around a church or a synagogue that worked hard to meet social and cultural needs as well as religious and economic ones. Religious and social institutions provided something small and familiar in a

---

Alleys and Row Houses

Many newcomers to Baltimore lived in alley housing, where rents were lowest. Although schools and many transportation and shopping facilities were segregated by race, housing was not. European immigrants and native-born African Americans frequently lived in the same alley block.

Some working-class families, including many immigrant families, realized the dream of owning their own home. Baltimore's reasonably priced row houses made home ownership more attainable than it was in most other cities. Families who bought these homes were often helped by loans from neighborhood building and loan associations. Buyers could usually pay off home loans in five years.

large city in a strange land. The most complex immigrant communities in Maryland developed in Baltimore, where most of the newcomers settled, but other Maryland cities followed the same pattern on a smaller scale.

Ethnic Communities: Immigrants and Blacks

Germans, who made up Maryland's largest immigrant group in the late 1800s, had the advantage of established and prosperous predecessors. The German Society, founded in the eighteenth century, continued to give assistance to immigrants from Germany, Austria, and Switzerland. The society helped people find jobs and provided financial aid in times of crisis. German savings and loan associations helped immigrants become homeowners instead of renters. The strong German community convinced the Maryland legislature in 1868 to have every general law published in German as well as in English, and to have German translators available at all trials. In both Baltimore and Cumberland, German-language churches, schools, and newspapers served the community. For example, one German-language newspaper, *Der Deutsche Correspondent*, was published in Baltimore from the 1840s until 1918 and continued as the *Baltimore Correspondent* until 1935. *Die Freie Presse*, one of several in Western Maryland, was published in Cumberland from 1891 to 1907.

Irish newcomers enjoyed the double advantage of a prior community and fluency in English. The Hibernian Society provided some financial and medical aid to the needy. The Hibernian Free School, founded by John Oliver in Baltimore, educated approximately 12,000 boys and girls. Respected religious leaders like Baltimore's Roman Catholic Archbishop James Cardinal Gibbons, whose parents were Irish immigrants, gave the community a strong voice. Still, many Irish immigrants faced poverty and discrimination all their lives.

Russians, Italians, Poles, Czechs, Greeks, and other "new immigrants" to America initially were not met by a group of their countrymen. The first to come tended to cluster together and build a church or synagogue as soon as possible. The largest numbers of all these groups settled in Baltimore, the port of entry for many of them. Early Italian immigrants in the 1870s rented housing near the Baltimore waterfront and then moved into the neighborhood still known as Little Italy. After Archbishop Gibbons dedicated St. Leo's Roman Catholic Church there in 1880, the church and its parochial school became the community's focal point. Lodges and self-help and social clubs grew as the population increased. Poles, Greeks, and others followed a similar pattern, creating churches and societies to support their communities. The Greek Orthodox Church also added a new religious denomination to Maryland's many existing congregations.

Jewish newcomers, mostly from Russia and central Europe, moved into the old German-Jewish neighborhood along Lombard Street. Eastern European Jews built their own synagogues that complemented the older ones established earlier by German-Jewish Baltimoreans. Many of the newcomers from eastern

Europe and Russia worked twelve to fourteen hours daily making clothing in the East Baltimore sweatshops. Several charitable groups raised substantial funds to help meet the needs of these people. Henrietta Szold, daughter of a Hungarian immigrant rabbi, was a pioneer in establishing a self-help program that was later adopted by cities throughout the nation. She initiated the first adult evening classes in Baltimore, which taught English and various skills to immigrants to enable them to get better jobs and thus move up the economic ladder.

Although Maryland African Americans were descended from many generations of people born in the United States, segregation and discriminatory practices led to the growth of institutions similar to those that aided immigrants. Black churches continued to play a particularly important role, as they had for many years. In Baltimore, several local black doctors raised the funds to build Provident Hospital, which opened in 1894. They believed that a black hospital was necessary because of the discrimination against black doctors and patients in white hospitals. In contrast, however, one of the founding doctors at the Annapolis Emergency Hospital, now the Anne Arundel Medical Center, was an African American physician, Dr. William Bishop Jr. Three black newspapers merged to form the *Afro-American*, which had a wide circulation across Maryland and in the region. It served as a source of news and a voice for the community, and its editors crusaded against the many injustices faced by African Americans.

■ Henrietta Szold, seen here in 1877, the year she graduated from the Western Female High School, convinced the Baltimore Hebrew Literary Society to open an evening school where immigrants from many countries could study English, American history, and government and could learn vocational skills. This school became a model that was copied all across the United States. Courtesy of the Ross J. Kelbaugh Collection and the Jewish Museum of Maryland.

Charities and Social Workers

In addition to ethnically based organizations, many private charities tried to ease the burdens of urban, industrial life. These organizations offered help to all racial, ethnic, and religious groups and led to the formation of a cadre of experienced and professional social workers. Before 1880, most charitable work throughout Maryland consisted of giving alms and other physical necessities to the poor. Allegany County charities, for example, opened soup kitchens during the depression of 1877–1878. This situation began to change with the founding of the Charity Organization Society in Baltimore in 1881. Mary Richmond, a pioneer in the field of social work and general secretary of the society, developed the techniques used in casework today. Social workers visited people in their homes and taught job skills, homemaking, and budgeting. Richmond kept records of clients' needs and progress.

Settlement houses, which had already succeeded in cities like New York and Chicago, opened in low-income neighborhoods in Baltimore after 1895. Volunteers and professionals conducted cooking and sewing classes, kindergartens, and clubs for all age groups. They offered English classes for speakers of other languages and emphasized skills for self-betterment.

Women, often upper- and upper-middle-class and white, led the way in many of the activities for improving the lot of working people. Local leaders like Elizabeth King Ellicott, Etta Haynie Maddox, and Anna Lloyd Corkran worked through groups such as the Maryland Federation of Women's Clubs and the Consumers' League. They fought to abolish child labor and to require inspection of health and safety conditions in factories. They campaigned to make water pure and milk safe to drink. They lobbied for underground sewers to get the filth off the streets. The Women's Cooperative Civic League, a black organization in Baltimore, worked for similar aims. They too wanted safe milk and drinking water for everyone. The organization sponsored a day nursery for working mothers run by Sarah Collins Fernandis, an early black social worker. Ida Cummings, a member of a prominent African American family, promoted the establishment of kindergartens for all children. Today's standards came only after long battles in which all these women took the lead.

Labor Unions

Workers joined together in labor unions to fight back in a different way. They sought higher pay, shorter hours, and better working conditions. They lobbied for legislation abolishing child labor and requiring compulsory education. They campaigned for laws to create workers' compensation for injuries received on the job. Many companies blacklisted employees who joined a union, firing them and putting their names on a list circulated among all area employers so that the activists would never be able to get work again. Workers organized to fight for change.

Unions grew nationally and in Maryland during the 1870s. Industrial workers in Baltimore and coal miners in Western Maryland formed the backbone of the state's union strength. The Knights of Labor organized its first local district assembly in Baltimore in 1878. This national union was unusual in that it welcomed all workers, skilled and unskilled, white and black, men and women. The Knights of Labor declined in the 1890s, however, partly because of labor violence elsewhere and partly because a nationwide depression in 1894 made workers less willing to risk their jobs for union activity.

In 1883, some thirty-two craft unions joined Baltimore's Federation of Labor. By 1900, sixty-five city trade unions were affiliated with the national American Federation of Labor (AFL). These unions generally included only skilled white male workers. They relied on strikes as their chief weapon, which frequently met with violence when factory owners hired private guards who rode on horseback into crowds of strikers, beating and sometimes killing the defenseless workers.

For the unions, gains came slowly and only after great struggle. In 1886, the building trades union won a nine-hour workday. In 1892, clothing workers failed to abolish sweatshops, but they did gain a ten-hour workday. By 1914, however,

■ Dr. William Bishop, a graduate of the Howard University Medical School, physician, and community leader, served on the board of trustees of the area's only public school for African American students, the Stanton Colored Public School. Collection of the Maryland State Archives, MSA SC 783.1.1.

The B&O Strike of 1877

In July 1877, railroad workers took home only half the wages they had earned monthly before 1873. Four pay cuts had reduced daily wages from $3.00 to $2.25 to $1.75 to $1.58. On the road, men had to pay 30¢ for a meal. Hard times in 1877 left the men working only fourteen to eighteen days a month, but the B&O appeared to be making a profit.

Accidents, against which there was no insurance, took a terrible toll. Railroad shop machinery mangled hands and cut off fingers. Landslides buried men who were digging tunnels. Railroad cars crushed men who were trying to couple them together.

The fourth pay cut was the last straw, and on July 16, B&O workers in Cumberland began the protest. Pennsylvania Railroad workers followed, and the strike spread nationwide. Strikers succeeded in stopping all freight traffic in Maryland.

B&O owner John Garrett asked the governor to send the state militia to Cumberland, where a train had been stoned, and persuaded the governor to issue a general alarm. As soldiers started to leave the 6th Regiment Armory in East Baltimore, a crowd turned them back. The soldiers lost control and fired into the crowd, killing nine people.

Another crowd disabled an engine and tore up track in South Baltimore. They cut fire hoses so the hoses could not be used to control the protesters. The following day was quiet as more than two thousand federal troops arrived. That night a crowd tried to burn the B&O foundry at Mount Clare and set fire to a coal oil train.

The company refused to make wage concessions. Rail traffic finally resumed, although trains required military escorts for safety. The workers had lost.

■ Violence characterized nineteenth-century labor protests such as the B&O strike of 1877. *Harper's Weekly*, August 11, 1877; Science History Images/Alamy Stock Photo.

one-third of all Baltimore workers still labored sixty hours a week, Monday through Saturday.

■ Modern Amenities: The Brighter Side of City Life

Utility services that we take for granted were virtually nonexistent in 1870. In the final decades of the nineteenth century, however, gas and electric service, telephones, and water systems began to modernize the major towns of Maryland. New educational and cultural institutions opened up to everyone opportunities that previously had been enjoyed only by the wealthy few. Popular amusements proliferated in parks and vacation areas, and movie theaters opened in the early part of the twentieth century. Commuter transportation allowed some people to enjoy the urban amenities while living in suburban spaciousness. Urban life improved slowly, first for those with money and then for many people.

Utilities and Sanitation

Utilities brought a new lifestyle to city dwellers who could afford the new conveniences. Instead of filling the stove with wood or coal, people could turn on a burner with the twist of a knob. Instead of filling lamps with kerosene and trimming wicks daily, people could flick switches that brought light to every room. Privately owned utilities opened for business in the late 1870s, and services spread quickly. Gas and electric power came to Annapolis, Baltimore, Cumberland, Frederick, Salisbury, and Westminster by 1890.

Baltimore's first telephone exchange began operating in 1879. Annapolis, Westminster, and Chestertown had exchanges in the 1880s and Salisbury and Rockville in 1895. Installations came slowly at first, however. Baltimore in 1890 had about two thousand telephone subscribers, in 1900 more than four thousand, and then, in 1910, almost forty thousand. Utility companies began small. They served wealthier citizens first, the masses later. Small companies gradually consolidated into larger ones, dominating increasingly wider areas. Soon the government began to take an interest in their rates and the quality of their service.

Improvements to water and sewer systems, two urban services essential to human health, began in the late nineteenth century, as cities looked for new sources of drinking water and opened water works to treat and pump the water. Wealthy homes in Baltimore had enjoyed running water for a number of years,

■ In public baths such as this one, urban working-class people whose homes did not have running water bathed themselves and washed their clothes. Courtesy of The Photography Collections, University of Maryland, Baltimore County, Hughes Collection #249, P75-54-0249g.

Modern Amenities: The Brighter Side of City Life

but after the Gunpowder River was dammed in 1881, relatively pure drinking water became widely available in the city for the first time. Baltimore's first sewage treatment plant opened at Back River in 1909. In towns throughout Maryland, running water became available in the late nineteenth century, but the quality of the water depended on its source.

Education

Cultural institutions also improved the quality of life in Maryland. Both private philanthropy and government legislation created institutions that benefited both cities and rural areas. Public education touched the greatest number of individuals. Baltimore City had created a school system in 1829, and the Maryland constitution of 1864 had mandated a statewide system of public schools. Nevertheless, Maryland lagged behind many states in public education because some counties and towns chose not to collect taxes to fund education. Baltimore's school system excluded black students until 1867 and the counties were even slower to open schools for black children. Although post–Civil War Baltimore operated several high schools for white students, for many years the Frederick Douglass High School in Baltimore, which opened in 1883, was the only high school in the state for African American students. Students from the coun-

■ The Tunis Mills one-room school in Talbot County in the 1880s. Many children attended such schools where a teacher taught all the grades in one classroom. Courtesy of the Talbot Historical Society, Easton, Maryland, 2011.2.2.

ties often had to commute long distances or spend the week living with friends or relatives in Baltimore, if they wanted a higher education. Annapolis High School, the first public high school for white students there, opened in 1907, but the first high school for black students, named for local African American philanthropist Wiley Bates, did not open until 1932. In Baltimore County, the first black high schools opened in 1939. Throughout Maryland, public education remained racially segregated until after the US Supreme Court's *Brown v. Board of Education* decision made that practice illegal in 1954.

Public schools at the turn of the century differed greatly from today's public schools. The General Assembly decided not to require attendance. Some children worked all day because their families needed their meager wages while others stayed home to help with household chores or to care for younger brothers and sisters. Some families could not afford the fees charged for books. The lack of free compulsory education reinforced economic and social inequities. In Baltimore City in 1870, only 28 percent of those ages 5 to 19 were enrolled in public schools. By 1900, the figure rose to 43 percent, still less than half, and the majority of those children did not receive a high school education. In 1902, the state legislature responded to political pressure from Baltimore City and Allegany County and required all children ages 8 to 12 in those jurisdictions to attend school. In 1912, the assembly extended compulsory attendance to all but six counties.

Philanthropy

Throughout the United States during this period, men and women who had grown rich from the profits of business and industry sponsored the building of institutions for the public benefit. Johns Hopkins, one of many such philanthropists in Maryland, donated funds to build a university and a hospital. The university opened to students in 1876 and quickly gained a worldwide reputation for its innovative scholarship. The hospital opened in 1889 and a medical school in 1893. The doctors who served both the hospital and the medical school contributed to the public wellbeing. Dr. William Osler and Dr. William Henry Welch brought their influence to bear on issues of pure water, sewage disposal, and treatment of infectious diseases. They were early activists whose work helped make the city a cleaner and healthier place to live.

Another philanthropist, George Peabody, a banker who had accumulated much of his fortune in Maryland, donated funds for a cultural center. The Peabody Institute, founded in 1858, included a library, an art gallery, and an academy of music. Enoch Pratt, a Baltimore merchant, gave the city money to open a free library. Pratt stated that the library's books were "for all, rich or poor, without distinction of race or color." During the same period, African American Methodists gave money to support historically black Morgan College as did the Reverend John and Mary Goucher, who also donated funds to start Goucher College, a leading institution in women's higher education.

Two Philanthropists

Johns Hopkins, born in 1795, grew up on a large farm in Anne Arundel County. The family performed the manual labor after Hopkins's father, a Quaker, freed his slaves. It is said that Hopkins always placed a high value on education because he had so little time for it. At age 18, Hopkins moved to Baltimore to work with his Uncle Gerard, a commission merchant and grocer. Later he opened his own provision company and invested his profits in the development of the city's port and in the B&O Railroad. At the time of his death, Hopkins was the railroad's largest single stockholder. He supported B&O President John Work Garrett's pro-Union stand during the Civil War and contributed $50,000 to furnish transportation facilities to the Union. Hopkins never married. When he died, he left $1 million to friends and various local charities. He divided the rest of his $8 million estate to establish the university and hospital that bear his name.

Mary Elizabeth Garrett, daughter of John Work Garrett, was active in and supplied financial support for the women's suffrage movement. A strong believer in education for women, she provided financial assistance to both the Bryn Mawr School in Baltimore and Bryn Mawr College in Pennsylvania, each of which offered high-quality education to girls and women. She played a major role in the opening of the Johns Hopkins School of Medicine. When funds were insufficient for the establishment of the medical school, Garrett and a group of local women formed the Women's Medical School Fund. She solicited donations from other wealthy women and contributed much of the needed cash herself. Two conditions went with the money: that the medical students be college graduates (at a time when that was not a requirement for admission to American medical schools) and that women students be admitted on an equal basis with men.

■ Johns Hopkins. Alfred Jacob Miller, *Johns Hopkins*, 1832, oil on canvas, 76.7 cm x 64.3 cm, Johns Hopkins University, gift of Mrs. Francis White; JH1992.61/JH1917.4.2.

■ Mary Elizabeth Garrett. The Alan Mason Chesney Medical Archives of The Johns Hopkins Medical Institutions.

■ The Washington County Free Library's bookmobile, first horse-drawn, then motorized, brought books to people in rural areas. Here it stops at the Old Road House in Indian Springs c. 1915. Courtesy of the Washington County Free Library.

Although the largest philanthropic gifts were made in Baltimore, where the greatest wealth was concentrated, a similar pattern prevailed throughout the state. Both private gifts and tax dollars supported an increasing variety of public institutions. For example, citizens of Frederick in 1888 collected money to build a public park around the county courthouse. In Cumberland in the 1890s, local women helped establish the Western Maryland Hospital to take care of victims of railroad accidents as well as other patients.

In 1901, Salisbury business leader William H. Jackson gave the land and money for construction of the second and modernized Peninsula General Hospital. In the same year, the Washington County Free Library, endowed by Benjamin F. Newcomer, opened in Hagerstown. Librarian Mary Lemist Titcomb made history when she established the nation's first bookmobile. The horse-drawn wagon, loaded with books, traveled throughout the rural areas of Washington County. In 1902, women in Annapolis worked with Mayor Charles DuBois to found the Annapolis Emergency Hospital, with ten women serving as the first board of managers. Philanthropy, large and small, added much to the quality of life at the turn of the century.

Transportation for Vacations and Suburban Living

Post–Civil War advances in transportation caused people's lives to change in several major ways. Trains and steamships, for example, opened vacation areas to city dwellers by carrying people to resorts throughout the state. The Deer Park Hotel, built in 1873 in the mountains of Garrett County by John Work Garrett, president of the B&O Railroad, provided an elegant escape from hot city summers. In Kent County, across the Chesapeake Bay from Baltimore, enterprising businessmen built beach resorts at Tolchester and Betterton. Hotel guests and day-trippers alike crossed the Bay on excursion boats throughout the summer months. Maryland's largest resort town, Ocean City, was one of a number of oceanfront subdivisions advertised in 1875. Several small hotels and a few cottages housed vacationers who traveled across the Bay by steamship and then across the Eastern Shore by train. By 1900, Ocean City supported two country stores, two churches, and one amusement center, where the Trimper family had installed a large merry-go-round.

Advances in transportation also made suburbs possible. First horse-drawn trolleys, then railroads and electric street railways, allowed people to live outside crowded center cities and still commute to work downtown and to enjoy urban culture. A large commuter operation, the Baltimore City Passenger Railway, received a state charter in 1858. Lines serving Catonsville, Hampden, Highlandtown, and Pikesville soon followed. These first lines radiated out from the city like the spokes of a wheel and transported residents to the new "streetcar suburbs."

More and more people moved into the "Belt," the area of Baltimore County that surrounded the city. Many of these residents used city services and sent their children to city schools but continued to pay the lower county taxes. After much conflict, in 1888, Baltimore City annexed 17 square miles of the Belt and its 35,000 residents. After further controversy, the city expanded its boundaries again in 1918. Both annexations required a favorable majority vote in the areas affected.

The national movement to build suburban communities affected more than just Baltimore City and County. In Anne Arundel County, towns like Severna

■ The *Emma Giles* was one of many steamboats that traveled on the Chesapeake Bay. She carried passengers and freight between Baltimore and communities along Anne Arundel County rivers, as well as city dwellers making excursions to Bay beaches. County residents shipped local produce—hogsheads of tobacco, bags of wheat, bushels of peaches and tomatoes—and seafood from local fish and oyster packing houses to city markets. Collection of John Conley.

Park grew after the railroad established connections with Annapolis and Baltimore. In Western Maryland, streetcars in Cumberland served the downtown and nearby areas in the 1890s. Workers from Washington, DC, who began moving to Montgomery and Prince George's Counties commuted on the newly built streetcar lines. One such streetcar suburb, Chevy Chase, had been farmland until 1890, when US Senator Francis Newlands, of Nevada, bought up land in northwest Washington and southern Montgomery County and built houses there.

■ The Baltimore, Chesapeake, and Atlantic Railroad Station in Mardela Springs in Wicomico County was a stopping point on a trip to the beach c. 1900. Passengers could take a ferry across the Chesapeake Bay, a train to Mardela Springs, and another train on to Ocean City. Courtesy of the Talbot County Free Library, Photo Binder 3—Buildings.

■ In Ocean City c. 1910, boardwalk strollers wore suits or dresses and hats. Bathers covered up also, as dictated by rules of modesty at the time. Marion Warren Postcard Collection, Talbot County Free Library.

Modern Amenities: The Brighter Side of City Life

■ New methods of transportation, both public and private, are evident in this postcard depicting the Hagerstown Public Square in 1912. Courtesy of the Washington County Free Library.

At the turn of the century, Marylanders living in cities and some suburban areas had begun to experience many elements of today's urban lifestyle. Utility services, public transportation, public education, a wide range of cultural institutions, popular entertainment, vacations, and spacious suburban living had all become familiar parts of life. These changes also touched Maryland's rural population, but they took place there more slowly than in urban areas.

■ Turn-of-the-Century Life outside the Cities

During the urban boom, many rural Marylanders continued to live close to the land in the manner of their parents and grandparents. Their lives centered on their farms and local communities. In Western Maryland, coal miners formed a distinct society that in some ways resembled an industrial community. Around the Chesapeake Bay, whole communities drew their livelihood from the bounty of the waters.

Maryland's Farms

Following the Civil War, the majority of Marylanders still lived in rural areas. Counties like Anne Arundel, Baltimore, Montgomery, and Prince George's, which today house dense suburban populations, were still mostly farmland in 1900.

Farm products varied across the state. On the Eastern Shore, Worcester County produced corn, wheat, and potatoes; Wicomico County grew corn, potatoes, melons, and berries. Peaches were Kent County's big crop in the 1880s, followed by tomatoes, pears, wheat, corn, and potatoes. First steamboats and then, beginning in the 1870s, railroads carried the produce to markets in Baltimore, Philadelphia, and New York. Railroads had an immediate economic impact. For example, when a railroad connected Easton to New York City, farmers from Talbot County received a much higher price for their chief fruit crop, peaches, than they had earned from customers in Baltimore.

The wages of Eastern Shore agricultural workers, whose employment was seasonal, were comparable to those of urban industrial workers. In Worcester County from 1890 to 1918, the average farm worker earned $1 daily. In peak seasons, good workers could do better. When canneries opened to process Eastern Shore produce, the demand for labor drew immigrants from Baltimore to work in temporary summer jobs. Four weeks in a tomato cannery could yield $175 in wages.

Montgomery and Prince George's Counties supplied much of the food for Washington, DC, with crops including wheat, corn, potatoes, fruits, and vegetables. Tobacco fields still covered significant areas of Prince George's and St. Mary's Counties. The transition from the pre–Civil War tobacco economy to a more diversified agricultural economy took place gradually. On farms from Frederick to Hagerstown, wheat was the dominant crop at the turn of the century, with dairy farming and animal husbandry growing in importance. Late in the nineteenth century, Baltimore County farmers still drove their sheep and cattle down the York Turnpike through Towson to market in Baltimore City.

■ Entire families worked in the fields harvesting crops. Laura Petty, 6 years old, earned two cents a box for berries she picked in Anne Arundel County in 1909. Courtesy of the National Archives, photo no. 523206, 102-LH-829.

■ A large condensed milk plant and ice cream factory for many years constituted the main industry in Greensboro, a town in Caroline County near the headwaters of the Choptank River. Collection of the Maryland State Archives, MSA SC 1477-1-4951.

From Harford County, trains carried dairy and meat products to Baltimore and returned with fertilizers and machinery. Canning houses in Havre de Grace and Aberdeen employed hundreds to process corn and tomatoes.

In rural Maryland, small general stores dotted the countryside. One-room schoolhouses served the larger towns, and high schools opened slowly. The county seats and larger towns began constructing utility networks soon after Baltimore did, but most rural areas did not enjoy gas, electric, telephone, public water, or sewer service before World War I. Many counties did not have hospitals until well into the twentieth century.

Mining in Western Maryland

Rapid growth spurred by coal mines and railroads lasted from 1865 to 1920. Population expanded so fast that the legislature carved a new county, Garrett County, named for the B&O's president, John Work Garrett, out of the western part of Allegany County in 1872. In 1900, Allegany County's continued growth still ranked it second in the state in county population.

In 1880, Maryland was the fifth largest coal producer in the United States. Maryland coal, shipped out first by barge along the C&O Canal and later by railroad, fueled East Coast industries and naval stations in the British West Indies, and was even shipped to Alaska during the gold rush there. Towns in the coal region, like Frostburg and Lonaconing, prospered. Agriculture, local timber, and the iron industry also made important contributions to the area's economy.

Maryland's miners enjoyed a better life than many coal workers elsewhere, with wages higher than those paid in neighboring Pennsylvania and West Virginia. One-third of Maryland mining families owned their homes. Most families raised a vegetable garden and kept some animals. Generally, they enjoyed the freedom to live and shop where they wanted. Elsewhere, miners often had to shop at a company-owned store and rent company housing, both at inflated prices.

Despite the relatively higher standard of living, Maryland miners shared numerous hardships with their colleagues in other states. At work for ten to twelve hours each day, they breathed in foul air in the dark, wet mines as well as toxic fumes from their oil lamps. Accidents killed miners suddenly. The coal dust that accumulated in their lungs killed them more slowly, as it still does today. Boys worked the same long hours at half the adult wage. Mining towns shared the sanitation problems prevalent at the time. Waste from houses and stables as well as runoff from the mines polluted Lonaconing's streams, for example.

One major problem miners faced was fluctuation in wages, as their pay rose and fell with the price of coal. Often they protested lowered wages with a strike. Strikes organized by the Knights of Labor and later by the United Mine Workers only occasionally resulted in higher pay. The miners' other avenue of influence lay in the political system. Beginning in the 1870s, miners elected sympathetic representatives to the state legislature, which passed laws that covered a variety of

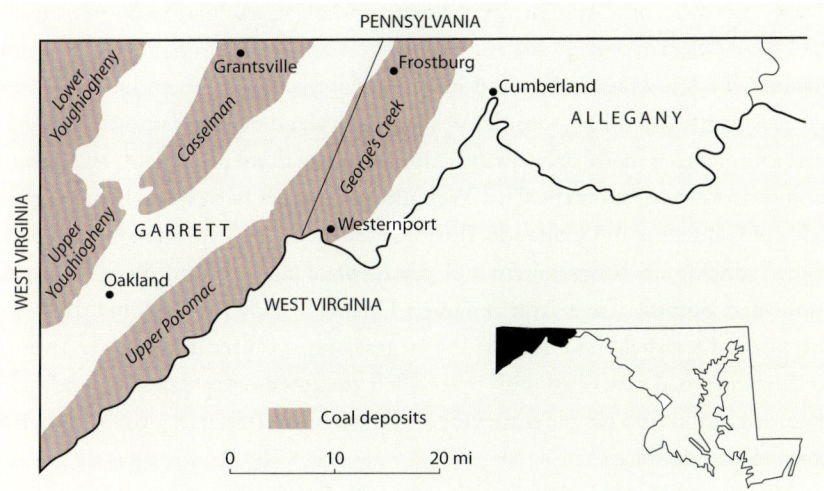

■ Major Coal Deposits in Maryland
Inset: The shaded area shows Garrett and Allegany Counties.

abuses. An 1876 law regulated ventilation in the mines and provided for an inspector, and the Mine Inspection Act of 1902 strengthened this law. In 1910, Maryland passed the first law in the nation requiring compensation for job-related injuries as well as for death on the job. In 1912, the state limited the age and regulated the working conditions of children in the mines. Despite the laws and regulations, mining remains a dangerous and unhealthy occupation today.

■ Early twentieth-century coal miners prepare to enter the mines of the Consolidated Coal Company, George's Creek, Allegany County. Many miners were young boys, paid only half of what men earned for their labor. Courtesy of the Allegany County Historical Society.

Turn-of-the-Century Life outside the Cities

Life on the Water

Around the Chesapeake Bay and its tributary rivers, watermen harvested the oysters, clams, and other seafood for which Maryland became famous. Refrigerated railroad cars made nationwide shipment of seafood possible. A steam canning process in use after the Civil War allowed oysters to be a staple in the gold fields of California and Colorado. Business took a major leap when John Woodland Crisfield, US congressman and president of the Eastern Shore Railroad, connected Somers Cove, later renamed Crisfield, with Philadelphia. By 1872, the town of Crisfield had become the largest oyster center in the state. Twenty to thirty railroad cars filled with oysters left the town every day but Sunday. In 1870, around 16,000 people statewide worked in oyster-related jobs; by 1891, the number had doubled.

Watermen, both black and white, were leaders in their communities. Men who braved the cold and dangerous Chesapeake Bay all winter long had to be strong and independent. In good times, oystering yielded a substantial income. In the 1870s, watermen earned 25¢ a bushel, shuckers 20¢ a bushel. The owners of the packing companies sold shucked oysters for $1 a bushel and invested their profits in other businesses like real estate and stores.

Not all workers on the water did well. Boat captains and their henchmen sometimes kidnapped newly arrived Irish, German, and Italian immigrants to work on the boats and sometimes did not pay them at all. Some of these men died of exposure and overwork and some were killed so they could not report the kidnapping and abuse. Other immigrants signed on voluntarily, hoping to earn money to get a start in America. One recently arrived German immigrant, Otto Mayher, in 1884 took a job on the oyster dredge *Eva*. He worked until he was too weak and sick to continue and then said he could work no longer. The captain and crew members drenched him with icy Bay water, strung him up by his thumbs, beat him with an iron bar, and, when he tried to escape, broke his neck.

Because their income depended on how much they harvested, watermen competed vigorously for the available supply. Boats with dredges that scraped oysters off the bottom tried to sneak into rivers where only tonging, using a pair of large rake-like tongs operated by hand, was legal. Marylanders and Virginians crossed state lines, often in the dark of night, to raid their neighbors' oyster beds. Illegal dredging and raiding resulted in widespread violence, now called the oyster wars of the Chesapeake Bay. Marylanders and Virginians shot each other and so did dredgers and tongers. In 1868, the Maryland General Assembly created the Oyster Navy to bring order on the Bay and its tributaries. Then all types of watermen shot at the oyster police.

One major cause of the rivalries and bloodshed was the increasing depletion of the oyster supply. Competing watermen plundered the oyster beds, which were not reseeded with baby oysters, called spat. A long decline in the size of the

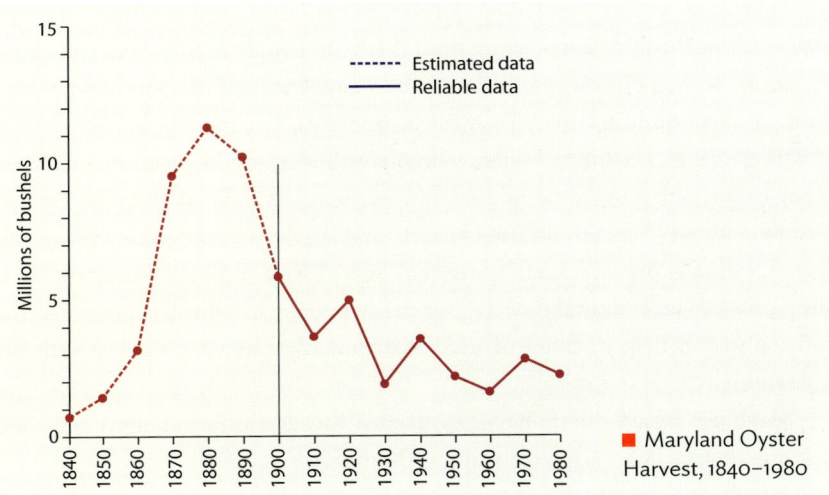

Maryland Oyster Harvest, 1840–1980

harvest began in 1885 and has continued into modern times. This depletion of resources led to hard times for oystermen and their families and helped cause the illegal and violent behavior. The oyster industry has never fully recovered from the overharvesting of the nineteenth century. Overharvesting, pollution, loss of habitat, and diseases have resulted in an early twenty-first-century harvest of about 1 percent of the peak numbers of the late nineteenth century.

Political Competition

Throughout the United States in the late nineteenth century, politics was complicated and often confusing. Men making political decisions faced the difficult problems of the period. Changes in many aspects of life left Americans struggling to decide what the proper role of government should be. National, state, and local governments gradually became more involved in social and economic problems as the years passed. The sectional politics that preceded the Civil War had undermined old alliances and new ones were still forming. African American men, enfranchised by the Fifteenth Amendment in 1870, added a new force in elections as did the large numbers of European immigrants and their American-born children. In many places, political organizations known as machines used a tight, structured hierarchy to bring order to the political process. The machines enjoyed considerable power and provided specific benefits to their supporters.

Political Machines

The organization of a political machine resembled that of the army. The "boss," who might or might not hold public office, resembled an army general in possessing the highest power. Under him came a hierarchy of ward leaders, precinct leaders, block leaders, and, at the bottom, ordinary voters.

Politicians wanted votes above all else. In exchange for votes, they met various needs of the people who supported them. To people at the lower end of the economic scale, political machines offered emergency aid like food and coal in times of economic trouble. To many supporters, the machines offered jobs: cleaning streets, teaching in public schools, and working in government offices. They oversaw the awarding of government contracts, helped shopkeepers and peddlers obtain licenses, and made sure streets got repaired and garbage collected. Political organizations sponsored boat rides and picnics and sent wedding presents and funeral flowers. For many people, machines represented the only source of help in times of need and the only contact they had with the government.

Machines raised the money they needed for election campaigns and their other activities in a variety of ways. Officeholders generally contributed a set percentage of their salary. Companies seeking contracts with city or state governments usually contributed heavily. Machine politicians and business leaders often worked closely together.

Democrats and Republicans: A Two-Party State

In Maryland a Democratic Party group known as the Old Guard came closest to the typical machine organization. Many urban workers, including immigrants and the children of immigrants, supported the organization, as did owners of utilities and other businesses that relied heavily on government contracts. Most Marylanders who had favored the South during the Civil War also voted Democratic. This rather odd coalition of urban workers, businessmen, and old Maryland conservatives provided the major support for the Democratic Old Guard.

Maryland's Republicans, the main opposition to the Old Guard, also united a coalition of several interest groups. These included many Western Marylanders and others who had favored the Union during the Civil War. Most African Americans voted for the party of Lincoln, emancipation, and Reconstruction. Businessmen who favored the Republicans' national economic policies often supported the party's local candidates as well. The Republican Party challenged the domination of the Old Guard. Never a majority party, it was nevertheless able to prevail in elections when enough Democrats defected to join its ranks. Issues of political corruption and social reform often moved many Maryland Democrats to do just that. Maryland did not become a true one-party state, as happened in states farther south.

Voters

By 1870, all male citizens, black and white, over 21 years of age were able to vote in Maryland. Maryland women, however, could not vote in the nineteenth century, with the exception of a few local elections in small jurisdictions with local voting rules. The General Assembly repeatedly spurned women's statewide ef-

THE RESULT OF THE FIFTEENTH AMENDMENT,
And the Rise and Progress of the African Race in America and its final Accomplishment, and Celebration on May 19th A.D. 1870.

This lithograph depicts the celebration in Baltimore of the passage of the Fifteenth Amendment. Courtesy of the Maryland Historical Society, Hambleton Print Collection, H85.

forts and, in fact, declined to ratify the Nineteenth Amendment to the US Constitution, which finally gave women the vote nationwide in 1920. Maryland did not ratify the amendment until 1941.

When black men began to vote after 1870, they sometimes provided the numbers needed to elect Republican candidates. Maryland Democrats, like many Democrats in the Deep South, wished to nullify that vote by disenfranchising the vast majority of African American men using devices like a literacy test and the grandfather clause. Many former slave states, which had large black populations, passed laws requiring voting registrars to administer a "literacy test" to potential voters, for example, to verify their ability to read and interpret parts of the Constitution or state laws. The local registrar judged the test and failed most black applicants. Those same states passed laws exempting a potential voter from the literacy test if his grandfather had voted, thus allowing most illiterate white applicants to vote. In the end, Maryland did not enact this combination of laws. Baltimore city politicians knew that the literacy tests could disenfranchise many immigrants and their children who, although true Democrats and staunch supporters of the machine, could not read and write English.

White Republicans and all black voters added their votes in opposition to the proposed laws. The coalition—of blacks, white Republicans, and Democratic machine leaders protecting their immigrant voters—prevented black disenfranchisement in Maryland.

The Old Guard at Work

From the 1870s until 1906, Arthur Pue Gorman headed Maryland's Democratic organization. Gorman, who was elected to the House of Delegates from Howard County in 1869, consolidated his power during the following decade. He chaired the Democratic State Central Committee, which controlled party nominations. In 1880, he was elected to the US Senate by the General Assembly which, at that time, still chose Maryland's US senators. Gorman gained national fame in 1884 from the major role he played in Grover Cleveland's successful bid for the presidency. Cleveland was the first Democrat elected president after the Civil War, and his victory gave Gorman a goodly number of political patronage jobs to hand out in Maryland.

Senator Gorman worked with a coalition of county Democratic leaders like Elihu Jackson of Wicomico County and John Walter Smith of Worcester County, both of whom later became governor. Fred Talbott of Baltimore County, another organization leader, enjoyed strong support from conservative countians. He had served with Harry Gilmor in the Confederate army.

Baltimore City's boss Isaac Freeman Rasin headed the largest and most powerful urban organization in the state, which worked closely with Gorman's statewide organization. Born in Kent County, Rasin moved to Baltimore and held jobs in the millinery and straw goods trade, while working his way up in the Democratic Party through ward politics. In 1867, he was elected clerk of the Court of Common Pleas, the only elective post he ever held. In the 1871 election Rasin was lucky enough to support two winners, William Pinkney White for governor and Joshua Vansant for mayor. Rasin thus came to control a great number of patronage jobs in Baltimore City. For many years these included teaching positions filled by political appointees who might or might not have had any real teaching credentials. Rasin served his working-class constituents by giving strong support to labor legislation. Although he had once supported the Know-Nothing Party, as boss he was responsive to the city's varied ethnic groups and worked closely with many businessmen.

■ Senator Arthur Pue Gorman headed Maryland's Democratic organization from the 1870s until his death in 1906. Collection of the Maryland State Archives, MSA SC 1545-1076.

Although the machines provided order during the post–Civil War period, they often used illegal means to assure their power. Elections held many temptations. In parts of Maryland, faithful supporters of the machine spent the whole day voting at different polling places across the state. "Vote early and often" was more than just a slogan. Sometimes dead people's names remained on the registration lists so party regulars could vote in their place.

In some states, machine leaders acquired personal fortunes through bribes, kickbacks from contracts, and other fraudulent means—actions that resulted in jail terms for many. Maryland's organization leaders generally avoided the worst abuses. Some of their appointees were competent men who served Maryland's interests well, but sometimes the public suffered because political allies got jobs that they were not qualified to perform.

Machine politics never totally controlled Maryland. The power of Gorman, Rasin, and their allies faced repeated challenges. After the deaths of Gorman in 1906 and Rasin in 1907, John J. "Sonny" Mahon assumed the position of boss but his influence was never as great as that of the earlier leaders.

■ Isaac Freeman Rasin, an ally of Arthur Pue Gorman, controlled the Baltimore City Democratic organization until he died in 1907. Courtesy of the Maryland Historical Society, PVF Z24.1215.

■ Reformers Challenge the Old Guard

Throughout the nation, reform groups quickly challenged the political machines. They decried the machines' corrupt practices, the political payoffs (called graft), and the favor swapping. They criticized politicians for tolerating dirty streets and hazardous working conditions. Most of all, reformers wanted to throw out the "bad guys" and put the reins of power into the hands of the "good guys," meaning themselves. Often reformers won elections on a popular issue only to be turned out of office two or four years later as the machine pulled together its supporters.

As their power grew, the reformers came to be called progressives. Early in the twentieth century, reformers dominated a number of state governments across the nation. Progressives like Republican Theodore Roosevelt and Democrat Woodrow Wilson were elected president. The reformers collectively known as progressives included Democrats, Republicans, and members of a third party called the Progressive Party.

Although the anti-machine effort in Maryland began in the 1870s, it gained much of its momentum in the 1880s and 1890s. In Baltimore County a coalition of reform Democrats and Republicans known as the Potato Bugs beat the machine in 1875, but the machine Democrats regained control in 1877. Progressives were active in many counties, including Prince George's, Montgomery, and Anne Arundel.

The Reform League

In Baltimore City in 1885, leading opponents of Gorman and Rasin joined together in an organization called the Reform League. This group gained enough strength to provide an effective challenge over the years. Its leaders, many of whom were prominent lawyers, came from educated upper-class and professional families.

Charles J. Bonaparte, the grandson of Napoleon's youngest brother Jerome and Betsy Patterson Bonaparte, daughter of a prominent Baltimore merchant of the Revolutionary period, was one leader of the Reform League. The organization crusaded for fair elections and supported efforts to enact civil service reform by putting government jobs under the control of a nonpolitical, nonpartisan commission instead of the bosses. Bonaparte later served as secretary of the navy and as attorney general in the cabinet of President Theodore Roosevelt.

Crusading Journalism

The Maryland reform movement gained momentum when Charles H. Grasty bought the *Baltimore Evening News* in 1891. Like many crusading journalists of the time, Grasty used his newspaper to attack abuses and reveal scandals about well-known public figures. The *News* attacked the high prices and poor service of the Consolidated Gas Company. It criticized the telephone and streetcar companies for their high rates and poor performance and suggested that a public utilities commission be created to regulate the operations of all such companies.

Grasty published an exposé on the city's street-paving contracts: who got them, why, and how much money changed hands as part of the deal. He ran a

---

The Spanish-American War, 1898

The United States had economic interests in the nearby Spanish colony of Cuba. Americans had invested more than $50 million in Cuba, most of that in sugar plantations. Much of the sugar produced was shipped to the United States and most Cuban imports came from the United States. In 1895, Cuban insurgents began a revolution to gain independence from Spain. Crusading journalists attacked abuses overseas as well as abuses at home. Reports of Spanish atrocities appeared frequently in American newspapers along with pressure to go to war to free Cuba from Spanish domination. In 1898, the United States did just that.

Fighting took place not only in the Caribbean but also in the Pacific. By December 1898, Cuba was independent and Spain had ceded the Philippines, Puerto Rico, and Guam to the United States. US army units called up during the conflict included two from Maryland, the First Maryland Infantry headquartered in Hagerstown and the Fifth Maryland Infantry headquartered in Baltimore.

The US navy played the most important role in the war effort, and its success helped guarantee a major expansion of the Naval Academy in Annapolis. Almost all of the original campus buildings were demolished and replaced by Ernest Flagg's Beaux Arts campus that is still the core of the academy's buildings today. The ripple effect changed the face of the city as well, with population increasing both as a result of construction and the influx of new faculty and other personnel.

This early twentieth-century aerial view of the United States Naval Academy shows the new campus created in the aftermath of the Spanish-American War, with buildings designed by Ernest Flagg in the Beaux Arts style. Only Gate 3 and its two guardhouses survived the rebuilding. Collection of John Conley.

series of articles on slums, pointing up the city's failure to regulate housing standards and to collect garbage in poor neighborhoods. He revealed the inner workings of the Policy, an illegal lottery run by the Democratic Party to raise cash for campaigns.

The Reformers' First Victory

Through the combined efforts of Republicans and reform Democrats, support for the progressive movement grew. Finally, in 1895, progressives won their first big victory as reform candidates swept elections across the state. Republican Lloyd Lowndes of Cumberland won the gubernatorial election, and Republican Alcaeus Hooper became mayor of Baltimore. Other Republicans won election to the state legislature and to many city and county council seats. In 1896, Maryland sent Republican congressional representatives to Washington; Democrat Gorman lost his Senate seat to Republican George L. Wellington from Allegany County.

Once they gained power, Republicans enacted several major laws that they hoped would change the state's political balance in their favor. In 1898, the General Assembly required the use of the Australian ballot in elections to replace the older, single-party ballots. The new type of ballot, still in use today, lists the names of all the candidates on one long ballot, allowing truly secret voting and making it easier to split votes among candidates of different parties.

The 1898 legislature also repealed the old requirement that one of Maryland's two US senators come from the Eastern Shore. The new law opened selection of both senators to men from the entire state. Republicans especially welcomed the change because the Eastern Shore was heavily Democratic.

The Old Guard Retaliates

When machine boss Gorman and the Democrats regained control of the General Assembly in 1901, they began to make plans to prevent another Republican victory. They figured, correctly, that Maryland's African American voters contributed substantially to the strength of the Republican Party. Their plans to prevent future Republican and reformer victories, therefore, centered on disenfranchising blacks through a series of schemes that they hoped would keep most black men from voting.

In 1901, legislators voted to remove party emblems from the ballot. Without the emblems, Democrats hoped, illiterate blacks might not know which party to choose. But Republicans opened schools to teach recognition of the word "Republican," and the black vote continued to be effective for them. In 1904, Democrats voted to remove all party identification from the ballot, but that effort also failed to confuse African American voters.

Finally, John Prentiss Poe, working with Arthur Pue Gorman, drafted a constitutional amendment that would require all Maryland voters, except those whose grandfathers had voted, to show an "understanding" of the state constitution when questioned by partisan voter registrars. Those registrars were to make up the questions and judge the answers. Poe stated outright that the grandfather clause would exempt most white voters from the test. African Americans and Republicans, Archbishop James Cardinal Gibbons, head of the Roman Catholic Church in Baltimore and a strong supporter of reform, as well as the Society of Friends and ministers of the Congregational Church publicly opposed the amendment, submitted to voters in a referendum.

A number of reform Democrats also campaigned against the disenfranchisement measure. Charles Bonaparte, a Republican leader of the Reform League, pointed out that the amendment would disenfranchise white, foreign-born voters, whose grandfathers had not voted and who might not be able to pass the "understanding" test. With that issue up for discussion, large numbers of German Americans, Italian Americans, Russian Jewish Americans, and other immigrant groups all opposed the amendment. In the end, Maryland's voting public rejected the Poe amendment and two similar proposals that followed. This is noteworthy because states farther south did, at this time, disenfranchise most black men and thereby assure Democratic control. Of the states that had previously permitted slavery, Maryland was one of the few to allow African American men to vote and run for public office continuously after 1870. Begin-

Brother and Sister: Leaders in the Black Community

Harry Cummings, the first African American to hold elected office in Baltimore City, graduated from Lincoln University in Pennsylvania and from the University of Maryland Law School. In 1890, he won election to the Baltimore City Council from the racially mixed Republican Eleventh Ward in West Baltimore. While on the City Council, Cummings fought against proposed housing segregation laws, which were eventually declared unconstitutional by the US Supreme Court. He convinced the Council to open the Colored Manual Training School, provide vocational education, and hire music and art teachers for the black schools. Cummings gave one of the speeches seconding the nomination of Theodore Roosevelt at the 1904 Republican Convention and later received an invitation to visit Roosevelt in the White House. Cummings was followed by five other African American Republicans on the City Council until the majority of black voters switched to the Democratic Party during the New Deal.

Ida Cummings, educated at Hampton Institute, Morgan College, and Columbia University, was a strong proponent of early childhood education and served as one of the first kindergarten teachers in the state. She convinced her brother Harry, who served on the Baltimore City Council, to introduce the bill that established kindergartens in all the city's schools, for both black and white children. She served as president of the Colored Empty Stocking and Fresh Air Circle, an organization that filled Christmas stockings for poor children and organized a summer week in the country for children from the inner city. She was active nationally as president of the National Association of Colored Women and organized campaigns for women's suffrage and against lynching. After women were enfranchised in 1920, she organized voter registration campaigns in African American neighborhoods. Women like Ida Cummings played a vitally important role in building community strength and welfare.

- Ida Cummings. Courtesy of the Maryland Historical Society, PP240.15.

- Harry Sythe Cummings. Private collection.

ning in 1873, African American men won election to the city councils in Annapolis, Baltimore, and Cambridge.

The voting rights of black men did not go unchallenged, however. The statewide success of Republican candidates in 1895 led to a decade of Democratic efforts to disenfranchise blacks once that party regained power in 1900. Although unsuccessful on the state level, in several Maryland cities, Annapolis among them, the party wrote disenfranchising provisions into the city charters and the General Assembly approved the charter changes. The 1908 Annapolis charter revision resulted in the loss of voting rights for most Annapolis blacks and a temporary end to black representation on the city council. A group of black voters, aided by the Republican Party, sued the city registrars. In 1910, the US Circuit Court of Appeals declared the disenfranchisement plan unconstitutional as a violation of the Fifteenth Amendment; the US Supreme Court upheld the ruling in 1915.

Decline of the Machine

Even before the Poe amendment's defeat, the solidarity of the Gorman-Rasin machine was cracking. In both 1903 and 1904, Gorman and Rasin supported opposing candidates and split the machine vote. By 1905, when the referendum on the Poe amendment came up, the Old Guard no longer worked as a tight unit. Arthur Pue Gorman died in 1906 and Isaac Freeman Rasin died the following year. Machine politics continued, but the Old Guard never recovered its earlier strength. Political organizations across the state had to nominate some reform-minded men for the top jobs and support some reform legislation or risk losing all their power.

The Progressive Program

In Maryland and across the nation, as reformers gained power they began to enact their programs. After 1895, a number of progressive measures became law in Maryland. These changes came during both Republican and Democratic gubernatorial administrations. Many reforms took place during the administrations of three progressive governors, Republican Lloyd Lowndes of Cumberland, Democrat Austin Crothers of Cecil County, and Republican Phillips Lee Goldsborough of Cambridge.

The variety of these programs reflects the wide interests of the reformers. They enacted measures to conserve natural resources and to provide people with a healthier environment. New laws regulated working conditions and protected laborers from some of the worst abuses. Other laws changed the political process to move power out of the hands of machine leaders and thus preserve the opportunity for further reforms. All these changes took place gradually.

The Environment and Health

Conservation of the environment was a priority for some progressives. Maryland's General Assembly in 1896 established a Geological and Economic Survey to investigate the potential for development of the state's resources. Ten years later, in 1906, the legislature passed the first of a series of oyster conservation measures designed to prevent the complete destruction of this valuable resource in the Chesapeake Bay and its tributaries.

Baltimore City in 1904 authorized a major park-building program that put green spaces in Baltimore's most heavily populated neighborhoods and added many acres to large parks like Druid Hill, Clifton, and Patterson. Maryland's State Forest and Park Service began to operate during the same period. In 1906, John and Robert Garrett, sons of B&O tycoon John Work Garrett, donated 2,000 acres in Garrett County to Maryland, and the state created a Board of Forestry, the first step toward scientific management of the state's forest lands. In 1910, the state Conservation Bureau came into existence.

Many environmental concerns focused on public health. Members of the state's medical community joined political reformers to effect change. Shortly after creation of the state Board of Health in 1888, local boards of health were developed to cooperate with the state board in planning local measures. Maryland gained national fame for its program to treat tuberculosis, a disease that was still a major killer well into the twentieth century. Construction of sewers and sewage treatment plants did much to improve public health. Baltimore was the last major city in the nation to build an underground sewer system. The new reservoir at Loch Raven and the new filtration plant at Back River finally provided the city with good-quality drinking water.

While improvements in the water and sewer systems led to improved public health, so too did improvements in medical care benefit many. The Johns Hopkins Hospital and Medical School brought pioneers in medicine and the scientific method to Maryland and much useful knowledge to the world of medicine and surgery. The "Big Four" doctors—pathologist William Henry Welch, surgeon William Stewart Halsted, internist William Osler, and gynecologist Howard Kelly—helped to lead the development of modern medical and surgical techniques.

Better Working Conditions

Progressives believed they had a responsibility to protect workers, children, and women, all of whom they saw as weaker members of society. Because working conditions posed grave dangers to the population's health and safety, progressives pushed for a number of reforms in this area. Maryland pioneered the development of a workers' compensation program. David J. Lewis, a state legislator and later a US congressman from Allegany County, led the fight to provide financial compensation to people who were disabled on the job and to families of people who were killed at work. The Maryland law benefited coal miners first, in 1910, and extended to workers statewide in a few years.

Progressives were eager to get children out of factories and mines and into schools. In 1906, the General Assembly prohibited all children under age 12 from working in factories and required that children ages 12 to 16 obtain work

David J. Lewis: Reformer

David J. Lewis, state legislator and US congressman, led the way in winning some early legislation to help working men and women. The son of a Welsh miner, he began to work in Allegany County coal mines at age 9. At age 19, he began studying law. He continued to work in the mines to support himself until he became a practicing attorney.

As a lawyer, he fought for the miners. When leaders of a 1900 miners' strike were tried for conspiracy, Lewis served as their defense attorney. Although the court decided against the strikers, Lewis became well known and admired. In 1901, he was elected to the state Senate as a Democrat from the predominantly Republican county.

Lewis pressed for and won passage of a mine inspection bill. He saw to it that Maryland enacted reform laws requiring compulsory education for children, primary elections, and a minimum age of 14 to work in mines and factories. After election to the US Congress in 1908, Lewis returned to Annapolis to lobby successfully for an injury compensation bill.

■ David Lewis. Courtesy of the Library of Congress, LC-DIG-hec-03555.

permits certifying their health and literacy. Specific laws came gradually, but by 1912 most of the state's school-age children were required to be in school. During Governor Goldsborough's administration, a new law was passed that prohibited women from working more than ten hours a day. Progressives argued that longer hours harmed the health of the women workers and the families dependent on them. A long series of complicated laws had been necessary to release people from the oppressive conditions of nineteenth-century labor.

Reforming the Political System

Much progressive effort went into reforming the political process. Reformers wanted to make politics more open and to assure the selection of qualified people for government jobs. The introduction of the Australian ballot across the state in the 1890s was part of this process. The establishment of a Board of Estimates and a Board of Awards to oversee Baltimore's budget and the awarding of city contracts was another step forward. Baltimore's charter of 1898 established a nonpartisan school board responsible for modernizing curriculum and facilities. Teachers and administrators were to receive appointments on the basis of merit, rather than through political connections. Similar reforms of the processes of budgeting and hiring were initiated across the state.

During Governor Crothers's administration, Maryland passed a Corrupt Practices Act, authored by Attorney General Isaac Lobe Strauss, which set punishments for politicians taking bribes and kickbacks. The assembly also established a Public Service Commission to draft regulations and set rates for railroads, shipping, gas and electric service, telephones, and telegraph service. A primary election law, establishing elections as the procedure for nominating candidates in all jurisdictions except Baltimore City, also passed by support of a majority of the legislature.

When Phillips Lee Goldsborough was governor, the state initiated presidential primaries. It also extended the right to petition state legislation to referendum, thereby allowing citizens to vote directly on certain measures. All these reforms were designed to put decision-making into the hands of professionals or to give more power to the voting public.

The Omissions of the Progressive Era

Despite these victories for reform, Maryland fell short in several areas. African Americans and women still suffered from severe discrimination at the end of the progressive era. By the outbreak of World War I, Marylanders still lived in a largely segregated society. Schools and most public facilities were both racially separate and unequal. The US Supreme Court, in the 1896 *Plessy v. Ferguson* case, ruled that "separate but equal" facilities were perfectly legal. But health care facilities and schools for blacks, for example, were often inferior, and blacks still faced discrimination in jobs and housing. Although African American men continued to win election to some local public offices, these few representatives often could not win majority support for the needs of their community. Despite the leadership of a growing African American professional class, blacks did not enjoy equality in any sense of the word.

Women as a group made some gains. For example, in 1882, when the legislature passed the Married Woman's Property Act, married women finally won the right to control their earned and inherited assets. But women failed to gain their major objective, the vote. During the late nineteenth century, as women won the franchise in some states, Maryland women, both white and black, generally separately but sometimes working together, organized to fight for enfranchisement. One group of white women formed the Maryland Woman Suffrage Association in 1894. This and similar groups across the state actively supported women's suffrage. Leaders like Emma Maddox Funck, who served as president of the Maryland Woman Suffrage Association for sixteen years, and Elizabeth King Ellicott, first president of the Maryland Federation of Women's Clubs, devoted many years to the cause of suffrage. Ida Cummings, who served as an officer in the National Association of Colored Women, was one of many black women to fight for women's suffrage in Maryland.

■ Hood College, founded in 1893 (as The Woman's College of Frederick), offered young women a liberal arts education intended to prepare them for roles in the home and, if they wished, in the workplace. These students are conducting experiments in the college's chemistry lab. Collection of the Maryland State Archives, MSA SC 1477-1-5418.

In 1910, leaders presented a women's suffrage bill to the General Assembly. Etta Haynie Maddox, the first woman to pass the Maryland bar exam and become a lawyer, drafted the bill. The measure never came to a vote because it was tabled in committee in the House of Delegates and never presented in the Senate. Maryland women finally gained the vote in 1920, with ratification of the Nineteenth Amendment to the US Constitution.

Suffrage leaders believed that women needed the vote to press effectively for reforms in many areas. Women all along had been strong proponents of change. Women's organizations had worked hard for the abolition of child labor, compulsory education, and safer and healthier living and working conditions. Even without the power of the vote, women were strongly influential in many of the reforms of this period.

The reforms accomplished by progressives often did not go far enough. At the outbreak of World War I, blacks and women remained unequal citizens. Many people still worked long hours under hazardous conditions, and many improvements still needed to be made in areas such as public health, educational opportunities, management of natural resources, and political reform.

Clearly progressivism did not bring about a perfect society. However, progressives did, for the first time, put responsibility for the general welfare into the hands of public authorities. In the future, government would play a role in every social change.

■ Toward a More Complex World

During the decades after the Civil War, American life grew more complex. New people, new industries, and bigger cities with all their problems had changed forever the old, agrarian way of life. As the nation moved into the second decade of the twentieth century, yet another force would make its impact felt. From 1870 to 1917, Maryland and the nation were occupied largely with their own problems and their own adjustments. Suddenly, in 1917, the outside world appeared in everyone's home in the form of World War I.

Maryland		The Nation and the World
	1917	United States declares war against Germany Bolshevik Revolution in Russia
Coldest winter on record Flu epidemic kills thousands in Maryland	1917–1918	
Washington Suburban Sanitary Commission created	1918	Armistice in Europe
Democrat Albert C. Ritchie elected governor	1919	Eighteenth Amendment ratified: prohibition
	1920	Nineteenth Amendment ratified: women's suffrage
	1920	Republican Warren G. Harding elected president
Mary Risteau becomes first woman elected to General Assembly in Maryland	1921	
United Mine Workers go on strike in Western Maryland	1922	
	1923	Harding dies; Calvin Coolidge becomes president
Potomac River flood destroys C&O Canal	1924	
	1925	Scopes trial
	1927	Charles Lindbergh flies solo across Atlantic Ocean
	1928	Republican Herbert Hoover elected president
Drought cripples Maryland farmers Baltimore Museum of Art opens	1929	Stock market crashes
Baltimore Trust Company fails	1931	
	1932	Democrat Franklin D. Roosevelt elected president
	1933	"100" Days programs of first New Deal Twenty-First Amendment ratified: prohibition repealed
Republican Harry Nice elected governor	1934	
Murray case overturns segregation at University of Maryland Law School	1935	Federal Relief Act creates Works Progress Administration Second New Deal begins
Congress of Industrial Organizations organized in Maryland Cambridge cannery workers go on strike	1937	
	1939	World War II begins in Europe
	1940	Peacetime Selective Service Act
	1941	Japanese bomb Pearl Harbor; United States declares war
	1945	Roosevelt dies; Harry S. Truman becomes president Germany surrenders (V-E Day) US drops atom bomb on Hiroshima and Nagasaki; Japan surrenders (V-J Day)

chapter six

Prosperity, Depression, and War
1917–1945

On April 6, 1917, the headlines of the Baltimore *Evening Sun* read "PRESIDENT PROCLAIMS WAR!" The changes that took place during World War I, and in the three decades that followed it, touched every aspect of Marylanders' lives. These crises-filled decades were marked by the death and destruction of two world wars and by the economic hardships of the United States' worst depression.

Lasting changes occurred during these years. Wartime industries brought economic expansion. Peacetime production introduced many new consumer goods. Americans continued their movement away from the countryside and into the cities. As cities became more crowded, people who could afford to began moving to the suburbs, which combined urban amenities with fresh air and green space.

War and depression both led to increased government involvement in people's lives. State and local governments undertook responsibilities they had never considered before, while the federal government played a more active role in state and local affairs. At the same time, the United States became increasingly more involved in the wider world. Despite all the changes, Maryland retained many of its local characteristics. Farming and mining in Western Maryland remained much the same, and Eastern Shore and Southern Maryland watermen and farmers kept their old ways, in sharp contrast to the modern industrialization of Baltimore City and the Baltimore and Washington, DC, suburbs.

■ Maryland during World War I

After war in Europe began in 1914, the United States became involved gradually, moving from a position of neutrality to one of close cooperation with England to full-scale war. When President Woodrow Wilson went before Congress in April 1917 and asked for a declaration of war, preparations had been under way for many months. Maryland industries had been producing ships, weapons, and ammunition for England as well as for the United States. Farmers increased the amount of land they cultivated to meet wartime needs. Citizens had been sharpening their marksmanship skills under the direction of the National Guard for almost a year. Two weeks before President Wilson signed the war resolution, the National Guard had been mobilized. Men with rifles guarded train tracks entering Baltimore. Companies of the 5th Regiment were on duty at Baltimore's Loch Raven, Clifton Park, and Montebello reservoirs to make sure that German spies did not drop poison into the city's drinking water. Fearing that German submarines would invade the Chesapeake Bay, the federal government placed the Maryland Oyster Navy under the command of the US Atlantic Fleet.

The war changed forever the lives of soldiers and civilians. Soldiers traveled abroad to fight, while the population at home became more concentrated around urban centers. Maryland activities became increasingly integrated into regional and national ones. At the same time, the federal government intervened in state and private activities to ensure efficient planning during wartime. The war brought prosperity to industry and agriculture as those segments of the economy met wartime production needs.

War Begins: America Chooses Sides

Few Marylanders foresaw the extent of the changes to come when war broke out in Europe in August 1914. Long before the United States declared war in April 1917, however, Maryland citizens had been drawn into the European struggle by economic and ethnic ties. Baltimore's status as a major port closely linked Maryland to European events and the city's shipping and manufacturing benefited from American trade as neutrals with Europe. After war broke out, Baltimore's labor force and exports tripled, while capital investment in manufacturing doubled. The Bethlehem Steel Company bought Sparrows Point in Baltimore County and began to expand its production capacity. The Baltimore Drydock and Shipbuilding Company purchased half of Locust Point. Many other industries bought land around Baltimore's outer harbor and expanded production. Across the state, industrial production grew as well. New military bases such as Camp Meade in Anne Arundel County and the Aberdeen Proving Ground in Harford County required the labor of many construction workers and the provision of building materials. Wartime building, farming, and trade brought prosperity to an economy that had been in the doldrums.

Maryland's mixed population of recent immigrants and older communities that still retained their ethnic identities was the second factor that pulled the European war closer to Maryland. Both sides in the struggle had Maryland supporters. Many Americans had good reason to sympathize with the Allied nations

Although by the time that the United States entered World War I in 1917 tanks were rapidly replacing cavalry units in offensive campaigns, army units of horses and mules still played a role in logistical support. At Camp George G. Meade training center, where these four cavalrymen posed in their new uniforms before being sent to France in 1918, the army processed 12,000 horses and mules for service and shipment overseas. Special Collections, University of Maryland Libraries.

of France, England, and Italy, to which they traced their ancestry. American Jews feared German anti-Semitism and hoped a Jewish homeland in Palestine would be established as the British had promised. Polish Americans, whose homeland had been occupied by Germany, waited hopefully for an American response. Irish Americans, however, who resented England's control of Ireland, generally opposed an American alliance with England. German Americans did not want to take up arms against friends and relatives from their homeland.

Many Americans hoped the United States would remain neutral, but American sympathy increasingly sided with the Allies. German use of submarine warfare against civilian ships shocked Americans. Propaganda appealed to emotions by portraying the Allies as fighting for democracy and making the German Kaiser and German soldiers seem like inhuman beasts. All things German became suspect. Although an 1868 state law requiring that every law passed be published in a German-language newspaper was not repealed until World War II, and two German newspapers continued to publish throughout the war, the German language disappeared in Baltimore schools. In Garrett County, the few Lutheran churches that had alternated sermons in German and English discontinued German services, and in Allegany County the German-language Cumberland *Freie Presse* stopped publishing in 1917. When the United States declared war, German Street in Baltimore was renamed Redwood Street, in honor of the first Maryland officer to fall in battle in World War I.

Maryland's Military Participation

Once the United States entered the war in 1917, Marylanders worked and fought to help the Allies achieve victory. The state provided more than 62,000 men and women who served in the US army, navy, and marine corps during World War I. A small number of women from Maryland, both black and white, served as nurses and clerical workers.

African Americans comprised about one-fifth of the Maryland military volunteers. For the state's black community, military service was a matter of pride. At first most served in noncombat jobs, and a few succeeded in becoming officers. Nationwide pressure from African American leaders led to the formation in 1917 of the 92nd and 93rd Divisions as US army black combat units, and in May 1917 the War Department established officers' training for African Americans at Fort Des Moines, Iowa, attended by more than 1,000 men before the war's end. African American National Guard units from Maryland became part of the 93rd Division. The navy had no black officers because it restricted African Americans to service positions like cook and mess man.

When the United States declared war in April 1917, the Maryland National Guard was already on duty in the state. The first Maryland unit of the Guard arrived in France in February 1918 and joined the regular army units already there, fighting in trenches alongside French soldiers. Trench warfare was particularly brutal, as men waited in deep muddy and cold ditches for the order to

Food and Fuel for Victory, 1917

Nothing brought wartime closer to home than the effort to reduce domestic consumption of scarce items. Fuel shortages caused the most hardship. Gasoline shortages did not affect the majority of citizens, for automobile ownership was not yet widespread. Scarcity of coal was a serious problem, however. Train transportation was needed for war matériel, and coal cars were put on sidings when troop transports needed to use the rails. Stores closed on Mondays to conserve electricity and fuel, and lights were blacked out on Mondays in parks, on streets, and in businesses. On special "lightless" Mondays and Thursdays, all but one light in each home had to be put out by 9:00 p.m.

Allied troops and the European civilian population badly needed agricultural goods. House-to-house canvasses were conducted to explain to American housewives how they could voluntarily conserve wheat, sugar, and milk products. Whole wheat bread was banned in homes and hotels. Instead, hungry citizens were limited to two ounces daily of "victory bread," made of 75 percent wheat and 25 percent substitutes.

During the war, all three meals on Tuesdays were meatless. On Thursdays and Saturdays, families agreed to eat one meatless and one wheatless meal. Fridays were porkless. Christmas 1917 was a meatless day, although the Food Administration announced that it did not classify turkey and other fowl as meats. "Your conscience will be perfectly patriotic if you eat them," the agency stated. But because many workers—carpenters, teamsters, longshoremen, clothing workers, laborers—earned between $10 and $15 a week, and turkey cost 60¢ a pound, only the well-to-do could afford a patriotic Christmas turkey.

fight. As the tide of battle turned, troops moved out of the trenches and marched toward Germany. The 115th Regiment, made up mostly of Marylanders and under the command of Maryland Colonel Milton A. Reckord, joined with other units of the 29th Division of the US army in breaking through the German lines north of Verdun, France. Another Maryland unit, known as "Baltimore's Own" because of its large contingent of Baltimore men, helped capture Montfaucon, one of the most strategically important French towns along the German front. Maryland also provided important noncombatant support units. Johns Hopkins Hospital and Medical School formed the 18th General Hospital Unit, and Hopkins School of Nursing graduates served in Red Cross units in Italy.

The army and the navy built forts, camps, and bases within Maryland to train soldiers, sailors, and officers from all over the United States. One important training base was Camp George G. Meade, located in the rural area of Anne Arundel County between Baltimore and Washington because of the number of railroads that passed nearby. More than one hundred thousand men received training there before the war ended. At Camp Holabird, located near the new town of Dundalk in Baltimore County, the army built a center to train soldiers to use its new motorized vehicles.

The War at Home

The "War to Make the World Safe for Democracy" was fought on the home front too. As the nation rushed to provide the food, clothing, and heavy artillery needed for war, shortages affected civilians in every part of their lives. Prices rose, and people began to hoard food, clothing, gasoline, and other necessities. Strikes in the coal fields and the heavy demand for coal for industry led to a fuel shortage in the winter of 1917–1918. The unusually cold winter made the fuel shortage particularly painful.

Most Marylanders plunged in to help the war effort. Women's clubs organized sewing parties and made miles of bandages to send "over there." Children grew victory gardens that supplied produce. Banks and schools throughout the state promoted war bond drives to help finance the war. Maryland farmers plowed and planted new fields and recruited schoolchildren and women as laborers to harvest the crops needed to feed the American armies and the European civilian population. African Americans and whites moved from rural areas to Baltimore to take industrial jobs.

Labor shortages brought a patriotic response from women, who moved into new types of work to free men for military service. Women became telephone operators, typists, and stenographers and some worked in factories. In

■ When Congress declared war on Germany in April 1917, advertising posters created by a Division of Pictorial Publicity within the United States Committee on Public Information played an important role in mobilizing ordinary Americans to change from passive neutrality to active participation in the war effort. This poster, designed by Lorraine Hazen and titled *Feminine Patriotism: Domestic Economy, Home Defense, Aid to the Suffering*, graphically illustrated for women the important roles they could play in support of the war. Courtesy of the National Archives.

Cumberland, women "hustled" freight cars, switching them from one train to another, and replaced war-bound men in local industries. The United Railways in Baltimore hired 150 women to drive streetcars.

The End of War

A transatlantic cable from Europe on November 7, 1918, announced the signing of an armistice. But Baltimore's celebration ended quickly when a later cable revealed that the first one had been false. When the real armistice was signed on November 11, the celebration began again, with singing and dancing in the city streets. The news did not arrive in Cumberland until early the next morning, but citizens partied in the streets until the following midnight. In Annapolis, schools that had closed during the flu epidemic and only reopened on November 4, closed again on November 7 as Annapolitans too celebrated early with whistles and sirens. On November 11, Mayor James F. Strange called on citizens to hold an impromptu parade honoring the "Dawn of Peace," led by midshipmen from the Naval Academy and men from St. John's College.

The "Spanish Flu" Epidemic of 1918–1919

The winter of the final victory by the Allied forces in November 1918 was marked by a grim battle against another foe: a worldwide pandemic caused by a deadly influenza virus. Worldwide, nearly 2 million people died. Flu deaths in the United States of 675,000 (out of a population of 105 million) exceeded by far the 117,000 military deaths during the war. The first case in Maryland appeared at Camp Meade in September 1918. By mid-October, state officials reported more than 24,000 cases; 41 percent of the population of Cumberland was ill and by the week ending October 18 there had been 1,357 deaths in Baltimore alone. Mailmen, shopkeepers, policemen, and gravediggers became infected and failed to show up for work. Funeral homes overflowed, and bodies began to be stacked up outside their doors. At Johns Hopkins Hospital influenza patients filled six wards and the hospital ultimately had to close its doors to more as staff physicians, nurses, and medical students too became ill. Frightened citizens wore masks in a futile attempt to prevent exposure. New cases of infection began to wane in November, although the disease continued through spring of the new year, finally disappearing in the summer of 1919. An estimated 12,000 people died in the 8 months from September 1918 through April 1919.

■ Nurses wearing masks to prevent infection tend patients in the flu ward of Walter Reed Hospital. Courtesy of the Library of Congress, hec2009000788.

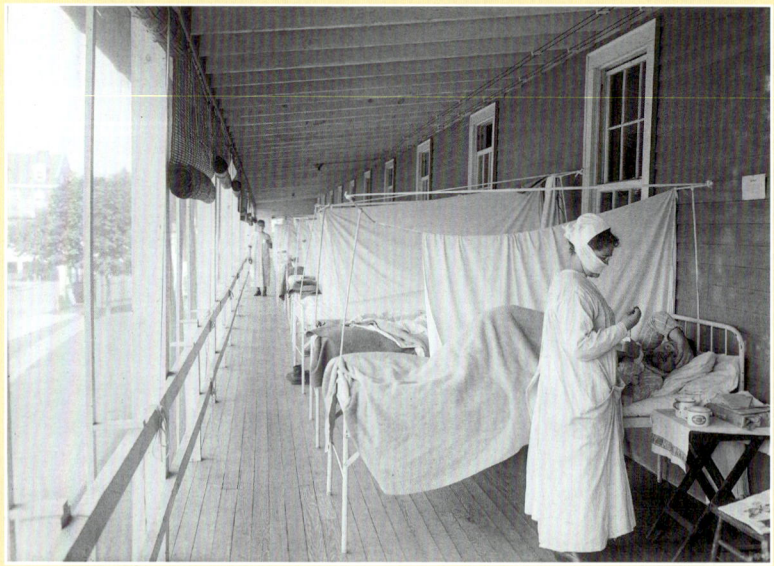

During the war nearly two thousand Marylanders lost their lives, half of them from disease unrelated to battle. By early in the summer of 1919, the troops who had survived had come home, ready to return to "normalcy."

■ Marylanders from the Eastern Shore to the Appalachian Mountains celebrated the end of World War I with parades honoring men from their communities as they returned home from Europe. In this victory parade in Easton in the summer of 1919, the use of automobiles instead of horse-drawn carriages signaled the growing importance of motorized vehicles in postwar Maryland. Courtesy of the Talbot Historical Society, Easton, Maryland.

■ Peacetime

Peacetime "normalcy," for most people, meant attempting to return to the way things had been before the war. For progressives, this meant enforcing the reforms already achieved. For businessmen, the postwar period meant expansion and prosperity. Business was stimulated in part by growth of transportation networks in the state. In every industry, new technology and new plants brought new jobs to the Maryland economy. For African Americans and women, as veterans returned home, it often meant losing the small gains they had made during wartime labor shortages.

Prohibition

The world war itself had helped to bring about some of the progressive reforms. Many reformers advocated prohibition, through the passage of an amendment to the US Constitution forbidding people to sell or consume alcoholic beverages.

■ The Jefferson Liquor Store in Baltimore held a sale of its stock just before prohibition of the sale of alcoholic beverages went into effect. The Eighteenth Amendment to the US Constitution was ratified by the states on January 16, 1919, to take effect on January 17, 1920. The Volstead Act, passed over Woodrow Wilson's veto in October 1919, provided for the prohibition's enforcement. During the thirteen years that prohibition was in effect before being repealed by the Twenty-First Amendment in December 1933, Baltimore was one of many large cities where the Volstead Act was widely flouted. Courtesy of the Maryland Historical Society, SVF.

Maryland Governor Albert C. Ritchie and Baltimore journalist H. L. Mencken were national leaders of the "wet" faction, which opposed prohibition. Methodist Bishop James Cannon was a leader of the national "dry" crusade. Most rural counties in Maryland voted themselves dry, but Baltimore citizens, among them immigrants or the children of immigrants whose cultural heritage included beer and wine, opposed prohibition. Rural county legislators dominated the Maryland General Assembly, however, and the state voted overwhelmingly in 1918 to ratify the Eighteenth Amendment to the US Constitution.

The amendment was ratified nationally in 1919, but Maryland did not pass a law of its own to provide for its enforcement. Governor Albert Ritchie believed that prohibition was an attack on the liberties of the individual. Maryland's attorney general ruled that local police could not arrest people who violated the Volstead Act, the federal law enforcing prohibition. Baltimore, the center of opposition to the law, disregarded it openly. Baltimore natives knew that a restaurant displaying a red hard crab sign served beer with its seafood. The thousands of miles of shoreline along the Chesapeake Bay and its tidal tributaries, including 42 miles in Baltimore, provided abundant opportunities for smuggling liquor from Canada or Cuba. Maryland became an eastern center for alcohol distribution. Ocean City served as a drop-off point for smuggled liquor and the road from Charles County to Baltimore was known as "bootlegger's boulevard" because of the liquor traffic. Federal agents arrested one thousand violators of the law each year without help from local law enforcement officers.

Women's Suffrage

Many of the same organizations of progressive women that supported a prohibition amendment also worked hard for women's suffrage. Although women could vote in a few states and even in local elections in a few towns in Maryland, women's suffrage leaders wanted a national constitutional amendment allowing women to vote. Male state officials, led by Governor Ritchie, opposed a federal amendment for women's suffrage, arguing that the issue involved states' rights, saying that each state should be able to decide which of its residents could vote in both state and national elections. In 1917, many American women used the patriotic rhetoric of wartime to argue for their right to participate in a democracy through voting. When the Maryland General Assembly met in special session to pass emergency wartime legislation, women again tried to get the legislators to pass a bill allowing women to vote in presidential and primary elections. On the first day of the session, 14-year-old Dorothy Ford, attired in red, white, and blue and "mounted on a spirited steed," rode into Annapolis as Pauline Revere to deliver a message to the governor in support of the bill: "Keep not liberty from your own household."

Women's suffrage gained moderate support among Maryland women but failed to convince the men who controlled the legislative processes that determined election rules. Maryland refused to ratify the Nineteenth Amendment to the US Constitution that guaranteed that "the right of citizens of the United States to vote shall not be denied . . . on account of sex." When thirty-six other states ratified it in August 1920, the amendment became the law of the land and Maryland women finally were able to vote (although Maryland did not officially ratify the amendment until 1941). The following year, Mary Risteau from Harford County won election to the House of Delegates. As in the case of Jewish men enfranchised in 1826 and African American men enfranchised in 1870, the expansion of the right to vote had quickly led to the election of a candidate from the newly enfranchised group, in this case a woman, to public office.

Transportation Changes in Maryland

Wartime demands had accelerated an expansion of highway and rail networks connecting Maryland to its neighbors. By the 1920s, Baltimore was shipping products from the entire nation to world markets. The city had ranked seventh in the nation in foreign trade in 1918, but by 1926 it was third, behind only New York and New Orleans. Baltimore became both more dominant in the state's economy and more important in the nation.

One of Maryland's two canals fell into disuse during this period. A flood in March 1924 destroyed many of the locks on the Chesapeake and Ohio Canal and made freight transportation impossible. The Baltimore & Ohio Railroad, which owned the canal, used the flood as an opportunity to end the expense of

Mary W. Risteau

Mary Risteau (1890–1978) was the first woman elected to the Maryland House of Delegates in 1921, where she served in 1922–1924, 1931–1933, and 1951–1954. She was also the first woman elected to the Maryland Senate in 1934, serving from 1935 to 1937. After graduating from high school in 1907, the Towson native taught elementary school from 1908 until 1917, the year in which she completed a special advanced course of study in mathematics at the Johns Hopkins University.

Although she left teaching to work on a family farm in Harford County, Risteau continued the political activity on behalf of better Maryland schools that she had begun while a teacher as a member of the Baltimore County Teachers' Association. She based her first campaign for public office in 1921 on issues of education, and remained a strong advocate for improvements to the state's educational system for the rest of her professional life. She served on the education committees of the Maryland House and Senate, and in both houses of the legislature sponsored and campaigned for bills that supported women's rights. Governor Albert C. Ritchie appointed Risteau as the first woman on the Maryland State Board of Education, where she served from 1922 to 1937. In 1938, she earned a law degree from the University of Baltimore.

A lifelong member of the Democratic Party, Risteau was a delegate to the Democratic National Convention in Philadelphia in 1936. She never married, but was active in the Harford County and statewide Homemakers' Clubs, and in the Grange, an important early twentieth-century farming organization. She also played the organ at the Christ Episcopal Church in Forest Hill. Ten years after her death in Cooptown in Harford County, she was inducted into the Maryland Women's Hall of Fame.

■ Mary Eliza Watters Risteau was selected for the Maryland Women's Hall of Fame in 1988. Collection of the Maryland State Archives, MSA SC 1545-1052.

running it. The canal remained "a magnificent wreck" until the National Park Service took it over in 1938 and turned it into an historic park and recreation path three decades later. Baltimore's growth brought new interest, however, in modernizing the Chesapeake and Delaware Canal, which connected the upper Chesapeake Bay to the Delaware River Basin. During World War I the federal government purchased the C&D canal and began extensive improvements on it, deepening its channel and eliminating locks, to enable heavier freight vessels to travel from Baltimore to Philadelphia by an inland waterway.

Consolidation that began during the war and accelerated afterward marked the development of rail transportation in Maryland. Two major lines, the Baltimore & Ohio Railroad and the Pennsylvania Railroad, dominated the state's rail transportation network by absorbing smaller lines. A third, the Western Maryland Railroad, became a B&O subsidiary in 1927. All three had grain elevators and port facilities in the Baltimore harbor, at Locust Point, Canton, and Port Covington, whose capacity doubled between 1914 and 1940. In addition to hauling freight, railroads provided passenger service, and regular commuter traffic developed between Washington and Baltimore.

■ Owned by the Tolchester Steamboat Company, *Louise* was a sidewheel steamer that operated on the Chesapeake Bay for forty years. She carried passengers from Pier 15 at Light Street in Baltimore to destinations that included the Tolchester Beach resort on the eastern side of the bay. An excursion steamer, *Louise* could carry as many as 2,500 passengers on day trips to enjoy the rides, beach, and other resort attractions. Collection of John Conley.

Prosperity brought with it increased leisure time for Maryland citizens, and railroads provided a link to the Atlantic Ocean beaches. Here, too, rail lines were consolidated in the early part of the century. The Baltimore, Chesapeake and Atlantic Railroad and the Delaware, Maryland and Virginia Railroad controlled not only rail lines but also the operations of thirty-three Chesapeake Bay steamers. These boats carried passengers and freight from Baltimore to Eastern Shore terminals at Love Point and Claiborne. During the 1920s, as many as one thousand passengers rode the train to Ocean City on hot summer weekends.

Existing rail and water systems in Maryland competed in this period with new modes of transportation, especially the automobile. In 1910, there were only 4,000 cars in Maryland; in 1914, there were 10,000; by 1917, there were 55,000 cars and 4,000 motor trucks. The prosperity of the 1920s made it easier for more people to own automobiles. The popularity of cars continued to grow despite the depression and World War II, so that by 1945, 375,000 owners registered automobiles in the state. Maryland spent a great deal of money, some of it from a 4¢-per-gallon gasoline tax, building a new system of highways. In 1938, the State Roads Commission claimed that the 3,000-mile state road system was one of the best in the nation.

Suburban Growth

Suburbs continued to grow and expand during and after World War I. The extension of streetcar and commuter rail lines and the increasing ownership of automobiles allowed many families to move to the greener and more spacious suburbs. Some industries and businesses also located new plants and offices on

■ Road building throughout the state of Maryland brought automobile transportation even to the mountainous western part of the state. By 1920, the old Cumberland Road, authorized by Congress in 1806 and later part of the National Road, had been partially paved from Cumberland westward. Photographer Leo Beachy's image captures a family enjoying an automobile outing along the "Pike." Courtesy of Ron Broadwater and the Ruth Enlow Library of Garrett County, Maxine Broadwater Collection.

large tracts of vacant land that were less expensive to buy and to build on than were downtown locations. Workers sought housing nearby. Returning veterans, often starting new families, further increased the suburban population. New roads, utility infrastructure, services such as police and fire protection, schools, and stores served this population. Construction, especially the housing industry, boomed.

Wartime government, particularly in the national capital area, resulted in both larger federal agencies with greater numbers of employees and new residential neighborhoods to house these people and their families. Wartime expansion of the government in Washington stimulated especially large growth in suburban Montgomery and Prince George's Counties. The two counties faced similar problems from the rapid expansion. Increased population resulted in more sewage that polluted local streams, including those that flowed into Washington, DC. Public health officials and citizens, working together, in 1918 created the two-county Washington Suburban Sanitary Commission to operate water supply and sanitary sewer systems and to control pollution. Initially serving less than 100 square miles, the WSSC grew over the years to serve most of the two counties. In 1927, the Maryland-National Capital Park and Planning Commission was formed with jurisdiction over both parks and planning and zoning. These commissions were pioneers in regional planning, a collaborative approach that is still expanding as new issues arise that encourage cooperation.

Baltimore City grew by annexing some of its surrounding suburbs. In 1918, the city, following a vote by residents of the city and Baltimore and Anne Arundel Counties, added 46.5 square miles of Baltimore County and 5.4 square miles of Anne Arundel County to its territory. Baltimore's residential areas stretched out into former farmlands. Annexation opened up new areas for industrial development as well. In the large and roomy industrial sites built in the 1920s, giant machinery took the place of closely packed workers.

Industrial Growth

Better land and water transportation spurred the growth of Maryland's manufacturing, trade, and food production. Baltimore led the way, although other areas of the state also prospered. Kelly-Springfield Tires introduced a new industry to the city of Cumberland and created many jobs when it opened a large and modern tire factory in 1921. The Kreider-Reisner Aircraft Company, formed in Hagerstown in 1923, operated a general flying service and built small aircraft. In 1929, it was bought out by the Fairchild Aircraft Company, which moved its headquarters to Hagerstown two years later. In St. Michaels in Talbot County, the Coulbourne and Jewett Seafood Company, founded and owned by African Americans, built a new cannery, operated a fleet of workboats, and employed a large number of local residents.

■ The Rubber Tire Wheel Company originated in Springfield, Ohio, in the 1890s and was later renamed the Kelly-Springfield Tire Company. In 1916, growth of the automobile industry led to an expansion of the business and the decision to build a new plant in Cumberland. The city provided the 81-acre site and $750,000 to help build the plant, which produced its first tire in 1921. Courtesy of the Library of Congress, VF, Folder of Cumberland Souvenir, Maryland.

At the new Bethlehem Steel plant at Sparrows Point, in Baltimore County, the number of workers declined after the end of the war, but steel production rose. The old industrial district of Canton in Baltimore City became a major center for growth because real estate was less expensive there. A new Standard Sanitary plant located there and Western Electric built a factory to make telephone parts on the site of the old Riverview Amusement Park. Across the outer harbor, the American Sugar Company built a modern new refining plant. In the inner harbor, Coca-Cola built a bottling facility and McCormick Spice opened a plant. In suburban Towson, Black and Decker Company opened a huge concrete and steel factory filled with the latest labor-saving mass production machinery.

Air travel had its start in Maryland in 1908, when the Wright brothers persuaded the US Army Signal Corps to experiment with flying machines at College Park, in Prince George's County. In 1918, the Post Office Department launched airmail service between Washington and New York from the field and in the 1920s vertical flight pioneer Emile Berliner experimented there with helicopter designs. Baltimore's Logan Field, built in 1919, was supplemented with a municipal airport in 1929. In the same year, the Glenn L. Martin Company obtained a loan from the Baltimore Trust Company to construct a major aircraft factory on land along the Middle River in Baltimore County that provided access to the Pennsylvania Railroad and room to build housing for workers. Both Glenn L. Martin and the Fairchild Aircraft Company in Hagerstown soon would play a major role in building military planes used in World War II.

■ Postwar Society in a Time of Change

The postwar period was accompanied by strains in Maryland society as different groups sought to share in the prosperity of the 1920s. People who wanted change and those who did not opposed each other bitterly. Many Maryland businesses found their workers determined to share in the new prosperity. Labor unrest raised fears of radicalism among some Americans. The Ku Klux Klan attracted some Marylanders, who joined partly to preserve their definition of "Americanism," which meant exclusion of a number of racial, ethnic, and religious groups. Bigotry directed at African Americans, immigrants, Catholics, and Jews intensified as a result of postwar fears. At the same time, the rise of a youth culture of new dances, clothes, and hairstyles caused concern for many older Marylanders.

Labor Unrest and Postwar Hysteria

During the war, labor had agreed not to strike. After the war, as business improved, wartime controls on prices were lifted, but controls on wages were not. The postwar years became an era of labor unrest and strikes as unions sought to preserve the gains won during wartime: union recognition, increased wages, and improved working conditions. Strikes often resulted in violent clashes between the strikers and the guards hired by the owners.

In 1922, the United Mine Workers in Western Maryland went out on an unsuccessful strike for union contracts and better wages. The strike lasted for eight months and shut down sixty-five mining companies. President Warren G. Harding urged Governor Ritchie to call out the National Guard to protect the mines when they reopened. Ritchie responded that the state could solve its own problems "without the aid of bayonets."

Other strikes, against the B&O Railroad, the Western Maryland Railroad, the Maryland Drydock Company, and Kelly-Springfield Tire, also ended in failure. Workers who participated sought to protect the union shop, a workplace in which unions enrolled all workers and bargained with factory owners for the workers' interests. During the early 1920s, the labor movement weakened as membership in the American Federation of Labor dropped. The steel, shipbuilding, and construction industries used new machinery to lower costs and as an excuse to weed "troublemakers" out of their workforce. Labor lost many key strikes, and the violence that accompanied the workers' demands to share in the postwar prosperity frightened many Maryland citizens.

Ethnic and Racial Issues

Many Americans blamed postwar labor violence on the influence of the "new immigration" patterns of the late nineteenth century. Coming from eastern and southern Europe rather than from northern and western Europe, in some cases speaking neither Germanic nor Latin-based languages, and predominantly Jewish, Roman Catholic, and Eastern Orthodox in religious beliefs, these new immigrants crowded into American cities between 1880 and 1914. The 1920 census data for Maryland and Baltimore City revealed that Russian-born residents for the first time outnumbered the German-born, whose numbers were the second highest, with Polish and Italian immigrants in third and fourth place.

During World War I, immigration from Europe almost stopped, disrupted by wartime conditions. Afterward, Congress adopted immigration restrictions, passing a temporary quota system in 1921 and then a permanent law in 1924 that limited immigration from nations based on the "national origins" of all Americans. This legislation effectively ended large-scale immigration from Russia, Poland, Greece, Italy, the Balkan countries, and Asia. At the same time that external immigration slowed dramatically, a new internal migration pattern of southern blacks, moving north and west, and rural white and black laborers, moving into urban industrial centers, had a profound effect on larger towns in Maryland and Baltimore City.

The Rise of the Ku Klux Klan

Labor unrest, wartime demands from African American leaders for better treatment of their people, and fears of the influence of "Bolshevists" among immigrants

■ The years between the two world wars saw a rebirth of the Knights of the Ku Klux Klan in Maryland as in the rest of the nation. Recruitment of members by local Klan groups began c. 1920. In the fall of 1922, 2,500 Klansmen marched to Annapolis, and in 1925, 10,000 held a state convention in Baltimore. The Klan rejected as un-American all Jews, Catholics, African Americans, and immigrants. Collection of the Maryland State Archives, MSA SC 1477-1-5619.

from Russia after the success of the Communist revolution there in 1917 all contributed to the resurgence of the Ku Klux Klan, or KKK. A secret organization formed after the Civil War to terrorize former slaves, the Klan experienced a major national revival during the 1920s when it blamed Communists, African Americans, immigrants, Catholics, Jews, and others for America's troubles.

In Maryland, the Klan attracted membership in both cities and countryside. A *Baltimore Sun* reporter concluded that many who joined were "mainly perfectly good, kindly people, generally without anything to occupy their minds when they quit work ... attracted by the idea of something mysterious, perhaps a little thrilled at the suggestion that they are members of a band pledged to support 'Americanism.'" In the early 1920s, robed Klansmen paraded in Frederick, Hyattsville, and Baltimore and held a huge rally in Annapolis. Frank Beale, a high-ranking Maryland organizer, boasted in 1925 that state membership had reached 33,000, a figure that might or might not have been correct because Klan leaders often exaggerated membership numbers. Recruiters generally received a portion of each new member's initiation fee as an incentive for their recruitment efforts.

Klan violence targeted African Americans, Catholics, and Jews and ranged from destruction of property to lynching. Cross-burning, especially in front of black churches, was one way the Klan declared its presence. Opposition to Klan activities came from Maryland's active Catholic organizations and Archbishop James Curley, Maryland's 75,000-member Jewish community, the growing black population, and many white Protestants as well.

African American Marylanders

During and after World War I, many Maryland African Americans moved from the state's small towns and rural areas into cities to try to find employment in expanding industries. Others from states farther south joined them as part of the "first Great Migration," which brought more than one million southern rural blacks into northern cities between 1910 and 1930. Germans, Jews, Italians, and members of other ethnic groups had begun to move out of the densely packed inner city, but African Americans remained squeezed into crowded segregated housing because of strictly enforced racial housing codes. Estimates put population density in these neighborhoods at 1,000 residents for every 113 homes. Across the state, African Americans were refused admission to many stores, theaters, restaurants, parks, and other public places. Many were kept in menial jobs. Children were crowded into schools, sometimes in buildings left abandoned when white children got newer ones, and students often received textbooks discarded by white schools. Violence against African Americans led to widespread concern for people's physical safety. In 1931 and 1933, two lynchings took place on the Eastern Shore. These were the last lynchings in the state.

Despite discrimination and violence, Maryland's African American community developed and maintained its own institutions and identity. The Baltimore branch of the Urban League, founded in 1924, joined the National Association for the Advancement of Colored People (NAACP) in fighting against racial injustice. Black women, like white women, fought to win the right to vote. They worked with organizations such as the national sorority Alpha Kappa Alpha, founded at Howard University in 1908, and the Baltimore-based Women's Co-operative Civic League, founded in 1913, to work for better education, health conditions, and other measures to benefit the community. Activists, including educator and social worker Sarah Collins Fernandis, led these efforts.

Pennsylvania Avenue in Baltimore became the focus of African American economic and cultural activity in the city and surrounding counties. Retail stores, laundries, theaters, a YMCA, and other businesses served needs that the larger business community would not meet. Near Pennsylvania Avenue stood Frederick Douglass High School, noted for its high academic standards. In 1916, there was only one black high school in the entire state, Baltimore Colored High School, founded in 1883. When it moved to Pennsylvania Avenue in 1925, community leaders changed its name to honor the abolitionist leader. Many of its teachers held advanced graduate degrees in the 1920s, and one-third of its graduates went on to college. Along Pennsylvania Avenue an entertainment district grew up that hosted a Baltimore "Harlem Renaissance," the term used to describe the flowering of the arts among urban African Americans in the 1920s.

Culture and Society: The Jazz Age

Most Marylanders showed little interest in the problems of working-class people and African Americans or concern about the Ku Klux Klan's excesses. They focused on their own lives. Transportation and communication networks brought new ideas and styles from the cities to the state's remotest corners. Telephone, radio, indoor plumbing, automobiles, and electricity steadily became necessities of daily life. After the intense idealism of the "War to Make the World Safe for

Democracy," the state joined the rest of the nation in a period of disillusionment with grand ideals and more concentration on self-indulgence.

Maryland's failure to enforce prohibition was both a cause and a symbol of a growing cynicism among many citizens. Young people began to question older values. The new values became embodied in fashions particularly attractive to the young. Women cut their hair and shortened their skirts. Young men and women rebelled against parental restraint by drinking homemade and smuggled liquor at illegal bars, called speakeasies, where older people often joined them. Jazz music,

■ Although he was born on Christmas Day in Rochester, New York, Cabell "Cab" Calloway III grew up in West Baltimore. After his graduation from Frederick Douglass High School, Calloway followed his sister into show business and became one of the leading singer–band leaders performing at New York City's famed Harlem Cotton Club in the 1930s. Courtesy of the Library of Congress, LC-GLB23-0101 DLC.

■ H. L. Mencken was first hired in 1906 as a book reviewer for *The Smart Set*, but in 1915 the magazine's new owners appointed him and George Jean Nathan as its editors. Under their direction, the magazine became the nation's leading literary magazine of the 1920s, introducing its readers to the fiction of F. Scott Fitzgerald, who lived in Baltimore in the 1920s, and publishing the work of authors such as Edna St. Vincent Millay, Theodore Dreiser, Aldous Huxley, Sinclair Lewis, and Eugene O'Neill. From the Matthew J. and Arlyn Bruccoli Collection of F. Scott Fitzgerald, Irvin Department of Rare Books and Special Collections, University of South Carolina Libraries, Columbia, SC.

with the sexy sound of the saxophone, moved out of the African American night clubs where it was born and became the rage of all the young. They danced with an abandon expressed both in the wild energy of the Charleston and in the shockingly close embrace of couples swaying to the slower music.

Maryland creative artists joined others in the nation who used themes of realism, rebellion, and explicit sex in music, literature, and the theater. F. Scott Fitzgerald, a novelist who celebrated this new morality, lived in Baltimore in the 1930s and finished *Tender Is the Night* during his time in the city. More than any other person, Henry Louis Mencken came to represent the cynicism of the nation. Born and raised in Baltimore's German community, he became one of the most influential critics of American life and literature in the 1920s. As an editor of *The Smart Set* and founder of the *American Mercury*, he ruthlessly satirized American middle-class complacency, religious bigotry, and intolerance. Although he believed women deserved the vote, he objected loudly to the actions of the suffragists. Mencken scorned many of the progressive era's reforms, and fought against prohibition and censorship. He was outraged by many of the moral inconsistencies of his day, and used his sharp wit to expose the absurdity of much of the older American "genteel tradition."

The prosperity of the 1920s gave many people the financial resources to spend on amusements. Improved transportation and the increase in private car ownership made it easier for people to take advantage of new entertainments. Film and sports celebrities became popular heroes. Moving pictures drew large crowds, and most Maryland towns opened movie theaters in the 1920s or 1930s. Baltimore built extravagant movie theaters that attracted thirty thousand patrons a week. Other spectator sports, especially baseball, grew in popularity. The best-known Maryland baseball players of their generation were George

■ James Emory "Jimmie" Foxx was born in Sudlersville, in Queen Anne's County, in 1907. In this photograph, Foxx wears the uniform of Easton's minor league baseball team, which played in the old Eastern Shore League. Foxx spent the summer of 1924, after his junior year of high school, with the Easton team before beginning his major league career with the Philadelphia Athletics at the age of 18. Courtesy of Gil Dunn.

■ Although a few African Americans had played on predominantly white baseball teams in the sport's early days, this was no longer permitted after about 1890. Talented players then played on all-black teams, including the Cumberland Cubs, founded in 1914, which had a strong following in Western Maryland. Collection of the Maryland State Archives, MSA SC 1744-1-5609.

Postwar Society in a Time of Change   233

Herman "Babe" Ruth and James Emory "Jimmie" Foxx, but many Maryland towns had their own local teams like the Salisbury Indians and the Centreville Orioles. Baltimore was the home of two Negro League franchises, the Baltimore Black Sox and the Elite Giants, and smaller towns and even neighborhoods throughout the state had black baseball teams as well, such as the Hot Sox sandlot team in Galesville in Anne Arundel County.

■ Maryland and the Great Depression

Economic expansion ended in the 1930s when a worldwide depression brought severe public and personal hardships that neither individual communities nor the state could remedy. The economic crisis of the Great Depression had been foreshadowed in the slowed agricultural economy of the late 1920s and the drop-off in demand for housing. As businesses lost customers and confidence, they began to lay off workers after the New York Stock Exchange crashed in 1929. By the end of 1932, one-fourth of Maryland farmers were near bankruptcy, one hundred thousand people in Baltimore had no income, and communities in Western Maryland had exhausted private relief funds.

Problems of Farmers and Watermen in the 1920s

For black and white farmers alike, the Great Depression began much earlier than 1929. At the end of World War I, overseas demand for crops dropped, and so did prices. Despite the nation's industrial growth during the war, one-fourth of Maryland's families still relied on agricultural income. Some farmers in central Maryland shifted from grain to dairy farming, while farmers in the western counties and on the Eastern Shore began producing more fruits and vegetables for urban markets. But the majority of farmers still depended on grain and tobacco crops, which were affected by the shrinking export market. Tenant farmers, both black and white, were hit especially hard, finding it difficult to pay the rent on their small farms and feed their families. Farmers already deeply in debt were in no shape economically to withstand the drought of the summer of 1929, the worst in the state's history. The blistering heat finally helped reduce the grain surplus that had kept prices down, but slightly higher prices did nothing for individual farmers whose crops shriveled and cattle died. Maryland farm losses that year reached $38 million.

For watermen, the 1920s saw a continuation of the decline in the supply of oysters. Oyster harvests had been falling at a nearly steady rate since the early 1890s, from more than 115 million pounds to 60 million pounds in 1920. Over the next decade, harvests declined precipitously to about 30 million pounds. Historically, the use of dredges and other destructive harvesting techniques had destroyed about three-quarters of the Bay's oyster reefs between 1860 and 1920. But a major 1924 outbreak of typhoid in Chicago, with smaller but significant

■ Maryland's seafood industry employed African American men and women in a variety of jobs. Men worked as crew for boats seeking oysters, crabs, and clams. Women, like the Crisfield workers shown here, picked crabs, and both men and women found work as oyster shuckers in packing houses along the shores of the Bay. Collection of the Maryland State Archives, MSA SC 1477-1-6720.

incidences of the disease in Washington, DC, and New York City, revealed a more critical long-term threat. Tracing most of the reported cases to contaminated raw oysters resulted in an immediate ban by the state of Illinois on the importation of raw oysters, a decree that affected all Atlantic seaboard oyster-harvesting areas. Maryland and the other states quickly joined the Public Health Service in establishing a program of oyster sanitation that involved adopting bacterial standards for oyster-growing waters as well as standards and practices for handling and processing oysters by harvesters, shuckers, and packers to prevent contamination.

Maryland authorities immediately closed oyster beds in polluted or questionable areas, most of them located near Cambridge, Crisfield, Salisbury, and Annapolis. The state brought the Illinois director of public health to Maryland to survey its oyster waters and processing plants. By October 1925, the governor of Illinois assured Maryland that it could certify its waters as safe. Markets for Bay oysters reopened, but the typhoid scare had brought to light the serious long-term threat to the industry. Unregulated growth of new suburbs around Baltimore and Washington without sufficient investment in sewage treatment brought increasing pollution of Chesapeake Bay waters. Growth necessitated adoption of public water systems for the region's cities, designed to provide pure drinking water and improve sanitation and safety by supplying water for street cleaning and fire fighting. The increased supply of fresh water and the spread of indoor plumbing amenities—the use of flush toilets and more frequent bathing and washing—meant that more fresh, but contaminated, water flowed into area streams and eventually into the Bay. The threat to the health of the oyster industry, and the Bay itself, contributed to a sizable campaign to build sewage treatment plants in Tidewater towns. By 1934, one-half of the state's population lived in areas with treated sewage, funded primarily by aid from the US Emergency Relief Fund and the Civil Works Administration.

The Great Crash and Its Initial Impact on Maryland

Newspaper headlines on October 29, 1929, shocked the nation with news of the great stock market crash. Nine million shares traded hands in one day, with losses totaling $14 billion. For many Marylanders, the stock market losses initially seemed far away. But as months passed, instead of investing in building new plants and buying new machinery, industries began to sell off their inventories of goods already produced and to lay off workers.

In 1930, the Baltimore Association of Commerce reassured the city that its "industry as a whole [was] in good shape," even though several important parts of the economy were working at only 70 percent of their normal levels. In Baltimore, several factors at first delayed the hard times that were hitting the nation. Because mortgages were often paid off in five years, many white and some black citizens owned their own homes and could not be put on the streets by foreclosures and evictions. The rate at which business dropped off varied from one industry or plant to another so that not all workers were laid off at one time. Maryland banks, like the Maryland government, had been fiscally conservative. Many of their holdings were city and federal bonds, which were more secure than many other investments. At first relatively few Baltimore banks failed, but those that did often took people's lifetime savings down with them.

Growth of Unemployment in Maryland

Although it came more slowly, when the Great Depression affected Maryland, it caused great distress in every part of the state. Women and African Americans were the first to lose their jobs. By 1931, almost one-third of all union workers were unemployed, and another one-third could find only part-time work. By Christmas 1933, 23,000 families in Baltimore, 1 family out of every 6, were on relief. Unemployment also grew in the counties, reaching a high of 46 percent in Somerset County during the winter of 1933–1934. People without jobs began to draw on their savings to pay for necessities. Between 1930 and 1935, the value of goods sold at retail to Maryland citizens dropped from $619 million to $462 million. Unemployed people could not afford to go shopping.

The Central Trust Company of Frederick, with assets of $8 million, went bankrupt in 1929 and shuttered its eleven branches. In September 1931, the Baltimore Trust Company, the second largest bank in Baltimore, with assets of $85 million and a thirty-two-story skyscraper, closed its doors. People whose life savings were in other banks began to panic and withdrew their money. If a bank could not meet the demand, it paid what it could and then closed. In all, three nationally chartered and fifteen state-chartered banks in Maryland failed by early March. On March 6, the new president, Franklin D. Roosevelt, having declared a bank holiday, closed all banks across the nation to give the federal government a chance to restore order.

Private Efforts to Provide Relief

A few Marylanders could not face the crisis. One bank manager shot himself. An Italian immigrant who was unemployed climbed up onto the Calvert Street Bridge in Baltimore City and jumped into the Jones Falls. Most people tried to cope with hard times by making do with individual resources. Families used up their savings, adult children moved back in with their parents, fewer people got married, and fewer babies were born. People who had migrated to the cities looking for work returned home to the farm if they could. Families tried to eat less food or less expensive food. Social workers in Baltimore reported that many children were coming to school without eating breakfast. Some children did not go to school at all because they did not have enough clothing or shoes. Such poverty existed across the state.

■ The multi-generation family of Wooly Bittinger lived in this log cabin in Garrett County when a photographer captured this family portrait in December 1937. Courtesy of the Library of Congress, fsa2000007539/PP.

Economic forces beyond the control of individuals caused the depression, but traditional means of helping people soon proved to be inadequate. In Maryland, as in much of the United States, relief for people who did not have jobs was organized initially at the local level. Most people believed that relief of poverty was a private, rather than a government, responsibility, and private charitable agencies distributed most of the relief funds in the early years of the depression. In 1930, the largest of Baltimore's relief agencies, the Family Welfare Association, spent $200,000; in 1931, it spent $600,000; and in 1932, it spent $3,400,000. The police became middlemen in the dispersal of charitable contributions for the needy, distributing food and fuel to families and providing meals at local station houses.

Unemployment and the need for relief expenditures also put a burden on private charities in the counties. Some had no agencies to supply unemployed families with funds for food, fuel, or rent. By June 1933, one of every seventeen inhabitants in the counties was on relief. Many of the mines in Garrett and Allegany Counties were closed. Two-thirds of all African Americans in Elkton were unable to find work.

State and Local Relief Efforts

As unemployment continued to rise, relief needs grew accordingly. Social worker Anna D. Ward, writing for the Family Welfare Association, urged the government to meet the needs of those affected by the depression. But Governor Albert C. Ritchie believed strongly in the principles of a balanced budget and local responsibility. Baltimore's newly elected Democratic mayor, Howard W. Jackson, was a "businessman's businessman." Worried property holders, who did not want their taxes raised, influenced both Ritchie and Jackson. Nevertheless, when the depression began, cities, counties, and the state responded by speeding up construction of roads and schools to provide jobs for the unemployed. Allegany County, for example, widened and paved Route 40 and other roads. Baltimore City responded before the state did in providing desperate city residents with food, fuel, and shelter. First it lent $150,000 to the Citizens' Emergency Relief Committee. In March 1932, Mayor Jackson asked Governor Ritchie to lend the city money backed by bonds to enable Baltimore to fund relief directly, a request that Ritchie refused.

By this time, the US government, under Republican President Herbert Hoover, was beginning to accept some responsibility for solving the problems of the depression. But Governor Ritchie thought that states ought to take care of their own people. Maryland relied on property taxes for its relief programs, but as the depression continued, property owners were less able to pay these taxes. In 1933, with other states getting their share, Ritchie finally decided to apply for federal help. "All hands agreed we ought to get all we can get" of federal money,

Albert C. Ritchie: Four-Term Governor

When Albert Ritchie graduated from the Johns Hopkins University in 1896, the yearbook predicted that he would be elected president of the United States by one vote and then reelected for life. Although he was only in the running for the presidency in 1924 and 1928, he did win the governorship of Maryland in 1919 by a narrow margin, and he was reelected three more times.

The role that Ritchie played in campaigns against prohibition and women's suffrage illustrates well both his skillful control of Maryland politics and his political philosophy. Ritchie entered politics in his native city of Baltimore in 1911 and became attorney general of Maryland in 1915. After he was elected governor in 1919, he remained the symbol of moderately progressive Maryland Democratic politics for the next decade and a half.

Ritchie believed in the responsibility of the state to solve its own problems and he opposed legislation like prohibition that interfered in individual rights. He also believed that the state must operate economically and efficiently to allow individual citizens and businesses to prosper. His programs succeeded well until the depression. Then, his opposition to the New Deal cost him many of his earlier supporters. In 1934, he failed to win a fifth term as governor.

■ Governor Albert C. Ritchie. Collection of the Maryland State Archives, MSA SC 1545-1103.

he told reporters. Responsibility for meeting the costs of relief from unemployment had gradually shifted from individuals, to charitable organizations, to cities, counties, and the state, and, finally, to the federal government.

■ Maryland and the New Deal

Early in 1933, a new administration took office in Washington and changed America's approach to the enormous problems of the depression. Under President Franklin D. Roosevelt, the national government created programs to provide relief for hungry families, to help the poor find employment, and to promote industrial and agricultural prosperity. An expanded federal government and its workforce spilled over from the District of Columbia into nearby Maryland counties. This stimulated suburban growth, which later increased rapidly during World War II.

The National Government Takes Charge

The New Deal programs created by Roosevelt's Democratic administration covered a variety of areas. Government-sponsored agencies encouraged industry to produce again. They set up a licensing and inspection system to ensure that banks lent money wisely and to assure citizens that their savings were safe. They limited the production of farm goods in an effort to help raise farmers' income. National government agencies provided work relief for many of the people who could not find jobs in private industry. The purpose of these jobs was to give the unemployed work rather than charity, usually on public projects like roads, parks, and federal buildings such as post offices. New Deal programs allocated money to the states as direct relief for people unable to work. They created new towns of inexpensive housing near areas where work could be found. They brought electricity to rural areas, and they created a new program, Social Security, to provide a regular income for senior citizens.

Almost all of these programs created controversy. The federal government became involved in many aspects of local government. When federal money was used to build roads, federal employees set rules about hiring and the kinds of roads to be built. Industries drew up agreements or codes about production and pricing to reduce the risks of competition and to get companies back on their feet financially. The federal government insisted that labor unions have some say in the codes and required companies to follow certain rules when dealing with unions.

To reduce farm production and thereby raise farm prices, the federal government paid farmers to plow under crops or to keep land idle. This caused outrage among city dwellers who were unable to afford enough food for their families. Labor unions in the city thought that the city pay rate of $45 per month for work relief was too low. Employers on the Eastern Shore complained that the lower pay scale there was twice the regular local wage rate.

The federal government required state and local governments to contribute to direct relief. State and federal officials quarreled constantly over the amount of the state contribution. Rural members, who controlled the state legislature, were particularly reluctant to provide as much as federal agencies said they should. They believed that any able-bodied man who really wanted to work could find a job. Federal programs, in their view, set dangerous precedents, leading people to expect higher pay for unskilled labor, or to accept public relief payments without working at all.

Early New Deal Work Relief Programs

In spite of the controversy, the New Deal had a profound effect on Maryland. The work relief programs affected the largest number of Marylanders directly. The state and local governments had already put some citizens to work by creating public jobs. Now through the Public Works Administration (PWA), the

Greenbelt

Maryland was the home of one of the most ambitious New Deal projects: the city of Greenbelt in Prince George's County. New Deal planners thought that federally funded "greenbelt towns" could solve several problems. Building the towns near large cities would provide work for unemployed, unskilled urban workers, and the new homes would provide inexpensive housing for working poor people. These homes would be in a healthy suburban atmosphere, rather than in the inner city. Fathers would be close to their work, and children would be surrounded by trees, parks, and gardens.

Better communities, it was thought, would result from advance planning. A "town center" would contain schools, stores, movie houses, libraries, gasoline stations, and beauty parlors, where everyone could gather. Only three such towns were ever built, of which Greenbelt, Maryland, was the first and most successful.

Greenbelt began in 1935 on 12,000 acres located 12 miles from Washington, DC. A federal Agricultural Research Center in nearby Beltsville provided jobs for Greenbelt residents. Completing the town took two and a half years and employed more than 13,000 people. The federal government became the town's landlord, renting each of the 885 homes for, on average, $31.23 per month. Tenants for the new town were carefully chosen from more than 5,700 applicant families.

In 1942, when Maryland became a center for wartime industries, housing had to be found for war workers. One thousand additional "defense housing" units were built in the undeveloped areas of Greenbelt. In September 1945, when the war was over, the federal government sold the row houses to a co-operative of Greenbelt tenants.

■ This 1936 photograph and 229 others documented construction under way at Greenbelt as part of the Resettlement Administration's creation of new communities. Courtesy of the Library of Congress, USF344-003772-ZB.

The Civilian Conservation Corps

The Civilian Conservation Corps (CCC), founded in 1933, was a popular New Deal program in Maryland. The CCC recruited unemployed young men, between the ages of 18 and 25 and from families on relief, for conservation, natural resources, and recreation projects, many of which still serve the public across the state. The program provided housing, food, jobs, and work skills training while lessening the economic burden on the families of unemployed young men. Participants earned $30 a month, but $22 had to be sent home. African American leaders had to push the federal government to include young black men, which it did although in segregated camps.

In Maryland, more than 30,000 young men worked across the state at many diverse sites, including Fort Frederick State Park, Elk Neck State Forest, and Pocomoke State Forest. They constructed 274 bridges, planted 4.5 million trees, and built golf courses and fire lookout towers. Local older men worked as camp supervisors, receiving a bit more than the regular stipend.

Young men in CCC camps were treated like army recruits. They were vaccinated, assigned to a company ruled over by a sergeant, marched around, and ordered to perform calisthenics. Many poor Baltimore families believed that the country was expecting war and was "taking these men to train for the first draft." But the young Maryland CCC corpsmen fought a different kind of war, a war against mosquitoes, fires, erosion, and vandalism in the state's parks and public lands.

■ The Civilian Conservation Corps hired young men to work outdoors on projects in Maryland. Here, CCC men use local stone to build a copy of an 1827 monument, originally built by the residents of nearby Boonsboro, which had fallen into disrepair in Washington Monument State Park. Collection of the Maryland State Archives, MSA SC 1477-1-6087.

Civil Works Administration (CWA), the Works Progress Administration (WPA), and the Civilian Conservation Corps (CCC), the federal government hired tens of thousands of Maryland residents.

The PWA was designed to complete large-scale projects. By July 1934, fourteen Maryland counties had proposed to Governor Ritchie public works projects worth $13 million. Baltimore City presented plans to spend an additional $16.1 million. Most of the state-sponsored PWA projects focused on roads, including a new major highway from Baltimore to Philadelphia, and government buildings such as schools, post offices, and courthouses. But PWA did not hire all the people who needed jobs, and it required more skilled than unskilled workers. At the height of PWA activity in Maryland, only 3,899 people were on its payroll. The CWA and WPA programs, on the other hand, sought to put the maximum number of people to work. Created in 1933, the CWA was an experiment in federal work relief. Half of the 51,000 Maryland workers hired for its projects came directly from the relief rolls. The other half were people who needed jobs but were not yet so destitute that they qualified for relief. In 1935, the CWA was replaced by a more permanent agency, the WPA.

The Works Progress Administration

Before it was dismantled in 1943, the WPA spent $58 million in Maryland. At one time or another, its payroll included nearly one-fifth of all workers in the state. Local communities provided equipment and supplies, and the WPA paid workers' salaries. The Service Division included the small number of women who qualified for WPA work. Black women trained as domestics. Both black

■ The federal Farm Security Administration made loans available to rural clients in Maryland. FSA supervisors in 1941 showed this La Plata farmer in Charles County how to replace the dangerous shallow well with a deeper, safer one. Courtesy of the Library of Congress, USF34-080002-D.

and white women worked in "sewing rooms," where they learned the skills of the garment industry. Some of the clothing they made was given away in the general relief program. The WPA Service Division also conducted a historical records survey, repaired library books all over the state, and held nursery school and adult education classes. A small group of WPA workers surveyed, measured, and photographed historic Maryland buildings as part of the Historic American Buildings Survey. WPA artists created posters and taught art classes; musicians, playwrights, and actors composed, wrote, and performed. A related "Fine Arts" program in the Treasury Department created murals in post offices of sixteen Maryland towns and cities.

The majority of Maryland WPA workers were unskilled male laborers who worked on construction projects in the Operations Division. Few local communities had resources to provide them with modern tools, so the men accomplished their jobs by manpower rather than by machinery. Using wheelbarrows and shovels, WPA workers on the Eastern Shore and in Western Maryland built or improved 1,300 miles of roads. On the Eastern Shore they cleared out drainage ditches and tidal rivers and built retaining walls to stop shoreline erosion. In Garrett and Allegany Counties they built floodwalls along the rivers after disastrous floods in 1936.

In towns all over the state, WPA workers built miles of curbs and sidewalks. Other community-sponsored WPA projects improved local parks and playgrounds. Many communities used WPA funds to install water mains and sanitary sewer systems. When WPA work was done, outhouses disappeared from the back alleys of towns from Garrett County to Worcester County. Long, straight sidewalks along tree-shaded streets provided safe places for children to play.

Politics, Labor, and African Americans in the 1930s

New Deal programs that brought Maryland citizens some relief from the depression also disrupted Maryland's political balance. As national programs were put into effect in the state, laborers used strikes to demand overdue improvements in their status. Maryland African Americans challenged discrimination in both state and federal courts.

Political Changes in Maryland

In Maryland, one of the most popular measures passed by President Roosevelt and Congress did not create a new program; it ended an old one. The new president had promised to end prohibition, and Congress moved immediately to pass the Twenty-First Amendment to the US Constitution. Maryland voters, particularly in Baltimore, voted overwhelmingly to approve the amendment repealing the ban on the manufacture, sale, and transportation of alcohol.

The end of prohibition accompanied a change in the state's political leadership. In 1934, when Albert Ritchie ran again for governor, prohibition was a dead issue and many Marylanders were still unemployed. Ritchie's insistence on a state's right to solve its own unemployment problems without federal interference had alienated many of his former supporters. His Republican opponent Harry W. Nice promised to seek full Maryland participation in New Deal programs. Nice won by a narrow margin, but the Democrats won most of the other Election Day contests. Without Ritchie's strong leadership, fiscally conservative rural delegates from Southern Maryland and the Eastern Shore dominated the state legislature. They blocked state tax increases needed to fund some of the New Deal programs that they opposed.

Organized Labor Makes Some Gains

From the beginning of the New Deal, President Roosevelt had insisted that organized labor ought to have a say in important economic decisions. Labor unions had been particularly hard hit by the loss of jobs for their workers. They won an important national victory in 1935 with passage of the Wagner National Labor Relations Act, which guaranteed labor the right to organize and bargain collectively. In Maryland, the struggle to establish a strong position for labor led to a series of strikes during the 1930s.

Organizers in a new national union voiced some of labor's demands. Skilled workers in Maryland had been members of craft unions that belonged to the American Federation of Labor (AFL). Many unskilled workers in Maryland's large industries did not have any union representation. The Congress of Industrial Organizations (CIO), organized in Maryland in 1937, represented workers on an industry-wide basis rather than on the basis of a single craft and included both skilled and unskilled workers, both blacks and whites. Young CIO labor leaders fought for collective bargaining rights in the large industries that had no unions. CIO-United Textile Workers and CIO-United Rubber Workers obtained union recognition, better wages and hours, and improved working conditions at large plants in Cumberland. In Baltimore, the CIO-United Auto Workers succeeded in organizing General Motors. Not all union successes were won by CIO unions. When two thousand poorly paid workers walked out of the Phillips Packing Company canning plant in Cambridge, they asked the AFL to organize and represent them.

In most strikes, violence on both sides heightened tensions. Earlier, the government had often intervened on behalf of industry when struggles between labor and management led to violence. But in each of these Maryland strikes, the federal government's National Labor Relations Board (NLRB) worked to enforce the right of workers to organize an independent union and insisted that the company bargain in good faith. Many Maryland workers became active sup-

Labor Unrest on the Eastern Shore: The Phillips Packing Company Strike of 1937

Vegetable crops—especially tomatoes—and canning were an important part of the Eastern Shore economy in the 1920s and 1930s. The largest and most prominent of the canneries was that of Cambridge's Phillips Packing Company, organized by Albanus Phillips in 1899. In the 1920s, he marketed his canned tomatoes all over the United States, but actively resisted all efforts of his workers to organize for better wages and conditions. More than two thousand striking white and black workers clashed with Phillips in the streets of Cambridge during 1937 as wages remained low and he refused to negotiate. Strikers overturned nineteen Phillips trucks before the state labor commissioner arrived to arrange a temporary truce to end the violence. Workers at the Phillips canneries did not unionize until World War II.

■ This photograph captures a striking worker at the Phillips Packing Company in Cambridge, Maryland, in June 1937. Courtesy of the Library of Congress, LC-USF34-025586-D.

porters of the Democratic Party, whose policies in support of union organization had won significant economic gains for workers.

Change for African Americans Comes Slowly

African Americans were hit particularly hard by the depression. They experienced the highest unemployment, both in Baltimore City and on the Eastern Shore, and often benefited less than whites from New Deal programs. A special study commissioned by the National Urban League in 1935 revealed that African Americans were concentrated in the poorest sections of Baltimore, crowded into deteriorating housing. They suffered such high rates of tuberculosis that one black neighborhood was known as Lung Block. Many were segregated in the lowest-paying jobs, usually those involving manual labor or difficult or unpleasant services. A large percentage of African American women worked for low wages as domestic servants, leaving their own homes and children to care for the homes and children of white families.

The tensions that accompany economic hard times often result in increased racial tensions as well. During the Great Depression, these tensions sometimes exploded in racial violence. On the Eastern Shore, a white mob lynched Matthew Williams in Salisbury in 1931, and two years later in Princess Anne, a mob seized and lynched George Armwood. When Governor Ritchie sent five hun-

In his 1938 painting titled *Dispossessed*, artist Mervin Jules captured the pain of the long-lasting effects of the Great Depression. Born in Baltimore, Jules studied art at Baltimore City College, at the Maryland Institute College of Art, and in New York. Because he was a realist, Jules's work often dealt with social themes. Courtesy of the American Art Museum, Smithsonian Institution, 1981.80.1.

dred Maryland National Guard soldiers to arrest the mob leaders, local firemen turned their hoses on the guardsmen. Black leaders, with the NAACP and the *Baltimore Afro-American* at the forefront, and their white allies continued to fight against lynching until it was made illegal.

Black leaders protested depression conditions in a number of ways. Some political leaders, like the former Republican Baltimore City Councilman William Fitzgerald, switched to the Democratic Party to help win New Deal benefits for blacks, and Democrats saw to it that black supporters received jobs from federal agencies such as the Post Office. During Roosevelt's presidency the majority of black voters changed their allegiance from the Republican Party to the Democratic Party, primarily for economic reasons. The NAACP, under the local leadership of Lillie May Carroll Jackson, and several other groups began to fight the problem of black unemployment directly. For example, they boycotted and picketed businesses along Pennsylvania Avenue that would not hire black workers. They urged people to buy only where they could work; in response, some merchants began hiring black workers. New chapters of the NAACP organized in the counties; the Prince George's County chapter, for example, led by Hester King, started in 1935.

The African American community always considered education essential in the struggle for equality. During the depression era black citizens did make some important gains in education for their children. Although schools remained segregated, Maryland schools for black children had begun to improve during the 1920s. Some counties bused black children across county lines to enable them to get a high school education. In 1928, 989 black Maryland stu-

African American women demonstrated on Pennsylvania Avenue in Baltimore to urge patrons to shop only in stores that would hire black employees. Courtesy of Afro Archives.

dents attended schools that offered a high school academic and vocational curriculum. Dunbar School, named after poet Paul Lawrence Dunbar, had begun as an elementary school in eastern Baltimore in 1918; by 1937, it had become the second full high school in the city for African Americans. Teachers in black schools taught black history and literature, instilled pride in their students, and served as community leaders.

Despite the improvements, by 1940, only 3.5 percent of all black students completed high school. The state spent less money to support black schools than it spent for white schools: in 1935, Maryland spent $48.01 to educate a black student, compared to $67.61 for a white student. Some counties paid black teachers lower salaries than white teachers. During the 1930s, black churches, the Maryland NAACP, and the *Baltimore Afro-American*, three powerful community institutions, all fought the inequity. Challenges in the courts finally won a federal injunction against the practice of unequal pay.

Segregation Is Challenged

In the area of higher education, only Morgan College offered a four-year liberal arts program. Bowie State Teachers College was the only state teachers' college for blacks. Princess Anne Academy, owned by Morgan, did not have a two-year college curriculum until 1927. Baltimore City ran Coppin Normal School to

Donald Murray, because he was African American, had to win a court order in 1935 to be admitted as a student at the University of Maryland Law School. Murray (*seated center*) was represented by NAACP lawyers Thurgood Marshall (*left*) and Charles Houston (*right*). They successfully argued, in this landmark case, that a "separate but equal" law school created for him in Maryland or a law school outside the state would not provide an equal education for someone who wanted to practice law in Maryland. Courtesy of the Library of Congress, ppmsca.09709.

provide black teachers for its schools. There were no provisions for educating African American students in law, medicine, or other professions.

In the spring of 1935, Donald Murray, a black Baltimore resident and an honors graduate from Amherst College in Massachusetts, applied to the all-white University of Maryland Law School and was refused admission. The state argued that it had provided equal professional educational opportunities by creating in 1933 a scholarship fund for blacks to defray the expenses of attending out-of-state professional schools. The NAACP hired lawyers Thurgood Marshall and Charles Houston to argue Murray's case.

The federal judge agreed with the NAACP that Maryland had failed to provide the legally required "separate but equal" education for Murray; stated that attendance at out-of-state schools was not, in fact, equal; and ordered the University of Maryland Law School to admit Murray. Murray graduated with an excellent record in 1938 and joined a Baltimore law firm. He was the first black student to integrate a state university south of the Mason-Dixon line in the twentieth century. The victory was a limited one, however. For the next fifteen years, only the law school admitted blacks. Fearful that it would be required to integrate other parts of the university, the state purchased Morgan College from the college's trustees and claimed that the purchase meant equal education for African American students.

■ World War II and the End of the Depression

Renewal of war in Europe in 1939, not New Deal programs, ended economic hard times in Maryland and the nation as the federal government and others prepared for war. Even before the United States entered the fighting, World War II placed heavy military and industrial demands on Maryland citizens. People from rural counties and nearby states flocked to Baltimore to work in the new jobs. Housing for workers and the opening of new industries resulted in a new ring of suburbs around Baltimore. Growth of the federal government and the military brought more people to the Washington suburbs. Factories making aircraft and weapons rapidly expanded, bringing new life to smaller cities like Frederick and Cumberland. Farms became more productive and more mechanized, producing greater quantities of food with a smaller workforce.

War Begins Again

Americans watched uneasily from 1935 onward as Germany under Adolf Hitler and Italy under Benito Mussolini rearmed and advanced into neighboring countries. Baltimore's German community had begun cautiously to celebrate its heritage again in the late 1920s as memories of World War I faded. But by the late 1930s, most Marylanders whose ancestors had come from Germany were as alarmed as other Americans by Hitler's actions in Europe. They were careful to identify themselves as Americans of German descent. By the time Hitler invaded Czechoslovakia, German-language broadcasts on WCBM had been dropped because of loss of advertising.

For the United States, the war began not in Germany but in the Pacific. On December 7, 1941, Japan, which had been conquering neighbors in Asia and the Pacific area to gain access to their resources, bombed the American naval base at Pearl Harbor in Hawaii in a preemptive strike. Americans, including Marylanders, responding to the unexpected attack, entered World War II more united and better prepared for war than they had been in 1917.

Wartime Industrial Growth in Maryland

Maryland's industrial expansion began long before its military participation in the war. In 1937, industries like Bethlehem Steel and the Glenn L. Martin Company were already receiving orders from overseas nations. Japan had become Bethlehem Steel's biggest customer. The *Baltimore Sun* observed in February 1937 that the junkman collecting scrap iron in Baltimore's alleys was "doing his bit for the Japanese war effort." When it became clear that the United States would take part in the war on the side of England and France, industrial activity speeded up even more.

The federal government invested $185 million to construct defense plants throughout Maryland. The government also ensured that factories in Balti-

more, Cumberland, and Frederick received raw materials to manufacture steel and rubber, build ships and airplanes, and refine oil. Maryland eventually filled war production contracts totaling more than $5.5 billion. This enormously expanded wartime production ended unemployment, the most stubborn problem of the depression. Total aircraft industry employment in 1940 was 11,000. By 1943, 50,000 people, many of them women, were making airplanes in Baltimore area and Hagerstown plants. The Glenn L. Martin Company in Baltimore County alone employed 37,000 workers.

In 1940, shipbuilding employed 4,000 workers; three years later, 77,000. Forty-seven thousand workers at Bethlehem Steel's Fairchild Shipyards built more than 500 Victory and Liberty Ships. Wartime production adapted automobile assembly-line techniques, cutting the time needed to launch a ship from 110 days to 52.

■ The Glenn L. Martin Company supplied bombers, such as this array of PBM Mariners (patrol bomber flying boats), for the United States and its allies in World War II. The jobs created by the massive demand for war matériel helped end the depression by putting men and women back to work. Courtesy of the Baltimore Museum of Industry, BGE.247.C.

Women's Work in Wartime

The US Employment Service heavily recruited women for war work. It promised unemployed homemakers in neighborhoods near war plants good pay and government-funded day care centers for their children if they would come to work. Recruiters also tried to make the work sound familiar, or *feminine*. They described women cleaning train passenger cars as "replacing men who have dropped the brushes and picked up guns. The ladies found it no harder than cleaning the woodwork at home." At the Fairchild Aircraft plant in Hagerstown, promotional signs extolled the superior ability of women to do the "delicate" work of riveting aircraft wings.

■ Woman riveting airplane wings at Fairchild Aircraft plant in Hagerstown. Courtesy of the National Archives, photo no. 86-WWT-13-22.

Women and African Americans as War Workers

Industries struggling to meet defense contracts could not find enough men to fill their production lines, so they turned to women for their labor supply. Posters told women that it was their patriotic duty to work in war industries. As more and more men were drafted or volunteered for the armed services, the proportion of women in the workforce grew. As they had in World War I, women learned to do many jobs that traditionally had been limited to men. Women became welders and riveters, operated heavy cranes, and drove trucks.

For African Americans, the war opened up economic opportunities that decades of protest had been unable to create. Federal Fair Employment Practices Committee members first attempted to overcome the prejudice of industrial managers who believed that black workers were not capable of performing highly skilled jobs. When persuasion failed, President Roosevelt issued an executive order to force defense industries to employ all Americans.

The US government followed a policy allowing no discrimination in employment of workers in defense industries because of race, creed, color, or national origin. This clause was included in all defense contracts. By the time Germany surrendered in May 1945, the number of African Americans working in industry nationally had more than doubled, and the percentage of blacks in the industrial workforce in the Baltimore area reached 17.6 percent, up from 8 percent before the war. But the improvement proved to be mainly a wartime phenomenon. African American employment in the industrial workforce began dropping off as war production ended, as did industrial work and other opportunities for women. As wartime protections disappeared, many workers, of all backgrounds, faced challenges in their right to organize and sometimes were offered lower salaries.

Demographic Changes during the War

Wartime demand for labor not only brought more women and blacks into the urban workforce, it also drew new people to the cities, as had wartime needs during World War I. The civilian population of Baltimore grew by 134,000 people between April 1940 and November 1943. The total migration of workers into the city in the war years totaled 210,000. Many of these people came from other parts of Maryland, but additional workers seeking industrial employment came from North Carolina, Virginia, West Virginia, and Pennsylvania.

■ This World War II poster promoted the idea of interracial cooperation on behalf of the war effort. Courtesy of the National Archives, photo no. 513533.

The War Effort in Annapolis

The Annapolis Yacht Yard on Spa Creek, using a British design, built 128 Vosper PT boats for the British and Russian navies under contract with the US government and 2 110-foot submarine chasers for the US Navy. More than five hundred men worked in 2 8-hour shifts while a night shift of women secured each day's planking. New buildings along the Eastport waterfront housed boat sheds and machine, welding, and other shops.

Late in the war, the yard built seventy PT boats in kit form for the Russian navy, translating plans and instructions with the assistance of officers with the Russian embassy. Three company officials spent nine months in Leningrad to direct the assembly of the boats.

On the other side of the Severn River, the navy's Engineering Experiment Station included chemical, metallurgical, welding, and internal combustion labs. The station expanded both labs and staff to solve problems for the navy's fleet and airplanes, including development, under the direction of Dr. Robert H. Goddard, of liquid-propellant jet-assisted take-off rockets to shorten the distance needed for launching heavy aircraft from carrier decks.

The naval radio station on Greenbury Point added transmitters, increased the number of enlisted personnel, and doubled the number of radio operators to 100. The 500-kilowatt station sent scheduled messages to ships and naval shore installations as far away as Guam, operating under tight security, with armed guards patrolling the perimeter of the point.

These new workers and their families arrived needing housing, transportation, food, health care, and educational services, and communities across Maryland scrambled to satisfy the needs. By the end of 1944, 28,000 wartime housing units had been built in Baltimore alone. Many war workers lived in makeshift trailer parks near the Martin Company plants. Long lines formed at laundries, and workers crowded buses and trolleys heading in and out of the city. In Baltimore, sightseeing boats were converted to marine buses to transport workers from crowded city neighborhoods to the Bethlehem Steel Shipyards; Chesapeake Bay pleasure boats similarly now served military needs. Defense plants built daycare centers for the children of their female employees. Public schools in Baltimore went on double shifts to accommodate all the new children.

Directing the enormous worldwide war effort caused a growth of the federal government's civilian workforce. These workers and their families began to seek housing in Montgomery and Prince George's Counties near Washington, DC. All these population shifts, or demographic changes, had political as well as economic and social consequences as population increased in urban areas and decreased in rural areas. These effects became clear in the years following World War II.

Soldiers and Civilians in Wartime Maryland

Thousands of Marylanders who worked overtime in war industries also followed closely the radio and newspaper reports from Europe, North Africa, and the Pacific. Many wondered if their sons or daughters, husbands, or brothers and sisters were involved in battle. Wartime shortages and rationing affected everyone, even those who had no relatives fighting in the war.

Maryland Military Participation in World War II

Maryland sent more than 240,000 men and women into service in the armed forces. They fought in the army, navy, marines, and coast guard. At the end of the war, more than five thousand of them were dead or missing. Many of the deaths in World War I had been due to disease, but most of the World War II dead were killed in action or died of wounds and injuries suffered in battle. African American Marylanders served in segregated army units that brought together men and women from across the country. The all-black 29th Infantry Division, with soldiers from Maryland, Virginia, Pennsylvania, and the District of Columbia, formed an important part of the Allied European invasion force at Omaha Beach on D-Day.

Marylanders formed five general hospital units in the army: the 18th and 118th, from the Johns Hopkins Medical School; the 42nd and 142nd, from the University of Maryland Medical School; and the 56th, organized by Baltimore physicians and serving as a front-line hospital in Europe. The Hopkins and University of Maryland units also provided medical care in the Pacific theater of war, in India, the Fiji Islands, Australia, and Manila and Leyte in the Philippines.

At the outbreak of World War II, the political and military establishments were still committed to complete segregation in the armed services, claiming that the separate units were, in fact, equal. African Americans, however, were coming to the conclusion that separation was inherently unequal and therefore not acceptable. Black Marylanders were not trained in hometown units, like their white counterparts, but placed with African Americans from across the nation. Responding to pressure from the NAACP, and persistent criticisms of segregation and discrimination in the armed forces voiced by the black press, including Baltimore's *Afro-American*, President Roosevelt promised that African American soldiers would be trained as officers and that they would play a combat role in all branches of the armed services. Many military leaders opposed full integration, however, and American armed forces did not desegregate until President Harry S. Truman issued Executive Order 9981 in 1948.

Even before World War I, many army and navy installations had been located in Maryland. By the end of World War II, military training bases, defense posts, testing sites, airfields, and medical centers formed an even more important part of the state's economy. The federal government spent $500 million in Maryland to expand older bases such as Fort Meade and to create new ones like Andrews Air Force Base, the Patuxent Naval Air Station, and the Bethesda Naval Medical Center. The army alone had sixty-five installations within the state. Most were small offices consisting of maintenance or service units, but others, like Aberdeen Proving Ground, covered hundreds of thousands of acres and became small cities in themselves.

■ The image of "Uncle Sam" challenging young men to enlist in the US army was so effective in World War I that it was adopted almost immediately to serve the same purpose during World War II. Courtesy of the National Archives, photo no. 513820.

Prisoners of War in Maryland

Not all of the military installations in Maryland were used for training American troops. As early as March 1942, the government interned Japanese, German, and Italian enemy aliens in stockades at Fort George G. Meade in Anne Arundel County. As wartime demands for labor became harder to meet, German and Italian prisoners of war (POWs) were allocated to Maryland farms and industry to meet the need. At one point eighteen camps in Maryland furnished POW labor. Ten thousand prisoners spent up to three years in Maryland before being repatriated, or sent home, at the end of the war.

The use of German prisoners as farm labor saved the Maryland tomato crop in 1943. At Fort Meade, Italian prisoners worked diligently in labor gangs. To improve their morale, Major General Philip Hayes asked Baltimore's Italian community to provide entertainment similar to that provided for American troops by the USO. When some three hundred Italian American girls over age 18 arrived at Fort Meade to participate in the dances, the American Legion protested that the prisoners were being "coddled."

■ On August 14, 1945 (V-J Day), Baltimoreans crowded the streets for festive celebration of the end of World War II. Permission from *The Baltimore Sun*.

Civilian Life during Wartime

The war effort affected every aspect of life in Maryland. Tires, gasoline, and food were rationed. Families turned to home gardens and public transportation for the duration of the war. Homemakers took classes in canning and preserving food; many also worked in war industries. To relieve the manpower shortage, older children worked after school, stocking grocery store shelves, waiting on tables, setting pins in bowling alleys, and caring for children whose mothers worked in war plants. High school boys and girls spent many Saturdays and summer vacations as farm laborers to harvest valuable crops.

Black and white college girls and women war workers volunteered as hostesses at USO dances for GIs far from home. Theaters and restaurants donated free tickets to servicemen to use on their off hours. Women all over the state rolled bandages for the Red Cross, knit wool sweaters for distribution to servicemen, and participated in letter-writing campaigns to boost the morale of

American soldiers. Newspaper advertisements promoted scrap metal collection drives. War bonds once again became the patriotic way for civilians to save the extra money they earned working overtime in war plants.

The news of "Victory!" in Europe in May 1945, and the atomic end of the war in the Pacific in August 1945, brought Marylanders thronging into the streets in celebration. But postwar readjustment threatened the seeming unity. By October 1945, nearly forty thousand war workers had been laid off. Returning soldiers entering the job market received priority over the women and African Americans who had entered the workforce during wartime.

Men who came home from war found that their wives and families had managed to run their affairs without a man in the house. Reunited families often faced unexpected strains. Thousands of women happily quit their war jobs and turned their attention to children and housework. But other women had become accustomed to working at a full-time job and earning decent pay, and wanted to stay in the workforce. African Americans had fought for equal treatment in the armed services and against an enemy that had carried racism to murderous extremes. They returned home determined to work for legal equality and an end to racism in civilian life.

■ 1945: A Pivotal Year

Maryland and the nation had lived through the crises of war, depression, and a second war. Everyone longed for better times. As the crowds cheered V-J Day, they looked ahead, hoping for peace and prosperity. Maryland at the end of 1945 was poised between its complex past, with all its rapid growth, and an uncertain future. The consolidation and growth of the preceding thirty years, as well as nostalgia for a colorful and unique Maryland identity, set the framework within which the postwar years would develop.

Maryland	Year	The Nation and the World
First suburban department store opens in Silver Spring Democrat William Preston Lane Jr. elected governor	1946	A national "baby boom" begins
	1947	Truman Doctrine and Marshall Plan
Ober Law	1949	NATO formed Communist revolution in China First Soviet nuclear test
	1950–1953	Korean War
Republican Theodore R. McKeldin elected governor	1950	
Chesapeake Bay Bridge opens	1952	Republican Dwight D. Eisenhower elected president
First Baltimore public schools desegregate	1954	*Brown v. Board of Education of Topeka*
Maryland Port Authority created	1955	
Baltimore Harbor Tunnel opens	1957	Soviet satellite *Sputnik* launched
Democrat J. Millard Tawes elected governor	1958	
Social Security Administration offices open in Woodlawn	1960	Democrat John F. Kennedy elected president
Charles Center construction begins in Baltimore	1961	
Baltimore Beltway opens	1962	Cuban Missile Crisis
	1963	Kennedy assassinated; Lyndon B. Johnson becomes president
Capital Beltway opens	1964	Civil Rights Act Gulf of Tonkin Resolution gives President Johnson authority to use force in Vietnam
	1965	Voting Rights Act
Republican Spiro Agnew elected governor	1966	
Convention attempts to revise Maryland constitution Wilde Lake, Columbia's first village, opens	1967	
Baltimore riots Democrat Marvin Mandel elected governor	1968	Martin Luther King Jr. and Robert F. Kennedy assassinated Republican Richard M. Nixon elected president Spiro Agnew elected vice president First man walks on the moon
Parren Mitchell is first African American elected to Congress from Maryland	1970	
	1973	Agnew resigns vice presidency US withdraws from Vietnam
Calvert Cliffs nuclear power plant built	1974	Nixon resigns presidency Vice President Gerald Ford becomes president Vietnam War ends
	1976	Democrat James Carter Jr. elected president
Democrat Harry Hughes elected governor	1978	
	1980	Republican Ronald Reagan elected president
	1982	First woman, Sandra Day O'Connor, appointed to the US Supreme Court
	1983	First multi-state Chesapeake Bay Agreement signed

chapter seven

Maryland after World War II

1945–1985

Many of the patterns of life that began early in the century continued in Maryland in the years after World War II, but at the same time there was much that was new. The movement of people away from farms and into cities and suburbs increased. The Industrial Revolution went through its final stages before being succeeded by an Information Revolution as the technology of television and computers came to dominate work and play. New bridges across the Bay and highways throughout the state tied Maryland's communities closer together. In politics, new groups and leaders from the cities and suburbs replaced the old bosses and organizations. The histories of the state and the nation in these postwar years contain strong parallels: Maryland changed in much the same way that the United States changed.

■ Return to Peace and Prosperity

When President Harry S. Truman announced the Japanese surrender at 7:00 p.m. on August 14, 1945, the people of Maryland joined the rest of the nation in celebration. For many, the greatest joy would be the return home from war of family and friends. Others rejoiced that the democracies of the world had defended their way of life, and everyone welcomed the end to years of worry and sacrifice. President Truman declared a two-day holiday for federal workers in recognition of their efforts during the war. For the first time since December 7, 1941, Marylanders looked forward to waking up in a nation at peace.

The Postwar World

After the initial excitement died down, the return to a normal life began in earnest. Streetlights came on again at night, ration lines disappeared from gas stations, and scarce consumer products began to reappear on store shelves. Fami-

With the end of World War II, manufacturing companies turned to making consumer goods. Bendix, headquartered in Towson, made radios, televisions, and washing machines as well as airplane and automotive products. Courtesy of magazine-advertisements.com.

lies could again buy rubber tires for their cars and bicycles. Women could buy nylon stockings once more, and fresh meat filled shelves in local grocery stores.

But for those who remembered clearly that the war had followed the Great Depression of the 1930s, peacetime brought fears that unemployment would return and spending money would decrease. The government canceled billions of dollars of contracts in defense industries like shipbuilding, ammunition manufacturing, and airplane construction. By October 1945, about 45,000 defense workers in Maryland had been laid off and 35,000 soldiers had returned home to begin to look for work. Many women who spent the war years employed in factories, government offices, and part-time defense jobs were encouraged to go back to doing housework. While some were happy to return to the role of wife and mother, others regretted the loss of income and the opportunity for a career.

The fears that Marylanders might have had about their future in the postwar world were quickly set aside as the state began a new period of growth and development. People soon discovered that the years ahead would be among the most prosperous the state had ever experienced. Instead of returning to depression, Maryland's economy improved, as wartime industries began to convert their factories from armaments to automobiles and from gunboats to consumer products. Bethlehem Steel at Sparrows Point stopped building ships for war and began scrapping them instead, to get steel for buildings and bridges. Westinghouse, which had been making torpedoes and weapons, switched to making electrical equipment for industrial use. Western Electric began to make parts for the new televisions, and factories that had made airplanes during the war began making products for the booming housing market.

Local and state governments helped the economy, too. In the four years following the end of World War II, the state's Department of Public Works spent more than $28 million on new projects. Construction of Friendship Airport cost the state $3 million, and $10 million built new schools to serve a growing population. Slum clearance and public housing projects also created jobs for workers in Baltimore and other Maryland cities. Many materials manufactured in Maryland or shipped overseas from Baltimore's port made their way to help rebuild war-torn Europe. The high wages and nearly full employment of the war years continued for the next quarter of a century in Maryland and much of the nation. Confidence in a more prosperous future replaced fear of a postwar depression.

War Again

The optimism of prosperity was soon marred by American participation in another war. In 1950, only five years after the end of World War II, the United States became involved in active warfare in Korea. This Asian nation had been divided into two zones of occupation, American and Russian, when the Japanese were expelled at the end of World War II. After the Americans withdrew their occupation troops from South Korea, North Korean forces crossed the border in an attempt to unite the country under North Korean Communist rule and Chinese forces soon joined the North Koreans. The United States and other countries sent troops, under the aegis of the United Nations, to fight for South Korean independence, which was finally affirmed by an armistice agreement in 1953. The day-to-day impact of this war was small compared to that of World War II, but for families of the more than five hundred Marylanders who died, this was not a minor conflict.

The Baby Boom

One important reason for the post–World War II prosperity was the baby boom. Between 1946 and 1964, the birth rate in the United States rose well above expected levels. Maryland's population had increased 12 percent during the 1940s, from 1,821,244 to 2,343,001. Between 1950 and 1960, however, it grew by 32 percent, and by 1970, increased another 27 percent. The state's population in 1980 stood at 4,216,446, having more than doubled in 40 years.

This population increase set off a buying binge. At first families bought diapers, baby food, and bassinets. Later this generation needed more schools, clothes, and toys. Mass consumer markets developed to provide education and housing and playthings such as hula hoops, Slinkys, Barbie dolls, Silly Putty, and Davy Crockett fur caps. In the late 1940s and 1950s, shopping centers sprang up across the state and the nation to serve a prosperous new generation.

New Marylanders

There was a boom in births in Maryland, but the population of the state increased after 1946 for other reasons as well. The state was a good place to work

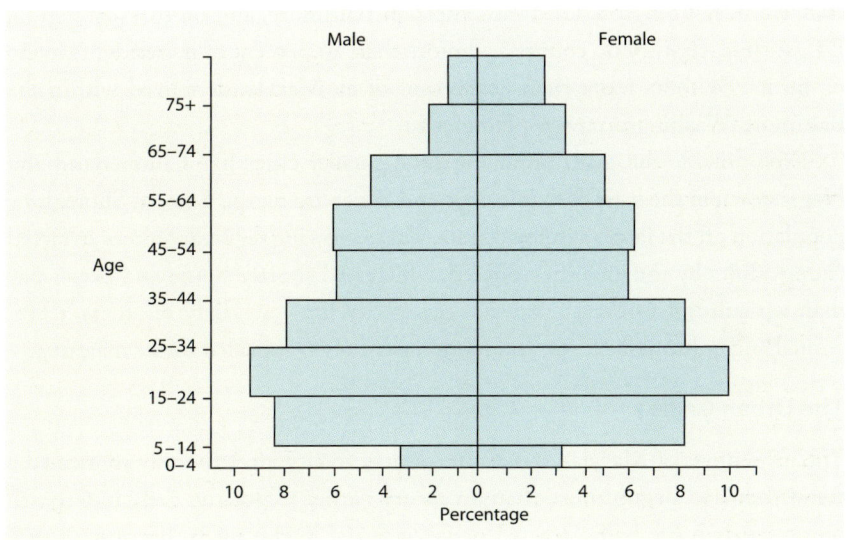

■ Age-Sex Pyramid of the Maryland Population, 1980

Return to Peace and Prosperity

and raise a family. Maryland became the fifth leading state in attracting new residents from other parts of the nation. Most came from nearby Mid-Atlantic states like New York, New Jersey, and Pennsylvania. Others came from the Middle West and the Deep South, seeking an environment that offered economic opportunity, a favorable climate, and good schools.

A small part of the population growth in this period resulted from immigration from abroad. The greatest increase in foreign-born population came after immigration laws were revised in the 1980s, but the cities of Maryland began to experience modest increases even before then. In 1950, there were 85,165 foreign-born residents (4 percent of the total population), and by 1980, the number more than doubled to 185,581 (5 percent). Immigrants still came from Europe, but now greater numbers arrived from Korea, Vietnam, and China in Asia and from El Salvador and Mexico in Latin America. Maryland attracted those with higher levels of education by offering jobs in medicine and the new technologies, while others with less preparation sought manual labor jobs. Although the newcomers placed a strain on schools and increased the demand for public services, they also contributed significantly to Maryland's economy by paying taxes, buying or renting housing, purchasing food and other goods for their families, and providing needed skills and labor.

■ Transition from Rural to Urban to Suburban

Whether native-born or migrant, the residents of Maryland in the 1940s and 1950s followed certain patterns of movement within the state. Movement at first was generally from countryside to city; later, movement was from city to suburb. The greatest rural shift was away from the farms of Western and Southern Maryland toward the large urban corridor that stretched across the center of the state from Wilmington, Delaware, through Baltimore, and on to Washington, DC. At mid-century no county had more than 20 percent of its residents living on farms. By 1980, more than 80 percent of all Marylanders lived within the Baltimore-Washington metropolitan area.

Even outside the main urban corridor, smaller cities like Cumberland and Hagerstown in the west or Cambridge and Salisbury on the Eastern Shore drew population off the farms at a steady rate. These growing regional centers attracted young adults by the jobs they offered, which had shorter hours and better pay than agricultural work. The advantages of city life—a variety of stores, recreational and cultural facilities, and modern schools—appealed to the majority.

The Urban Crisis

The movement of Marylanders from country to city after the war continued a trend that had begun more than a century earlier. Since the early nineteenth century, urban life had attracted new residents. In the 1950s, however, a new change occurred. As the cities grew older, their cores began to decay, and people began to leave the cities for the suburbs, just as earlier they had left the farms for the cities.

Maryland's urban crisis of the postwar period pointed up the economic and racial divisions that still plagued society. As cities grew in the first half of the twentieth century, their problems became more intense. Overcrowded or unsafe housing, uncollected garbage, poor sanitation, rising crime rates, pollution, and steeper tax rates were all unpleasant features of Maryland's larger cities by mid-century, as was true across the country. Those who could afford to moved outward toward the more spacious urban fringe or beyond to the suburbs. Left behind, usually, were the poor and the nonwhite populations. By the 1950s, Baltimore and other Maryland cities had become "two cities," divided by economic and racial barriers.

Early Attempts at Urban Renewal

Large cities across the nation looked for ways to change the trend toward decay. Demolition offered one solution to this urban crisis. Believing that new was always better, Baltimore began tearing down slum housing. This early attempt to solve urban problems by destroying old buildings, however, soon proved to be a failure. New public housing projects quickly developed the same problems of overcrowding and poor sanitation. Worst of all was the loss of the sense of community. Many residents of Maryland's cities became angry when old neighborhoods were torn apart and replaced with concrete expressways and commercial developments.

By the 1960s, the outward flight of middle-class whites had become almost a stampede. In 1962, before passage of federal civil rights and housing laws, Baltimore County was 96.5 percent white, but Baltimore City had the second largest percentage of black residents in any American city, ranking behind Washington, DC. The median income of county families was $7,098, compared to $5,659 in the city. Baltimore also had twenty times more people receiving welfare than did the suburban counties. Yet people in Cumberland and Hagerstown also moved toward the suburbs, indicating that white flight was not the sole motivation. Other factors, such as the availability of home loans, the attraction of new homes with more amenities, and new roads providing convenient access, played a part.

Violence motivated by poverty and racial discrimination brought the urban crisis to the point of explosion in the late 1960s. The governor called up National Guard troops to halt the looting and burning of sections of Baltimore after the 1968 assassination of Martin Luther King Jr. in Memphis, Tennessee. Racial violence also struck the town of Cambridge on the Eastern Shore. Urban crime rates increased, the number of welfare recipients grew, and the conflict between ethnic and racial groups seemed to reach a peak in the early 1970s, at

---

in the inner city

in the inner city
or
like we call it
home
we think a lot about uptown
and the silent nights
and the houses straight as
dead men
and the pastel lights
and we hang on to our no
 place
happy to be alive
and in the inner city
or
like we call it
home

Lucille Clifton, "in the inner city," from *The Collected Poems of Lucille Clifton*. Copyright © 1987 by Lucille Clifton. Reprinted with the permission of The Permissions Company, Inc., on behalf of BOA Editions Ltd., www.boaeditions.org.

the height of the war in Vietnam. The fear of violence led some people to avoid going into the center cities even to shop or attend cultural events. Critics across the nation warned of the death of America's older central cities.

After the Vietnam War ended, the federal government enforced fair housing laws passed to prevent racial discrimination by real estate companies, mortgage bankers, and developers. Now many African Americans who could afford to also abandoned the center cities. By 1980, the number of nonwhites in suburban Baltimore and Baltimore County had risen to 24 percent of the total population. Prince George's and Montgomery Counties, located near Washington, had similar increases in nonwhite residents.

Suburbia

Middle-class whites, and later blacks as well, looked for newer homes and better schools far away from the more crowded centers of the cities. Few had any desire to return to the countryside, but the suburbs and, eventually, whole new towns offered what they considered a better type of urban life. The cities of Baltimore and Washington had peaked in the 1940s, and then, like the rural areas, began to decline steadily. By 1970, Baltimore no longer ranked among the nation's ten largest cities. Too much of its population had fled from the city into the suburban counties of Anne Arundel, Baltimore, and Harford. Similarly, Washington lost residents to nearby Montgomery and Prince George's Counties. Howard County, lying between the two cities, grew the fastest of all, especially after construction of the new town of Columbia.

Those who left the city sought to escape the crowded conditions of urban life and the fear of rising crime and taxes, but they also hoped to find in suburbia more space, privacy, and control over their lives. Parents wanted good schools, clean streets, back yards, and neighbors with values similar to their own. Some critics considered the suburbs dull and monotonous places, but the thousands who moved there saw them as safe havens.

Washington Suburbs

The Maryland suburbs of Washington, DC, were among the fastest growing areas of the state after 1945. Returning war veterans and new government workers flocked to the attractive countryside of Montgomery and Prince George's Counties. Rockville, Wheaton, College Park, Bladensburg, and other communities at first developed as "bedroom suburbs."

By the 1950s, business, government, and industry followed the population shift to the suburbs. Silver Spring was the site of the state's first shopping center. In the 1950s, the federal government spread into suburban Maryland with the National Institutes of Health in Bethesda, the Atomic Energy Commission headquarters in Germantown, and the Bureau of Standards in Gaithersburg. Private corporations like IBM, Comsat, Control Data, Bechtel, Kodak, and Xerox all established new offices and factories in Rockville along Route 270. By the 1980s, these Maryland suburbs had become a key part of Washington's and the state's growth.

The rapid growth of Maryland's suburbs resulted also from their proximity to Baltimore and Washington. With completion of the beltways around both cities in the 1960s, industries, businesses, and consumers moved to suburban counties. Transportation in the suburbs was easy for residents with automobiles, and land prices and taxes were lower than in the cities. The federal government encouraged the move by providing money for new housing through the GI Bill, passed to help veterans get re-established after the war, and by constructing more highways. Later, new public transit systems made movement between city and suburb even easier. Washington launched its Metro in 1976 and Baltimore's Metro line followed in 1983.

To serve the growing population of suburban consumers, the shopping center appeared as a new phenomenon on the American scene. The Hecht Company opened its first suburban store in 1946 in Silver Spring, and one year later Edmundson Village opened in Baltimore with a variety of shops and ample parking to serve its customers. Covered malls, of which Harundale Mall in Anne Arundel County was the first in Maryland in 1958, became both a social and a shopping center.

New Towns

The shift of population also led to the creation of entirely new urban centers. Americans had always been fascinated with new town planning, and Maryland was one of the leading states in this type of urban experimentation.

During the New Deal of the 1930s, President Roosevelt's administration tried to create an environment that blended together the best of city and country life in Greenbelt, in Prince George's County. In 1960, the Levitt Company opened Bowie, a residential community for middle- and working-class families with similar objectives. By 1968, Bowie boasted nearly 33,000 residents, mainly commuters to nearby Washington and Annapolis.

Columbia, in Howard County, took shape as a more complete model town. Started by developer James W. Rouse, Columbia opened in the mid-1960s and rapidly grew to 57,000 residents by 1980. This new town, which received national attention, consisted of a carefully planned mixture of village clusters, shopping centers, industrial sites, and recreational and open space. Racial mixing was more successful than economic mixing; about 20 percent of Columbia's population was nonwhite by the 1980s and the vast majority, both black and white, was middle class. By design, all its facilities were open to all its residents.

By the 1970s, the interest in finding better ways of urban living led to a revival of some of Maryland's older towns. Small towns began to discover a new vitality that emphasized their historic past and their unique character. Towns on the Eastern Shore, like Easton, St. Michaels, and Salisbury, gradually developed new life as centers for tourism and recreation as new highways made long-distance commuting easier. Cities of central and Western Maryland, like Fred-

> ### James Rouse: Urban Pioneer
>
> James W. Rouse (1914–1996), a native of Easton and a graduate of the University of Maryland Law School, became a key figure in the state's urban growth. He built his first shopping center, Talbottown, in Easton in 1957. The following year, his company created Harundale Mall, the first enclosed shopping mall in Maryland. Rouse was a leader in bringing together private businessmen and public officials in new projects like Baltimore's Charles Center. Both the Village of Cross Keys and his Harborplace project in downtown Baltimore won praise from city planners and the general public. Rouse's new town of Columbia in Howard County was one of the largest and most talked about experiments in community planning in the twentieth century.
>
> Rouse combined social activism with his business ventures. His urban malls were designed to draw people of all incomes and racial backgrounds to the central city. His residential projects encouraged racial integration in pleasant surroundings. A man of imagination and business success, Rouse left the company he established in 1979 to head the Enterprise Foundation, a nonprofit organization founded to raise funds to house the urban poor.

erick, began to attract residents who found the larger suburbs monotonous, crowded, or too expensive. Industries and businesses also found Maryland's smaller towns and cities attractive.

■ The Urban Renaissance

Despite the fact that many critics predicted the death of America's large cities, a new effort sought to revive them. The failures of urban renewal and slum clearance in the 1950s taught planners, politicians, and citizens valuable lessons. By the end of the decade, business and political leaders in cities across the state joined forces. They worked to revive the downtown core and to renew and renovate urban residential housing. Across the nation, beginning in the 1950s, residents, usually working-class families, began to protest the urban renewal efforts that were tearing down their neighborhoods.

Baltimore

In 1955, a group of local businessmen formed the Greater Baltimore Committee under the leadership of men like James Rouse. The committee collected financial resources, hired an urban planner, and began to define its objectives. The effort first sought to restore Baltimore's port to a prominent place in the nation's economy. Second, they planned to improve the area's transportation infrastructure that served the port and the city. Third, they hoped to construct a new civic center. And lastly, they called for a more comprehensive plan for urban renewal.

The construction of Charles Center in the heart of the business district symbolized the new outlook. Planned by the Greater Baltimore Committee in 1958 and designed by the internationally known architect Mies van der Rohe, this complex of high-rise offices, apartments, and stores reflected Baltimore's self-confidence and expectations for renewed growth. The carefully designed plazas and elevated walkways once again made the center of the city an interesting and pleasant place to work and shop. At the same time that Charles Center was being built, a cluster of state office buildings was constructed on North Howard Street. Together these two major projects illustrated the value of cooperation between private and public sectors.

In 1963, Mayor Theodore McKeldin announced an even larger plan to revitalize Baltimore's inner harbor. Once again private capital and public planning combined to renew 240 acres around the harbor at a cost of $200 million. Even the federal government joined in by granting the city $19 million in 1964 to help start the inner harbor redevelopment. When Harborplace opened in 1981, it attracted 18 million visitors in the first year. In the 1980s, the Inner Harbor of Baltimore was one of the most attractive city centers in the country. It contained the National Aquarium, a convention center, and several hotels, as well as older attractions, like the Maryland Science Center and the battleship *Constellation*.

The urban renaissance had an equally important consequence for Baltimore's residential neighborhoods. The key to progress again proved to be close cooperation between private and public interests. Progress was slow during the 1950s, but improved after creation of a Department of Housing in 1968. Robert D. Embry Jr., the first commissioner of this new city department, became a key figure in the improvement of the city's housing.

■ Baltimore celebrated its first City Fair at Charles Center in 1970. After the turmoil of the late 1960s, the fair provided a showcase for the city's diverse neighborhoods and ethnic groups in the rebuilt downtown center. By 1973, the fair had moved to the Inner Harbor area, where it remained through the 1980s. Courtesy of the Maryland Historical Society, Large Posters, folder 2.

■ Baltimore's highly successful urban renaissance during the 1980s featured the revitalized Inner Harbor where new shops, eateries, and tourist attractions drew crowds. Private collection.

The Urban Renaissance

■ As mayor of Baltimore, William Donald Schaefer worked for cooperation between the government and the private sector to benefit the city. Schaefer served as the city's mayor from 1971 to 1987, governor of Maryland from 1987 to 1995, and state comptroller from 1995 to 2007. Collection of the Maryland State Archives, MSA SC 4383-285-1-0002.

Luckily, much of Baltimore's older housing, particularly its unique row houses, had not been destroyed by earlier urban renewal projects. In 1973, Baltimore became one of the first cities in the nation to start an urban homesteading program. The city government acquired houses from delinquent taxpayers and sold them to the public for $1. By 1980, more than five hundred houses had been reclaimed under this program. Other government-supported programs helped restore nineteenth-century neighborhoods and funded new housing projects.

By the 1980s, Baltimore, Maryland's largest urban center, had gained a reputation as a very livable city. Urban planners from all over the country visited Baltimore, not only to view the spectacular Inner Harbor, but, more importantly, to observe how neighborhood life had been preserved. The involvement of citizens through strong community organizations was often emphasized as a key factor. Likewise, the effective leadership of Mayors Theodore McKeldin, Thomas D'Alesandro III, and William Donald Schaefer was recognized. Baltimore still suffered serious difficulties with unemployment, poverty, racial conflict, urban crime, and pollution, but it had achieved a new sense of pride and confidence in progress.

Across the State

Although Baltimore received the most national attention for its renewal efforts, many of Maryland's cities underwent planned changes. Some, like Annapolis, Easton, and Frederick, emphasized preservation of historic buildings. Others, like Cumberland and Cambridge, turned to new construction. As in Baltimore, these efforts usually combined public and private resources and interests.

As the capital of Maryland since 1695, Annapolis had a rich heritage to preserve. Nevertheless, local groups that hoped to restore the historic district along the city's waterfront and around the State House faced strong opposition. Private developers saw greater profits in building new, efficient buildings than in restoring the old. Despite the opposition, city voters approved a historic district ordinance that protected existing buildings and regulated new construction. At the same time, the city moved ahead with plans for urban renewal in the largely African American neighborhood west of the historic district, accompanied by construction of new office buildings and parking garages. By the late 1970s, Annapolis had protected and restored much of its historic core and had become a favorite stop for tourists. But gentrification had pushed out longtime residents, many of whom ended up in public housing projects, and local businesses, in favor of wealthier newcomers and stores catering to tourists.

In Easton similar conflicts occurred between blacks and whites and between those who wanted to give Easton a "colonial" look to attract tourists and those who wanted to build in more contemporary styles. As in many places, the renewal process displaced working-class and African American residents. Through careful zoning laws Easton succeeded in encouraging many new buildings constructed in a style that matched that of the past and did become a popular tourist destination. Cambridge was another Maryland city that fought urban decline with planned restoration. Cambridge rebuilt sections of its downtown shopping area and constructed new luxury townhouses along its waterfront in order to achieve what local planners called the "Bay Country look."

In the western part of the state, Cumberland experienced much of the same conflict over urban renewal that other Maryland cities faced. Through the 1950s and early 1960s, Cumberland's population declined as unemployment increased. In 1973, under the direction of the city's Urban Renewal Agency, local and federal governments joined resources to restore 83 acres in the downtown area, spending $21 million to tear down or restore old buildings and to construct new ones. The urban renaissance in Frederick began in 1973, after the election of Ronald N. Young as mayor. By combining historic preservation of buildings, like the Roger Brooke Taney House and the Barbara Fritchie House, with new construction, Frederick revived its downtown area. A new county courthouse in the center of the city and an attractive park along Carroll Creek kept businesses and residents from relocating to the suburbs.

■ In an area reserved for pedestrians in downtown Cumberland, this outdoor market sold vegetables and other produce. Courtesy of the Maryland Office of Tourism.

■ The old and the new exist side by side in Cambridge. Traditional workboats are tied up in view of new residences along the city's waterfront. Photo by Jill Jasuta.

The Urban Renaissance

The Technological Revolutions

Wherever Marylanders lived in the second half of the twentieth century, they saw their world grow smaller and their lifestyles become more alike. Rapid changes in transportation and communications reduced the separations and differences that had made some parts of the state so unique. Before World War II, watermen of the Chesapeake Bay had little connection with farmers near the Appalachian Mountains. But bridges, highways, television, and communications networks now brought them closer together.

The Transportation Revolution

For years Marylanders had argued the pros and cons of building a bridge across the Chesapeake Bay. Opponents cited the immense cost of such a project, fear for the Bay's ecological balance, and threats to the fishing industry. Finally, after Governor William Preston Lane Jr. made the bridge a reality by introducing a state sales tax of 2¢ for every dollar spent by consumers, construction began on October 1, 1949. The spectacular Chesapeake Bay Bridge opened with a ribbon-cutting ceremony on July 30, 1952. Former Governor Lane and Governor Theodore McKeldin led ten thousand celebrants in song as the band played "Maryland, My Maryland." At a cost of $112 million, the bridge was one of the largest public works projects ever undertaken in Maryland up to that time. Almost two million travelers passed over the bridge in its first year of use. In 1973, the state had to open a second, parallel span to handle the volume of traffic.

Political leaders wave to boaters below at the opening of the William Preston Lane Memorial Bridge (the Chesapeake Bay Bridge) in 1952. Former governor William Preston Lane Jr., Governor Theodore R. McKeldin, Delaware Governor Elbert N. Carvel, and Baltimore Mayor Thomas D'Alesandro Jr. (with Lane closest to the camera). Permission from *The Baltimore Sun*.

With their annual traffic surpassing ten million travelers by 1982, the bridges over the Bay had a tremendous impact on Maryland's Eastern Shore. A boom in real estate, retail sales, land development, and tourism changed the traditionally rural lifestyle of the region. In addition to the hundreds of thousands of

Ocean City

The Chesapeake Bay Bridge brought tremendous changes to Maryland's Eastern Shore. Ocean City, which had been a small town before World War II, blossomed into the state's major resort by the 1960s. Even fierce Atlantic hurricanes like the one in 1962 did not stop the rapid development of Fenwick Island, where Ocean City is located. Each year tourists from Maryland and many other states spend millions of dollars enjoying the beaches and pleasures of Ocean City.

The massive development has also had a downside as building along the shoreline destroyed the dunes that provided a natural protection from storms for the barrier island and resulted in widespread pollution of the ocean and bays. Resort sprawl has displaced the habitat of native animals and birds, especially as wetlands have been filled in to make space for homes, hotels, stores, and other businesses. Developers and environmental advocates often disagree over policy issues that affect Ocean City and the coastal area.

■ Generations of Maryland children have enjoyed this merry-go-round, installed at Trimper's Rides in Ocean City at the turn of the century. Collection of John Conley.

■ Postwar prosperity, the widespread purchase of cars, and the ease of driving to the beach resulted in rapid development of Ocean City and nearby beach resorts. Hotels and homes were built where wetlands and dunes stood formerly. Courtesy of the Town of Ocean City, Tourism Department.

The Technological Revolutions

weekend and holiday visitors to the beaches, new permanent residents came to build homes along the shore. Towns like Salisbury and Cambridge saw modest growth, while Ocean City grew more like a boomtown.

Similarly, a new network of highways drew Maryland's western and central cities closer together. Beginning with the Baltimore–Washington Parkway, which opened in 1952, and continuing for the next thirty years, state and federal governments built an interstate road system that linked all parts of the region. Beltways around Baltimore and Washington and local expressways helped commuters travel ever-greater distances from home to work with relative ease. Asphalt ribbons of highways and steel beams of bridges tied Maryland's communities more closely together. No part of the state was more than a few hours away from any other part by automobile. By 1979, Maryland had more than 26,000 miles of highway.

The dependence on highways and the automobile meant that mass public transportation tended to decline. Buses replaced streetcars and train stations fell into a state of decay. By 1980, about 1.2 million Marylanders commuted to work by car, but only 170,000 used public transportation. Maryland, like the rest of the nation, became a society on wheels, despite unhealthy and unpleasant side effects like air pollution and traffic congestion.

Air travel proved more popular and successful than efforts to encourage mass transit. In 1972, the state purchased Friendship Airport from the city of

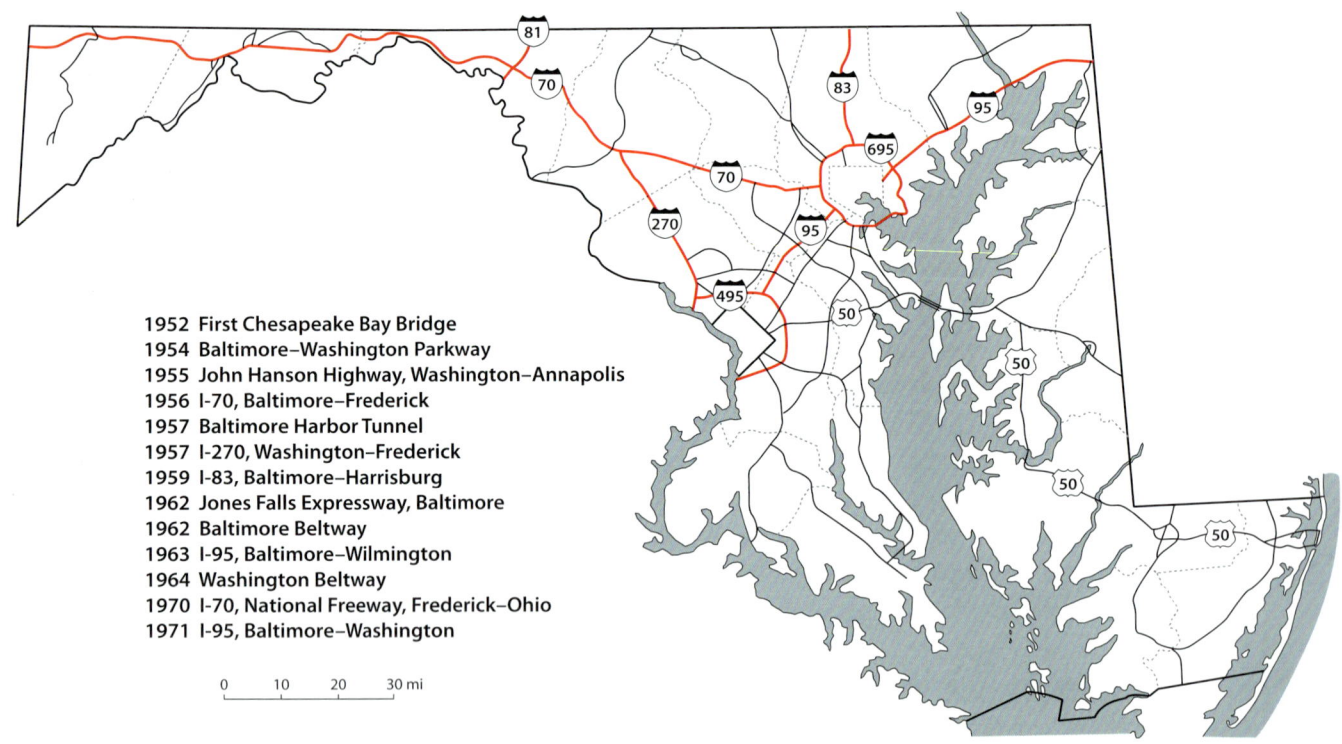

■ State Primary Highway System, 1978

1952 First Chesapeake Bay Bridge
1954 Baltimore–Washington Parkway
1955 John Hanson Highway, Washington–Annapolis
1956 I-70, Baltimore–Frederick
1957 Baltimore Harbor Tunnel
1957 I-270, Washington–Frederick
1959 I-83, Baltimore–Harrisburg
1962 Jones Falls Expressway, Baltimore
1962 Baltimore Beltway
1963 I-95, Baltimore–Wilmington
1964 Washington Beltway
1970 I-70, National Freeway, Frederick–Ohio
1971 I-95, Baltimore–Washington

Baltimore for $36 million, renamed it Baltimore/Washington International Airport, undertook a program of expansion, and renamed it again in 2005 BWI Thurgood Marshall Airport. Smaller regional airports, like the Hagerstown Municipal Airport and the Wicomico County Airport at Salisbury, served other areas of the state. Along with the rest of the nation, Marylanders accepted air travel as a normal part of their business and personal worlds.

The Information Revolution and the Loss of Isolation

New communications networks, like transportation systems, drew the people of Maryland closer together. By 1980, Marylanders shared information in 14 daily newspapers, 80 weekly papers, 10 television stations, and 50 AM and 50 FM radio stations. Newspapers and television stations in the District of Columbia supplemented these communications media. Multiple-channel cable television systems and new technologies in telephone and computer communications promised to expand the available information facilities even more. Metropolitan Baltimore and the Washington, DC, area constitute the state's two major media markets.

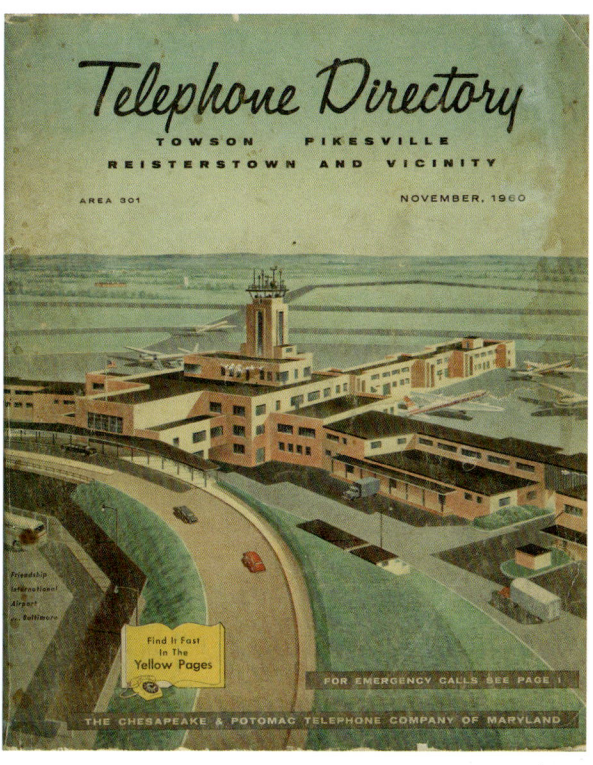

■ The City of Baltimore's Friendship International Airport was dedicated in 1950 by President Harry S. Truman. The C&P Telephone Company of Maryland recognized the airport's growth and importance to the regional economy when it featured Friendship on area phone books in 1960. The state purchased Friendship in 1972 and renamed it the Baltimore-Washington International Airport. In 2005, the facility once again received a new name to honor Supreme Court Justice Thurgood Marshall, a Baltimore native. Courtesy of DexYP, Verizon, and the Enoch Pratt Free Library.

By 1980, few homes in any part of the state escaped the influence of the revolution in communications. Coal miners' families in Western Maryland and watermen's families on Smith Island could receive the same news and watch the same television network entertainment shows. The powerful forces of the new information technologies shaped fashions, taste in entertainment, political opinions, and general lifestyles in rural Maryland, small towns, suburbs, and large cities alike.

The Modernization of Farm Life

The impact of the new technology in Maryland could also be seen in the farmer's way of life. At the end of World War II, it was still possible to find a few farmers in rural Maryland living in homes without electricity and plowing their fields with teams of oxen. By 1954, the vast majority of farms had electricity and tractors, and approximately two-thirds had telephones and televisions. Like watermen and miners, farmers became less isolated as they shared in the culture of the urban and suburban society.

Once the technological revolution began, change came rapidly. Although the number of farms in Maryland declined by about half between 1950 and 1970, productivity increased greatly. Farmers became more like businessmen, depending heavily on price supports from the federal government and joining organizations like the Farm Bureau to improve their economic condition. Besides using new machinery, farmers used more artificial fertilizers, insect controls, hybrid seeds, and selective breeding. At the time, most people did not understand that the chemicals in the pesticides and artificial fertilizers harmed the natural environment and human health nor did they understand that displacing natural seeds, which could reproduce themselves, with hybrids would diminish the varieties of plants available and the ability of farmers to save their own seeds for the next year's planting.

Maryland's agricultural production was a mixture of the old and the new. Tobacco farmers still brought their crops to auction at Hughesville, Waldorf, or Upper Marlboro, as their ancestors had done. Corn, wheat, and barley remained the typical field crops of central Maryland. Farmers tended livestock as well; dairying made up 70 percent of the total farm production for Frederick County, for example. Eastern Shore truck farming supplied nearly 80 percent of Maryland's vegetable crop in 1978. The production of broiler chickens added a new element to the state's agricultural mix. By 1978, Maryland produced more than 900 million pounds of chickens, making it the sixth largest producer in the nation.

■ Maryland's New Economy

In the post–World War II years, Maryland's growth and change were clearest in its economy and in the way its people made a living. Not only did farming become less important, but there was also a gradual shift away from industry and other blue-collar jobs and toward a greater dependence on jobs in services, government bureaucracy, and new technology.

The Port of Baltimore

When the United States passed the Marshall Plan in 1948 to help rebuild Europe after the war, millions of tons of materials passed through Baltimore. The Korean War of the early 1950s also resulted in much activity for Maryland's busy port. Baltimore built an international trade that sent coal to Japan, grain to India, and steel and fertilizer to Brazil. In return, Baltimore received iron ore from Venezuela, copper from Chile, and textiles from the Far East. By 1966, studies showed that port activities contributed more than $1.5 billion to Maryland's economy.

Every ship that passed into and out of Baltimore needed many services. Pilots, who guided vessels through the channel; radio and radar operators; tugboat captains; and longshoremen, who loaded and unloaded cargo, were directly involved. Port operations provided work for clerks, customs and immigration officials, ship cleaners and repairers, and doctors, who quarantined vessels that

■ Mayor William Donald Schaefer commissioned the *Pride of Baltimore*, a replica of the Baltimore clippers that had played such an important role in the War of 1812. Built using the techniques and materials of the time, this ship visited ports around the world until it capsized and sank in high winds in 1986. A new ship, the *Pride of Baltimore II*, launched in 1988, continues the mission of representing Baltimore in near and distant places. Courtesy of Creative Commons, Pride101981.jpg.

carried disease. The port also needed inspectors, truck drivers, warehouse managers, bankers, and foreign-language interpreters. The port was not only a major economic engine for Maryland, but in 1980, it was one of the six largest ports in the United States.

The Maryland Port Authority, with responsibility for coordinating state, city, and private business interests to make the port's operations more efficient, controlled the activities of this busy center. In 1977, the authority opened the World Trade Center to house the services of international businesses, bankers, and government officials. The port activity is another important example of the way Maryland's economy depends on the relationship between public and private interests.

To promote trade and extend the reputation of Baltimore and its port, the city built the *Pride of Baltimore*, an authentic reproduction of a clipper ship and a symbol of Maryland's close connection to the sea. This ship sank in a sudden squall in 1986, with the tragic loss of its captain and three crew members. Several years later, a new ship, the *Pride of Baltimore II*, took over the job of ambassador for the city and port.

Blue-Collar Workers

At the end of World War II, when Maryland industries changed back to peacetime production, blue-collar workers found the most jobs in the metal and food industries. In the Baltimore area large corporations like Bethlehem Steel, Martin-Marietta Aircraft, and Kennecott Refining built ships and made railroad rails, metal barrels, petroleum products, parts for airplanes, and steel for buildings or bridges. Three out of every four blue-collar workers in the state worked in factories in the Baltimore metropolitan area.

Elsewhere men and women earned a living by canning food in Cambridge, making men's clothing in Salisbury, or producing explosives in Elkton. In Western Maryland blue-collar workers found jobs in Cumberland at the Kelly-Springfield Tire Company, in Allegany County at the Westvaco paper mills, or in Hagerstown making Mack trucks. Many of these industries in both Baltimore and elsewhere were located in industrial parks outside the cities. Industries followed their workers to the suburbs after the war, attracted by the lower cost of suburban land.

Watermen and Miners

Maryland's watermen form a more distinctive element of its population than its farmers and industrial workers. Although urban growth and industrial pollution took a heavy toll on the Bay's production, there were still 17,504 licensed watermen and waterwomen in Maryland in 1978. Hardshells—oysters, clams, and crabs—were the most important harvest from the Bay. Hardy Marylanders

■ Watermen harvesting clams from the bottom of the Chesapeake Bay. The seafood and recreational resources of the Bay provide employment for many Marylanders. Courtesy of the Office of Maryland Tourism.

gathered more than 2 million bushels of oysters each year and millions of dollars worth of other seafood. The Chesapeake Bay was the world's largest producer of the Atlantic blue crab.

Rivalry between Maryland and Virginia for Chesapeake seafood continued in the years after World War II. A new agreement, drawn up in 1958, finally helped to reduce conflict and divide the oyster catch between the two states. Although in the late twentieth century the annual catch of oysters, crabs, and other seafood was only a fraction of what it had been earlier in the century, it still contributed nearly $20 million a year to Maryland's economy.

Mining, one of the state's oldest industries, continued to be important in this period, as workers mined and quarried various stone, sand, gravel, and limestone deposits. Bituminous coal, soft coal that yields pitch or tar when it burns, continued to be one of the state's most valuable natural resources, mined in five major coal basins lying in Garrett and Allegany Counties, the most important being George's Creek Basin. A few large coal companies that supplied fuel to urban utility companies dominated modern coal mining. In 1973, the international oil embargo highlighted the importance of America's coal resources to the national economy and encouraged new efforts to improve Baltimore's role as a coal-exporting port. But, while coal provides an important, domestically produced fuel, it also creates health problems for the miners and has serious environmental consequences, including poisoned water and air pollution. These problems became better recognized, although not solved, during the postwar years.

White-Collar and Service Workers

Although many GIs returning home in the 1940s went to work in Maryland factories, others found jobs in nonmanufacturing occupations. Maryland reflected the national trend as its economy grew less dependent on heavy manufacturing and more dependent on services and white-collar work. By 1950, one out of every two wage earners held a nonmanufacturing job, and in 1980, the proportion rose closer to two out of every three.

Several factors accounted for this change in the state's economy. The baby boom between 1946 and 1964 created huge demands for all kinds of new services, from medical care to education. Because this was a time of prosperity, the economy needed many workers to serve the vast consumer market. Clerks, salespersons, appliance repairmen, insurance and real estate agents, restaurant servers, car dealers, and many others helped satisfy the demand for more consumer goods and services. While the service economy provided new kinds of work and a decent living for many, its less skilled jobs often paid lower salaries than the old industrial jobs had, making it difficult for some full-time workers to provide for their families, especially on a single income.

Maryland's economy also changed as more women entered the labor market beginning in the 1960s. There was a trend toward greater independence and

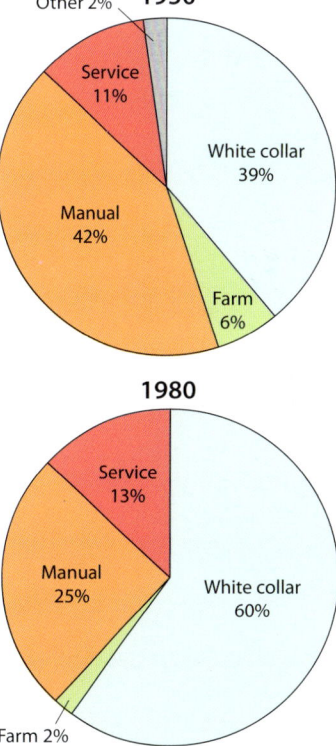

■ Types of Employment in Maryland as a Percentage of the Total Labor Force, 1950 and 1980

equality for women throughout the nation, and the numbers of women employed outside the home increased dramatically. After 1960, the percentage of women in the workforce grew three times faster than the rate of increase for men. Most of these women worked in service or nonmanufacturing occupations. As more women than ever before graduated from Maryland's universities and colleges, the numbers of women in medicine, law, and business also increased rapidly.

Government at all levels—local, state, and federal—constituted one of the largest employers in the postwar decades, with the number of jobs multiplying several times over. The growth of government services that began during President Roosevelt's New Deal in the 1930s continued on a large scale, with support from both Republicans and Democrats. After accepting responsibility for the health, welfare, and security of all citizens, the government had to increase the size of its bureaucracy to meet those commitments.

Because Maryland bordered the nation's capital, it benefited more than most states from the expansion in federal jobs. The large Social Security complex in Baltimore County and the many military bases in the state were major employers of Maryland white-collar workers, and many residents of Prince George's, Montgomery, and Howard Counties worked in federal offices in Washington, DC. By 1980, nearly 1 out of every 4 Maryland wage earners held a government job. The federal government employed 145,000, the state 80,000, and local governments another 150,000. The largest private employer, Bethlehem Steel, had about 40,000 workers.

The New Technology and a New Middle Class

Another change in Maryland's economy after 1945 came about as the result of new technology. When the war ended, few Marylanders were familiar with either televisions or computers. Children born in the 1970s and 1980s, however, found it hard to imagine life without these and other technological "necessities." Children of the 1980s could awaken to stereo music from their digital clock radio, eat a breakfast heated in a microwave oven, and rush off to a school where learning was assisted by slide projectors, video cassettes, electronic calculators and, soon, computers. Their parents withdrew money from electronic banktellers, used plastic credit cards to buy groceries in stores with automatic price scanners, and conducted business with word processors and computers. The older Industrial Revolution had been replaced by a newer revolution in technology and information.

These revolutionary changes meant new ways of earning a living. Many people who had been employed in older types of manufacturing had to retrain in order to take jobs in new companies requiring new skills. Between 1970 and 1975, for example, more than forty thousand jobs disappeared from the manufacturing sector of the state's economy. At the same time, new jobs were created in other areas.

The most impressive concentration of new industries occurred along I-270 near Rockville and Gaithersburg in Montgomery County. Nicknamed "Satellite Alley," this area between Washington and Frederick became the home of telecommunications, electronic, biomedical, and genetic engineering companies. Comsat, IBM, Hewlett-Packard, General Electric, American Satellite, and Litton Bionetics all had offices and laboratories there. The National Institutes of Health, the Department of Energy, and the National Bureau of Standards were also located in this area, where they could draw on the knowledge of many research firms. The Goddard Space Flight Center of the National Aeronautics and Space Administration in Greenbelt, the Johns Hopkins Applied Physics Laboratory near Columbia, and several army and navy research centers helped to make Maryland one of the leading states in the new technological economy.

For most Marylanders the changes in the economy meant a higher standard of living. As the number of white-collar and government workers increased, observers pointed to the rise of a new middle class. The typical Maryland family of the second half of the twentieth century was better educated, earned higher wages, and spent more on consumer and luxury goods than the previous generations. The average income for families steadily rose, reaching $26,521 by the 1980 census. This was more than double what it had been only a dozen years earlier. In per capita income, Maryland ranked thirteenth in the nation and its standard of living placed it among the country's best.

■ Postwar Politics

Maryland's politics reflected the changes in the nation as much as did its economic growth. The decline in power of the old political bosses, the rise of a new middle-class bureaucracy, and the tremendous growth of both government spending and services represent a part of Maryland's history after 1945. The unreasonable fear of Communism, the conflict over civil rights, and the spread of corruption that plagued the nation also could be found in Maryland.

The Politics of Growth

The first major change came after voters elected William Preston Lane Jr. as governor in 1946. With the war over, Lane wanted to turn the state's attention to the need for better public services. The state needed new schools to serve the baby boom's children. New highways and bridges had to be built to connect different parts of the state. The state's sick and poor needed better health care and welfare programs. This demand for more government services continued the trend started before the war by Roosevelt's New Deal and, some would say, reached back to the changes championed by early twentieth-century progressives.

The problem Governor Lane faced, however, was that more services cost more money. A bridge across the Bay, new state mental hospitals, higher salaries for teachers, and 1,100 miles of new highways were all expensive. Maryland's budget increased from $60 million to more than $200 million during Lane's administration. To pay for the new programs and facilities, Lane persuaded the General Assembly to pass a 2 percent sales tax in 1947. Unfortunately for Governor Lane, this tax also cost him reelection in 1950. Although the public wanted more services, it did not want to pay for them.

McCarthyism in Maryland

Maryland shared in the anxieties of the Cold War between the United States and the Soviet Union. The late 1940s and early 1950s were a time of fear in both the state and the nation as Americans felt threatened by the spread of Communism. Some people claimed that American government officials had sold out to the Communists at the end of World War II by allowing Russia to occupy parts of Europe and Asia. The success of Communists led by Mao Tse-tung (Mao Zedong) in China and the war in Korea seemed to some proof that Communists wanted to expand to all parts of the world. In Washington, Senator Joseph McCarthy of Wisconsin led a movement that he claimed intended to rid the government of subversives, or people who worked to overthrow the US government and bring the country under Communist domination. McCarthy used scare tactics to intimidate, and unfairly and inaccurately accused people of being Communists. Because McCarthy seemed more interested in gaining power and recognition for himself than in finding the truth about the people he accused, "McCarthyism" became a term used to refer to the practice of depriving people of their rights through false accusation.

In Maryland the fear of Communism was particularly strong. Although there were few Communists in the state, Maryland passed the infamous Ober Law in 1949 requiring public officials and teachers to take an oath swearing their loyalty to the United States. Even the Boy Scouts called for an investigation to make sure there were no subversives in their organization.

Maryland also had a particular interest in anti-Communist activities because several of its residents played major roles in national events. In 1948, writer and editor Whittaker Chambers accused Alger Hiss, a former high-ranking official in the State Department, of being a Communist; both men lived in Maryland. The whole nation closely followed the dramatic trial that convicted Hiss of perjury for making misleading statements about stolen documents and his relationship to Chambers.

In 1950, Joseph McCarthy accused another Marylander, Owen Lattimore, who taught at Johns Hopkins University's Walter Hines Page School of International Relations, of being a Communist. When Maryland Senator Millard Tydings conducted an investigation that concluded McCarthy was a fraud, Marylanders were shocked. In that year's fall election, McCarthy campaigned actively against the reelection of Tydings, using a doctored photograph that linked Tydings with a Communist party leader; voters sided with McCarthy by voting Tydings out of office. The fear of subversives had become a powerful force in Maryland politics.

By the mid-1950s, the anti-Communist hysteria faded. The public and politicians alike began to realize that there was more to fear from ignoring people's civil liberties than there was to fear from Communism in America. A truce in Korea, the steady leadership of President Dwight D. Eisenhower at the national level, and capable government at the state level helped restore people's confidence.

The Politics of Stability

In the 1950 election, Maryland voters chose Theodore R. McKeldin as governor. Although Maryland was usually a Democratic state, voters switched to the Republican McKeldin because they opposed any further increases in taxes. But the new governor continued many of the programs started by Governor Lane and increased government spending and services even more. McKeldin's administration built Patuxent Institution and Clifton T. Perkins State Hospital in Jessup and the Western Mayland State Hospital near Hagerstown. Spending for education, including a new campus for Coppin State College, increased. New state office buildings were constructed in Baltimore and Annapolis, and the state spent $130 million to complete the Harbor Tunnel Expressway System. However, the Republican administrations of Governor McKeldin and President Dwight D. Eisenhower shared a similar commitment in the 1950s to the concept that governments held responsibility for the security and wellbeing of their citizens.

In 1958, Maryland voters returned to tradition by electing a Democrat as governor again. Two years later, the nation followed by electing John F. Kennedy president. Voters selected J. Millard Tawes from the Eastern Shore's Somerset County as the state's new governor. As the long-time comptroller of the Treasury, Tawes was experienced in state politics. He continued the expansion of government by adding departments, like the Department of Economic Devel-

Theodore R. McKeldin: Popular Republican

Theodore Roosevelt McKeldin was an unusual Maryland Republican in that he won election twice as the mayor of Baltimore, in 1943 and 1963, and he served two terms as governor of Maryland, from 1951 to 1959.

The son of an Irish immigrant father and a German American mother, the Baltimore-born McKeldin was a master of popular politics. A moving orator and a humanitarian, he won the support of many workers, blacks, and liberals who normally voted Democratic. He benefited from splits within the Democratic Party, and on occasion he received help from some of that party's leaders.

Like President Dwight Eisenhower, McKeldin was a liberal Republican. He supported a program to improve the state highway system and encouraged the creation of the Maryland Port Authority to improve the state's economy. He worked with black leaders like Lillie May Carroll Jackson to implement civil rights programs. In 1952, McKeldin, the only Republican governor south of the Mason-Dixon line, gave the speech nominating Dwight Eisenhower for president at the Republican National Convention in San Francisco.

opment, and a Regional Planning Council to the state government. He encouraged the expansion of the state's education system and promoted new industry and business. During the Tawes administration Maryland phased out of existence the state's final slot machines.

Tawes was not an activist leader, but some of his policies were controversial nevertheless. For example, he initiated reform that brought legislative reapportionment, or the redistribution of representatives among equal numbers of voters. This reapportionment brought voting power more in line with the growth of cities and suburbs, at the expense of rural areas.

In response to a federal court of appeals decision, Maryland became one of the first states south of the Mason-Dixon line to pass a Public Accommodation Law requiring equal treatment for people of all races in public places. Governor Tawes also took the lead in attacking economic problems by inviting governors from eleven states to come to Annapolis for the Conference of Appalachian Governors. On the whole, the administrations of both Theodore McKeldin and Millard Tawes provided effective leadership through the growth years between 1951 and 1967.

The Rise of Spiro Agnew and the Politics of Corruption

One of the best-known names in all of Maryland politics in the second half of the twentieth century was that of Spiro Agnew, the product of the new middle-class, suburban America. After graduating from the University of Baltimore Law School, Agnew eventually set up a modest law practice in suburban Towson, the county seat of Baltimore County. His rise in politics was casual and undistinguished, as he moved from president of a junior high school PTA to a seat on the county zoning appeals board. Agnew won the race for Baltimore County executive in 1962 because no other Republican would agree to run and because the Democrats, who usually controlled the county, were split.

Agnew's election as governor in 1966 was again a case of being at the right place at the right time. Running on a campaign that called for honest government, he defeated the racially conservative Democratic candidate, George P. Mahoney, who ran on the slogan "Your home is your castle—defend it." Everyone knew he meant that blacks should not be encouraged or permitted to move into the all-white suburbs of Baltimore and Washington. Because his racist views drove away liberal Democrats, Mahoney lost the 1966 election to Agnew by a vote of 455,318 to 373,543.

Republicans chose Agnew to run for vice president on the ticket with Richard Nixon in 1968 in part because he was a Republican governor of a normally Democratic state and had as governor pushed back against civil rights activists—part of Nixon's southern strategy. Nixon and Agnew won the election and the first four years of Agnew's vice presidency went well. He acquired a reputation as a sharp-tongued speaker who criticized the liberal opponents of Nixon's policies. But after the incumbents' reelection in 1972, Agnew's career came to an abrupt and disgraceful end. An investigation of corruption among public officials in Baltimore County uncovered a pattern of bribery in Agnew's administration. Even as vice president he had continued to accept bribes, called kickbacks, in return for political favors. Agnew resigned as vice president after this information became known. The courts later required him to pay back to the state nearly $250,000 for the alleged kickbacks. Within a year, charges that he had covered up illegal activities by members of his staff during the election campaign forced Nixon to resign his office.

When Spiro Agnew gave up the governorship of Maryland to run for vice president, the legislature chose Marvin Mandel to fill the vacancy. Mandel seemed well suited for the job. A product of Baltimore politics, he had worked his way up the ladder until he became Speaker of the House of Delegates. In January 1969, he took office as governor of Maryland.

During his first two years in office, Mandel demonstrated his skills as a politician. The legislature passed ninety-three of the ninety-five bills proposed by the governor's office. The governor's cabinet was revised and streamlined, with the creation of twelve departments: Agriculture, Budget, Economic Development, General Services, Health, Licensing, Natural Resources, Personnel, Planning, Police and Corrections, Transportation, and Welfare. Accusations of Mandel's involvement in a web of corruption soon overshadowed his achievements, however.

Left to right: Marvin Mandel, Louis Goldstein, and Harry Hughes. Hughes and Mandel, both Democrats, each served two terms as governor. Louis Goldstein served as the chief financial officer of Maryland from 1959 to 1998. Collection of the Maryland State Archives, MSA SC 4975-12-189-28.

Postwar Politics

In November 1975, Governor Mandel was indicted, or formally accused by a grand jury, for accepting bribes of $415,000 in gifts from friends. In return, the indictment said, he had influenced the passage of bills in the legislature to help these friends. After a lengthy and confusing trial, the jury convicted Mandel, who went off in July 1980 to serve fifteen months in prison. Mandel's conviction was later overturned on appeal and he was exonerated of all charges.

The next governors of Maryland, Blair Lee III, who served for one and a half years after Mandel's conviction, and Harry Hughes, elected in 1978 and again in 1982, compiled good records while in office. After the controversies of the Agnew and Mandel administrations, many voters welcomed Hughes's quiet manner. Nevertheless, the collapse of several of the state's savings and loan companies marred the administration of the less controversial Hughes.

The late 1970s and early 1980s were a time of limitations rather than expansion. The postwar era of growth and prosperity seemed to be coming to an end. Instead of the usual confidence in the future, Americans had doubts. Sources of fuel and other natural resources seemed to be dwindling. Fighting in Asia, the Middle East, Africa, and Central America threatened world peace and security. Concern over inflation and unemployment undermined social and civil rights reforms. Governor Hughes had to answer the voters' demand for less spending, fewer government programs, and lower taxes.

■ The Challenge of Equality

The second half of the twentieth century was a time of significant change for African American Marylanders. At the end of World War II, Maryland resembled southern states in its racial segregation and discrimination. By the 1980s, however, its schools and public places had been desegregated; African Americans held important positions in state and local government; and a greater percentage of blacks had joined suburban whites in a middle-class style of life. Racial prejudice and bigotry had by no means disappeared from Maryland, but their influence was dramatically reduced.

The Black Revolution

The racism and Jim Crow laws that still prevailed in 1945 had been weakened by the war. African American migration into Maryland and especially into Baltimore increased in response to the plentiful new jobs in wartime industries. In some places, blacks and whites worked side by side. When the war ended and workers retrained for peacetime employment, many black men and women built their careers in state and federal jobs or in jobs with city services and utilities, such as bus lines and telephone companies, where there was less discrimination in hiring than was the case in many private companies. The improvement in job opportunities in the 1940s, however, was overshadowed by poor housing and sanitation, overcrowding, lack of recreation facilities, and segregated schools. African Americans still were not allowed to try on clothes in many department stores or to eat in "white" restaurants. As a border state, Maryland experienced a mixture of discriminatory racial traditions and liberal change. Although blacks had pressed for reforms before the war, leaders now picked up the pace.

The Civil Rights Struggle

Maryland		The Nation
St. John's College admits first black resident student	1948	President Truman desegregates armed forces
Commission on Interracial Problems and Relations established	1951	
Ford's Theatre in Baltimore desegregated	1952	
Baltimore City public schools desegregated First African Americans elected to General Assembly	1954	*Brown v. Board of Education of Topeka*
	1955	Montgomery, Alabama, bus boycott
Baltimore Fair Employment Ordinance All Baltimore City public swimming pools desegregated	1956	
Sit-ins at College Park, Baltimore, and Salisbury	1960	Sit-in movement begins in Greensboro, North Carolina
Cambridge Riot Verda Welcome becomes first black woman elected to state Senate Public Accommodation Law Demonstrations at Gwynn Oak Amusement Park	1963	March on Washington
	1964	Civil Rights Act
	1965	Voting Rights Act
	1967	Thurgood Marshall becomes first African American appointed to the US Supreme Court
Baltimore Riot Maryland Commission on Human Relations organized	1968	Martin Luther King Jr. assassinated
Maryland Commission on Afro-American History and Culture established	1969	
	1971	US Supreme Court's *Swann v. Charlotte-Mecklenburg Board of Education* decision upholds busing as a way to achieve integration
Busing begins in Prince George's County	1973	

The Challenge of Equality

In 1947, the University of Maryland agreed to accept more blacks into its law school and professional programs. That same year Baltimore appointed its first African American police sergeant. Over the next seven years Maryland's barriers to racial equality gradually weakened. In 1949, Baltimore's first black plumber received his license, and both the Baltimore County and Frederick County medical societies admitted African American physicians. Even on the Eastern Shore, with its more rigid tradition of segregation, hospitals in Cambridge and Salisbury opened their doors to black doctors.

The election of Theodore McKeldin as governor marked an important event in the struggle for civil rights, as he became a strong spokesman for racial equality. Governor McKeldin appointed African Americans to most state commissions and to several courts. Robert B. Watts became the first black traffic court magistrate and George L. Russell the first African American magistrate-at-large of Baltimore; both men later became judges. In 1952, McKeldin appointed a new Maryland Commission on Interracial Problems and Relations.

Lillie May Carroll Jackson: Civil Rights Leader

Lillie May Carroll Jackson was born on May 25, 1889, in West Baltimore. According to family history, she was a descendant of Charles Carroll of Carrollton, a signer of the Declaration of Independence. She taught school until 1910, when she married Keiffer Jackson.

In the 1930s, she became one of Maryland's leading black activists for civil rights. She served as the head of the state's branch of the National Association for the Advancement of Colored People for thirty-five years. She led the fight to employ black clerks in supermarkets and stores, and for Baltimore to hire black policemen, firemen, and bus drivers.

She and Governor McKeldin often agreed on civil rights issues and worked together for change.

Together with Carl Murphy, editor of the *Afro-American* newspaper, she helped bring about the desegregation of the city's restaurants, department stores, and theaters. Her daughter Juanita Jackson Mitchell became the first black woman to graduate from the University of Maryland Law School. When Lillie May Carroll Jackson retired from the NAACP in 1970, she was widely recognized for her courage and her persistent fight for equal rights.

■ Civil rights leader Lillie May Carroll Jackson, longtime head of the Baltimore NAACP, meets here with Henry Parks, the co-founder of the Parks Sausage Company, a multimillion-dollar, black-owned business established in Baltimore in the 1950s. Courtesy of the Maryland Historical Society, HEN.05.07-033.

In the black community, several leaders were especially influential. One of the most prominent was Lillie May Carroll Jackson, the head of the local branch of the National Association for the Advancement of Colored People (NAACP). Her organization became a powerful force in breaking down barriers in hiring, housing, and the use of public facilities. Others who stepped forward to take leading roles were Walter Carter and Edward Chance of the Congress of Racial Equality (CORE); Furman Templeton of the Baltimore Urban League; and Carl Murphy, owner of the *Afro-American*. Thurgood Marshall, who later became the first person of African descent appointed to the US Supreme Court, got his start fighting for equal civil rights in Maryland.

School Desegregation

In 1954, the US Supreme Court ruled in the test case *Brown v. Board of Education of Topeka* that the doctrine of "separate but equal" had no place in American education. Schools had been legally segregated throughout the South, but they had never been equal in practice. Earlier challenges had questioned the lack of equality, but Thurgood Marshall, Charles Houston, and the other NAACP lawyers targeted segregation itself. The Supreme Court's unanimous decision stated that to separate children by race "generates a feeling of inferiority as to

■ Marylander and future US Supreme Court Justice Thurgood Marshall in 1954 led the legal team that won the *Brown v. Board of Education of Topeka* decision that desegregated schools across the country. Marshall and George E. C. Hayes and James M. Nabrit Jr., the two attorneys for the companion case, *Bolling v. Sharpe*, celebrate their victories on the steps of the US Supreme Court building. Courtesy of the Library of Congress, ppmsca.38654.

their status in the community that may affect their hearts and minds in a way unlikely ever to be undone."

In Maryland the decision received mixed reactions. Baltimore City immediately began transferring black students to previously all-white schools. Baltimore County delayed school integration until 1955. Residents of Montgomery County asked the state Board of Education in 1955 to reverse its ruling that would send thirty-two blacks to a formerly white school. Most colleges in Maryland admitted black students, although some were not enthusiastic about the change. H. C. (Curly) Byrd, a past president of the University of Maryland who had resisted earlier integration reform, ran for governor against McKeldin in 1954 on a campaign platform that opposed desegregation. Byrd lost at a time when many southern states were digging in their heels to resist desegregation in all ways possible.

After the first steps toward desegregation, real progress toward racial equality was slow. One problem was that children attended schools near their homes, so that as long as blacks and whites did not live together in the same neighborhoods, schools continued to be largely segregated. By 1978, because of white flight to the suburbs, African Americans accounted for two-thirds of Baltimore's schoolchildren. In 1954, less than half had been black. The other problem was the continuing presence of racial prejudice. At Deale, in Anne Arundel County, for example, threats of physical violence forced a black physician to withdraw his son from a white elementary school.

Pressure from black parents and community leaders sometimes led to improvements. New schools were built and curricula were strengthened. In the 1970s, beginning with Prince George's County in 1973, courts ordered children to be bused to achieve better racial balance. But the progress toward racial equality in education as well as in jobs and housing proceeded more slowly than many had hoped.

The New Militancy

By the 1960s, the lack of significant progress led to greater frustration and a more militant level of protest. Organized demonstrations (which often included white as well as African American protesters), like those to integrate Baltimore's Gwynn Oak Amusement Park in 1963, signaled the growing impatience of black Marylanders. Many whites, on the other hand, found unsettling the violence that occurred in Cambridge that same year.

A new state law that prohibited discrimination in hotels, restaurants, and other public places had exempted the counties of the Eastern Shore. Frustrated with the slow pace of change, peaceful protesters became more militant in the summer months. Sit-ins and demonstrations led to mass arrests and growing anger on both sides. In Cambridge, Gloria Richardson led the protests. On the night of June 11, 1963, fighting broke out between black and white citizens of

Marylander Clarence Mitchell Jr. (*right*) headed the Washington office of the National Association for the Advancement of Colored People for many years. Here he meets with Roy L. Wilkens, executive director of the NAACP from 1955 to 1977. Permission from *The Baltimore Sun*.

Cambridge, with stores firebombed, cars overturned, and several people wounded by gunfire. Peace was restored only when National Guard troops were called in. The events in Cambridge were a forewarning of the violence that would continue in Maryland and throughout the nation for the rest of the decade.

In 1964, Congress passed the Civil Rights Act in an attempt to correct some of the nation's racially based inequality. An important part of the bill outlawed discrimination in hotels, motels, restaurants, theaters, and other public places. Other parts increased the federal government's authority to stop discrimination in schools, elections, and the workplace. The following year the Voting Rights Act strengthened protections against voting rights abuse. As a result, by the end of 1965, black registration in the Deep South had increased by 40 percent. Marylanders took leading roles in this on-going battle for civil rights. Clarence Mitchell Jr., for example, played a key part in persuading congressional representatives to vote for the new legislation. A graduate of Douglass High School in Baltimore, Mitchell made a career of working for better civil rights laws. As the director of the NAACP's Washington bureau, he was a strong lobbyist for the new guarantees against discrimination in the 1960s.

Even with the successes of the civil rights movement, however, the decade continued to be characterized by protest and violence. The worst year was 1968. The first crisis occurred at Bowie State College, where students boycotted classes to protest state authorities' neglect of the historically black school. When the students attempted to take over the college, Governor Agnew called in the Maryland National Guard and had the protesters arrested. More serious rioting

The Challenge of Equality

■ Representative Parren Mitchell, brother of Clarence Mitchell, served in Congress from 1971 to 1987. Maryland's first African American congressman, he took strong stands in favor of civil rights legislation and against the war in Vietnam. Collection of the US House of Representatives.

broke out in April 1968 after the assassination of Dr. Martin Luther King Jr. Baltimore African Americans, frustrated by overcrowded housing, high unemployment, and poverty-level incomes, took out their anger in violent protest, looting stores and firebombing buildings. After four days of rioting, the casualties included 6 people dead, 700 people injured, 1,000 businesses damaged, and more than 5,000 people arrested. Violence returned to Cambridge in the summer of 1968. H. Rap Brown, a nationally known protest leader, encouraged local residents to protest poor living conditions and inadequate schools. Before the rioting ended, two square blocks of Cambridge had been burned. This marked the end of major racial violence in Maryland during the turbulent 1960s.

In the 1970s, public attention turned away from the civil rights struggle. Concern for the economy and protests over the war in Vietnam distracted many reformers. Also, by the 1970s, civil rights legislation began to have some effect. Federal and state laws made discrimination in jobs and housing more difficult. And black Marylanders had more spokespersons. By 1973, there were fourteen African Americans in the Maryland House of Delegates and four in the state Senate. Parren Mitchell, the first black admitted to the University of Maryland's graduate program in sociology, took on a leading role in the US House of Representatives, to which he was first elected in 1970.

■ The Turbulence of War

The United States began to send military advisors into Vietnam shortly after World War II when the former colonial power, France, could no longer maintain its dominance there. Like Korea, Vietnam came to be divided into a northern half controlled by a Communist government and a southern half dominated by a government allied with the West. The American military presence began to increase sharply after 1964, reaching a height of more than five hundred thousand in 1968. Almost sixty thousand Americans died in the Vietnam War, including more than one thousand from Maryland.

A large number of Americans opposed this war, including many who had experience in direct action protests as part of the civil rights movement. They believed the war to be morally wrong, that too many innocent people were dying, and that the government should be "making peace, not war." Antiwar protests, both on and off college campuses, grew violent. The University of Maryland and other campuses in Maryland were the sites of numerous protests in the late 1960s and early 1970s. Some antiwar action in Maryland attracted national attention, such as the protest of the Catonsville Nine in 1968. Nine men and women, including several Roman Catholic priests, broke into the office of the Catonsville draft board, carried draft files out to the parking lot, dumped napalm on them, and set the files afire. The protesters were arrested, tried, and sentenced to prison terms. The bitter divisions of the Vietnam era persisted long after the United States ended its active participation in the fighting, with proponents of the pro-peace and pro-war sides tending to demonize each other. Even though this was a national rather than a state issue, it had an enormous impact on many Marylanders and much that happened in the state.

■ The Catonsville Nine, a group that included several Roman Catholic priests, protested the war in Vietnam in ways that generated much controversy. In 1968, they entered the draft board office in Catonsville in Baltimore County, put draft files into a wire basket, took them outside, poured napalm on them, and set them on fire. Antiwar groups protested the arrests of these activists. Courtesy of the Enoch Pratt Free Library, Fire and Faith: the Catonsville 9 File on Digital Maryland, Dean Pappas contributor.

■ Environmental Concerns

Environmental deterioration became a growing issue of public concern after the late 1960s. One basic problem stemmed from the fact that Maryland's population doubled between 1945 and 1980, placing land, air, water, and energy resources under heavier use. Discharges of waste and runoff from paved surfaces grew at a rapid rate and increasingly fouled the environment. New and often toxic chemicals came into widespread use.

Preservation of the Land

As early as 1945, Maryland had two agencies with responsibility for the environment. A Water Pollution Commission joined the older Health Department in trying to regulate pollution from industries and urban communities. These two agencies gave Maryland a head start over many other regions. In 1955, for example, Maryland became the first state to pass a strip mining law. This law required companies that mined coal by stripping the top layers of soil away to restore the land to its original condition. The law did not, however, provide for cleaning up waterways polluted by mining operations. Maryland also began early to protect its land by creating state parks and forests. State protection of wildlife led to an increase in the numbers of animals in Maryland's woodlands. Cities and counties established parks and playgrounds for tennis, baseball, soccer, swimming, and picnicking.

By the late 1960s, however, Marylanders, along with the rest of the nation, realized the need for greater measures to stop environmental deterioration. Marylander Rachel Carson aroused concern nationwide with her book *Silent Spring*. She warned of the dangers of pesticides and other chemicals that were polluting America's land and water, and she showed how they killed wildlife and endangered human health.

In 1968, Maryland responded to the need for better control by establishing the Department of Natural Resources. This government department coordinated the actions of all state agencies that regulate parks, forests, and wildlife and worked to solve pollution problems. It helped get passage of new laws to control oil spills, chemical dumps, industrial pollution, and even noise pollution. The creation of the Environmental Protection Agency by the federal government in 1970 was another important step toward better but still imperfect control.

Efforts to Save the Bay

The deterioration of the Chesapeake Bay, considered the state's greatest natural resource, was an issue of special concern in Maryland. Pollution from several sources contributed to a decline in the Bay's water quality. Cities and towns dumped millions of gallons of untreated sewage into its waters. Industrial waste discharges included chemicals, oil, grease, and metals. Commercial shipping and recreational boating contributed more pollution. Farms added to deterioration of water quality because their pesticides, herbicides, chemical fertilizers, and animal waste eventually washed down to the Bay. The Water Pollution Control Commission, created by the legislature in 1947, had little effect on the Bay's steady deterioration.

Only after 1960 did Maryland begin to make any progress toward saving the Bay. The Department of Natural Resources under the direction of former Governor Tawes and then James B. Coulter pushed tougher legislation through the

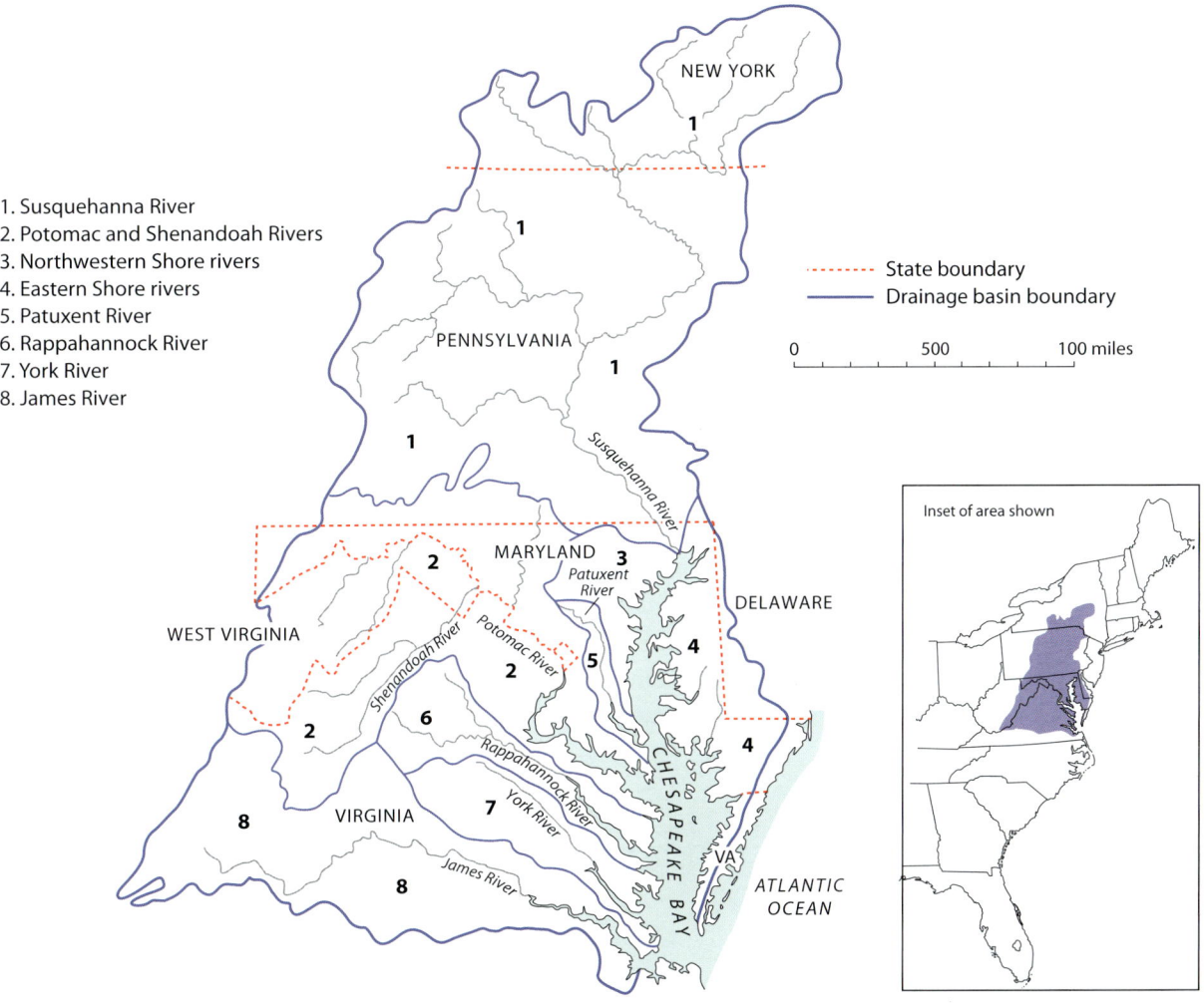

1. Susquehanna River
2. Potomac and Shenandoah Rivers
3. Northwestern Shore rivers
4. Eastern Shore rivers
5. Patuxent River
6. Rappahannock River
7. York River
8. James River

■ Major Drainage Basins of the Chesapeake Bay System

General Assembly. These state laws, combined with federal action by the Environmental Protection Agency, helped to slow the decline in water quality. The Maryland Environmental Service helped towns and cities improve their waste-disposal systems. The Chesapeake Bay Foundation, founded in 1967, led citizens' efforts to protect the Bay through education, hands-on programs, legal actions, and legislative advocacy. In 1984, the state took a major step toward preservation with the passage of the Chesapeake Bay Critical Area Law. This law established a resource protection program to improve the Bay's water quality and to reduce pollution by regulating land use along the shores of the Bay and its tributaries. Pennsylvania, Virginia, and the District of Columbia joined Maryland to protect the Bay, agreeing to work together when they signed the first multi-state Chesapeake Bay Agreement in 1983.

Although Maryland and its neighboring states did much to slow the rate of deterioration, new studies in the 1980s showed that more needed to be done. Estimates of population growth in the Bay region predicted an increase from 3.6 million to 9 million people by the end of the century, with all of these people and their workplaces adding pollutants into the natural environment. Because of demand for water by industry, homes, and agriculture, the Bay would not receive as much fresh water as it had in the past. The salinity of the Bay's water would increase, threatening the health of oysters, crabs, and fish. More money, knowledge, and public commitment would be needed to save the Bay for future generations.

Sources of Energy

Diminishing sources of energy constituted another cause for concern about the environment. At the end of World War II, Maryland depended largely on coal mined in the nearby Appalachian Mountains. By the late 1960s, the Baltimore Gas and Electric Company, the Potomac Electric Power Company, Potomac Edison, and Delmarva Power and Light, major suppliers of energy in the state, had begun to use oil and natural gas in addition to coal. By the 1970s, Maryland imported fuel from all over the world. Oil came from Venezuela, and natural gas was piped and tanked in from Texas, Algeria, and the Arctic Sea. Coal still came from Appalachian mines.

At the same time, more people used more energy. Unfortunately, the dependence on international sources also raised the cost of Maryland's energy. Prices

■ The Calvert Cliffs Nuclear Power Plant, near Lusby in Calvert County, began providing electric power in 1975. Although nuclear power does not pollute the air, the danger of accidents and the problem of waste disposal pose threats. Courtesy of *DECD Wikimedia*.

gradually increased to many times the prices of the 1940s. Baltimore Gas and Electric, which spent $25 to $30 million for fuel supplies per year in the 1950s, was spending about $250 million each year by the 1970s. Some of the increased cost for energy resulted from construction of the Calvert Cliffs Nuclear Power Plant in 1974. As one of the world's largest power-producing plants, this new facility supplied 11 percent of the state's energy by 1979. The new source of energy also brought with it fear of nuclear accidents and radiation pollution.

■ Life in Maryland

As Maryland passed its 350th anniversary in 1984, its citizens liked to describe their state as the "Land of Pleasant Living" because of its amenities and as "America in Miniature" because of its geographic diversity. Education, arts and culture, and sports and recreation all formed an important part of life in the state.

Education

For many, education provided the key to a good life. Like other states, Maryland faced the need for more and better schools. The postwar baby boom swelled the demand for classroom space, teachers, and books. The sales tax begun by Governor Lane provided revenue needed for buildings and better teachers' salaries. Enrollment in public schools increased by more than 50 percent during the 1950s, and salaries in education also rose by about that percentage, while the inflation rate for the decade stood at about 25 percent.

In this period there was also an ongoing debate over the quality of education. When the Soviet Union put the first satellite into space in 1957, Americans worried that the United States might fall behind in engineering and the sciences. Student rebellions and demonstrations on college campuses in the late 1960s, however, turned a significant segment of public opinion against education. By the 1970s, an economic recession undermined efforts to improve the quality of schools.

In Maryland there was a modest attempt to expand opportunities for higher education. The state's former normal schools, which had become state teachers colleges, then full liberal arts colleges, were brought together under a single governing board, the State Colleges System, in 1963 with Governor Tawes's support. With campuses across the state from Frostburg in Western Maryland to Salisbury and Princess Anne on the lower Eastern Shore, the system grew to almost 37,000 students by the 1980s. The University of Baltimore joined the system in 1975, an expansion marked in 1976 by a new name, the State University and College System of Maryland. In addition, by 1978, the 20 community colleges around the state enrolled 28,000 in classes for both students planning to transfer to complete an undergraduate degree and those seeking certification for a wide variety of careers. About 42 percent of all Maryland students attended college by the 1980s.

Arts and Culture

The post–World War II era saw an increase in cultural opportunities for Marylanders. Each of the two-year and four-year colleges offered classes, exhibits, lectures, and other activities for adults. Baltimore and Washington remained the dominant cultural centers, but all of Maryland's smaller cities and suburban areas also expanded their cultural activities during this period. Baltimore's urban renaissance in particular included a new blossoming of the arts. The Morris Mechanic Theatre, for example, was a popular part of Charles Center in the heart of the city. Dozens of small theaters and drama groups drew audiences from the entire metropolitan area.

Maryland's growth in the arts and culture resulted from both private and public efforts. In 1967, Governor Agnew established the Maryland Arts Council, whose budget by 1979 reached $1.7 million. These public dollars joined private funds to offer Marylanders a better quality of culture and entertainment. The Meyerhoff Symphony Hall, home of the Baltimore Symphony Orchestra and built with a large contribution by philanthropist Joseph Meyerhoff, opened in 1982 in Baltimore. It symbolized the enthusiasm for the arts that existed in the second half of the twentieth century. The Merriweather Post Pavilion in Columbia, the Harford Opera Company in Bel Air, the Weinberg Center for Performing Arts in Frederick, the Washington County Museum of Fine Arts in Hagerstown, and the rebuilt Peale Museum in Baltimore were other examples

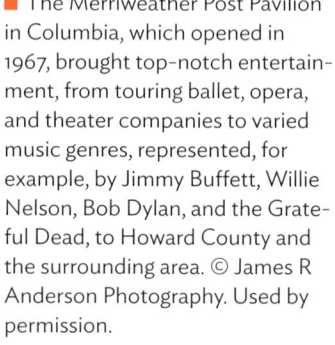

■ The Merriweather Post Pavilion in Columbia, which opened in 1967, brought top-notch entertainment, from touring ballet, opera, and theater companies to varied music genres, represented, for example, by Jimmy Buffett, Willie Nelson, Bob Dylan, and the Grateful Dead, to Howard County and the surrounding area. © James R Anderson Photography. Used by permission.

of renewed support for culture. Music by groups like the Montgomery Symphony Orchestra and theatrical performances by local companies in College Park and Salisbury offered Marylanders alternatives to the national artists who came to the metropolitan areas.

Maryland became better known, too, as a home for writers. John Barth, a Johns Hopkins University professor, gained a national reputation with his novels *The Sot-Weed Factor*, *Giles Goat-Boy*, and *The End of the Road*. Anne Tyler's novels, many set in Baltimore, such as *Searching for Caleb* and *Celestial Navigation*, were also read by a national audience. Gilbert Byron became the best-known poet of the Eastern Shore. In Baltimore, poetry flourished in the 1970s and 1980s with many excellent writers like Lucille Clifton and Josephine Jacobsen, who became poet-in-residence at the Library of Congress.

Sports and Recreation

As Maryland's population increased after World War II, demand for more recreation and sports facilities also grew. Because of the diverse environment, Marylanders could choose between the mountains of Western Maryland and the beaches of the Atlantic and the Chesapeake Bay. In Allegany and Garrett Counties favorite pastimes consisted of skiing, fishing, hunting, camping, and hiking. On the Eastern Shore, traditional sports included horse shows, yacht regattas, log canoe races, and hunting geese and ducks. After the Chesapeake Bay Bridge was built, taking in the sun and waves along the beaches of Maryland's Atlantic Coast brought pleasure to hundreds of thousands each weekend.

Baltimore's rebuilt downtown harbor became a major recreation site in the 1970s. The City Fair, started under Mayor Thomas D'Alesandro III, attracted crowds of half a million. Ethnic festivals, children's concerts, and parades made the urban landscape a playground for Marylanders and encouraged suburbanites to come downtown again. Communities across the state organized ethnic festivals, food festivals, and other events to bring people together in addition to the county fairs and state fair that had drawn crowds for many years.

Maryland also had two of the most successful spectator sports teams in America. When the Baltimore Colts won "the greatest game ever played" to become the National Football League champions in 1958, Maryland had a new set of folk heroes. Johnny Unitas, Lenny Moore, Raymond Berry, Art Donovan, and Gino Marchetti—these were names that every schoolchild knew well in the Colts' glory days of the 1950s and 1960s. Even more successful were the Baltimore Orioles. New to the city in 1954, the team won a world championship in 1966 with the help of star players Jim Palmer, Boog Powell, Brooks Robinson, and Frank Robinson, among many others, Orioles who remained important in the Maryland sports world well into the twenty-first century. In their first twenty-five years in Baltimore, the Orioles became the winningest team in all of baseball.

On the Occasion of Maryland's 350th Birthday

from the Ark
of refuge,
from the Dove
of peace,
we have become.

we celebrate
three hundred fifty years
of learning.

turning
watermen and women,
hill folk and city,
into citizens.

safe now and at peace
in this proud state
named for a woman

we blend our brown
and yellow, red
and black and white
into a greater We.

Maryland,
heiress to refuge
and to peace,
We celebrate.

We praise.

Lucille Clifton
Poet Laureate of Maryland

From the collection of the Maryland State Archives, Papenfuse Topic File Collection, 350th Anniversary Poem, MSA SC 1916-B29-F548, copyright © 1984 by Lucille Clifton.

■ The Baltimore Orioles have been a source of pride for Marylanders since they came to the city in 1954. The team enjoyed notable success, winning eight American League Championships, appearing in six World Series, and winning three titles in 1966, 1970, and 1983. The 1970 team, led by manager Earl Weaver, defeated the Cincinnati Reds. Standout members of the team during these years included Brooks Robinson, Boog Powell, Elrod Hendricks, and Dave McNally. Private collection.

Marylanders loved tradition in their sports. The running of the Preakness stands out as one of the longest and richest traditions. This event, held each May, gave Maryland an honored place in horse racing as a site of one of the Triple Crown races. The annual Hunt Cup Race and the popular jousting tournaments proved that Maryland's love of fine horses had not diminished since the eighteenth century.

■ Toward a New Millennium

By 1985, World War II seemed long past, as did the conflicts in Korea and Vietnam, as Maryland moved swiftly toward full participation in the new era of information technology. With the new millennium in view, the state, like the nation, looked toward the twenty-first century. The promise of technological and scientific advances, however, would be counter-balanced by a growing gap between the wealthy and the poor and middle classes as well as by new threats to the nation's safety and wellbeing. New challenges and new opportunities faced the generation of young women and men rising to leadership positions in the late twentieth century.

Maryland		The Nation and the World
William Donald Schaefer elected governor Elizabeth Bobo, Howard County, elected first woman county executive	1986	
Clarence "Du" Burns becomes first African American mayor of Baltimore Kurt Schmoke elected mayor of Baltimore	1987	World stock market decline
	1988	Republican George H. W. Bush elected president
	1989	*Exxon Valdez* oil spill in Alaska Berlin Wall falls
	1990	Launch of Hubble Telescope
	1991	Gulf War, Operation Desert Storm, follows Iraqi invasion of Kuwait World Wide Web debuts
Baltimore light rail service begins	1992	Democrat William Jefferson Clinton elected president
Democrat Parris N. Glendening elected governor Wayne Curry, Prince George's County, elected first African American county executive	1994	
Western Correctional Institution opens in Cumberland	1996	
Smart Growth and Neighborhood Conservation Act becomes law	1997	
State and Allegany County invest $48 million in Rocky Gap Resort and Golf Course	1998	
	1999	Dow Jones stock market average closes above 10,000 for the first time Massacre at Columbine High School in Colorado
	2000	Republican George W. Bush elected president
Bethlehem Steel declares bankruptcy	2001	September 11 terrorist attacks cause approximately three thousand deaths
Robert L. Ehrlich Jr. elected first Republican governor in thirty-six years Tornado causes major damage in La Plata	2002	Department of Homeland Security created
Hurricane Isabel kills one person and destroys thousands of homes	2003	United States and other nations invade Iraq
	2005	Hurricane Katrina causes major damage and leaves almost two thousand dead in Louisiana, Mississippi, and Alabama
Democrat Martin J. O'Malley elected governor	2006	
	2007	Massacre at Virginia Polytechnic Institute
Voter referendum approves state licensing of slot machines	2008	Democrat Barack Obama elected first president of African descent Stock market crashes, followed by global financial crisis
	2010	*Deepwater Horizon* oil rig explodes in Gulf of Mexico
Intercounty Connector opens in Prince George's and Montgomery Counties	2011	
Voter referendum approves Dream Act, providing eligibility for in-state tuition at public colleges and universities for some undocumented immigrants Voter referendum approves Civil Marriage Protection Act Derecho, a major storm, causes two deaths and massive power outages Hurricane Sandy causes eleven deaths and widespread damage in Crisfield	2012	Massacre of twenty-six children and adults at Sandy Hook Elementary School in Connecticut
General Assembly abolishes the death penalty Takoma Park becomes first municipality to allow 16-year-olds to vote	2013	Terrorists attack Boston Marathon
Republican Lawrence J. Hogan Jr. elected governor	2014	
	2015	US Supreme Court decision makes same-sex marriage legal throughout the country

chapter eight

Maryland

1985–2015

With a population of approximately six million people in 2015, Maryland was characterized by a wide range of America's social, economic, racial, and ethnic diversity. Maryland stood out because its population was wealthier and better educated than that of most other states. During these years, which saw both prosperity and recession, technical knowledge became vital in some segments of the job market. Science, technology, electronics, health care, and other fields based on advanced skills and knowledge grew in importance, making formal education more relevant for employment in those fields.

The diversity of Maryland's population increased during the years from 1985 to 2015. As the state's African American population grew, many African Americans held prominent positions in the government and the economy. Newcomers, especially from Asia and Central America, marked a continuation of the American pattern of immigration followed by assimilation into the wider society. Widespread advocacy for equal rights for all people, without discrimination based on race, ethnicity, gender, or sexual orientation, resulted in major, although incomplete, social changes.

Maryland and the nation as a whole faced the threat of terrorism and suffered through several prolonged wars overseas. Nationally, people had to find ways to deal with this new reality while governments, especially the federal government, debated possible actions with which to respond. Environmental issues moved into major prominence as the consequences of pollution, environmental destruction, and climate change became increasingly apparent and the need for planning more urgent.

Politically, the majority of voters in Maryland cast ballots for Democrats during this period, but certain regions of the state were heavily Republican while others were heavily Democratic. Voters elected three Democratic and two Re-

Table 8.1. Maryland Population Growth, 1980–2010

Year	Total Population
1980	4,216,933
1990	4,780,753
2000	5,296,486
2010	5,773,552

Source: US Census.

publican governors during these years, while Democratic state senators and delegates controlled the General Assembly throughout the period. Government leaders and citizen advocates worked on the interconnected issues of economy, education, growth, environment, public safety, and human rights, among others.

■ Maryland's Economy

In 2000 and 2010, Maryland ranked first nationally in median household income, moving up from fourth in 1990. The state retained its top AAA bond rating throughout the period, one of only ten states in the nation to do so. Economic growth in Maryland in the 1980s and afterwards was led by information technology, telecommunications, biotechnology, and the aerospace and defense industries. The state was a leader in medical and scientific research. Although Maryland was prosperous in relation to many states, a close look reveals both ups and downs in the state's economy and wide disparities in the distribution of income and wealth. Traditional industries declined and many industrial workers lost jobs that were not replaced. Newer manufacturing establishments often could not find workers with the needed skills, such as computer literacy. Income disparities thus reflected both educational level and geographic distribution. Bank failures and short recessions hit in the 1980s and early 1990s. Prolonged growth in the 1990s and early 2000s ended with an economic and banking crisis in 2007–2008. The banking crisis led to a major recession in 2009 that resulted in increased unemployment, large numbers of home foreclosures, and financial hardship for many, in both the state and the nation.

Decline of "Old Economy" Industrial Jobs

In Maryland, as in other states, many old manufacturers closed their factories and many industrial jobs moved overseas or simply disappeared. At the same time, owners of a number of manufacturing companies complained that they could not find enough workers trained to fill available new jobs, which often required skills such as computer literacy.

Parts of Western Maryland still dealt with the hardships of poverty and the disappearance of jobs for factory and mine workers. In Allegany County, for example, industrial jobs accounted for 28 percent of the workforce in 1979 and coal mining had been one of the county's mainstays. By 2010, manufacturing employed only 8 percent of Allegany's workers and mining accounted for only 0.3 percent.

One notable setback occurred in 1986 when the Kelly-Springfield Tire Company announced the closing of its Cumberland factory and corporate offices. Maryland's governor, William Donald Schaefer, took steps to save some of the jobs by pledging $15 million in state funds to build a new corporate headquarters. While he could not save the tire factory, this step did protect six hundred jobs in Allegany County until 1998, when the company closed its Cumberland offices.

In and around Baltimore, former steel mill and factory workers faced joblessness, underemployment, and low wages. In Baltimore County, Bethlehem Steel and its Sparrows Point shipyard once employed thousands of workers. During a recession in 1982, steel production fell to 50 percent of capacity and the company registered a $67 million deficit in just one quarter of the financial year. The company laid off more than five thousand workers, more than at any time since the Great Depression of the 1930s. Bankruptcy came in 2003. The property then passed from one owner to another until 2012, when it was sold for scrap to a company specializing in industrial waste. By 2014, plans were in the works for a new use for the old waterfront site.

Industrial workers during the second half of the twentieth century had earned good wages, in large part because of union activities and wartime demand for skilled workers. As these jobs disappeared, many people faced hardships. Without education in the needed new skills, some men and women found no work at all while many others had to accept lower-paying jobs, often in service industries such as food and retail, and, with those jobs, a lower standard of living. Discrepancies between job training and job availability caused other difficulties. For example, shortages of men and women trained in plumbing, electrical, and mechanical jobs—that paid good wages for those qualified to fill them—caused widespread angst among homeowners and small businesspeople who could not obtain the services they needed.

■ Levi Watkins, MD, was a pioneer both as the first African American chief resident in cardiac surgery at Johns Hopkins Hospital, where he performed the world's first human implantation of the automatic implantable defibrillator, and as a recruiter and mentor for minority students in the medical school. The Alan Mason Chesney Medical Archives of The Johns Hopkins Medical Institutions.

The "New" Science and Technology Economy

Biosciences, medicine, and technology as well as technology-based manufacturing and international trade occupied a prominent place in Maryland's modern economy. Private companies, nonprofit institutions, and government agencies all played a major role in these fields. By 2010, almost fifteen thousand high-tech firms operated in Maryland, the majority in Anne Arundel, Baltimore, Howard, Montgomery, and Prince George's Counties and Baltimore City. The numbers of professional and technical workers increased over the years, making up approximately 28 percent of the state's workforce in 2013.

The Johns Hopkins University and Medical Institutions and the University of Maryland Medical System conducted medical research, developed new treatments, and cared for patients. Johns Hopkins expanded throughout the region and operated medical programs around the world. Significant work in mapping the human genome also took place in Maryland. In the early twenty-first century, both Johns Hopkins and the University of Maryland built biotechnology

■ The NASA Goddard New Horizons Spacecraft flew the first mission to reach and study Pluto and its moon Charon. The Johns Hopkins University Applied Physics Laboratory manages the mission for NASA and designed, built, and operates the spacecraft. Courtesy of the National Aeronautics and Space Administration.

parks in Baltimore that attracted nonprofits and for-profit companies, making collaboration easily possible.

The space industry also grew during this period and by 2009 employed more than ten thousand Maryland women and men. In the 1980s, the Space Telescope Science Institute opened on the Hopkins campus in Baltimore to develop the Hubble Space Telescope, launched by the National Aeronautics and Space Administration (NASA) in 1990. This advanced telescope provided the most detailed views of space up to that time. In 2006, the University of Maryland, the University of Maryland Baltimore County, and NASA established the Center for Research and Exploration in Space Science and Technology, one of a number of projects on which NASA and universities partnered. Similar collaborative ventures expanded Maryland's place in this economic sector.

Federal agencies located in Maryland acted as a catalyst for the state's science and technology industries. Among these were the National Institutes of Health (NIH) in Montgomery County and the NASA Goddard Space Flight Center in Prince George's County. These and other federal agencies contracted with private companies in Maryland as well as around the nation. The defense industry employed large numbers in Maryland both in government agencies such as the Department of Defense and the National Security Agency and in private companies such as BAE Systems, Northrup Grumman, and Raytheon.

The Search for Prosperity

As the old economy weakened, all regions of the state searched for alternative sources of income and growth, with solutions that varied from region to region.

Western Maryland

Tourism became one mainstay in Western Maryland's economy. Deep Creek Lake, the Wisp Resort, and the state parks in Garrett County attracted people for skiing, white water rafting, hiking, boating, and other outdoor sports. In Allegany County, the Rocky Gap Lodge and Golf Resort opened with backing from the state government. The resort added slot machines when they became legal, but still did not draw as many tourists as its supporters had hoped. Historic sites such as Antietam National Battlefield and Harpers Ferry in Washington County as well as the Appalachian Trail and the Chesapeake and Ohio Canal helped

> ### Working for the Government
>
> As the federal government grew during and after World War II, so too did state and local governments across the nation. Women and men working for the government made up an important part of Maryland's workforce. In 1990, civilian and military federal workers in Maryland numbered 225,790. By 2010, the figure had declined to 218,416, still a significant part of the workforce, and approximately 500,000 Marylanders worked for the federal, state, and local governments combined. More than 80,000 were working for the US Armed Services as military or civilian employees. The federal civilian agencies with the most employees in Maryland in 2010 were Health and Human Services, Social Security, and the Department of Commerce. Federal government employees living in Maryland earned a total of more than $25 billion. Maryland's federal government procurement contracts totaled $10.6 billion in 2000 and $26.2 billion in 2010. While federal spending often buffered the state from the worst ups and downs of the economy, cuts in federal spending affected the state disproportionately when compared to other states.

bring tourists to the region. Frostburg State University, with more than five thousand students, as well as arts and entertainment in Frostburg and Cumberland, also attracted people to Allegany County. Spending by the many visitors supported local businesses and increased employment opportunities.

The Western Maryland Health System (WMHS), with a 2014 workforce of more than 2,300, was the largest regional employer in the early twenty-first century. Formed in 1996 by uniting several existing medical facilities, WMHS was designed to serve residents of Maryland, Pennsylvania, and West Virginia. In 2009, WMHS opened a new state-of-the-art 275-bed hospital, which served as the headquarters of the area's trauma center.

The Maryland Department of Public Safety and Corrections located a number of facilities in Western Maryland. These prisons became large employers. In Cumberland, the Western Correctional Institution opened in 1996 and in 2014

■ Whitewater rafting is one of many tourist attractions that depend on the natural resources of Western Maryland. The Youghiogheny River in Garrett County attracts both novice and experienced rafters. Courtesy of Precision Rafting.

Maryland's Economy

received authorization for more than 560 staff members. The Western Correctional Training Center and the North Branch Correctional Institution together employed approximately 1,200 by 2014. The state authorized the Maryland Correctional Institution, the Maryland Correctional Training Center, and the Roxbury Correctional Institution, all in Hagerstown, to employ almost 1,600 staff members in 2014. Exceedingly controversial because of the numbers of people being incarcerated, these institutions did absorb some of the employment gap created as industries closed.

The Eastern Shore

Much of the Eastern Shore's economy depended its natural resources—fertile soil, open spaces, the Chesapeake Bay and its tributary rivers, and beaches. The natural environment played an essential role in farming, fishing, and forestry, and growth in the region's population threatened all three. The completion of the Chesapeake Bay Bridge in 1952 represented a critical turning point for the Eastern Shore, and its consequences continued to unfold well into the twenty-first century as regional tourism accelerated and the local economy grew.

For the Eastern Shore as a whole, the Bay Bridge and new and wider highways opened new markets for the area's farmers and watermen. Before the bridge, Philadelphia was the biggest consumer of Eastern Shore produce and seafood. After the bridge, farmers and seafood companies could easily ship to Baltimore and Washington. As a result, trucking—already a key element in the Eastern Shore's economy—became even more important.

Over the years, people living in and around Baltimore and Washington increased their spending throughout the Eastern Shore and, in turn, increased profits for old and new businesses. Multitudes of vacationers poured into Ocean City each summer to enjoy the beaches, boardwalk, and time away from work. They spent money on hotels, restaurants, and consumer goods. Some tourists headed to historic towns like Chestertown, St. Michaels, and Oxford. Other outsiders became residents as thousands built vacation homes or retired there. The increase in regional population entailed not only construction of houses and condominiums but an increase in shopping centers, parking lots, health care facilities, marinas, gas stations, and the industries that build and maintain the infrastructure. The growth in population and the parallel destruction of natural land contributed to the runoff that contaminates the Chesapeake and the Atlantic coastal bays and threatens the livelihoods of watermen. Environmental leaders and local residents formed new organizations and enlarged existing organizations to work for environmental protection.

As was the case in Western Maryland, several major institutions played an important role in the economy of the Eastern Shore in the late twentieth and early twenty-first centuries. The Peninsula Regional Medical Center, based in Salisbury, became a regional trauma center and offered medical care to residents of and visitors to the three states of the Delmarva Peninsula. In the early twenty-first century, the medical system workforce included more than 3,300 physicians, staff, and volunteers and served nearly 500,000 patients.

Salisbury State University had a faculty of more than 570 among 1,600 employees and a student population of more than 8,600 in 2013. The University of Maryland Eastern Shore (UMES), in Princess Anne, a historically African American institution that became racially diverse, grew to an enrollment of more than 4,000 students during the early twenty-first century. Both Salisbury and UMES

Tourism: The Beach

Water in all its forms draws visitors to enjoy its pleasures. Rivers, the Chesapeake Bay, the coastal bays near the Atlantic, and Ocean City all lured tourists. Ocean City continued to be the most lucrative tourist attraction in Maryland, as it was during earlier years as well. Although the town had a small number of permanent residents, 5,146 in 1990 and 7,102 in 2010, its location, directly on the Atlantic Ocean, attracted millions of vacationers each year. About 8 million visited in 2010 when the resort town offered more than 9,500 hotel rooms, 25,000 condominiums, and 200 restaurants. Seasonal employment helped many students find temporary jobs while they attended school. In the late twentieth and early twenty-first centuries, new communities around the coastal bays, such as Ocean Pines, offered amenities like boating and golfing. The rapid growth brought with it serious environmental concerns. For example, the physical expansion of the resort involved the destruction of sand dunes that had provided some protection from flooding and the filling in of wetlands that had provided habitat for a wide variety of species.

■ The popularity of Ocean City as a vacation spot resulted in development from the ocean to the back bays as well as across the bays on the mainland. Some Marylanders point to the economic benefits of tourism while others worry about the environmental impact of paving dunes and wetlands. Balancing economic benefits with the need to protect the environment is a major dilemma in today's world. Courtesy of the University of Maryland Center for Environmental Studies.

contributed to the Eastern Shore's economy as employers and purchasers and by providing an educated workforce.

The Baltimore Region's Economy

Baltimore worked to restart economic growth by upgrading its central business district and by giving commuters and visitors easy access to the office buildings and attractions at the city's core. Governor William Donald Schaefer, always loyal to the city of which he had been the mayor, persuaded the legislature to approve a 22.5-mile light rail line connecting Baltimore to suburban areas. By 1997, the light rail extended north to Hunt Valley's office and shopping complex in Baltimore County and south to Glen Burnie in Anne Arundel County. Branches linked the system to Baltimore/Washington International Thurgood Marshall Airport (BWI) and the Baltimore Amtrak station. The path of the light rail system intentionally paralleled construction of a new baseball stadium for the Baltimore Orioles, for which Governor Schaefer had won legislative approval at the end of his first year in office. Both the light rail line and the stadium

■ Oriole Park at Camden Yards, built adjacent to the old B&O Railroad warehouse, won praise for its fan-friendly design that draws crowds to downtown Baltimore. Courtesy of the Baltimore Orioles.

The Blue Crabs, a baseball team affiliated with the Atlantic League of Professional Baseball, play in this stadium in Waldorf. The rapidly growing population in Southern Maryland provides the team's fan base. Courtesy of the Southern Maryland Blue Crabs Professional Baseball Club.

opened in 1992. Four years later, an additional light rail stop opened to serve the Baltimore Ravens' new stadium authorized under Governor Parris Glendening.

Baltimore's stadiums were designed to produce growth downtown, and thus contrasted with stadiums built in other cities on the outskirts of the urban area. The Washington Redskins, for example, in 1997 opened their new football field in Landover, Maryland, in Prince George's County, linked to the metropolis by the Washington Metro. Whereas Redskins games drew fans out of the District into its Maryland suburbs, Baltimore's stadiums drew them in. The Baltimore stadiums and light rail stops also provided convenient access to the Inner Harbor, with its restaurants and hotels, the National Aquarium, the Maryland Science Center, and other attractions that Baltimore had created since the 1970s to bring visitors to its downtown. The Horseshoe Casino, which opened in 2014 near the stadiums, brought additional visitors and money to the city while also tempting locals to gamble.

Despite the new facilities, the 2010 census showed that the city continued to lose population. The new rapid transit lines contributed to the emergence of "edge cities," such as Owings Mills and Hunt Valley, that drew businesses and their customers away from the central city. One important positive trend in the early twenty-first century, however, was the return of young professionals to the city, many settling in trendy neighborhoods such as Federal Hill and Harbor East.

Service-sector jobs generated by tourism and sports facilities did not make up for the manufacturing jobs lost by cities like Baltimore. In 1970, Baltimore had 499,000 employed workers, 20 percent of them in manufacturing. By 2005, workers in manufacturing accounted for fewer than 5 percent of employed Baltimoreans. The shift to jobs in restaurants, hotels, and similar businesses reduced earnings for many Baltimore workers. One study of wages in Baltimore, based on 2001 data, estimated that jobs in manufacturing paid an average of $14.80 an hour while service-sector jobs related to tourism averaged only $8.40.

Baltimore also became home to a number of nonprofit organizations such as the National Association for the Advancement of Colored People (NAACP), Catholic Relief Services, and Lutheran World Relief. Health care and higher education also played a vital role in developing and maintaining the city's economy. The Johns Hopkins Hospital, the University of Maryland Hospital, and other medical institutions brought doctors, researchers, and patients to the city. The Baltimore area contained the highest concentration of universities in the state as well as professional schools, including two medical schools, two law schools, a school of dentistry, and a school of social work. In 2002, both Johns Hopkins and the University of Maryland announced plans to bring biotechnology companies to Baltimore by building "biotechnology parks" in the city. They aimed to bridge the distance between research and the market by establishing research laboratories and production facilities in close proximity to one another.

The Washington Suburbs

In the Washington suburbs, the federal government provided the engine for much of the local economy. While the size of the federal workforce increased only modestly after the 1960s, the number of federal contract workers grew rapidly, and staff members of national organizations with headquarters or lobbying offices in Washington also contributed to the growth of the city's suburbs. The recession of the early twenty-first century resulted in the loss of some government and contractual jobs, with an especially negative effect on Maryland's Washington suburbs.

■ The National Institutes of Health, headquartered in Bethesda, conducts a wide range of medical research and treatment. Here, research fellow Youngmi Ji, PhD, is working on a better translation of lab results to medical therapies in the area of orthopedics. National Institute of Arthritis and Musculoskeletal and Skin Diseases, National Institutes of Health.

Federal grants and contracts with private enterprises helped power the growth of the Washington suburbs. Biotechnology firms clustered around the Bethesda headquarters of NIH. As early as 1990, Maryland was home to about 150 biotechnology companies, but few of them earned any profit initially. The state's scientific workforce ranked among the biggest and best in the nation, especially in the biosciences, and Maryland ranked highly in competition for government research grants. However, Maryland's twentieth-century science establishment lacked a market orientation. Many of Maryland's biotechnology firms served only one customer: the federal government. That was the case not only for biotech companies but also for the Johns Hopkins Applied Physics Laboratory in Laurel, which relied primarily on secret research for the Department of Defense. The Goddard Space Flight Center in Greenbelt and its parent agency, NASA, provided support for development of spacecraft and satellites. The economy prospered, however, as new companies opened in Maryland. These included biotechnology giants like Medimmune, with facilities in Gaithersburg and Frederick, and information technology companies like Digicon, with a headquarters office in Rockville. By 2010, Maryland's five hundred bioscience companies in both the Washington suburbs and the Baltimore area accounted for approximately 8 percent of the national industry.

Infrastructure, Transportation, Trade, and Agriculture

Transportation, trade, and agriculture have always played an important role in Maryland's economy, just as the movement of people and goods from place to place remains vital to the functioning of any economy. Maintaining the state's infrastructure represents one of government's major jobs.

Infrastructure and Transportation

Maryland's main modes of transportation during this period included motor vehicles on the highways, public transit via both buses and trains, shipping in trucks and on boats, and passenger and freight traffic by air.

By the early twenty-first century, the state's Department of Transportation oversaw approximately 30,000 miles of highways, more than 2,400 bridges, and several important tunnels including the Fort McHenry Tunnel, opened in 1985 as part of Interstate 95, the major East Coast highway. Interstate 68, completed in 1991, replaced Route 40 as the main route to Western Maryland with the goal of encouraging more business development there. The Department of Transportation oversaw light rail, subways, railroads, and the track systems. By 2000, much of the aging twentieth-century infrastructure needed significant repair and upgrading. Safety concerns grew paramount, but the expense to state and local governments frequently resulted in deferral of much-needed maintenance. It did not help that the state transportation fund, with monies theoretically designated for transportation projects, was raided regularly to support other endeavors.

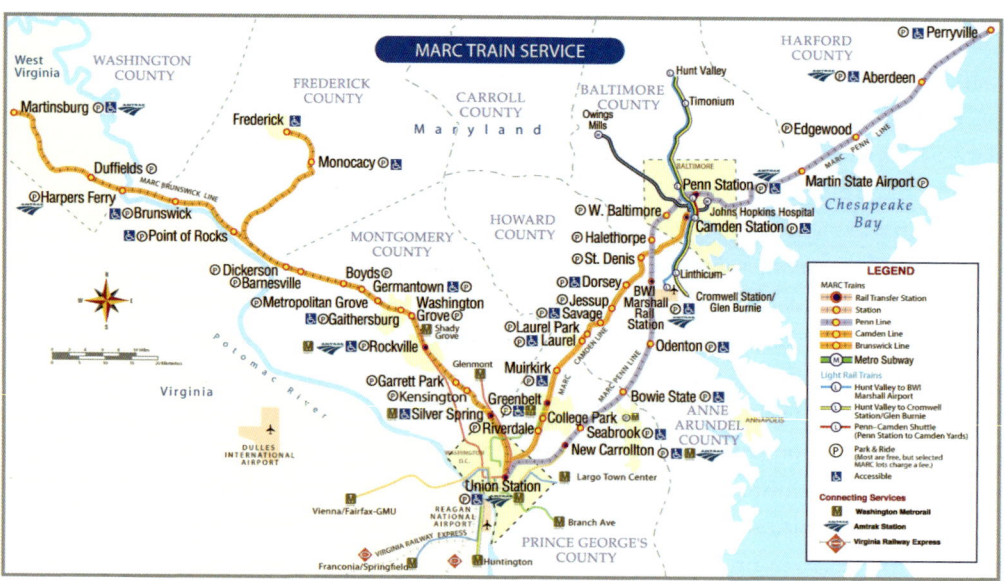

■ This Maryland Transit Administration MARC train system map shows the distances suburban commuters traveled to jobs in metropolitan Baltimore and Washington and points in between in 2015. The routes extend from Washington northwest through Montgomery, Frederick, and Washington Counties to Martinsburg, West Virginia, and northeast through Baltimore and Harford Counties to Aberdeen and Perryville. Development of much former agricultural land has brought additional population for residential and business uses. Courtesy of the Maryland Transit Administration.

In the second half of the twentieth century, crowded highways became a major problem for commuters, long-distance travelers, and truckers. Problems did not cease despite widening the beltways around Washington and Baltimore and constructing new roads, including the Intercounty Connector in Montgomery and Prince George's Counties, controversial because of its environmental impact. Expansion of commuter railroads, the Washington and Baltimore Metro systems, and the Baltimore Light Rail, and extension of bus lines served some commuters well, but many people still chose to drive, often alone, sometimes for more than an hour in each direction.

Beginning in 1983, the state had responsibility for the Maryland Area Rail Commuter (MARC) lines, which connected Baltimore and Washington and expanded outward as both commuters and employers moved farther from those urban centers. By 2014, MARC lines ran north to Perryville and west to Martinsburg, West Virginia. Throughout the period, transportation experts and environmentalists found that use of public transportation did not increase rapidly enough to solve existing problems despite people's complaints about traffic jams and bad air. Funding for future public transportation improvements remained controversial because the projects carried large price tags during a period of budget shortfalls and opposition to tax increases.

At BWI, in Anne Arundel County, first US Airways and then Southwest Airlines made the airport a hub. Passenger traffic increased from 6.7 million in 1984 to 19.6 million in 2000 and to 22.5 million in 2013. In 2001, the airport generated 85,000 direct and indirect jobs and provided $6.5 billion in economic impact. In 2010, it generated almost 100,000 direct and indirect jobs and $11.2 billion in economic impact.

Trade

Trade remained a mainstay of Maryland's economy. The hub continued to be the Port of Baltimore, which had handled both domestic and international cargo for more than two hundred years. In the early twenty-first century, the value of trade through the port increased from more than $20 billion in 2000 to almost $54 billion in 2012.

Modern facilities encouraged much of this growth. The Seagirt Marine Terminal, opened in 1990, provided a 275-acre site for automated cargo handling. Foreign waterborne commerce included automobiles and light trucks, farm and construction machinery, sugar, and iron ore as well as coal, petroleum, sand, and gravel. In the second decade of the twenty-first century, the port generated more than 50,000 jobs and more than $3 billion in annual revenue and local purchases. Passenger cruising increased in the early twenty-first century with the opening of a new terminal and year-round offerings. The port was renamed the Helen Delich Bentley Port of Baltimore in 2006 in honor of the congresswoman who was a longtime advocate for the port.

■ Shipping containers constitute a major component of the cargo shipped through the Port of Baltimore. Courtesy of *Wikimedia Commons*.

Maryland's Economy

New Ways of Eating

Marylanders, along with people across the nation, became consumers of increasing amounts of locally grown and organic food for reasons of health, nutrition, and taste. Farmers markets opened across the state, with 139 listed by the Maryland Office of Tourism in 2015. At these markets, farmers sold directly to customers, allowing them to keep a greater share of their profits than they would selling through a wholesaler. The markets enabled consumers to buy freshly harvested fruits, vegetables, and flowers as well as locally produced meats, eggs, cheeses, and baked goods.

A second trend, increasingly popular since the late twentieth century, was the consumption of organically grown foods. Growing numbers of consumers decided that they preferred to eat foods grown without the use of chemical pesticides and fertilizers for both health and environmental reasons. The Maryland Organic Food and Farming Association was founded in 1991 to build a network of individuals and organizations that support organic farming. The Maryland Department of Agriculture is accredited by the US Department of Agriculture to give organic certification to farms that meet the federal organic standards.

During the early twenty-first century, community-supported agriculture (CSA) grew in popularity. CSA farms sell shares to customers, who pay a set fee during the winter, when the farmers buy their seeds and other necessities. In exchange, the customers receive a share of the crops harvested that spring, summer, and fall. If it is a good season, the customers receive a lot of produce. If the season does not produce a good harvest, the customers receive smaller amounts of food, sharing the risk with the farmers.

■ At the Bird's Eye View Farm in Pocomoke City, Carole Morison raises organic free-range chickens. Her eggs sell out rapidly because of rising demand for such products in recent years. Private collection.

■ The Gurleys gave up city life to raise organic vegetables and fruits on Calvert's Gift Farm in northern Baltimore County. Here they are selling their produce at the Kenilworth Farmers Market in Towson. Private collection.

Agriculture

Although fewer and fewer families lived on farms as the twentieth century progressed, both small farms and large commercial establishments continued to be an important sector in Maryland's economy. In 1992, 13,037 farms with an average size of 171 acres occupied 2.2 million acres of land. In 2011, Marylanders farmed 2.05 million acres on 12,800 farms with an average size of 160 acres. Agricultural revenue in 2011 was more than $2 billion, up from $1.5 billion in 2000. Corn and soybeans were major field crops, while major fruit and vegetable crops included watermelons, peaches, apples, and beans. In 2011, more than 50,000 cows produced milk and Maryland growers sent more than 65 million chickens to market. Almost half of the state's agricultural acreage lay east of the Chesapeake Bay, but Frederick, Carroll, and Washington Counties also devoted extensive land to agriculture. In Southern Maryland, as tobacco sales declined due to greater knowledge of the health hazards of smoking and government regulation, farmers suffered, but the state's Tobacco Buyout program helped farmers shift to other crops. The area's proximity to Washington, DC, helped provide a ready market for fresh produce but also resulted in an increase in land prices that made it attractive to farmers to sell their acreage for development. Marylanders across the state continued to celebrate the sweet taste of the summer's peaches, corn, and tomatoes which, like blue crabs, remained a part of the local culture.

Just as transportation-based pollution continued to be a problem, so too did agriculture contribute to serious pollution. Studies revealed that excessive use of fertilizers containing nitrogen and phosphorus harms the Chesapeake Bay by encouraging the growth of algae that block sunlight from underwater plants. Other studies showed the damage caused by chemicals; in particular, those used to kill various weeds and pests cause harm to both human beings and wildlife.

Agriculture faced serious challenges to its survival in Maryland. As suburbia expanded, developers bought up farmland to build houses, businesses, roads, and other facilities, covering formerly arable land with impermeable surfaces. Farmers themselves were an aging population as many young people chose careers off the land. The state initiated measures to aid farms and farmers such as subsidizing the protection of agricultural land and zoning certain areas for agriculture only. Subsidies made farming viable for families that might otherwise have sold their land to developers.

Poverty and Economic Inequities

An increase in economic inequities during the late twentieth and early twenty-first centuries took place both nationally and in Maryland. The old saying "the rich get richer and the poor get poorer" described the reality of these years. The decline of "old economy" industrial jobs played a role in this trend. Inequities in education also contributed to the growing income gaps as the best jobs in industry, business, science, education, and other fields required specialized education and technical training.

The recessions of the 1980s and early 2000s contributed to a loss of jobs that left many people with no source of income and others with part-time instead of full-time work. Lower-level service jobs such as work in fast food restaurants and caregiving for the elderly and disabled stood out as paying low wages; so too did many retail jobs. Part-time jobs often meant not only low take-home pay but also lack of benefits, such as health insurance and retirement plans.

According to the state's Department of Labor, Licensing, and Regulation, Maryland mandated a minimum wage of $3.80 an hour in 1991, $5.15 in 1998, and $6.15 in 2007. The state's early twenty-first-century minimum wage of $7.25 (the national minimum) was insufficient to support a full-time worker, especially a single parent. In 1990, the US census counted almost 10 percent of Maryland's population living below the poverty level. In 2000, that rate had fallen to 7.7 percent, but in 2010 the rate rose again to the 1990 level, with more than 80,000 families living in poverty. The situation was particularly dismal during the early twenty-first-century recession when Maryland's unemployment rate more than doubled from 3.3 percent in January 2008 to 8 percent in January 2010. By July 2014, as the job market picked up, unemployment fell to 6.1 percent, but many working people still earned wages too low to support their families. Responding to pressure for reform, the state in 2014 passed a law gradually raising the minimum wage to $10.10 by 2018. Several Maryland counties mandated an even higher minimum wage, with Montgomery and Prince George's Counties requiring a rate of $11.50 per hour by 2018.

Throughout the 1980s, 1990s, and early 2000s, income inequality increased. The middle-class share of the total income declined while the wealthiest Marylanders made gains. The poor in Maryland also lost ground from their already precarious financial position. Growing income inequality meant reduced buying power for all but the wealthiest, affecting sales and business income across the state.

Table 8.2. Income Inequality in Maryland by Household, 1980–2010

All Households	Bottom 20%	Middle 60%	Top 20%
1980	4.2%	52.3%	43.5%
1990	4.1%	50.6%	45.3%
2000	3.9%	48.9%	47.2%
2010	3.5%	48.6%	47.9%

Source: US Census: American Community Survey.

Note: The decades of the late twentieth and early twenty-first centuries saw an increase in the share of the total income earned by Maryland's wealthiest households and a decrease in the share earned by the poorest households.

Maryland's highest poverty rates occurred in urban centers such as Baltimore City and in rural areas such as Somerset, Wicomico, and Allegany Counties. Howard and Montgomery Counties enjoyed the highest income levels in the late twentieth and early twenty-first centuries. In 1990, Maryland ranked fourth nationally in median household income. At the extremes, however, households in Howard and Montgomery Counties enjoyed the highest annual income whereas those in Allegany and Garrett Counties averaged the lowest. In 2010, Maryland ranked first nationally in household income. Again, as in 1990, sharp variations existed among regions and subdivisions. While the 2010 median household income in Howard County exceeded $100,000, Allegany County's stood at just over $35,000 and Baltimore City's at slightly more than $38,000.

■ Maryland's Diverse People

Demography is the discipline that studies characteristics of groups of people. Awareness of these characteristics, including ethnicity, age, education level, and income as well as geographic distribution, is essential to understanding the society, economics, and politics of any period and place. The general population and the women and men elected to represent that population in state and local government determine the issues and policies that are prominent in any historical period and influence how governments deal with those issues. It is important, therefore, to understand the makeup of Maryland's population.

Racial, Ethnic, and Linguistic Diversity

Although Maryland's total population grew at about the same rate as the nation's, the state's growth, especially in the early twenty-first century, reflected an increase in diverse population groups with non-European backgrounds. In 2010, Maryland had the fourth largest proportion of African American residents—following behind Mississippi, Louisiana, and Georgia. In addition, whereas late nineteenth- and early twentieth-century immigrants to Maryland had come primarily from Europe, newcomers in the late twentieth and early twenty-first centuries came primarily from non-European countries. As immigration increased and as immigrants had children, the national and ethnic origins of Maryland's population became more diversified.

The median age for Marylanders in 2010 was 38 years, virtually the same as the national median, but the median age varied sharply among different racial and linguistic groups within the state. For non-Hispanic whites the median age was 43; for Asian Americans 35.9; and among African Americans 34.7 years. The youngest by far were Maryland's Latino Americans, whose median age was 27.8 years. Latinos also had the highest percentage of young children (ages 0–4), a sign of a high birth rate and a rapidly growing population. In 2010, the greatest numbers of Latinos resided in Montgomery, Prince George's, Baltimore, and

Table 8.3. Racial and Ethnic Origins of Maryland Residents, 1990–2010

	1990	2000	2010
Non-Hispanic white	71.0	64.0	58.2
African American	24.9	27.9	29.4
Hispanic	2.6	4.3	8.2
Asian	2.9	4.0	5.5
Native American	0.3	0.3	0.4
Two or more races	not asked	2.0	2.9

Source: US Census.
Note: The number of people with African American, Hispanic, and Asian backgrounds increased in Maryland during the decades from 1990 to 2010. When responding to the census questionnaire, individuals choose their own category. Some individuals with multiracial or multiethnic backgrounds, an increasing category, do not list this on the census.

Kent Counties. Some observers calculated that Maryland would soon be a "majority-minority" state where non-Hispanic whites no longer constituted the majority. Montgomery and Charles Counties reached this point by 2010.

Immigration

One significant source of American diversity has always been immigration from outside the country. During the period of large-scale immigration between 1880 and 1910, roughly 10 percent of Maryland's people had been born in other countries, many of them the "new immigrants" from eastern and southern Europe, from countries such as Russia, Poland, and Italy, discussed in chapter 5. In more recent times, according to the US census, approximately 6.5 percent of Maryland's people in 1990 had been born in another country. Two decades later, the percentage doubled to approximately 14 percent, a figure slightly higher than the proportion of immigrants nationwide. Immigration to the United States from countries plagued by violence, discrimination, and poverty is a long-term, integral part of American history.

A close look at the state's foreign-born population reveals differences that distinguish Maryland's recent immigrants from one another. Spanish-speakers and Asians, for example, are not homogeneous groups. While most Latinos speak Spanish, they belong to a multiplicity of nationalities from countries such as El Salvador, Guatemala, Honduras, and Mexico. Immigrants from Brazil speak Portuguese. People coming from Asian nations, such as Korea, India, China, and the Philippines, speak many different languages. Black immigrants came from many African nations, with more than half arriving from countries in West Africa such as Nigeria and Liberia, as well as from Caribbean nations such as Jamaica. Other immigrants arrived from Russia and other parts of the former Soviet Union. As of 2010, almost half of Maryland's immigrants had

Many localities across the state offer classes and assistance to newcomers. The Charles W. Gilchrist Center for Cultural Diversity in Montgomery County provides classes in English language, citizenship preparation, and other useful skills for immigrants from around the world. Courtesy of Montgomery County, Maryland.

become naturalized citizens. Others stated their intention to become citizens when they completed the required five years of residency.

The state's foreign-born residents have always made important contributions to Maryland. A 2006 study found that immigrants accounted for 27 percent of Maryland's scientists, 21 percent of health care practitioners, and 19 percent of the state's mathematicians and computer specialists. Immigrants made up 12 percent of the state's labor force in 2000 and almost 18 percent in 2010. Foreign-born workers helped to produce economic growth in many areas, including construction, retail sales, transportation, farming, and fishing. Historically, immigrants have taken many of the lowest-paying, often unpleasant jobs that native-born Americans do not want.

The composition of Maryland's population differs sharply from region to region. In 2010, about 1 million of the state's 1.7 million African Americans lived in just 2 subdivisions: Baltimore City and Prince George's County. In 2010, Maryland's Latino population was similarly concentrated, with more than 62 percent of the state's 470,000 Latinos residing in Montgomery and Prince George's Counties, but with growing numbers in the Baltimore area and parts of the Eastern Shore. The greatest numbers of immigrants from Asia lived in Howard and Montgomery Counties. Western Maryland counties had the highest percentage of native-born whites.

Education and Income

Education and earnings are closely linked. People whose skills are in demand tend to earn good salaries. People with a low literacy level or without market-

Diversity in Government

Earlier chapters have chronicled diversification among elected officials as immigrants, women, and African Americans took their place in local, state, and national government. The first woman was elected to the Maryland General Assembly in 1921 and the first African American in 1954. In the late twentieth and early twenty-first centuries, as the electorate became more diverse, elected officials reflected this new heterogeneity, often first as local officials and as members of Maryland's House of Delegates with its relatively small districts. In the 1990s, 2000s, and 2010s, legislators born in countries as diverse as the Philippines, Jamaica, El Salvador, the Dominican Republic, and Lebanon were elected to the House of Delegates. Sons and daughters of immigrants from countries including India, China, Pakistan, and Korea also served as did Maryland's first Muslim delegate, Saqib Ali of Montgomery County.

■ These immigrants and children of immigrants have chosen to serve the state in the Maryland General Assembly. Courtesy of the offices of the individual delegates.

Kumar Barve, Montgomery County. His father was born in India.

Susan Lee, Montgomery County. Her mother and her paternal grandparents were born in China.

Shirley Nathan-Pulliam, Baltimore County, born in Jamaica.

Joseline Peña-Melnyk, Anne Arundel County, born in the Dominican Republic.

Victor Ramirez, Prince George's County, born in El Salvador.

able skills tend to be paid less, if they can find a job at all. Skills include not only professional knowledge gained through a college education but also competence in fields such as plumbing, electrical, or mechanical work. Maryland's state and local governments have had major responsibility for providing residents with appropriate educational opportunities since the second half of the nineteenth century.

■ Community colleges play a major role in educating men and women for today's economy. Harford Community College partners with local plumbing, heating, and air conditioning contractors on apprenticeship programs and offers training in newer technical fields such as photovoltaic (solar) installation shown here. Workers trained for these jobs earn good salaries because of the demand for their skills. Courtesy of the US Bureau of Labor Statistics, US Department of Labor.

Marylanders overall can claim an increasingly high level of education relative to the nation as a whole based on 2010 census figures. Of Maryland's adult population, 88 percent had high school diplomas, up from 78 percent in 1990. College graduates comprised 36 percent of the state's adults as compared with 26 percent in 1990. Among the state's African American population, 24 percent of people over age 25 were college graduates in 2010, the third highest proportion of black college graduates in the nation. Maryland Latinos, at 21 percent, ranked fourth nationally in the percentage of college graduates. Just under 40 percent of the state's non-Hispanic whites over age 25 were college graduates, the third highest proportion in the country.

■ Local school students work as a team in a robotics competition organized by the College of Southern Maryland, a public community college that serves Charles, St. Mary's, and Calvert Counties. Courtesy of the College of Southern Maryland.

Employers complained in the late twentieth and early twenty-first centuries that they could not find enough men and women with the skills and work habits they needed, even among high school graduates. Ongoing discussions of educational standards and priorities sought to address this problem. School systems instituted frequent testing to help remedy the situation, but testing itself became controversial. Some educators and parents asserted that the tests did not evaluate useful knowledge while others complained that "teaching to the tests" took too much time away from meaningful education. Testing in a few basic subjects often led to the neglect of important but non-tested subjects such as history, geography, some fields of science, and the arts.

Although Maryland's standard of education remained generally high, some students maintained higher achievement levels than others. Students from lower-income families, as determined by their eligibility for free school lunches, generally performed less well on tests than did students from higher-income families. To help remedy this situation, a commission appointed by Governor Parris Glendening and chaired by Dr. Alvin Thornton proposed a new funding formula for the state's public schools. This recommendation was implemented in the 2002 Bridge to Excellence in Public Education Act. The poorest county districts and Baltimore City would receive the largest increases in state aid. Fearing budget problems, legislators passed an amendment that allowed the General Assembly to take an annual vote on whether the state had sufficient funds to meet the monetary goal. The education funds could be cut if the legislature determined that the state could not afford the money in a given year. To help pay for this school aid, the legislature enacted a 34¢ per pack increase in the cigarette tax.

■ Maryland's Environment

Problems of land use, declining water quality, energy use, air pollution, and climate change all posed threats to the way of life in Maryland and to the welfare of the world as a whole. Marylanders disagreed about both the seriousness of the problems and the ways to improve the situation. Pressures for state regulation sometimes succeeded and sometimes did not.

Choosing Sides

Environmentalists and medical experts pointed out the hazards to the environment and to human health caused by pollution from factories, mines, chemical plants, and other industrial sites. Physicians and researchers also concluded that the pollution in poorly made homes with lead in the paint and rodent feces in the floors made people sick. They noted, for example, the prevalence of breathing disorders such as asthma in areas with high levels of air pollution and poor housing conditions. The owners of many mines, industrial sites, and urban real estate, however, often cited the economic benefits of their businesses and resisted the imposition of regulations.

Maryland took steps to abate the danger of lead poisoning with the passage of regulations and the specific Reduction of Lead Risk in Housing Act that passed in the 1990s. The law requires owners of rental properties built before 1978 to register their units with the Maryland Department of the Environment and to meet specific lead paint risk reduction standards. It also requires the owners to distribute educational materials to their tenants. Lead poisoning in children has declined as this law has been enforced.

Environmentalists and agricultural producers differed on policy priorities. Animal waste, from chickens and hogs especially, caused conflict between environmental leaders who wanted it regulated to prevent water pollution and growers who considered it a good fertilizer and did not want to pay the cost of removing it from fields, even as it washed into local streams and thence into the bays and ocean. Although agricultural fertilizers and chemical pesticides often increase short-term profits for farmers, overuse has a negative impact on the larger environment and on the health of people who consume the chemicals through food they eat.

Protecting the "Land of Pleasant Living"

In recent decades, Marylanders and people around the world began paying more attention to the condition of the natural environment and to the impact of environmental pollution on human health. Maryland has been one of the more active states in environmental protection in recent decades. During the late twentieth and early twenty-first centuries, environmental advocates and many government officials worked to create viable solutions to environmental problems. The Chesapeake Bay continued to be one focus of such efforts in Maryland.

The Chesapeake Bay

For Marylanders, the Chesapeake Bay is a source of crabs, oysters, and other seafood, a mainstay of local cuisine and culture, and a favorite place for recreation. A local beer company used to boast that its product was brewed in the "Land of Pleasant Living . . . on the shores of the Chesapeake Bay."

The Chesapeake Bay brings much of Maryland together. Into its waters flow the agricultural wastes from farms, oil and dirt-laden runoff from streets and parking lots of cities and suburbs, and sewage from septic tanks and leaky sew-

■ Acidic mine drainage pollutes streams near the Savage River State Forest in Garrett County. Courtesy of the University of Maryland Center for Environmental Studies.

■ Plastic trash like the bags in this landfill in 2006 present a particular problem because, rather than decomposing, they can persist in the environment for centuries. Courtesy of the University of Maryland Center for Environmental Studies.

Maryland's Environment

■ Patuxent Riverkeeper Fred Tutman, left, is one of many waterkeepers across the state and nation. He preserves, protects, and replenishes the Patuxent through advocacy, restoration, and education. Here, Tutman takes a photographer out on the river. Private collection.

ers and treatment plants. The Potomac and Susquehanna Rivers bring effluents from out of state into the Bay. All of these can create "dead zones," oxygen-deprived areas where nothing can live except certain algae and bacteria. Oxygen levels in the water typically decline during the summer when fertilizers and animal manure provide nutrients that foster algae growth. Algae blooms on the water's surface block sunlight, killing the underwater grasses that, while alive, increase the level of dissolved oxygen in the Bay's waters. When the algae and grasses die, the bacteria that consume them remove oxygen, depriving fish and shellfish of the oxygen they need to survive. The Chesapeake Bay Foundation, founded in 1967, took the lead in educating the public and advocating with the government on behalf of the Bay.

A comprehensive monitoring program introduced in 1986 tracked changes in key indicators. Some years showed improvement but other years saw declines in the health of the Bay. In 1998, Governor Glendening proposed legislation to impose mandatory controls on nutrient (nitrogen and phosphorus) runoff. He encountered determined opposition but a compromise passed that gave farmers up to five years to file plans with the state for reducing the runoff from their fields. Nonetheless, the debate over runoff continued into the twenty-first century.

The Chesapeake Bay Restoration Fee

In the summer of 2003, Chesapeake watermen reported unusually large numbers of dead fish in their nets. Blue crabs actually abandoned the water, crawling onto land because of insufficient oxygen in the Bay. Residents around the Chesapeake refer to such occurrences as "crab jubilees." The fish kill, the crab jubilee, and popular demand encouraged the Ehrlich administration to propose a tax of a $2.50 a month to be added to Marylanders' sewer and water bills. The controversial tax, called the "Flush Tax" by opponents, approved in 2004, would contribute an estimated $1.4 billion needed to upgrade the sixty-six Maryland sewage treatment plants whose discharges ended up in the Chesapeake Bay.

Multi-State and Federal Efforts

In 1983, the governors of Maryland, Virginia, and Pennsylvania and the mayor of the District of Columbia met to discuss the Bay. They agreed that the Bay's problems had roots in all jurisdictions from which water flowed into the Bay and that all would have to work together to ameliorate the situation. They hammered out the first of several Chesapeake Bay Agreements, but none resulted in enough pollution reduction to achieve the goal of sufficiently clean, productive water. Maryland's US senators and congressional representatives pressed for federal action, and the federal government played a growing regulatory role over the decades that followed.

Early in the Obama administration, the Environmental Protection Agency (EPA) required states whose waters fed the Bay to submit plans for reducing pollutants and nutrients in runoff and rivers. Under this program, the EPA got the right to reject plans deemed insufficient. Under federal supervision, the state made progress in reducing Bay contamination from specific "point sources" like sewage and wastewater treatment plants. When some critics maintained that this progress would soon be erased by runoff from "non-point sources" such as farm fields and paved and built-up areas of new and old developments, efforts began to moderate those sources as well.

Sprawl

Sprawl is the name given to the spreading out of residential and commercial areas across what once was farmland, forests, or other open spaces. The counties nearest Washington and Baltimore were the earliest victims of sprawl, but soon more distant counties such as Calvert and Frederick followed the same pattern. Commuters bought homes in areas that still had pleasant open space and often lower home prices. Wider roads and shopping malls followed. Suburban sprawl increased the distances traveled to work and shop, and rush-hour traffic jams prolonged the time needed to cross those distances. Increased burning of fossil fuels caused a rise in air pollution.

Suburban sprawl meant increased paving over of land, resulting in greater runoff of polluted water; no longer absorbed into the ground, it fed into streams, rivers, and eventually the Bay. Sprawl also resulted in cutting down trees that had both absorbed air pollution and lowered air temperature, two beneficial methods of countering climate change and rising global temperatures. Sprawl also meant less good farmland available for production of food crops. Clearly sprawl had become a major problem by the late twentieth century.

Smart Growth

Governor Parris Glendening proposed a program called Smart Growth that took shape in 1996. Instead of stretching superhighways to reach new developments that were consuming farms and woodlands, Glendening proposed concentrating the state's infrastructure investments in existing communities to conserve open space and reduce state expenditures. Rather than build new roads and sewage lines to facilitate outward migration, Smart Growth would finance the repair or replacement of infrastructure in existing neighborhoods to make them more desirable places in which to live.

The Smart Growth bill passed by the General Assembly made incorporated cities and towns "priority funding areas" for state expenditures on public works, including schools. The land encircled by the Baltimore and Washington beltways

Table 8.4. Population of Maryland's Largest Cities, 1990–2010

	1990	2000	2010
Maryland	4,780,753	5,296,486	5,773,552
Baltimore	736,014	651,154	620,961
Frederick	40,148	52,767	65,239
Rockville	44,830	47,388	61,209
Gaithersburg	39,676	52,613	59,933
Bowie	37,642	50,269	54,727
Hagerstown	35,306	36,687	39,662
Annapolis	33,195	35,838	38,394
College Park	23,714	24,657	30,413
Salisbury	20,592	23,743	30,343
Laurel	19,086	19,960	25,115
Greenbelt	20,561	21,456	23,068
Cumberland	23,712	21,518	20,859

Source: US Census.
Note: These cities were the largest incorporated cities in Maryland between 1990 and 2010. Only three of these cities are not within easy commuting distance of Baltimore or Washington.

also qualified for priority funding. Counties could approve developments outside these areas, but they would have to proceed without state support for new roads, sewers, water supply, and schools. The program provided loans and tax incentives to clean up and reuse old industrial and commercial sites. Cumberland's vacant Kelly-Springfield tire factory, for example, was refurbished to accommodate a manufacturer of blankets. Smart Growth also allocated state money to protect forests and farmland from development. Although the legislation met some serious opposition, it passed without being significantly weakened.

Priority Places

During his successful gubernatorial campaign in 2002, Republican Robert Ehrlich declared his support for Smart Growth, though he expressed concern that it might undermine local autonomy in land-use zoning. Once in office, Governor Ehrlich instituted a program called Priority Places and moved Glendening's once independent Office of Smart Growth into the state's Department of Planning.

Ehrlich portrayed his Priority Places program as a mere shift of emphasis within the framework of Smart Growth. Given the state's budget problems, he proposed to reduce expenditures for protecting open space and to concentrate on encouraging development in industrial brownfields and established communities. Critics argued that preserving open space was essential to the success of Smart Growth. A number of organizations, 1000 Friends of Maryland prominent among them, continued to fight for the joint principles of improving existing towns and cities while preserving open farms and forests and taking care of the natural environment.

Suburban sprawl continued despite efforts to control development. Between 2000 and 2010, Frederick, Charles, Calvert, and St. Mary's—all outer-ring suburbs of Washington—experienced the state's highest rates of population increase. Smart Growth and Priority Places may have slowed the pace of suburban sprawl, but the consumption of open space for residential and commercial development continued as the twenty-first century moved beyond its first decade.

Land Preservation Programs

In 1969, the Maryland General Assembly established the nationally recognized Program Open Space (POS) and instituted a one-half of 1 percent transfer tax on every real estate transaction to protect land and create parks and recreation areas. The Department of Natural Resources administered POS, with sites to be chosen by both state and local governments. From its inception through 2014, POS preserved more than 360,000 acres. The program helped protect the Bay by preventing runoff, the air by preserving vegetation, wildlife by safeguarding animal homes and food sources, and human quality of life by making recreational facilities available in all parts of the state. But one difficulty POS faced was that the General Assembly and the governor, in the process of state budgeting, often raided the designated funds, as they raided the Transportation Trust Fund, to pay for other government programs.

A similar program, the Rural Legacy Program, was designed to protect farmland. The program allowed local governments and land trusts to purchase easements that restrict use of selected land to agricultural purposes. From 1999 to 2014, this program protected more than 80,000 acres of farmland. Despite this and other programs designed to protect agricultural land, Maryland in the early twenty-first century lost an average of 25,000 acres of fertile agricultural land to development every year. Once such land is paved over, it is extremely difficult to convert it back to food production.

Powering Maryland: Energy

Maryland, like the rest of the nation, used and also wasted a lot of energy during recent decades. Historically, the state moved from wood and water to coal to petroleum products, natural gas, and nuclear energy by the second half of the twentieth century. Petroleum products powered most vehicles. Coal and nuclear fuels generated most of the electricity used in Maryland in the late twentieth and early twenty-first centuries. Both coal and petroleum products polluted the environment. Nuclear plants, many of which were built across the country in the 1970s, posed the threat of accidents that could release radioactivity. Maryland has one nuclear plant, located at Calvert Cliffs on the shore of the Chesapeake Bay in Calvert County. Two nearby plants, Three Mile Island and Peach Bottom, both located in Pennsylvania near the Maryland line, experienced serious accidents in the late twentieth century. Such accidents resulted in a nationwide pause in construction of new nuclear plants.

Controversies over Fossil Fuels

Fossil fuels, which come from the remains of plants and animals that lived millions of years ago, contain carbon which, when burned, produces energy. Although fossil fuel deposits have been used up faster than they can be made, coal, the dirtiest of the fossil fuels, continued to be widely available, with large reserves that will last for many decades to come. Burning coal pollutes the air and produces chemicals that harm human health. The process of mining coal, dangerous for miners and causing illnesses such as black lung disease, also affects the wider population by degrading the land and poisoning waterways. Petroleum, produced in the United States but also imported from other nations, made the nation dependent on foreign sources while producing pollution when used to power cars and supply electricity. Natural gas provided an alternative that could be used to heat homes and power appliances, vehicles, and machinery. While cleaner than coal or petroleum, natural gas also pollutes. Marylanders used natural gas increasingly during the latter part of the twentieth and early twenty-first centuries. A natural gas terminal at Cove Point in Calvert County, where ships carrying liquefied natural gas can dock to offload supplies, had fallen into disuse but was revived as an import facility in 2003. During the second decade of the twenty-first century, the state approved Cove Point as a facility for the export of natural gas.

One source of contention about the building of an export facility at Cove Point centered on a process called fracking, short for hydraulic fracturing. Fracking involves the use of sand, water, and chemicals injected at high pressures to blast open shale rock deep underground to release the gas trapped inside. The process requires millions of gallons of fresh water and large swaths of land. Fracking can pollute ground water, including water people rely on for drinking; there is also some evidence that it can trigger earthquakes. The first proposals for fracking operations in Maryland involved Garrett and Allegany Counties. Studies identified other areas in the state where fracking would also be profitable, but the process could not begin if Maryland banned it. The dispute over allowing fracking continued beyond 2015.

Climate Change

The use of fossil fuels also adversely affects the world's climate. An increasing awareness of the resulting hazards grew during the past three decades. Warming temperatures in many parts of the world, along with concomitant droughts, floods, and other weather events, wreaked havoc on agricultural land and urban

In September 2003, Hurricane Isabel swamped the City Dock area in Annapolis with so much water that people came out to play. Despite the levity shown here, the storm severely damaged many homes and businesses. Courtesy of the Federal Emergency Management Agency, 42061.

environments. In some places, climate changes threatened the availability of drinking water. Although Maryland has a good supply of potable water, any major drought or decrease in the food supply affects the state. As global warming melted polar glaciers, sea levels began to rise, threatening low-lying Maryland communities like Smith Island and land along the Atlantic Ocean coast, coastal bays, and the Chesapeake Bay.

Scientists have attributed a worldwide increase in serious storms to climate change. Hurricanes, typhoons, blizzards, and other extreme weather events have increased in frequency and intensity in recent decades both nationally and worldwide. Maryland has been affected directly by such storms, particularly by hurricanes. In 2003, Hurricane Isabel, with storm surges of more than 8 feet along the Bay's shore and 6.5 feet of ocean water in Ocean City, resulted in flooding and other destruction, causing one death and property damage valued at more than $530 million. The deadliest hurricane of the period, 2012's Hurricane Sandy, caused eleven deaths in the state and enormous hardship north of Maryland.

Many people see climate change as the most serious existential problem of the twenty-first century. Although some people still denied the reality of climate change in the early twenty-first century or disputed the role of humans as agents of the change, most by then agreed that the dangers were real; governments around the world were beginning to take steps to reduce production of the fossil fuels that contributed to the havoc.

New Energy Sources

Just as Marylanders began talking about Smart Growth, they came to recognize the possibilities of Smart Energy from renewable and less polluting sources. In 2008, the General Assembly set a goal that 20 percent of Maryland's energy use by 2022 would come from renewable sources rather than from increasingly depleted fossil fuel supplies. Examples of non-polluting energy sources include solar panels that collect energy directly from the sun and geothermal energy that makes use of underground water pumped through buildings to add winter heat and reduce summer temperatures.

Wind power is another source of energy that began to grow in popularity at the end of the twentieth century, but not without arousing some serious controversy. Wind turbines can kill birds and bats, while the noise generated by turbines placed at sea harms marine life, especially mammals with keen hearing such as whales and dolphins. Some researchers also assert that turbine noise on land is harmful to human health. A major controversy erupted over a proposed wind farm in Somerset County when the Defense Department contended that the turbines would interfere with work done at the nearby Patuxent Naval Air Station. Further controversy broke out over whether wind turbines miles out at sea would destroy the view from Ocean City's beaches.

■ Politics: Office Holders, Elections, and Issues

During the decades near the turn of the twenty-first century, Maryland faced challenges and made decisions on many fronts. For the most part, officials elected by the people and their appointees made the decisions about how to deal with the various issues, a number of them contentious. In some cases, the political majority prevailed; in others, opposing sides reached compromises.

Maryland's Political Scene

Maryland was a majority Democratic, or "blue," state from 1986 to 2015. In all presidential elections, Maryland gave a majority of its votes to the Democratic candidates. The two US senators and the majority of members of the US House of Representatives were also Democrats. Although voters elected two Republican governors during this period, the General Assembly remained under Democratic control. Both Democrats and Republicans served as county executives, as members of county councils, and in other local capacities. Generally, the heavily populated metropolitan areas such as Baltimore City, Montgomery County, and Prince George's County elected Democrats while the Eastern

■ Governor Larry Hogan, a Republican, won a clear majority in the 2014 election, enjoying personal popularity across the state despite Maryland's normally Democratic majority. In this photograph, Governor Hogan and his wife Yumi are escorted on January 21, 2015, his inauguration day, by Major General Linda Singh, whom Hogan appointed as adjutant general of Maryland. Courtesy of govpics.maryland.gov, DSC_7737.jpg.

Shore and Western and Southern Maryland often voted for Republicans. Baltimore County provided the swing vote in a number of elections.

Maryland elections resulted in three Democratic and two Republican governors since 1985. In the election of 1986, Baltimore's Mayor William Donald Schaefer was elected by 82 percent of the votes, a huge victory and tribute to his popularity across the state. He easily won reelection in 1990. Democrat Parris Glendening won election in 1994 and 1998 and Democrat Martin O'Malley in 2006 and 2010. The Republican victories by Robert Ehrlich in 2002 and Larry Hogan 2014 were considered surprising results because of Maryland's heavily Democratic registration. Low turnouts by normally Democratic voters played an essential role in the Republican victories as did larger than usual support for the Republicans who won. In both cases, some political pundits blamed the Democratic losses on poor campaigns run by outgoing Lieutenant Governors Kathleen Kennedy Townsend and Anthony Brown. In 2014, analysts concluded that Hogan's moderate pronouncements and positive ads boosted his campaign while Brown's negative ads weakened his support.

Marylanders elected a majority of Democrats and a minority of Republicans to the state General Assembly in all the elections from 1986 to 2014. Thomas V. "Mike" Miller, a Democrat, became president of the Senate in 1986 and continued to serve into the second decade of the twenty-first century. Democrats Benjamin Cardin, R. Clayton Mitchell, Casper Taylor, and Michael Busch held the office of Speaker of the House during the same period.

One important trend during these years was the increase in the number of Republicans elected to local offices. In 1986, Republicans represented only 25 percent of local officials. By 1998, they accounted for 38 percent, and by 2010, for fully 50 percent of local office holders. The large populations of the Democratic

■ Community leaders and children came together to celebrate the opening of the K–8 Henderson-Hopkins Public School in East Baltimore in 2014. Adults from left to right: Morgan State University President Dr. David Wilson, Representative John Sarbanes, Senator Barbara Mikulski, Governor Martin O'Malley, Johns Hopkins University President Ronald Daniels, and Representative Elijah Cummings. Courtesy of Homewood Imaging and Photographic Services, 20140210_JHU7932_a-print.

strongholds of Montgomery and Prince George's Counties and Baltimore City dominated statewide elections, but voters in some of the less populated counties chose Republicans in many local elections.

Another trend with important implications for the political process was the amount of money spent on election campaigns. Many feared that this infusion of money would put political control in the hands of a few wealthy donors. Total gubernatorial campaign expenditures grew from around $8 million in 1994 to more than $24 million in 2014. However, the biggest spenders did not always win. One case in point is the contest between Republican Larry Hogan and Democrat Anthony Brown in 2014. Hogan, who accepted public funding and its accompanying limits, spent millions of dollars less than Brown, but still won.

Some Major Issues

Many policy issues occupied the attention of Marylanders during the years from 1986 to the beginning of 2015. These include topics already discussed such as the economy and economic development, transportation, education, land use, and the environment. Taxes always constitute a major issue for voters, who generally prefer to pay lower taxes and fewer fees while not giving up any government services from which they benefit. Other issues that concerned Maryland's citizens during this period included the death penalty; slots and casinos as a source of increased revenue for the state; the Dream Act to allow some noncitizen immigrant residents to attend college while paying reduced in-state tuition; and the Same-Sex Marriage Act to allow people of the same sex to marry legally in Maryland. Positions of support for or opposition to these issues often reflected people's cultural heritage and religious beliefs.

> ### War and Terror around the World
>
> The nation and the world have experienced the horrors of war and terror in recent decades. These national and international tragedies impacted Maryland and its people extensively. Marylanders fought in wars in places like the Persian Gulf, Iraq, and Afghanistan, suffering injuries, illness, and death. School shootings and homegrown terrorism made Marylanders fear for their safety as they went about their everyday business. The horror of the 2001 attacks on the World Trade Center in New York and the Pentagon in nearby Virginia changed Marylanders' lives in many ways, from the imposition of greater security measures for simple things like entering government buildings to cyber-security measures to the insecurity of never knowing when or where violence might occur next. Most actions to deal with these crises occurred on a national or international level, but state action did include increased security in public places and government facilities, debate over and the passage of gun laws, and added security in schools, among other measures to help keep people safe. No history of Maryland in the late twentieth and early twenty-first centuries can be complete without an awareness of the problems of the wider world.

Death Penalty

The death penalty had been in use in Maryland since the colonial period. Worldwide controversy over the morality and the effectiveness of its use increased during the twentieth century. Some nations and some states abolished the death penalty for a variety of reasons that included a belief that one person did not have the right to take the life of another; that the penalty was inhumane; that it did not prevent the most heinous crimes; and that the process itself, including the inevitable appeals, was expensive. As the issue came to the fore in Maryland, opponents offered two key arguments: that innocent people were sometimes executed and that the punishment was not fairly applied. Statistics showed that African Americans received the death penalty more often than whites and that some counties imposed the death sentence more frequently than others. A wide-ranging public discussion continued for several decades. Governor Glendening halted executions by executive order in 2002 while a study was being done; Governor Ehrlich resumed executions in 2004. A study commission established in 2008 by the General Assembly concluded that there were both racial and geographic disparities in the imposition of the death penalty. In 2013, a bill abolishing the death penalty in Maryland became law and, shortly before the end of his term, Governor O'Malley commuted the sentences of the four remaining death row prisoners to life in prison without parole.

Slots and Casinos

Various forms of gambling and laws regulating the practice existed from the colonial period. Slot machines, located even in grocery stores, were popular and legal in Southern Maryland from the 1940s to the 1960s. In the 1970s, a new state lottery became the instrument for legal gambling. Beginning in 2010, slot machines and then full-scale casinos became a new revenue source for Maryland. Several proposals preceded the reality. Racetrack owners, who pointed to a decline in horse racing and breeding in the state, suggested that slots at tracks would draw bigger crowds and greater revenues to support the racing industry. Soon, others suggested that money from gambling could be used to support education. Robert Ehrlich, when running for governor in 2002, proposed legalizing slots and said that his electoral victory signaled that Marylanders supported this effort. Many lawmakers, including powerful House of Delegates speaker Michael Busch, opposed gambling and the measure did not pass. Governor O'Malley succeeded in getting the bill through the legislature; when it was submitted for referendum in 2008, a majority of voters approved the measure. Opponents had argued that gambling harmed families by draining money from spending on necessities and that casinos would attract organized crime to the state. Religious leaders testified that gambling was an avoidable evil, but the argument that casinos would raise money for government programs won out. After the first new slots opened in 2010, it quickly became apparent that more money could be raised if casinos could also operate games such as blackjack and roulette. This expansion received legislative and referendum approval in 2012.

The first slots casino opened in Perryville in Cecil County in 2010. By 2014, some racetracks also had slot machines and five casinos across the state had licenses for both slots and gaming tables. In addition to the Hollywood Casino in Perryville, the casinos were located in Allegany, Anne Arundel, and Worcester Counties and in Baltimore City, with a sixth licensed to open in Prince George's County in 2016. Money did pour into the casinos, with about two-thirds of the proceeds returned to gamblers as winnings. Between 2010 and 2014, more than $700 million went into the state's Education Trust Fund. However, as this money generally replaced other allocations, it did not actually increase the total available for schools. Other monies went to general state expenses and to casino owners. Critics argued that with many states legalizing casino gambling, Maryland's revenues would over time decline.

The Dream Act

In 2011, the General Assembly passed the Maryland In-State Tuition Act allowing certain foreign-born residents of the state to attend state and local colleges and universities at the in-state or in-county tuition rate, lower than the tuition charged to non-Maryland residents. This measure was designed primarily to benefit undocumented immigrant children brought by their parents to this country at a young age. To qualify for in-state tuition, students had to have attended a Maryland high school for at least three years and to prove that they or their parents had filed tax returns. Students would begin their higher education in a community college and, after two years, could transfer to a four-year institution. The students would be admitted from an out-of-state pool of applicants to ensure that they did not displace any qualified in-state resident citizens.

United Food and Commercial Workers union members rallied in Annapolis in 2014 as Marylanders campaigned for the state to mandate a higher minimum wage. The General Assembly passed a law requiring that the minimum wage be raised to $10.10 by 2018. Courtesy of MdGovPics, 11971487973.

Supporters argued that it was only fair to allow young people who had grown up in Maryland and considered it their home to get a college education. Furthermore, an advanced education would enable such students to contribute to the state's economy. Opponents asserted that these young people did not deserve such benefits because of their illegal status. After the bill became law, it was submitted for referendum in 2012 and approved by approximately 60 percent of the voters.

Civil Marriage Protection Act

When same-sex marriage became a topic of nationwide discussion in the 1970s, Maryland law established that a legal marriage was specifically the union of one man and one woman. In 2001, Maryland's Antidiscrimination Act provided equal protection for gays and lesbians in housing, employment, and accommodations. For several decades, a political debate raged between supporters and opponents of the right of same-sex individuals to marry in the state. Religious denominations debated the same question, with some liberal mainline Protestant groups and liberal Jewish groups supporting same-sex marriage while the Roman Catholic Church and many conservative denominations opposed it. A number of individuals brought court cases that, among other claims, asserted that outlawing same-sex marriage denied equal rights to all individuals. In 2006, the state legalized civil unions, which extended to same-sex couples some but not all of the rights of married people. In 2008, the General Assembly approved bills allowing certain rights to unmarried domestic partners, including hospital and nursing home visits, end-of-life choice participation, and joint property ownership provisions. After defeats of several similar bills, the 2012 Civil Marriage Protection Act, which allowed religious leaders and institutions to choose whether they would perform same-sex marriages, passed the legislature and was signed into law by Governor O'Malley. The law was petitioned to referendum and, in November 2012, won approval from 52 percent of the voters. As of January 1, 2013, same-sex marriages became legal in Maryland.

■ Maryland's Culture

Both within the state and because of proximity to the District of Columbia, Maryland residents had access to a wide array of cultural, recreational, and entertainment choices catering to a broad variety of tastes and incomes. Some cultural institutions had a long history while others were quite new.

Music and Theater

The Baltimore Symphony Orchestra, which in 2007 appointed Marin Alsop the first female music director and conductor of any major American symphony, commanded international respect under her leadership. Symphony orchestras played in Hagerstown, Frederick, Columbia, Annapolis, and other towns as well. The Music Center at Strathmore in Bethesda, the Meyerhoff Symphony Hall in Baltimore, and the Merriweather Post Pavilion in Columbia provided performance spaces for a variety of artists from rock, blues, and bluegrass bands to symphony orchestras and ballet companies. Maryland supported with pride internationally known musicians including pianist Leon Fleisher, violinist Hilary Hahn, and guitarist Manuel Barrueco. Popular musical artists of the early twenty-first century included singer Toni Braxton and the members of the band Good Charlotte from Waldorf.

Baltimore residents looked to the Everyman and Center Stage theaters for live drama, and patronized the Hippodrome, a former movie theater that re-opened in 2004 to host touring Broadway shows. Many of Maryland's smaller cities and towns had thriving local theaters of their own. These included the Colonial Players in Annapolis, the Chesapeake Shakespeare Company in Ellicott City, Olney Theater in Olney, and the Port Tobacco Players in La Plata.

Museums and Artists

Museums both expanded and proliferated across the state. Baltimore's well-known Walters Art Museum and Baltimore Museum of Art had attracted visitors from far away since the early part of the twentieth century, and Bethesda, Easton, Fred-

The Music Center at Strathmore in North Bethesda, which opened in 2005, can seat 1,976 patrons for each of the more than 150 concerts presented annually. Kirkegaard Associates, Chicago, IL, 2015.

erick, Hagerstown, Hyattsville, Rockville, and Solomons, as well as several of Maryland's colleges and universities, established art museums. Some newly opened museums represented distinctive departures from more traditional collections.

The Visionary Art Museum opened at the site of a former whiskey warehouse and copper paint factory at the foot of Federal Hill in Baltimore. Its permanent collection held works of "grassroots genius" by self-taught "outsider" artists. Founder Rebecca Alban Hoffberger conceived the museum while volunteering in a program that prepared psychiatric patients to return to the community. Hoffberger raised $7 million, the city of Baltimore donated the land, and the state issued $1.3 million in revenue bonds to start renovation of the first two buildings, which opened in 1995.

Baltimore's National Great Blacks in Wax Museum provided a sculptural representation of black history and culture. Exhibits included more than one

Maryland's Culture

The Chesapeake Bay Maritime Museum in St. Michaels offers exhibits, demonstrations, boat rides on the Miles River, and annual festivals that celebrate Chesapeake Bay culture, boats, seafood, and history. Photo: Mark Sandlin for the Talbot County Office of Tourism.

hundred wax figures of African Americans who have played prominent roles in the nation's history. Established in 1983 by Drs. Elmer and Joanna Martin, the museum attracted approximately three hundred thousand visitors a year in the early twenty-first century. The Reginald F. Lewis Museum of African American History and Culture in Baltimore, established in 2005, featured both permanent and temporary exhibits as well as educational programs. In Annapolis, the Banneker-Douglass Museum, established in 1984, highlighted the contributions of famous black Marylanders and the state's African American heritage. Its collections included samples of African and African American art. In Prince George's County, the African American Museum and Cultural Center formed part of the Gateway Arts District. In addition to the museum, the District included affordable studio and living space for active artists. The Center also provided space for poetry readings, musical performances, and public lectures.

The Jewish Museum of Maryland, founded in Baltimore in 1960 and enlarged in the twenty-first century, presented exhibits on Jewish history and culture in Maryland as well as the history of the East Baltimore neighborhood where many Jewish immigrants first settled. The organization preserved the historic Lloyd Street and B'nai Israel Synagogues and conducted educational programs open to all. In Bethesda, the Ratner Museum, the shared creation of two cousins, Philip and Dennis Ratner, featured sculpture and paintings that embody the narrative of the Old Testament and the spirit of Jewish tradition.

Renowned artists shared their talents with Maryland's students and with the wider community as faculty members at the Maryland Institute College of Art, a major state educational institution that thrived for several decades under the creative direction of President Fred Lazarus until his retirement in 2014. Highly respected artists of the late twentieth and early twenty-first centuries included painter Grace Hartigan, whose works were displayed at the Baltimore Museum of Art along with the Metropolitan and Whitney Museums in New York; Connie Imboden, whose photographs resided in the permanent collections of many museums worldwide, including the Museum of Modern Art in New York and the Bibliothèque Nationale in Paris; and Joyce Scott, whose beaded sculptures addressed social issues such as race, gender, and class and whose works were displayed in a number of Maryland venues as well as at the Smithsonian, the Philadelphia Museum of Art, and the American Craft Museum in New York.

Literature and Film

Although Maryland is a small state, it produced a number of notable writers during this period. Anne Tyler won the Pulitzer Prize for Fiction in 1989 for her novel *Breathing Lessons*. Historian Taylor Branch, whose trilogy about the civil rights struggle during the King years and whose biography of President Bill Clinton won him international fame, received the Pulitzer Prize for History for *Parting the Waters: America in the King Years, 1954–1963*.

National Book Award winner and Hopkins faculty member John Barth gained worldwide renown for his diverse works of fiction. Laura Lippman's mysteries set in Baltimore and Christopher Tilghman's novels set on the Eastern Shore attracted national as well as Maryland readers. David Anthony Durham's novels, including *Gabriel's Story*, about African American settlers in the American West, were prominent among the works of the new generation of black writers. Journalist Ta-Nehisi Coates won the National Book Award for his 2015 nonfiction book *Between the World and Me*, about living black in America. Poets Mary Jo Salter and Daniel Epstein as well as sportswriter Frank Deford made their mark nationally. Many noted print and broadcast journalists made Maryland, especially suburban Washington, their home.

In the 1980s, the Maryland Film Office began promoting Maryland as a good location for making movies and television shows. In 1995, when the office joined the Department of Business and Economic Development, its staff began estimating the economic impact of filmmaking in Maryland. The figure calculated for 1995 was $56 million. The numbers varied from year to year, reaching $123.5 million in 2012.

Films of note with local writers and locations included *The Accidental Tourist*, based on a novel by Anne Tyler; *Tin Men* and *Avalon*, written and directed by Barry Levinson; and *Cry-Baby* and *Hairspray*, musical romantic comedies written and directed by John Waters. The award-winning television shows *Homicide: Life on the Streets* and *The Wire* were located and filmed in Baltimore, with scripts written by former *Baltimore Sun* reporter David Simon. *The Wire*'s portrayal of the sale of drugs and the prevalence of crime in Baltimore made it controversial, but both it and *Homicide* were critical successes. In the early twenty-first century, Maryland-filmed productions included hit shows *Veep* and *House of Cards*. Government financial incentives played a role in attracting the film companies, and the allotment of tax breaks and other incentives became a political football, which also resulted in ups and downs in the filmmaking business in Maryland.

Sports

Sports continued to be an important source of both entertainment and tourism income. The Baltimore Orioles and the Washington Nationals baseball teams drew large crowds. Baltimore built a new downtown stadium to replace the old

■ Marylanders quickly became fans of the new Ravens football team, which began playing in Baltimore in 1996, several years after the shocking departure of the Colts. Here, Ravens Ray Lewis (*left*) and Shannon Sharpe (*right*) flank owner Art Modell. Courtesy of the Baltimore Ravens.

■ The 139th running of the Preakness Stakes at Pimlico Race Course in Baltimore in 2014. Horse racing has been a favorite sport in Maryland since the colonial years. Courtesy of MdGovPics, 14042907527.

Memorial Stadium and bring people to the neighborhoods around the Inner Harbor. The Nationals, supported by many Marylanders, built a new stadium in southwest Washington. Pro football drew huge crowds during the fall and winter months. In 1984, Baltimore's Colts angered most fans by loading up trucks and moving to Indianapolis in the middle of one night. After several years, a new team came to Baltimore, taking Ravens as their name. The Ravens built a new stadium next to Oriole Park at Camden Yards, drawing even more fans downtown and quickly becoming hugely popular. The Washington Redskins football team also built a new stadium in the Maryland suburb of Landover and attracted large crowds as well.

Increased interest in a diversity of sports marked the early twenty-first century. Basketball, lacrosse, soccer, and tennis enjoyed popularity across the nation. A number of Marylanders won Olympic gold medals, among them Pam Shriver in tennis, Michael Phelps and Katie Ledecky in swimming, Jessica Long in Paralympic swimming, Dominique Dawes in gymnastics, Kimmie Meissner in ice skating, and Bernard Williams in track.

■ From Past to Present to Future

The line from past to present moves inevitably toward an unknown future. Maryland in 2015 was a vastly different place from Maryland in 1634. A modern technological society, with all of its advantages and all of its problems, had replaced the colonial wilderness. The once sparsely populated land had grown crowded with the great variety of people that makes the United States distinctive. Many challenges remain for Marylanders in the years to come. Some of them will simply be repetitions or continuations of old challenges. Others cannot yet be imagined.

The economy will have to adjust periodically to new conditions, while social customs change constantly. Recent years have witnessed strong campaigns for greater equality, yet discrimination and inequities still remain. Increasing population and past failure to care for the environment have put a strain on the natural resources that have served the state well and on the overall health of the planet. The decisionmakers of the future can benefit from the experiences of the past. Past successes give clues about how to proceed while the failures of the past indicate what to avoid. Marylanders, while looking forward to the future, will benefit by glancing backward at the state's rich history.

appendix A

Supplementary Maps

See following pages.

Political Map of Maryland, 2015

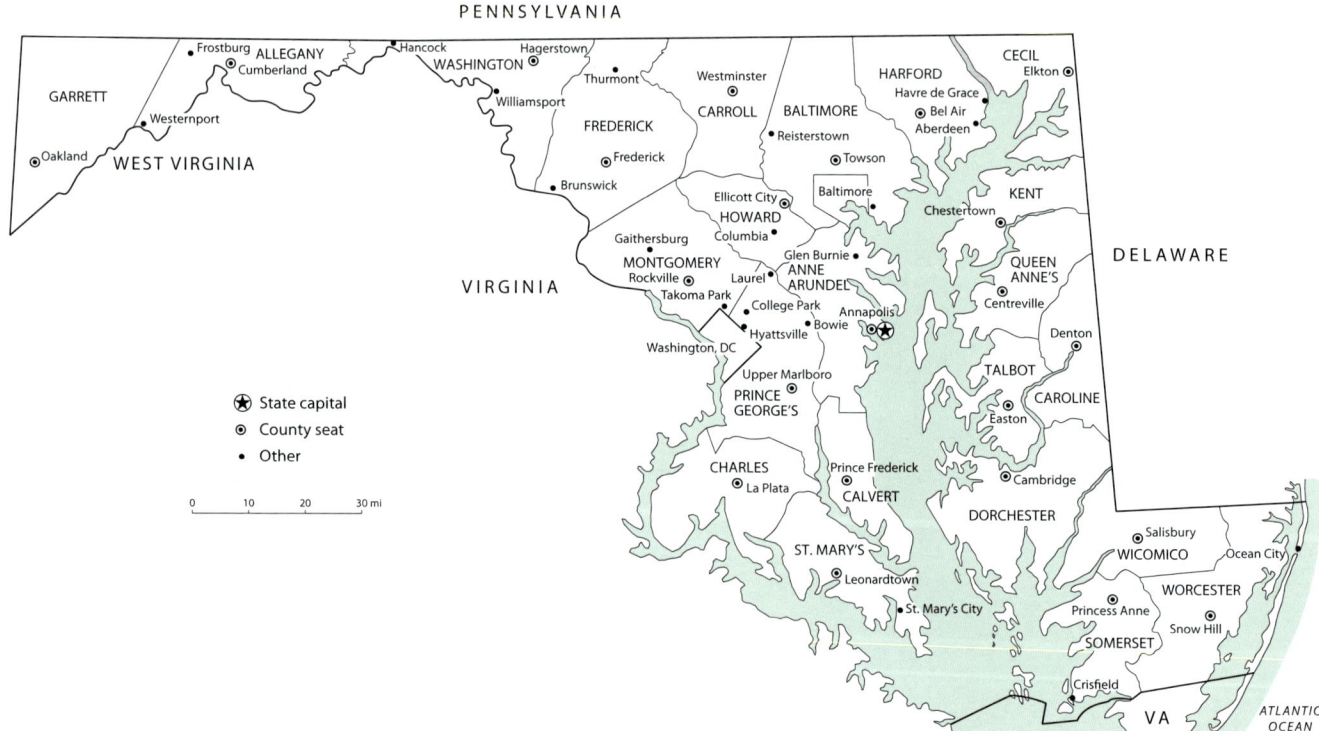

Geographic Regions of Maryland

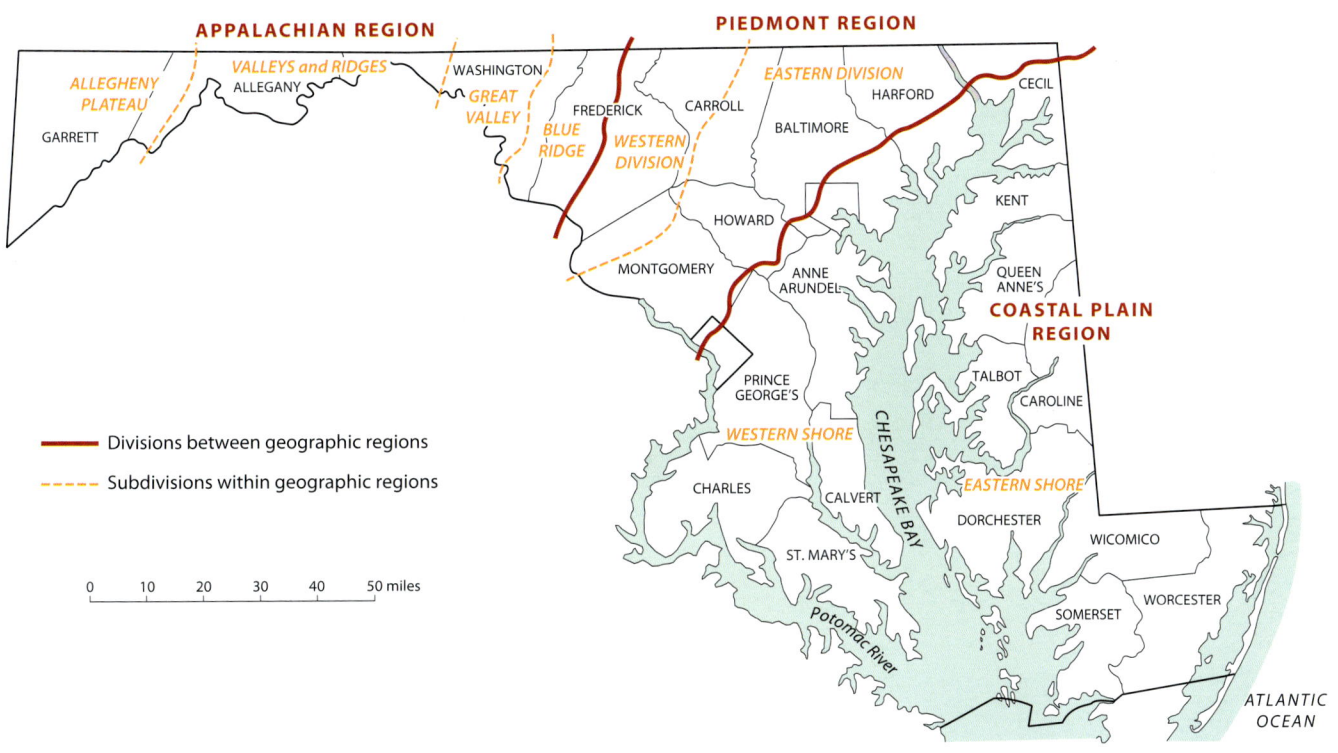

Supplementary Maps

Progress of Settlement in Maryland, 1631–1800

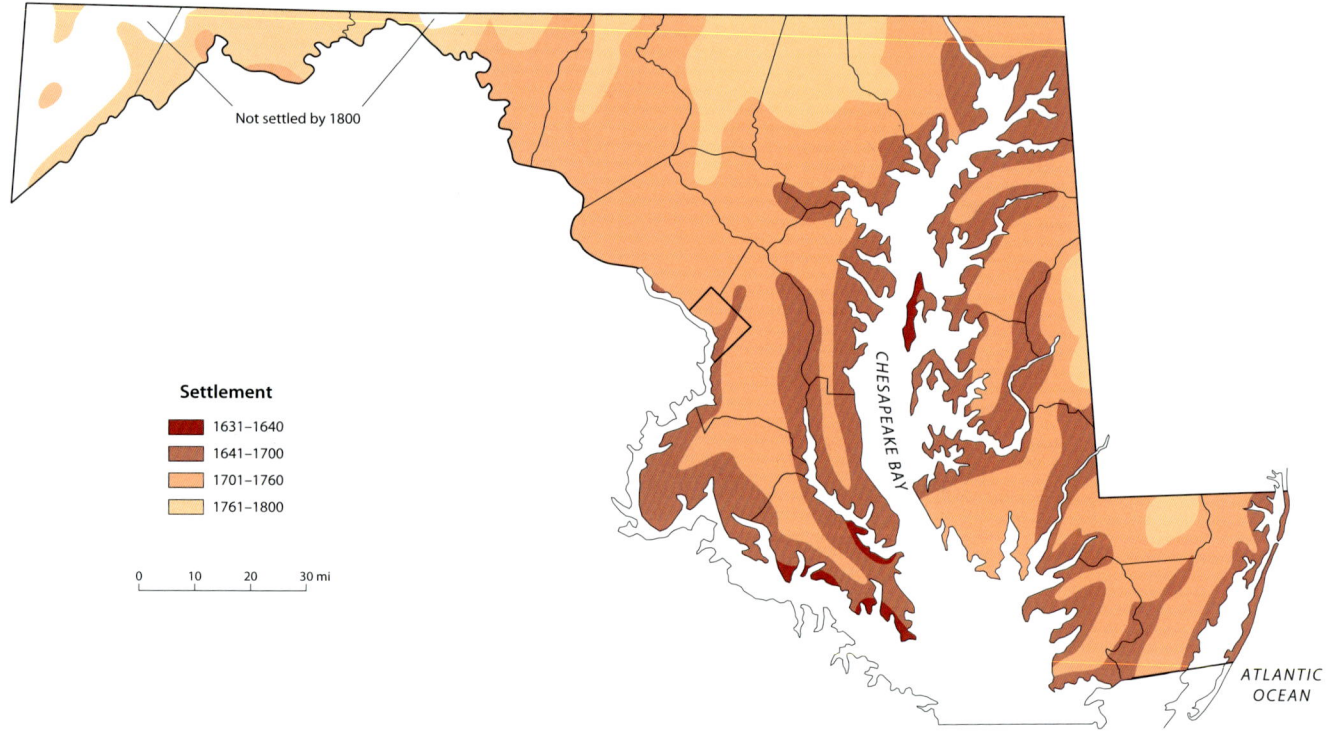

Evolution of Maryland Counties, 1755, 1860, and 2015

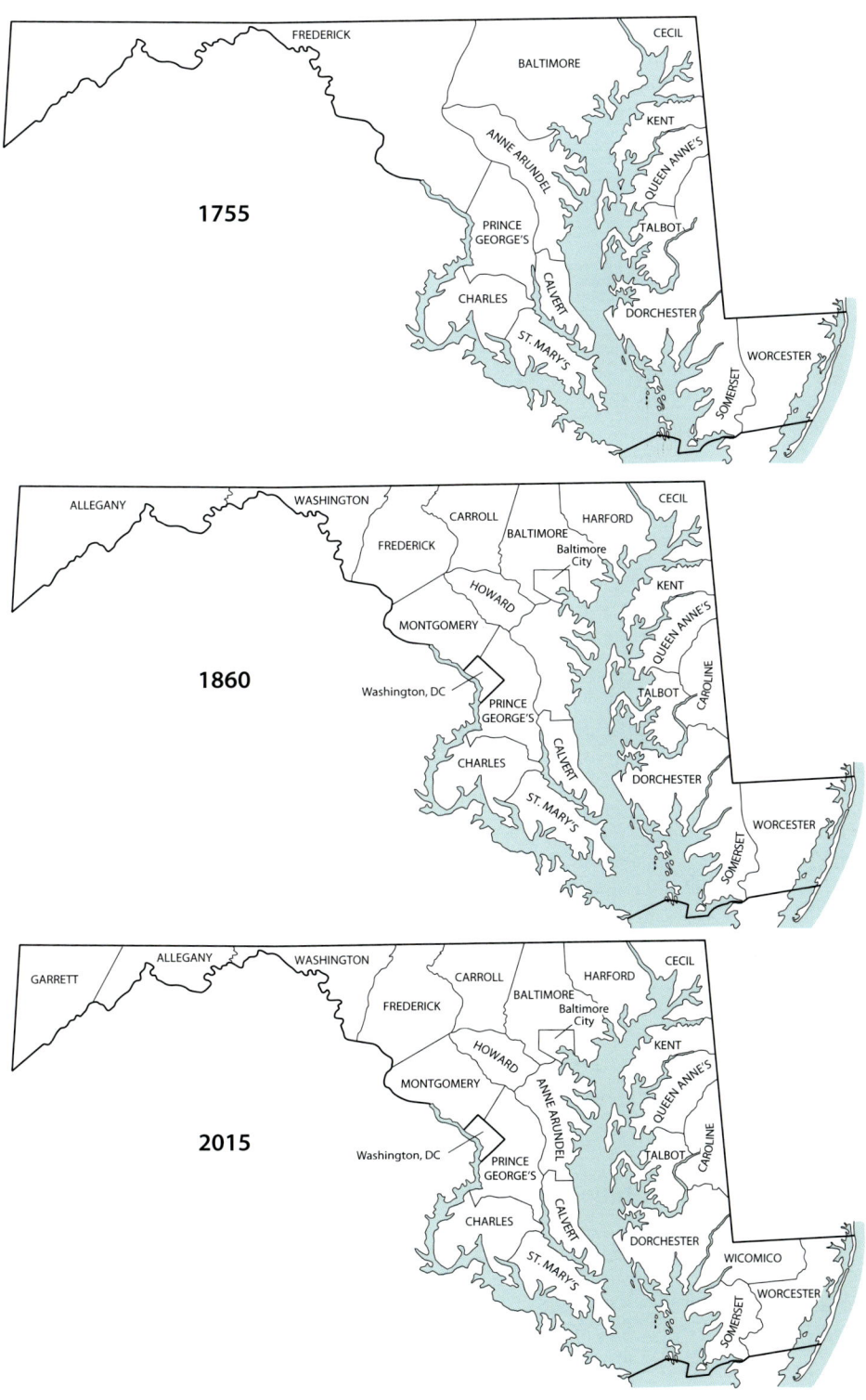

Supplementary Maps

appendix B

Governors of Maryland

Colonial Governors

1634–1647	Leonard Calvert		1693–1694	Colonel Nicholas Greenberry
1647–1649	Thomas Greene		1694	Sir Edmund Andros
1649–1652	Captain William Stone		1694	Sir Thomas Lawrence
1652	Parliamentary Commissioners		1694–1699	Francis Nicholson
1652–1654	Captain William Stone		1699–1702	Colonel Nathaniel Blackiston
1654–1657	Commissioners appointed by the Parliamentary Commissioners		1702–1704	Thomas Tench
			1704–1709	Colonel John Seymour
1657–1660	Josias Fendall		1709–1714	Major General Edward Lloyd
1660–1661	Philip Calvert		1714–1720	John Hart
1661–1676	Charles Calvert		1720	Thomas Brooke
1676	Jesse Wharton		1721–1727	Charles Calvert
1676–1679	Thomas Notley		1727–1731	Benedict Leonard Calvert
1679–1684	Charles Calvert, Third Lord Baltimore		1731–1732	Samuel Ogle
1684–1688	Benedict Leonard Calvert (Council of Deputy Governors during his minority)		1732–1733	Charles Calvert, Fifth Lord Baltimore
			1733–1742	Samuel Ogle
1688–1689	William Joseph		1742–1747	Thomas Bladen
1689–1690	John Coode		1747–1752	Samuel Ogle
1691–1692	Nehemiah Blackiston		1752–1753	Benjamin Tasker
1692–1693	Sir Lionel Copley		1753–1769	Horatio Sharpe
1693	Sir Thomas Lawrence		1769–1776	Robert Eden
1693	Sir Edmund Andros			

Governors Elected under the Constitution of 1776 by the Legislature for One Year

		Party	Birthplace
1777–1779	Thomas Johnson	None	Calvert County
1779–1782	Thomas Sim Lee	None	Prince George's County
1782–1785	William Paca	None	Harford County

1785–1788	William Smallwood	None	Charles County
1788–1791	John Eager Howard	Federalist	Baltimore City
1791–1792	George Plater	Federalist	St. Mary's County
1792–1794	Thomas Sim Lee	Federalist	Prince George's County
1794–1797	John Hoskins Stone	Federalist	Charles County
1797–1798	John Henry	Federalist	Dorchester County
1798–1801	Benjamin Ogle	Federalist	Anne Arundel County
1801–1803	John Francis Mercer	Democrat	Stafford County, Virginia
1803–1806	Robert Bowie	Democrat	Prince George's County
1806–1809	Robert Wright	Democrat	Queen Anne's County
1809–1811	Edward Lloyd	Democrat	Talbot County
1811–1812	Robert Bowie	Democrat	Prince George's County
1812–1816	Levin Winder	Federalist	Somerset County
1816–1819	Charles Ridgely of Hampton	Federalist	Baltimore County
1819	Charles Goldsborough	Federalist	Dorchester County
1819–1822	Samuel Sprigg	Democrat	Prince George's County
1822–1826	Samuel Stevens Jr.	Democrat	Talbot County
1826–1829	Joseph Kent	Democrat	Calvert County
1829–1830	Daniel Martin	Anti-Jackson	Talbot County
1830–1831	Thomas King Carroll	Jackson Democrat	Somerset County
1831	Daniel Martin	Anti-Jackson	Talbot County
1831–1833	George Howard	Anti-Jackson	Anne Arundel County
1833–1836	James Thomas	Anti-Jackson	St. Mary's County
1836–1839	Thomas W. Veazey	Whig	Cecil County

Governors Elected by the People for Three Years under the Constitution of 1776 as Amended in 1837

		Party	Birthplace
1839–1842	William Grason	Democrat	Queen Anne's County
1842–1845	Francis Thomas	Democrat	Frederick County
1845–1848	Thomas G. Pratt	Whig	Georgetown, DC
1848–1851	Philip Francis Thomas	Democrat	Talbot County
1851–1854	Enoch Louis Lowe	Democrat	Frederick County

Governors Elected under the Constitution of 1851 by the People for Four Years

		Party	Birthplace
1854–1858	Thomas Watkins Ligon	Democrat	Prince Edward County, Virginia
1858–1862	Thomas Holliday Hicks	Native American	Dorchester County
1862–1866	Augustus W. Bradford	Unionist	Harford County

Governor Elected under the Constitution of 1864 by the People for Four Years

		Party	Birthplace
1866–1869	Thomas Swann	Unionist	Alexandria, Virginia

Governors Elected under the Constitution of 1867 by the People for Four Years

		Party	Birthplace
1869–1872	Oden Bowie	Democrat	Prince George's County
1872–1874	William Pinkney Whyte	Democrat	Baltimore City
1874–1876	James Black Groome	Democrat	Cecil County
1876–1880	John Lee Carroll	Democrat	Baltimore City
1880–1884	William T. Hamilton	Democrat	Washington County
1884–1885	Robert M. McLane	Democrat	Wilmington, Delaware
1885–1888	Henry Lloyd	Democrat	Dorchester County
1888–1892	Elihu E. Jackson	Democrat	Somerset County
1892–1896	Frank Brown	Democrat	Carroll County
1896–1900	Lloyd Lowndes	Republican	Clarksburg, West Virginia
1900–1904	John Walter Smith	Democrat	Worcester County
1904–1908	Edwin Warfield	Democrat	Howard County
1908–1912	Austin L. Crothers	Democrat	Cecil County
1912–1916	Phillips Lee Goldsborough	Republican	Dorchester County
1916–1920	Emerson C. Harrington	Democrat	Dorchester County
1920–1935	Albert C. Ritchie	Democrat	Richmond, Virginia
1935–1939	Harry W. Nice	Republican	Washington, DC
1939–1947	Herbert R. O'Conor	Democrat	Baltimore City
1947–1951	William Preston Lane Jr.	Democrat	Washington County
1951–1959	Theodore R. McKeldin	Republican	Baltimore City
1959–1967	J. Millard Tawes	Democrat	Somerset County
1967–1969	Spiro T. Agnew	Republican	Baltimore City
1969–1979	Marvin Mandel	Democrat	Baltimore City
1979–1987	Harry R. Hughes	Democrat	Talbot County
1987–1995	William Donald Schaefer	Democrat	Baltimore City
1995–2003	Parris N. Glendening	Democrat	Prince George's County
2003–2007	Robert L. Ehrlich Jr.	Republican	Baltimore County
2007–2015	Martin J. O'Malley	Democrat	Baltimore City
2015–	Lawrence J. Hogan Jr.	Republican	Prince George's County

Source: Information from the *Maryland Manual*, courtesy of the Maryland State Archives.

Glossary

abolitionist: A person who wanted to end slavery.

Anglican Church: The Church of England. This was the legally established church in Maryland from 1692 until the American Revolution. An established church is supported by public monies collected from the taxpayers. After the Revolution, the Anglican Church became the Protestant Episcopal Church and existed on an equal basis with all other churches, with no public funding.

antebellum: Before the American Civil War.

Australian ballot: The long ballot listing all the candidates in an election. This allows truly secret voting. It replaced the one-party ballot, which, when it was carried to a voting box, made a voter's choice obvious to all observers.

baby boom: The rapid increase in the birth rate in the United States between 1946 and 1964.

bankruptcy: The legal status of a person or business that is unable to pay its debts, usually imposed by a court order. The bankrupt individual's or company's remaining assets are divided up and distributed among creditors, who generally get less than they are owed. The bankrupt entity then starts fresh, free of debts.

biotechnology: A technology that uses biological systems or living organisms, often in the fields of medicine, agriculture, and food science.

blockade runner: A ship or person who tries to go through a blockade. A blockade is a shutting off of a place or region by hostile troops or ships.

bond rating: A grade given to bonds to indicate the issuer's financial strength, the ability to pay back a bond's principal and the interest in a timely way. The highest rating is AAA, the lowest C or D, depending on the organization making the rating.

brownfield: A piece of land, generally a former industrial or commercial site, polluted during its previous usage. Generally, brownfields must be cleaned up before being used for a new purpose.

capital: Assets that produce income. In the colonial economy, these included land, laborers, crops, livestock, buildings for storing crops and sheltering animals, orchards, and farm equipment. As the economy modernized, capital came to include factories, machinery, and stocks and bonds.

charter: The document that confirmed the grant of the Maryland colony to Cecilius Calvert and his heirs. The charter defined the powers given to Lord Baltimore as the colony's proprietor.

colonization: The establishment of a colony in territory that is distant from the homeland of the colony's settlers.

consolidation: Merging together of many companies into a few or one.

Continental army: Established in June 1775; the regular troops of the American army during the War of Independence. General George Washington served as commander-in-chief. The number of army troops never amounted to more than 25,000. The Continental army was disbanded in 1784.

contraband: Unlawful or prohibited trade; smuggled goods. During the Civil War, an enslaved person who fled to or was smuggled behind Union lines.

country and court parties: Neither was a political party in the modern sense. The "country" party consisted of a group of men who united on various issues in opposition to the proprietor and his officials in Maryland. Proprietary supporters made up the "court" party.

demagogue: A political leader who gains power and popularity by arousing the emotions, passions, and prejudices of the people.

demography: The study of people, their distribution, and their characteristics.

direct relief: Funds or goods given to the poor without obliging them to work in exchange for the funds or goods.

diversification: A usually desirable economic strategy, in which many different kinds of industry are operating. In Baltimore, for example, factories manufactured items ranging from clothing and soap to iron and steel. Thus, Baltimore had a diverse economy.

electors: People elected in order to select other officers of government. The Senate established under the first Maryland constitution was chosen by electors rather than directly by voters. The use of electors was viewed as a check against excessive democracy.

embargo: An order from the central government stopping all foreign commerce in and out of the ports.

enfranchisement: The act of admission to full citizenship, especially the right to vote.

external tax: Duties, or taxes, levied on items of commerce. External taxes were charged on most items imported into the American colonies from England. The selling price of these goods included the amount of the tax.

extralegal government: A government that functions without a basis in existing law. The convention government that came into being in Maryland in 1774 was extralegal; the legally established government under the charter of Maryland was that of the proprietor, but it no longer had the power to rule.

foreclosure: A forcible sale of a home, farm, or business when the owners are unable to meet mortgage payments.

freemen: In colonial Maryland, men who had paid for their own passage to the New World and thus enjoyed full legal rights. As indentured servants worked off their terms of service, they also became freemen.

General Assembly: The state legislature, or representative branch of the Maryland government. *See also* Lower House; Upper House.

genome: All the genetic information, such as DNA, in a person or other living entity, including animals and plants.

gentry: The upper or elite strata of colonial society, usually the large planters as well as government officials, professional men, and merchants. Gentry men controlled most local offices, sat in the Upper House, and filled most of the seats in the Lower House of the Assembly.

graft: Money acquired dishonestly in exchange for political favors.

Great Britain: The kingdom formed by the union of the Kingdom of England (England and Wales) with the Kingdom of Scotland in 1707.

habeas corpus: A legal expression first used in medieval England meaning "you have the body." In law it is a written requirement that a court decides the legality of a prisoner's detention.

Harlem Renaissance: A remarkable flowering of the arts in the black community in the 1920s. Although the term originated in the Harlem section of New York City, it came to include black cultural and artistic accomplishments throughout the United States.

impressment: The practice or act of forcing men or property into service.

indentured servant: An individual who signed a legal document, known as an indenture, agreeing to serve for a term of years in exchange for passage to the colonies. The term generally ranged between four and seven years.

indict: Formally accuse by a grand jury.

infrastructure: Basic facilities and installations, including dams, power lines, railroads, roads, and sewers.

internal improvements: A term describing transportation infrastructure projects, such as roads, turnpikes, canals, and railroads.

internal taxes: Taxes charged on goods and services at the time of sale or use. The Stamp Act was an internal tax because it required that tax stamps be purchased in the colonies for various commodities, newspapers, and documents filed in court.

inventory: A stock of goods already produced or acquired and held in reserve or in storage until needed for sale or use.

ironclad oaths: The oaths used in the Civil War that included swearing that aid or support had never been given to the Confederate government.

Ku Klux Klan (KKK): A secret organization formed after the Civil War to terrorize newly freed slaves. It experienced a major national revival during the 1920s, when its campaign of hatred was extended to immigrants, Roman Catholics, and Jews.

lieutenant governor: Office holder similar to a vice president, but at the state level.

Lower House: In the colonial period, the elected branch of the General Assembly. Now the House of Delegates.

Loyalist: A person who remained loyal to England during the War of Independence; also called a Tory.

manor: A large holding of land, carrying special privileges. In colonial Maryland, the owner could call himself lord of his manor and could hold special manorial courts.

manumission: A legal act that freed an enslaved person.

mercenary: A foreigner hired for pay to serve in another country's army.

mobilization: Getting men and military equipment ready to enter a war.

moveable wealth: Wealth in the form of moveable goods, such as farm animals, silverware, or furniture.

nativism: Anti-Catholic, anti-immigrant prejudice and actions; especially prevalent in the 1850s in Maryland.

naturalization: The process by which foreign-born immigrants become citizens of the United States.

nonexportation: Prohibition against exporting goods abroad. Although the colonies depended heavily on exports for income, nonexportation was added to nonimportation to heighten the economic impact of the protest against English policies.

nonimportation: Prohibition against importing goods from abroad. In the years before the War of Independence, colonists used this tactic to bring economic pressure against England. Nonimportation hurt British merchants who specialized in exporting goods to the colonies.

nonpartisan: Not controlled by any single party; beyond party interests.

nonprofit institutions: Also called not-for-profit institutions. These organizations and companies work for the public good. They do not make a profit to distribute to their owners. Their employees do, generally, receive salaries. Many small nonprofits rely on volunteer labor and a small paid or volunteer staff.

Parliament: The legislative branch of the British government, consisting of the hereditary House of Lords and the elected House of Commons.

party convention: A gathering to nominate candidates to run for office that came into use during the Jackson administration. An official party nomination was intended to discourage independent candidates and to unify various factions behind a party's choice.

patronage: The granting of favors, such as offices, contracts, or similar benefits. Patronage jobs are positions received through political favoritism.

peonage: A system of bond labor that some white Marylanders tried to install after emancipation. Blacks were to be forced to work for individuals and could not leave the employ of their "master."

per capita income: Income for each "head" or person, calculated by dividing total income for a given area by population.

perjury: Lying while under oath in a court of law.

philanthropy: The practice of helping others, especially through acts of service or charitable donations.

pogrom: An organized massacre or attack on Jews, especially in czarist Russia.

primary election: An election to choose party nominees to run in the general election. Voters, rather than party leaders, choose among all candidates seeking nomination by a particular party.

privateers: Ship captains licensed to attack and harass an enemy's commerce. During the War of 1812, many sailed from Baltimore.

progressives: Reformers in the late nineteenth and early twentieth centuries who were especially concerned with ending political corruption and improving social conditions. The Progressive Party was a short-lived political party that embraced these principles.

prohibition: The political reform movement for passage of a constitutional amendment forbidding the sale or consumption of alcoholic beverages. Also the period of time during which the Eighteenth Amendment was in effect.

propaganda: Biased appeals to emotional fears, often used in time of war to portray an enemy as evil or uncivilized.

proprietary official: An officer, such as the governor, appointed by the proprietor to oversee his affairs and protect his interests in the colony.

proprietor: A person holding legal title to property. Maryland's proprietor was Lord Baltimore, owner of the colony's land under the 1632 charter that gave the colony to Cecilius Calvert, second Lord Baltimore, and his heirs forever, with specific powers of governance.

quitrent: A small monetary payment made by the owner of land to the person who originally granted title to the land. The payment replaced certain obligations, holdovers from the feudal system, which would otherwise have been owed to the proprietor.

ratification: The act of confirming or approving. The Treaty of Paris ending the War of Independence, for example, was negotiated and signed by representatives of all countries involved in the war but could not take effect until formally confirmed or approved by the appropriate authorities in each country (France and Spain as well as Great Britain and the United States). Congress ratified the Treaty of Paris for the United States in 1784 when meeting in Annapolis.

reapportionment: Recalculation of the distribution of representatives among equal numbers of voters; required after each decennial census.

referendum: Submission of a law to a direct vote by the people for approval or rejection.

salinity: The saltiness or amount of salt dissolved in a body of water.

seasoning: A period of adaptation to a new land, often a time of hardship and great adjustment. Many colonial settlers and enslaved Africans did not survive the time of seasoning.

separate but equal: A provision of a US Supreme Court decision in the 1896 case of *Plessy v. Ferguson*. The Court ruled that it was legal to provide segregated facilities for blacks as long as they were of equal quality to those provided for whites. In practice the facilities tended to be separate but unequal.

sharecropper: A person who farms another person's land in return for payment of a set portion of the crop.

silting: The choking up of a body of water by fine particles of earth.

Social Darwinism: A belief that the fittest people will survive and prosper, while the weak will fall by the wayside, an especially popular philosophy in the late nineteenth and early twentieth centuries. The rich often cited this belief to justify their wealth, explaining away poverty as the result of being "unfit" to prosper in the new industrial society.

subsistence: The ability of a farm or plantation to produce virtually everything its residents needed for survival. Subsistence farmers or planters did not produce extensively for a market and earned little, if any, profit.

subversives: People who work to overthrow the government.

suffrage: The right to vote.

tayac: The leader of a loose association of Native American groups. Europeans thought of this individual as an "emperor" and attributed more power to him than he actually possessed.

tenant: A person who farms another person's land in return for an annual rent payment to the owner. In colonial Maryland rent was generally calculated in pounds of tobacco.

truck farming: Growing fruits and vegetables to be marketed locally, generally in nearby urban areas that can be supplied by trucks.

union shop: A workplace in which unions enroll all the workers and represent their interests in bargaining with the owners.

Upper House: In the colonial period, the appointed branch of the General Assembly, with members chosen by the proprietor and serving at his pleasure. Members of the Upper House also served as the governor's advisory council. Replaced by the Senate, whose members are now elected by popular vote.

work relief: Government-created jobs whose purpose is to provide work, rather than charity, for the unemployed. The term usually refers to public works projects like roads and parks.

Further Reading

The following list of readings is not meant to be all-inclusive. Interested readers will discover a wealth of information at the Maryland Historical Society in Baltimore, the Maryland State Archives in Annapolis, local historical societies, and local libraries, and through other local groups and associations. Online resources, newspapers, magazines, government documents, and papers of organizations as well as county and local histories available through these sources will fill in some of the detail that more general works do not cover. The *Maryland Historical Magazine*, published by the Maryland Historical Society, every year prints an extensive Maryland History Bibliography listing books and articles on all aspects of Maryland history published during the previous year.

Chapter One
Maryland's Formative Years, 1634–1763

Carr, Lois Green, and David W. Jordan. *Maryland's Revolution of Government, 1689–1692*. Ithaca, NY: Cornell University Press, 1974.

Carr, Lois Green, Philip D. Morgan, and Jean B. Russo, eds. *Colonial Chesapeake Society*. Chapel Hill: University of North Carolina Press, 1988.

Clemens, Paul G. E. *The Atlantic Economy and Colonial Maryland's Eastern Shore: From Tobacco to Grain*. Ithaca, NY: Cornell University Press, 1980.

Hoffman, Ronald, with Sally D. Mason. *Princes of Ireland, Planters of Maryland: A Carroll Saga, 1599–1782*. Chapel Hill: University of North Carolina Press, 2000.

Land, Aubrey C. *Colonial Maryland—A History*. Millwood, NY: KTO Press, 1981.

Quinn, David, ed. *Early Maryland in a Wider World*. Detroit, MI: Wayne State University Press, 1982.

Rice, James D. *Nature and History in the Potomac Country: From Hunter-Gatherers to the Age of Jefferson*. Baltimore, MD: Johns Hopkins University Press, 2009.

Russo, Jean B., and J. Elliott Russo. *Planting an Empire: The Early Chesapeake in British North America*. Baltimore, MD: Johns Hopkins University Press, 2012.

Seib, Rebecca, and Helen C. Rountree. *Indians of Southern Maryland*. Baltimore: Maryland Historical Society Press, 2014.

Stiverson, Gregory A. *Poverty in a Land of Plenty: Tenancy in Eighteenth-Century Maryland*. Baltimore, MD: Johns Hopkins University Press, 1978.

Tate, Thad W., and David L. Ammerman, eds. *The Chesapeake in the Seventeenth Century: Essays on Anglo-American Society*. Chapel Hill: University of North Carolina Press, 1979.

Weslager, C. A. *The Nanticoke Indians: Past and Present*. Newark: University of Delaware Press, 1983.

Chapter Two
The Revolutionary War Era, 1763–1789

Barker, Charles A. *The Background of the Revolution in Maryland*. New York: Archon Books, 1967.

Clarkson, Paul S., and R. Samuel Jett. *Luther Martin of Maryland*. Baltimore, MD: Johns Hopkins Press, 1970.

Eller, Ernest McNeill, ed. *Chesapeake Bay in the American Revolution*. Centreville, MD: Tidewater Publishers, 1981.

Haw, James, et al. *Stormy Patriot: The Life of Samuel Chase*. Baltimore: Maryland Historical Society, 1980.

Hoffman, Ronald. *Princes of Ireland, Planters of Maryland: A Carroll Saga, 1500–1782.* Chapel Hill: University of North Carolina Press, 2000.

———. *A Spirit of Dissension: Economics, Politics, and the Revolution in Maryland.* Baltimore, MD: Johns Hopkins University Press, 1973.

Land, Aubrey C. *The Dulanys of Maryland.* Baltimore: Maryland Historical Society, 1955.

Letzer, Mark B., and Jean B. Russo, eds. *The Diary of William Faris.* Baltimore: Maryland Historical Society, 2003.

Papenfuse, Edward C. *In Pursuit of Profit: The Annapolis Merchants in the Era of the American Revolution, 1763–1805.* Baltimore, MD: Johns Hopkins University Press, 1975.

Steffen, Charles G. *The Mechanics of Baltimore: Workers and Politics in the Age of Revolution, 1763–1812.* Urbana: University of Illinois Press, 1984.

Stiverson, Gregory A., and Phebe R. Jacobsen. *William Paca: A Biography.* Baltimore: Maryland Historical Society, 1976.

Chapter Three
Maryland in the New Nation, 1789–1850

Browne, Gary Lawson. *Baltimore in the Nation, 1789–1861.* Chapel Hill: University of North Carolina Press, 1980.

Cassell, Frank A. *Merchant Congressman in the Young Republic: Samuel Smith of Maryland, 1752–1839.* Madison: University of Wisconsin Press, 1971.

Crowl, Philip A. *Maryland during and after the Revolution.* Baltimore, MD: Johns Hopkins Press, 1943.

Deutsch, Alexandra. *A Woman of Two Worlds: Elizabeth Patterson Bonaparte.* Baltimore: Maryland Historical Society, 2016.

Eshelman, Ralph E., and Burton K. Kummerow. *In Full Glory Reflected: Discovering the War of 1812 in the Chesapeake.* Baltimore: Maryland Historical Society and Maryland Historical Trust, 2012.

Garitee, Jerome R. *The Republic's Private Navy.* Middletown, CT: Wesleyan University Press, 1977.

Grivno, Max. *Gleanings of Freedom: Free and Slave Labor along the Mason-Dixon Line, 1790–1860.* Urbana: University of Illinois Press, 2011.

Livingood, James W. *The Philadelphia-Baltimore Trade Rivalry, 1780–1830.* Harrisburg: Pennsylvania Historical and Museum Commission, 1947.

Lord, Walter. *The Dawn's Early Light.* New York: W. W. Norton, 1972.

Preston, Dickson J. *Young Frederick Douglass: The Maryland Years.* Baltimore, MD: Johns Hopkins University Press, 1980.

Renzulli, L. Marx. *Maryland: The Federalist Years.* Rutherford, NJ: Fairleigh Dickinson University Press, 1972.

Ridgway, Whitman H. *Community Leadership in Maryland, 1790–1840: A Comparative Analysis of Power in Society.* Chapel Hill: University of North Carolina Press, 1979.

Risjord, Norman K. *Chesapeake Politics, 1781–1800.* New York: Columbia University Press, 1978.

Rockman, Seth. *Scraping By: Wage Labor, Slavery, and Survival in Early Baltimore.* Baltimore, MD: Johns Hopkins University Press, 2009.

Sander, Kathleen Waters. *John W. Garrett and the Baltimore and Ohio Railroad.* Baltimore, MD: Johns Hopkins University Press, 2017.

Sanderlin, Walter S. *The Great National Project: A History of the Chesapeake and Ohio Canal.* Baltimore, MD: Johns Hopkins Press, 1946.

Whitman, T. Stephen. *The Price of Freedom: Slavery and Manumission in Baltimore and Early National Maryland.* Lexington: University Press of Kentucky, 2015.

Chapter Four
Maryland in Peace and War, 1850–1870

Baker, Jean H. *Ambivalent Americans: The Know-Nothing Party in Maryland.* Baltimore, MD: Johns Hopkins University Press, 1977.

———. *The Politics of Continuity: Maryland Political Parties from 1858 to 1870.* Baltimore, MD: Johns Hopkins University Press, 1973.

Berlin, Ira, et al., eds. *Freedom: A Documentary History of Emancipation, 1861–1867.* Series 1, Volume 2, *The Wartime Genesis of Free Labor: The Upper South.* New York: Cambridge University Press, 1993.

Series 2, *The Black Military Experience.* Ibid., 1982.

———. *Free at Last: A Documentary History of Slavery, Freedom and the Civil War.* New York: The Free Press, 1985.

Brackett, Jeffrey. *The Negro in Maryland: A Study of the Institution of Slavery.* Baltimore, MD: Johns Hopkins Press, 1889; reprinted Leopold Classic Library, 2015.

Diggins, Milt. *Stealing Freedom along the Mason-Dixon Line: Thomas McCreary, the Notorious Slave Catcher from Maryland.* Baltimore: Maryland Historical Society, 2015.

Dorsey, Jennifer Hull. *Hirelings: African American Workers and Free Labor in Early Maryland*. Ithaca, NY: Cornell University Press, 2011.

Evitts, William. *A Matter of Allegiances: Maryland from 1850 to 1861*. Baltimore, MD: Johns Hopkins University Press, 1974.

Fuke, Paul. *Imperfect Equality: African Americans and the Confines of White Racial Attitudes in Post-Emancipation Maryland*. New York: Fordham University Press, 1999.

Kelbaugh, Ross J. *Maryland's Civil War Photographs: The Sesquicentennial Collection*. Baltimore: Maryland Historical Society, 2012.

Mitchell, Charles, ed. *Maryland Voices of the Civil War*. Baltimore, MD: Johns Hopkins University Press, 2007.

Wagandt, Charles. *The Mighty Revolution: Negro Emancipation in Maryland, 1862–1864*. Baltimore, MD: Johns Hopkins Press, 1964.

White, Jonathan. *Lincoln and Treason in the Civil War: The Trials of John Merryman*. Baton Rouge: Louisiana State University Press, 2011.

Chapter Five
A New Century, 1870–1917

Brackett, Jeffrey. *Notes on the Progress of the Colored People in Maryland since the War*. Freeport, NY: Books for Libraries Press, 1971.

Brown, C. Christopher. *The Road to Jim Crow: The African American Struggle on Maryland's Eastern Shore, 1860–1915*. Baltimore: Maryland Historical Society, 2017.

Callcott, Margaret Law. *The Negro in Maryland Politics, 1870–1912*. Baltimore, MD: Johns Hopkins Press, 1969.

Crooks, James B. *Politics and Progress: The Rise of Urban Progressivism in Baltimore, 1895–1911*. Baton Rouge: Louisiana State University Press, 1968.

Fee, Elizabeth, Linda Shopes, and Linda Zeidman. *The Baltimore Book*. Philadelphia, PA: Temple University Press, 1991.

Gibson, Larry S. *Young Thurgood: The Making of a Supreme Court Justice*. Amherst, NY: Prometheus Books, 2012.

Hart, Richard H. *Enoch Pratt: The Story of a Plain Man*. Baltimore, MD: Enoch Pratt Free Library, 1935.

Harvey, Katherine A. *The Best-Dressed Miners: Life and Labor in the Maryland Coal Region, 1835–1910*. Ithaca, NY: Cornell University Press, 1970.

Hirschfeld, Charles. *Baltimore, 1870–1900: Studies in Social History*. Baltimore, MD: Johns Hopkins Press, 1941.

Kent, Frank. *The Story of Maryland Politics, 1864–1910*. Baltimore, MD: Thomas and Evans Printing, 1911.

Lambert, John. *Arthur Pue Gorman*. Baton Rouge: Louisiana State University Press, 1953.

Mencken, H. L. *Happy Days, 1880–1902*. Baltimore, MD: Johns Hopkins University Press, 2006.

———. *Newspaper Days, 1888–1906*. Baltimore, MD: Johns Hopkins University Press, 2006.

Peterson, Peter B. *The Great Baltimore Fire*. 2nd ed. Baltimore: Maryland Historical Society, 2004.

Sander, Kathleen Waters. *Mary Elizabeth Garrett: Society and Philanthropy in the Gilded Age*. Baltimore, MD: Johns Hopkins University Press, 2008.

Thom, Helen Hopkins. *Johns Hopkins: A Silhouette*. 2nd ed. Baltimore, MD: Johns Hopkins University Press, 2009.

Wennersten, John. *The Oyster Wars of the Chesapeake Bay*. Centreville, MD: Tidewater Publishers, 1981.

Chapter Six
Prosperity, Depression, and War, 1917–1945

Anderson, Karen. *Wartime Women: Sex Roles, Family Relations, and the Status of Women during World War II*. Westport, CT: Greenwood Press, 1981.

Argersinger, JoAnn Eady. *Toward a New Deal in Baltimore: People and Government in the Great Depression*. Chapel Hill: University of North Carolina Press, 1988.

Arnold, Joseph L. *The New Deal in the Suburbs: A History of the Greenbelt Town Program, 1935–1954*. Columbus: Ohio State University Press, 1971.

Brown, Dorothy. "Maryland between the Wars." In *Maryland, A History: 1632–1974*, edited by Richard Walsh and William Lloyd Fox. Baltimore: Maryland Historical Society, 1974.

Callcott, George. *A History of the University of Maryland*. Baltimore: Maryland Historical Society, 1966.

Hayward, Mary Ellen, and Charles Belfoure. Chapter 4, "The Daylight Rowhouse: 1915–1955." In *The Baltimore Rowhouse*. New York: The Princeton Architectural Press, 1999.

Jefferson, Robert F. *Fighting for Hope: African American Troops of the 93rd Infantry Division in World War II and Postwar America*. Baltimore, MD: Johns Hopkins University Press, 2008.

Kimberly, Charles M. "The Depression in Maryland: The Failure of Voluntarism." *Maryland Historical Magazine* 70 (1975): 189–202.

Kirwin, Harry W. *The Inevitable Success: Herbert R. O'Conor.* Westminster, MD: Newman Press, 1962.

Knepper, Cathy D. *Greenbelt, Maryland: A Living Legacy of the New Deal.* Baltimore, MD: Johns Hopkins University Press, 2002.

Maryland Historical Society, War Records Division. *Maryland in World War II.* Baltimore: Maryland Historical Society, 1950–1958.

Olson, Karen. *Wives of Steel: Voices of Women from the Sparrows Point Steelmaking Communities.* University Park: Pennsylvania State University Press, 2005.

Reid, Ira De A. *The Negro Community of Baltimore.* Baltimore, MD: Urban League, 1935.

Schulz, Constance B. *Maryland in Black and White: Documentary Photography from the Great Depression and World War II.* Baltimore, MD: Johns Hopkins University Press, 2013.

Skotnes, Andor. *A New Deal for All? Race and Class Struggles in Depression-Era Baltimore.* Durham, NC: Duke University Press, 2012.

Starks, Glenn L. *Thurgood Marshall: A Biography.* Santa Barbara, CA: Greenwood Press, 2012.

Watson, Denton L. *Lion in the Lobby: Clarence Mitchell, Jr.'s Struggle for the Passage of Civil Rights Laws.* New York: Morrow, 1990.

Chapter Seven
Maryland after World War II, 1945–1985

Bambrilla, Robert, and Gianni Longo. *Learning from Baltimore.* New York: Institute of Environmental Action, 1979.

Bard, Harry. *Maryland: State and Government.* Centreville, MD: Tidewater Publishers, 1974.

Baum, Howell S. *"Brown" in Baltimore: School Desegregation and the Limits of Liberalism.* Ithaca, NY: Cornell University Press, 2010.

Brooks, Richard O. *New Towns and Communal Values: A Case Study of Columbia, Md.* New York: Praeger, 1974.

Callcott, George. *Maryland, 1940–1980.* Baltimore, MD: Johns Hopkins University Press, 1985.

Durr, Kenneth D. *Behind the Backlash: White Working Class Politics in Baltimore, 1940–1980.* Chapel Hill: University of North Carolina Press, 2003.

Elfenbein, Jessica I., Thomas Hollowak, and Elizabeth Nix. *Baltimore '68: Riots and Rebirth in an American City.* Philadelphia, PA: Temple University Press, 2011.

Gibson, Larry. *Young Thurgood: The Making of a Supreme Court Justice.* Amherst, NY. Prometheus Press. 2012.

Hughes, Harry Roe, with John W. Frece. *My Unexpected Journey.* Charleston, SC: History Press, 2006.

Jacobs, Bradford. *Thimbleriggers: The Law v. Governor Marvin Mandel.* Baltimore, MD: Johns Hopkins University Press, 1984.

Lippman, Theo, Jr. *Spiro Agnew's America: The Vice-President and the Politics of Suburbia.* New York: W. W. Norton, 1972.

Maryland Historical Trust. *New Life for Maryland's Old Towns.* Annapolis, MD: Department of Economic and Community Development, 1979.

Maryland Population Data. Baltimore: Maryland Department of State Planning, 1981.

Meyer, Eugene L. *Maryland Lost and Found: People and Places from Chesapeake to Appalachia.* Baltimore, MD: Johns Hopkins University Press, 1986.

Orser, W. Edward. *Blockbusting in Baltimore: The Edmondson Village Story.* Lexington: University of Kentucky Press, 1994.

Peters, Shawn Francis. *The Catonsville Nine.* New York: Oxford University Press, 2012.

Stebenne, David, and Joseph Rocco Mitchell. *New City upon a Hill: A History of Columbia, Maryland.* Mt. Pleasant, SC: History Press, 2007.

Tennenbaum, Robert, ed. *Creating a New City: Columbia, Maryland.* Columbia, MD: Perry Publishing, 1998.

Thompson, Derek, Joseph W. Wiedel, and Associates. *An Economic and Social Atlas of Maryland.* College Park: University of Maryland, 1974.

Warner, William. *Beautiful Swimmers: Watermen, Crabs, and the Chesapeake Bay.* New York: Penguin, 1976.

Witcover, Jules. *A Heartbeat Away: The Investigation and Resignation of Vice President Spiro T. Agnew.* New York: Viking, 1974.

Chapter Eight
Maryland, 1985–2015

Chapelle, Suzanne Ellery. *Maryland Government.* Layton, UT: Gibbs Smith Publishers, 2010.

Frece, John W., and Gerrit-Jan Knaap. *Sprawl and Politics: The Inside Story of Smart Growth in Maryland.* Albany: State University of New York Press, 2008.

Smith, C. Fraser. *William Donald Schaefer.* Baltimore, MD: Johns Hopkins University Press, 1999.

Smith, Herbert C., and John T. Willis. *Maryland Politics and Government: Democratic Dominance*. Lincoln: University of Nebraska Press, 2012.

General Works

Arnett, Earl, Robert J. Brugger, and Edward C. Papenfuse. *A New Guide to the Old Line State*. Baltimore, MD: Johns Hopkins University Press, 1999.

Arnold, Joseph, and Anirban Basu. *Maryland: Old Line to New Prosperity*. Sun Valley, CA: American Historical Press, 2003.

Bode, Carl. *Maryland*. New York: W. W. Norton, 1978.

Brooks, Neil A., and Eric G. Rockel. *A History of Baltimore County*. Towson, MD: Friends of the Towson Library, 1979.

Brugger, Robert J. *Maryland: A Middle Temperament, 1634–1980*. Baltimore, MD: Johns Hopkins University Press, 1988.

Capper, John, Garrett Power, and Frank Shivers Jr. *Chesapeake Waters: Pollution, Public Health, and Public Opinion, 1602–1972*. Centreville, MD: Tidewater Publishers, 1983.

Chapelle, Suzanne Ellery Greene. *Baltimore: An Illustrated History*. Sun Valley, CA: American Historical Press, 2000.

Chapelle, Suzanne E., and Glenn O. Phillips. *African American Leaders of Maryland: A Portrait Gallery*. Baltimore: Maryland Historical Society, 2004.

Corddry, Mary. *City on the Sand: Ocean City, Maryland, and the People Who Built It*. Arglen, PA: Schiffer Publishing, Ltd., 2011.

Cottom, Ric. *Your Maryland*. Baltimore, MD: Johns Hopkins University Press, 2017.

Crenson, Matthew. *Baltimore: A Political History*. Baltimore, MD: Johns Hopkins University Press, 2017.

Cronin, William B. *The Disappearing Islands of the Chesapeake*. Baltimore, MD: Johns Hopkins University Press, 2005.

Cunz, Dieter. *The Maryland Germans*. Princeton, NJ: Princeton University Press, 1948.

Curtin, Philip D., Grace S. Brush, and George W. Fisher. *Discovering the Chesapeake: The History of an Ecosystem*. Baltimore, MD: Johns Hopkins University Press, 2001.

Davison, Steven, Jay Merwin, John Capper, Garrett Power, and Frank Shivers Jr. *Chesapeake Waters: Four Centuries of Controversy, Concern, and Legislation*. Centerville, MD: Tidewater Publishers, 1997.

DiLisio, James. *Maryland Geography: An Introduction*. Baltimore, MD: Johns Hopkins University Press, 2014.

Ernst, Howard R. *Chesapeake Bay Blues: Science, Politics, and the Struggle to Save the Bay*. Lanham, MD: Rowman, Littlefield Publishers, 2003.

Fein, Isaac M. *The Making of an American Jewish Community: The History of Baltimore Jewry from 1773 to 1920*. Philadelphia, PA: Jewish Publication Society of America, 1971.

Fields, Barbara Jerome. *Slavery and Freedom on the Middle Ground: Maryland during the Nineteenth Century*. New Haven, CT: Yale University Press, 1985.

Fitzpatrick, Vincent. *H. L. Mencken*. Macon, GA: Mercer University Press, 2004.

Goldstein, Eric L., and Deborah R. Weiner. *On Middle Ground: A History of the Jews of Baltimore*. Baltimore, MD: Johns Hopkins University Press, 2018.

Harvey, Katherine A. *Best Dressed Miners: Life and Labor in the Maryland Coal Region, 1835–1910*. Ithaca, NY: Cornell University Press, 1969.

Helmes, Winifred G., ed. *Notable Maryland Women*. Centreville, MD: Tidewater Publishers, 1977.

Hildebrand, David K., and Elizabeth M. Schaaf. *Musical Maryland: A History of Song and Performance from the Colonial Period to the Age of Radio*. Baltimore, MD: Johns Hopkins University Press, 2017.

Horton, Tom. *An Island Out of Time: A Memoir of Smith Island in the Chesapeake*. New York: W. W. Norton, 1996.

MacMaster, Richard K., and Ray Eldon Hibert. *A Grateful Remembrance: The Story of Montgomery County, Maryland*. Rockville, MD: Montgomery County Government and Historical Society, 1976.

Maryland Manual. msa.maryland.gov/megafile/msa/speccol/sc2900/sc2908/html/manual.html.

McWilliams, Jane W. *Annapolis, City on the Severn*. Baltimore, MD: Johns Hopkins University Press, 2011.

Olson, Sherry H. *Baltimore: The Building of an American City*. Baltimore, MD: Johns Hopkins University Press, 1997.

Papenfuse, Edward C., and Joseph M. Coale III. *Maryland State Archives Atlas of Historical Maps of Maryland, 1608–1908*. Baltimore, MD: Johns Hopkins University Press, 2003.

Phillips, Christopher. *Freedom's Port: The African-American Community of Baltimore, 1790–1860*. Urbana: University of Illinois Press, 1997.

Pietila, Antero. *Not in My Neighborhood: How Bigotry Shaped a Great American City*. Chicago, IL: Rowman & Littlefield, 2010.

Preston, Dickson J. *Talbot County: A History*. Centreville, MD: Tidewater Publishers, 1983.

Reutter, Mark. *Sparrows Point and the Rise and Ruin of American Industrial Might*. Urbana: University of Illinois Press, 2004.

Rice, Laura. *Maryland History in Prints*. Baltimore, MD: Johns Hopkins University Press, 2001.

Sanger, Martha Frick Symington. *Maryland Blood: An American Family in War and Peace, The Hambletons, 1657 to Present*. Baltimore: Maryland Historical Society, 2016.

Scharf, J. Thomas. *A History of Baltimore City and County*. 3 vols. Philadelphia, PA: Louis H. Everts, 1881.

———. *A History of Western Maryland*. 2 vols. Philadelphia, PA: Louis H. Everts, 1882.

Scheckels, Theodore F. *Maryland Politics and Political Communication, 1950–2005*. Lanham, MD: Lexington Books, 2006.

Sewell, Jane Eliot. *Medicine in Maryland: The Practice and the Profession, 1799–1999*. Baltimore, MD: Johns Hopkins University Press, 1999.

Smith, Herbert C., and John T. Willis. *Maryland Politics and Government: Democratic Dominance*. Lincoln: University of Nebraska Press, 2012.

Spalding, Thomas W. *The Premier See: A History of the Archdiocese of Baltimore, 1789–1989*. Baltimore, MD: Johns Hopkins University Press, 1989.

Stegmaier, Harry, Jr., David Dean, Gordon Kershaw, and John Wiseman. *Allegany County: A History*. Parsons, WV: McClain Printing Company, 1976.

Tilghman, Oswald, comp. *A History of Talbot County, Maryland, 1661–1861*. 2 vols. Baltimore, MD: Williams and Wilkins, 1915.

Warner, Nancy M., Ralph B. Levering, and Margaret Taylor Woltz. *Carroll County, Maryland: A History, 1837–1976*. Westminster, MD: Carroll County Bicentennial Committee, 1976.

Warren, Mame, and Marion E. Warren. *Maryland Time Exposures, 1840–1940*. Baltimore, MD: Johns Hopkins University Press, 1984.

Warren, Marion. *Bringing Back the Bay*. Baltimore, MD: Johns Hopkins University Press, 1994.

Weeks, Christopher, ed. *Between the Nanticoke and the Choptank: An Architectural History of Dorchester County, Maryland*. Baltimore, MD: Johns Hopkins Press, 1984.

Wennersten, John R. *The Oyster Wars of the Chesapeake Bay*. Centreville, MD: Tidewater Publishers, 1981.

———. *Maryland's Eastern Shore: A Journey in Time and Place*. Centreville, MD: Tidewater Publishers, 1992.

White, Frank. *The Governors of Maryland*. Annapolis, MD: Hall of Records, 1971.

Williams, Thomas J. C. *A History of Frederick County, Maryland*. 2 vols. 1910; Baltimore, MD: Regional Publishing Company, 1967.

———. *A History of Washington County, Maryland*. 1910; Baltimore, MD: Regional Publishing Company, 1968.

Wright, James M. *The Free Negro in Maryland, 1634–1860*. New York: Columbia University Press, 1921.

Index

Page references to illustrations are in *italic* type.

Aberdeen, 196
Aberdeen Proving Ground, 216, 255
abolitionists, 106, 113–14, 131, 142–45
"Act Concerning Religion," 16
Adams, John, 56, 88, 90
Africa, 20, 114, 116, 144
African Americans, 140–47, 162–64, 284–90; antebellum communities, 115; baseball teams, *233*, 234; churches, 114, 115, 118, 120, 140, 184; and Civil War, 162, *163*, 200; colonization movement, 114, 116, 144; community leaders, 185, 207, 231, 248, 288; during 1930s, 236, 238, 244–49; early 19th century, 112–16, 120; education, 83, 106, 140, 185, 188–89, 207, 231, 247–49, 287–88, 289; free blacks, 36–37, 107, 112–16, 120, 134, 140, 144–45; impact of Civil War, 127–28, 169; late 19th century, 174–75, 183–84; late 20th and early 21st centuries, 301, 317–21; mid-18th century, 35–37; museums, of history and culture, 337–38; population, 97–99; poverty among, 181, 290; Reconstruction era, 164; Revolutionary War era, 63–64, 75–76; role in Baltimore economic life, 107; rural-urban migration, 230–31; suffrage, 167, 169, 199, 206–7, 223; and World War I, 218, 230–31; and World War II, 252–53, 254, 255, 257. *See also* civil rights movement; slavery

African immigrants, 318
African Methodist Episcopal Church, 114, 118, 120, 140
Agnew, Spiro T., 282–84, 289, 296
agriculture: colonial period, 14, 18–21, 24–26, 36–40; diversification, 29, 98–102, 103, 315; during Great Depression, 234, 240, 243; late 20th and early 21st century, 314, 315; mid-19th century, 132–34; Native Americans and, 9–10; post–World War II, 273–74; turn of 20th century, 194–96. *See also* tobacco; wheat
air pollution, 272, 277, 322, 325
air travel, 228, 272–73
aircraft industry, 227, 228, 250–52, *251*, *252*, 276
airports: Friendship Airport, 260, 272; Hagerstown Municipal Airport, 273; Logan Field, 228; Wicomico County Airport, 273. *See also* Baltimore/Washington International Thurgood Marshall Airport
Alexandria, VA, 81, 83, 93, 99
Allegany County: charities, 184; coal mining, 196, *197*, 210, 277, 302; compulsory school attendance, 189; foreign-born residents, 175; formation of (1789), 101; fracking operations, proposals for, 328; German language, 183, 217; and Great Depression, 238; industrial jobs, 302–3; median household income, 317; newspaper, 217; sports and recreation, 297;

tourism, 304, 305. *See also* Cumberland; Frostburg; George's Creek
Allen, Bennet, Rev., 48–49
Almanac (Banneker), 83, *83*
Alsop, Marin, 336
American Federation of Labor (AFL), 185, 229, 245
American Red Cross, 219, 256
American Revolution. *See* Independence, War of
American Visionary Art Museum, Baltimore, 337
Anglican Church, 23–24, 47, 65, 68, 116–17, *117*
Annapolis: arts and culture, 336, 338; and Civil War, 131, 135, 149, 151, 160; colonial period, 23, 30; early 19th century, 115; education, 119, 120, 121, 189; end of World War I, 220; fire (1883), 181; flood (2003), 329; free blacks, 114; "golden age," 34, 43; historic preservation, 268; mid-18th century, 34, 35; mid-19th century, 135; newspapers, 34, 48, 121; oyster beds, 235; post–Revolutionary period, 71–73, 75, 79–80; railroads, 193; rallies, 230, 335; Revolutionary War era, 43–50, 52–55, 55, 60, 64–70, 82; state office buildings, 69, 281; turn of 20th century, 207–8; urban renewal, 268; utility services, 187; view of, c. 1800, *80*; and World War II, 253. *See also* King William's School; St. John's College; State House; US Naval Academy

Annapolis Convention (1786), 79–80
Annapolis Yacht Yard, 253
Anne Arundel County: Baltimore Light Rail connections, 308; colonial period, 16, 21, 30, 35; covered mall, first, 265; education, 189; farmland, 194; high-tech firms, 303; land annexation, by Baltimore City (1918), 227; medical care, 184, 191; railroads, 192–93, 219; shipyards, 30; steamboats, 192; suburbia, 264. *See also* Annapolis; Baltimore/Washington International Thurgood Marshall Airport; Fort George G. Meade; Severna Park
annexations, by Baltimore, 192, 227
Antietam National Battlefield, Sharpsburg, 304. *See also* Battle of Antietam
Antifederalists, 81
Appalachian Mountains, 8, 34, 75, 221, 270, 294
Appalachian region, 8, 34, 143
Appomattox, VA, 159
apportionment, 166, 282
apprenticeship, 105–6, 320, 321
Ark (ship), 6, *6*, 7–8, 11, 297
armed forces, British: convoy for tobacco fleet, 24; during French and Indian War, 34; during War of 1812, 82, 89–97; during War of Independence, 56, 61–64, 69–71
armed forces, Confederate: at Antietam, 157–58; campaign diary, 155; Maryland regiment, 150
armed forces, US: Civil War, 155, 156, 160, 162; desegregation of, 255; Spanish-American War, 204; War of 1812, 89–97; War of Independence, 56, 61, 62, 64, 65, 70, 82, 89; World War I, 217–19; World War II, 250–57
Articles of Confederation, 73, 78–80, 83
artisan system, 105
artists: Grace Hartigan, 338; Connie Imboden, 338; Joshua Johnson, 114, 122; Mervyn Jules, 247, *247*; Charles Willson Peale, 20, *47*, 70, 67; Rembrandt Peale, 122; Joyce Scott, 338
arts and culture, 34–35, 121–22, 231–33, 296–97, 336–39. *See also* artists; concert halls and theaters; music; musicians; writers

Asian immigrants, 206, 301, 317–20, *320*
Association of Freemen, 55–56
athletes, baseball: James Emory "Jimmie" Foxx, 233, *234*; Elrod Hendricks, 298; Dave McNally, 298; Jim Palmer, 297; John Wesley "Boog" Powell, 297, *298*; Brooks Robinson, 297, *298*; Frank Robinson, 297; George Herman "Babe" Ruth, 233–34; Earl Weaver, 298
athletes, football: Raymond Berry, 297; Art Donovan, 297; Ray Lewis, *340*; Gino Marchetti, 297; Lenny Moore, 297; Shannon Sharpe, *340*; Johnny Unitas, 297
athletes, Olympics, 341
automobiles: effects of, 225–27; and mass transit, 272; ownership, expansion of, 218, 221, *221*, 225, 260; and recreation, 226; and suburbs, 265
Avalon Nail and Iron Works, *111*

baby boom, 261, 277, 279, 295
Baltimore, 103–8; annexations of suburbs, 192, 227; antebellum free black community, 114–15, 120, 122; arts and culture, 121–22, 232, 296, 336–39; blue-collar workers, 276; city council, 182, 207; and Civil War, 131, 150, *151*, 160; colonial period, 30, 31, 32, *32*, 34; and constitution of 1851, 125; as Democratic stronghold, 330, 331–32; Dickeyville, 101; early political parties, 87–88; economy of, 74, 134–35; education, 119–20, 140, 188, 189, 248–49, 322; end of World War II, 256; enslaved people, 141, 142; fire of 1904, 180, *180*, 181; foreign-born residents, 86, 122, 175, 176, 229; grain center, 32, 103; and Great Depression, 238, 246; high-tech firms, 303; homesteading program, 268; household income, median, 263, 317; immigrants, 122–23, 317, 319; Ku Klux Klan parades (1920s), 230; park-building program, 209; population statistics, 263, 319; poverty, 107, 181, 317; and prohibition, 222, *222*; protest demonstrations, 247, *248*, 288; railroads, 193; Revolutionary War era, 62, 65, 74, 103–4; riot of 1812, 90, 91; riot of 1861, 150–51, *151*; riot of 1968, 290; rural-urban migration, 229; school integration, 288; settlement houses, 184; state office buildings, 281; street celebrations, *201*, 220, 256; tourism, 267; urban renewal, 263, 266–68; urban-rural conflict, 108; utility services, 187; and War of 1812, 90, 91, 93–95, 97, 104–5, 275. *See also* Canton; Federal Hill; Fells Point; Fort McHenry; Inner Harbor; Locust Point; Mount Vernon Place
Baltimore, Lord. *See* Calvert (family members)
Baltimore Afro-American, 164, 184, 247, 248, 255, 286
Baltimore and Ohio (B&O) Railroad, 133, 135, 190, 223, 308; construction, 111; funding, 112; strikes, 186, *186*, 229
Baltimore City Fair, 267, 297
Baltimore City Passenger Railway, 192
Baltimore Colts, 297, 340, 341
Baltimore County: African Americans, 115, 189, 286; colonial period, 16, 35; Confederate support, 149; "edge cities," 308, 309; education, 189; elections, 167, 331; farms and farmers, 134, 153, 194, 195, 314; flour mills, 135; foreign-born residents, 175; high-tech firms, 303; ironworks, 30; land annexation, by Baltimore City (1918), 227; population statistics, 263, 264; reform groups, 203; school integration, 288; soil fertility, 99; suburbia, 264; textile mills, 137. *See also* Joppa; Sparrows Point; Towson
Baltimore Drydock and Shipbuilding Company, 216
Baltimore Federation of Labor, 185
Baltimore Gas and Electric Company, 294, 295
Baltimore Hebrew Congregation, 119
Baltimore Hebrew Literary Society, 184
Baltimore Iron Works, 28, 30
Baltimore, Lord. *See* Calvert (family members)
Baltimore Orioles, 297, 298, 308, *308*, 339
Baltimore Ravens, 309, 340, 341
Baltimore Sun, 128, 230, 250, 339
Baltimore Urban League, 287
Baltimore/Washington International Thurgood Marshall Airport (BWI), 273, 308, 312
Baltimore–Washington Parkway, 272

bank failures: Great Depression, 236–37; during Jackson's presidency, 124; late 20th century, 302
Bank of the United States, 86, 107, 124
banking crisis (2007–2008), 302
banks and banking, 107
Banneker, Benjamin, 81, 83, *83*
Barney, Joshua, 62, 93, 94, *94*
Barney, Mary Chase, 121
baseball, 233, *233*–34, 297, *298*, 309, 339; Memorial Stadium, 339, *341*; Oriole Park at Camden Yards, *308*, 308, *341*
Battle of Antietam (1862), 156, 157–58, *158*
Battle of Harlem Heights (1776), 61
Battle of Long Island (1776), 61–62, *62*
Battle of New Orleans (1814–15), 95–96
Battle of the Severn (1655), 16
Bel Air, 296
Bendix Corporation, 260, *260*
Bentley, Helen Delich, 313
Berkley, 115
Bethel African Methodist Episcopal Church, Baltimore, 114, 120
Bethesda, 255, 336, *337*, 338. *See also* National Institutes of Health
Bethlehem Steel, 170, 216, 228, 254, 260, 276, 278; bankruptcy, 303; wartime growth, 250, *251*. *See also* Sparrows Point
Betterton, 192
Bill of Rights (MD), 81, 113
Bishop, William, 184, *185*
Bittinger family, *237*
Black and Decker Company, 228
black lung disease, 328
Bladensburg, 93, 94, 96, 264
Blue Crabs (baseball), *309*
Bolling v. Sharpe, 287
Bonaparte, Betsy Patterson, 204
Bonaparte, Charles J., 204, 206
Booth, John Wilkes, 152
Boston, MA, 34, 50, 113
Boston Port Act, 53
Boston Tea Party (1773), 53
Bowie, 265
Bowie, Oden, 166
Bowie State University, 164, 248, 289
Bradford, Augustus, 131, 152, 158
Breckinridge, John, 147–48
Britain. *See* Great Britain
Brown, Anthony, 331, *332*

Brown, George, 111, 132, 150, 151
Brown, H. Rap, 290
Brown, John, 145
Brown v. Board of Education of Topeka, 189, 287, *287*
Burnside's Bridge, Antietam Creek, *158*
Busch, Michael, 331, 334
Butler, Benjamin, 152

Calloway, Cabell "Cab," 232
Calvert, Benedict Leonard, Fourth Lord Baltimore, 22, 26
Calvert, Cecilius, Second Lord Baltimore, 4–6, *5*, 7, 11, 15–17
Calvert, Charles, Fifth Lord Baltimore, 26, 27, 28, 76
Calvert, Charles, Third Lord Baltimore, 22–23
Calvert, Charles Benedict, 133–34
Calvert, Frederick, Sixth Lord Baltimore, 48–49, 52
Calvert, George, First Lord Baltimore, 4, 5–6, 7, 13
Calvert, Leonard, 11, 13, 15
Calvert Cliffs, Calvert County, 294, *295*, 327–28
Calvert County: creation of (1654), 16; natural gas terminal, 328; nuclear power plant, 294, *295*, 327–28; schools and colleges, 164, 321; sprawl, 325, 327
Calvert family tree, *22*
Cambridge: Bay Bridge impact, 272; blue-collar workers, 276; canneries, 245, *246*, 276; city council, 207; hospitals, 286; newspapers (1830s), 121; oyster processing plants, 172; racial violence (1960s), 263, 288–89, 290; rural-urban migration, 262; urban restoration, 268, 269; waterfront, 269, *269*; workers' strike (1937), 245, *246*
Camden Street, Baltimore: army hospital, 160
Camden Yards. *See* baseball
Camp Holabird, 219
Camp Meade. *See* Fort George G. Meade
Canada, 91, 95, 96, 143, 222
canals, 97, 108, 110–11, 122, 124, 132, 133, 223–24. *See also* Chesapeake and Delaware Canal; Chesapeake and Ohio (C&O) Canal

canning, 171, 172, 179, 196, 198, 276; child labor, *179*; strike (1937), 245, 246, *246*
Canton, Baltimore, 181, 224, 228
Cardin, Benjamin, 331
Caribbean immigrants, 176, 318, 320, *320*
Carmichael, Richard Bennett, 154
Caroline County, 16, 144, 195
Carroll, Anna Ella, 161, *161*
Carroll, Charles, Barrister, 28, 66
Carroll, Charles, of Annapolis, 32, 58
Carroll, Charles, of Carrollton, 57–60, *58*, 66, 81, 88, 117, 123; newspaper debate, 51–52
Carroll, Charles, the Settler, 32
Carroll, Daniel, 32, 80
Carroll, Dr. Charles, 27–28
Carroll, John (Archbishop), 117, *117*–18
Carroll County, 96, 101, 102, 127, 315. *See also* Westminster
Carson, Rachel, 292
casinos, 309, 333–34
Catonsville, 192, 291
Catonsville Nine, 291, *291*
Cecil County, 16, 36, 103. *See also* Elkton; Perryville
censorship, 233. *See also* civil liberties
Chambers, Whittaker, 280
charities and benevolent societies, 104, 107, 120, 182, 184–85, 190, 238, 239
Charles Center, Baltimore, 266–67, 296
Charles County, 78, 125, 222, 318, 321, 327; colonial period, 16, 18, 30–31; tobacco, 18, 100, 274. *See also* La Plata; Waldorf
Charles I, King (England), 4–5, 15
Charles II, King (England), 15
Charter, of Maryland, 4–5
Chase, Samuel: career, 59, *59*, 60; as Continental Congress delegate, 53, 57; politics, 47, 66, 78, 81; signer, Declaration of Independence, 57, 59
Chesapeake (frigate), 90
Chesapeake and Delaware Canal, 99, 103, 224
Chesapeake and Ohio (C&O) Canal, 110–11, 112, 133, 196, 223, 304
Chesapeake Bay, 8, 10, 323; algae, 315, 324; efforts to save, 292–94, 323–25; exploration of, 10–11; fugitive slaves and, 143; during 1920s, 234–36; Oyster Wars, 198–99; during prohibition, 222;

Index 363

Chesapeake Bay (*cont.*)
  recreation, 192, 225; sea level rise, threat from, 329; seafood resources, 8, 10, 276–77; shipyards, 30, 31; steamboats, 151, 192, 195, 225, 225; during War of 1812, 92–93, 94; during War of Independence, 61, 62. *See also* canals; Chesapeake Bay Bridge
Chesapeake Bay Agreements, 293, 324
Chesapeake Bay Bridge, *270*, 270–71, 297, 306
Chestertown, 30, 31, 117, 187, 306. *See also* Washington College
child labor: agriculture, 36, 195; factories, 137, 179, *179*, 185, 212; laws regulating, 209–10, 212
Choptank River, 40, 195
Church of England. *See* Anglican Church
civil liberties, 20, 153–54, 280–81
Civil Marriage Protection Act (2012), 335–36
Civil Rights Act (1964), 289
civil rights movement, 106, 282, 284–91
Civil War (England): effect on Maryland, 15
Civil War (US), 127, 148–63, 167, 200; African American Maryland regiments, 162, *163*; Baltimore riot of 1861, 150–51, *151*; John Brown's raid, 145; prisoner of war camps, 156, *163*; Union occupation of Federal Hill, *152*
Civil Works Administration (CWA), 236, 243
Civilian Conservation Corps (CCC), 242, *242*, 243
Claggett, Thomas John (bishop), 117, *117*
Claiborne, William, 11, 15
clams, 198, 235, 276, *276*
Clifton, Lucille, 263, 297
climate change, 301, 322, 325, 328–30
C&O Canal. *See* Chesapeake and Ohio Canal
coal and coal mining, 128, 196–97, *197*, 219, 277, 292, 294, 302; dangers of, 328; environmental and health concerns, 133, 328; labor unions, 185; working conditions, 209
coastal plain. *See* Tidewater region
Coca-Cola bottling facility, 228
Cohen, Jacob, 118

Coker, Daniel, 114, 120, *120*
College Park, 228, 264, 297
Columbia, 264, *265*, 336. *See also* Merriweather Post Pavilion; Rouse, James
Communists, 230, 261, 279, 280–81, 291
company towns, 170, 196. *See also* factory towns
concert halls and theaters, 296–27, 336; Baltimore Center Stage, 196; Chesapeake Shakespeare Company, 336; Colonial Players, 336; Everyman Theatre, 336; Harford Opera Company, 296; Hippodrome Theatre, 336; Merriweather Post Pavilion, 194, *194*, 336; Meyerhoff Symphony Hall, 296; Morris Mechanic Theatre, 296; Music Center at Strathmore Hall, 336, *337*; Olney Theatre Center, 336; Peabody Institute, 189; Port Tobacco Players, 336; Weinberg Center for Performing Arts, 296
Consolidated Coal Company, 197
Consolidated Gas Company, 204
Constellation (ship), 267, *267*
Constitution, US. *See* US Constitution
Constitutional Convention (1787), 59
Constitutional Union Party, 147–48
constitutions (MD). *See* Maryland Constitution (date)
Consumers' League, 185
Continental Congress, 53, 56–58, 60, 62, 70, 73, 78
convict servants. *See* servants, indentured and convict
Cooper, Peter, 110
Coppin State University, Baltimore, 248, 281
Country Party, 26, 27, 28
crabs, 8, 10, 235, 276–77, 294, 315, 323, 324
crime, 163, 263–64, 268, 333, 334, 339
Crisfield, 172, 198, 235, *235*
Crothers, Austin, 208, 211
Cumberland, 33, 109–12, 172, 186, 191, 226, 305; C&O Canal, 110, 133; coal, 112, 135, 172; factories, 227, *227*, 229, 245, 251, 276, 302, 326; fires, 181; German community, 183; market, 269; newspapers, 121, 183, 217; rural-urban migration, 262; streetcars, 193; urban renewal, 268, 269; utility services, 187; water supply, 181;

and World War I, 219–20; and World War II, 250
Cumberland Cubs (baseball team), 233
Cummings, Elijah, 332
Cummings, Harry, 207, *207*
Cummings, Ida, 185, 207, *207*, 211
Czech immigrants, 176, 183

daily life: early settlers, 14; mid-19th century, 136–37; Native Americans, 9; Revolutionary War era, 43; rural areas, 194–97; slaves, 36, 142; turn of 20th century, 172–73, 177–79, 194–97; working class, 177–79, 182, 187
D'Alesandro, Thomas, Jr., 270
D'Alesandro, Thomas, III, 268, 297
Davis, Henry Winter, 130, 147, 150
de Sousa, Mathias, 7, 19
Declaration of Independence, 57–60, 77, 102, 113
defense industries, 250–54, 251, 253, 260, 302, 304
Delmarva Peninsula, 99, 103, 110–11, 307. *See also* Eastern Shore
Democratic Party: African American voters, 207, 247; Civil War period, 128–32, 147–48, 163, 165; late 19th to mid-20th century, 281–84; late 20th to early 21st century, 330–32; lottery, 205; New Deal, 239–40, 245–47; political machines, 199–200, 202–8; predecessors of, 85–86; and Whigs, 123–25
Democratic-Republican Party, 85, 86–87, 90–91, 96, 123
Depression, Great, 215, 234–39, 260, 303
development, 271; colonial period, 19, 28, 30; environmental issues, 306, 315; protection from, 327; rural land, cost advantage of, 228, 264. *See also* suburbs; urban development
Dorchester County, 16, 21, 24, 29, 38, 125, 143. *See also* Cambridge
Douglass, Frederick, 106, *106*, 107, 115, 135, 140, 146
Dove (ship), 6, *6*, 7–8, 11, 297
Dream Act (MD; 2012), 332, 334–35
Dred Scott v. Sandford decision, 145
Druid Hill Park, Baltimore, 165, 209
Dulany, Daniel, the Elder, 27, *27*, 28, 31
Dulany, Daniel, the Younger, 45, 51–52, 58

Early, Jubal, 158
Eastern Shore, 69, 98–102, 112, 114, 262; early settlers, 7, 11, 15, 16, 20, 21; fruit and vegetables, 135, 234, 246, 274; fugitive slaves, *146*; government and politics, 65, 67, 87, 166, 330–31; Native Americans, 10, 11, 16, 41; navigable rivers, 98, 102; Quakers, 21, 99; rural-urban migration, 262; slavery, 99, 100; state offices, 69, 99; tobacco, 98–99, 100, 112; wheat, 99; white population, 101–2
East India Company, 52, 53
Easton, 115, 221, 265, 266, 268, 269; baseball team, 233; circuit court, 154; historic preservation, 268, 269; museum, 336–37; newspapers, 99, 121; parade (1919), 221; railroad, 195; state offices, 69, 99; Third Haven Meeting House, 24; tourism, 265, 269; urban renewal, 268–69
economy: antebellum period, 98–102; diversification of, colonial period, 29–31; 18th century need for paper money, 28–29; manufacturing, late 19th–early 20th centuries, 172; during War of Independence, 64–65, 75; during World War I, 216; during World War II, 250–51, 274–79; post–War of Independence, 78; post–World War II, 259–60, 261. *See also* industry and industrialization
Eden, Robert, *51*, 51–52, 53, 54, 57, 71
education: 105; African Americans, 83, 106, 185, 188–89, 207, 231, 247–49, 287–88, 289, 321; art, 338; colonial period, 76; compulsory, 185, 189, 210, 212; early 20th century, 224; late 20th century, 295–96, 321; link with income, 76, 319–22; mid-19th century, 139–40; one-room schoolhouses, 139–40, *188*, 196; post–Revolutionary period, 119–21; Quakers, 83, 115, 139; school desegregation, 248–49, 287–88; turn of 20th century, 188–89, 207; 21st century, 321–22, 332. *See also under* African Americans; women
education, higher: integration of, 249, 290. *See also names of individual institutions*
Ehrlich, Robert, Jr., 324, 326, 331, 333, 334
Eight Million Dollar Act (1836), 112
Elkton, 121, 172, 238, 276
Ellicott, Andrew, 81, 82, *82*, 83
Ellicott, Elizabeth King, 185, 211

Ellicott City, 101, 172, 336
Ellicott's Mills, 82, 83, 110, 111
Emancipation Proclamation, 162
Embry, Robert, Jr., 267–68
Emma Giles (steamboat), 192
energy sources, 294–95, 327–30; solar, 321; water, 32; wind, 330. *See also* coal and coal mining; mills; natural gas; nuclear power
Engelbreck, Jacob, 158–59
environment: changes during colonial period, 21; concerns in late 1960s, 291–95; late 19th and early 20th centuries, 208–9; late 20th and early 21st centuries, 322–30; problems of city life, 179, 181
Environmental Protection Agency (EPA), 292, 293, 325
Erie Canal, NY, 108
Etting, Solomon, 118
exploration, 4; 17th century, 10–11

factory towns: Avalon, 101, *111*; Dickeyville, 101; Hampden-Woodberry, 101; Oella, 101; Savage, 101. *See also* Sparrows Point
Fairchild Aircraft Plant, Hagerstown, 227, 228, 251, 252
farmers markets, *314*, 314
farming. *See* agriculture
Federal Hill, Baltimore, 97, 104, 152, 309, 337
Federalist Party, 81, 85–91, 96, 123
Fee Proclamation, 51–52, 58
Fells Point, Baltimore, 32, 105, 106, 107, 135, 181
filmmaking, 339
fish, 8, 34, 192, 294, 324
fishing, 4, 9, 10, 270, 297, 306, 319
Fitzgerald, F. Scott, 232, 233
football, 297, 309, 340, 341
Fort Cumberland, 33, *33*
Fort George G. Meade, 216, 217, 219, 220, 255
Fort McHenry, 93–95, 96, 97, 153, 154
Fort McHenry Tunnel, Baltimore, 311
fossil fuels, 325, 328, 330
fracking, 328
France, 4, 24, 29, 89, 96; French and Indian War, 33, 34, 43, 44; War of Independence, 69–71, 104; World War I, 217, 218, 219; World War II, 250, 291

Franklin, Benjamin, 34, 53
Frederick: arts and culture, 121, 296, 336; biotech companies, 311; and Civil War, 131, 151, 156, 158; diphtheria (1880s), 181; early development, 31, 34, 48; economy, 102, 172, 250, 251; German immigrants, 102, 122; and Great Depression, 236; Ku Klux Klan parades (1920s), 230; philanthropy, 191; railroad, 111; as regional trading center (1860), 135; urban renewal, 268, 269; utility services, 187
Frederick County, 36, 99, 195, 274, 286, 315; colonial period, 16, 31, 35, 36, 40, 47; enslaved workers, 36; farming, 36, 195; German population, 33, 102, 122; politics, 88; Revolutionary War era, 47, 62; soil fertility, 99; sprawl, 325, 327. *See also* Frederick
Frederick Douglass High School, Baltimore, 188, 231, 232, 289
Frederick Town. *See* Frederick: early development
Fredericksburg, VA, 158
Freedmen's Bureau, 164
French and Indian War, 32, 33–34, 44
Frenchtown, 92
Friends, Society of. *See* Society of Friends
Friendship Airport, 260, 272, 273. *See also* Baltimore/Washington International Thurgood Marshall Airport
Frostburg, 181, 196, 295, 305
Fugitive Slave Act (1850), 86, 143, 144, 162
Funck, Emma Maddox, 211
fur trade, 4, 5, 11, 34

Gaithersburg, 264, 279, 311
Galesville Hot Sox (baseball team), 234
gambling, 309, 333–34
Garrett, John Work, 186, 190, 191, 196, 209
Garrett, Mary Elizabeth, 190, *190*
Garrett County: coal, 277; creation of (1872), 196; floods, 244; fracking operations, proposals for, 328; geography, 8; household income, 317; log cabin, *237*; Lutheran churches, 217; mines, 238; resorts, 191–92; sports and recreation, 297, 304, *305*. *See also* Savage River State Forest
Garrison, William Lloyd, 113
gentry, 39–40, 124, 132

geography, 8; drainage basins, 293; regions, 345
George I, King (England), 26
George's Creek, *197*, 277
German (language), 102, 122, 183, 217
German immigrants, 20, 31–32, 56, 86, 102, 122, 134–35, 167, 175, 183, 198; ethnic associations, 167; industrial workers, 31, *134*, 135
Germany: World War I, 216, 217; World War II, 250, 253, 255. *See also* German immigrants
Gettysburg, PA, 158
Gibbons, James Cardinal, 183, 206
Glendening, Parris N., 309, 322, 324, 325, 326, 331, 333
Glenn L. Martin Company, 228, 250, 251, *251*, 254
global warming, 325, 329
Glorious Revolution (1689), 23
Goddard, Mary Katherine, 48
Goddard, Robert H., 253
Goddard Space Flight Center, Greenbelt, 279, 304, 311
Goldsborough, Phillips Lee, 208, 210, 211
Goldsborough, Robert, 53, 66
Goldsborough, William, 155
Goldstein, Louis, 283
Good Intent (brigantine), 50, 54
Gorman, Arthur Pue, *202*, 202–6, 208
Gorsuch, Edward, 145
Goucher College, Towson, 189
government: colonial period, 13–14, 15–17, 27; early 19th century, 89; legal establishment of slavery, 19; overthrow of proprietary government, 15–17, 22–23; Revolutionary War era, 53–54, 56; royal period, 22–24; rural v. urban, 67–68; under charter, 4–5; under constitution of 1776, 65–69; under constitution of 1851, 125; under constitution of 1867, 166
governor's office: regional rotation of, 124, 125
Grasty, Charles J., 204–5
Great Britain, 41, 57, 65, 68, 86, 112, 116, 117. *See also* armed forces, British; Parliament
Greek immigrants, 229
Green, Anne Catharine (Anne Catherine Hoof Green), 47, 48

Green, Jonas, 47, 48
Greenbelt, 241, *241*, 265, 279, 311
Gruber's German Almanac, 102
Gunnison, William, 144

Hagerstown, 31, 34, 87, 102, 121, 128, 172, 273; aircraft plant, 227, 228, 251, 252; airport, 273; army units, 204; arts and culture, 296, 336, 337; blue-collar workers, 276; and Civil War, 157; correctional facilities, 306; farms, 195, 262; fire (1871), 181; library, 191; Public Square, *194*; rural-urban migration, 262; suburbs, 263
Hamilton, Alexander, 86, 87, 88
Hanson, Alexander C., 90, 91
Hanson, John, 73, *73*
Harborplace, Baltimore, 266, 267, *267*
Harford, Henry, 52, 75
Harford Community College, Bel Air, 321
Harford County, 78, 99, 196, 264, 296, 312. *See also* Aberdeen; Aberdeen Proving Ground; Bel Air; Berkley; Havre de Grace
Harper, Frances Ellen Watkins, 121, 122, 140
Harpers Ferry, WV, 145, 157
Harpers Ferry National Historical Park, MD-VA-WV, 304
Havre de Grace, 92, *93*, 103, 196
health and health care: cost of, 279; environmental issues, 328; immigrants, as workforce in, 319; inferiority for African Americans, 211; influenza epidemic (1918–19), 220; Johns Hopkins, later 19th-century leadership, 189, 209; malaria, 25; mid-19th century, 137–38; military, during World War II, 254; sanitation, 179–81, 185; smallpox, 21, 181. *See also* tuberculosis; typhoid fever
Hecht, Simeon, 136
Henrietta Maria, Queen (England), 4
Hibernian Society, 122, 183
Hicks, Thomas, 131, 132, 149–51
Hogan, Lawrence J., Jr., 331, *331*, 332
Hood, Zachariah, 44
Hood College, Frederick, 212
Hopkins, Johns, 189, 190, *190*
horse racing, 34, 35, 334; Pimlico Race Course, 340; Preakness, 299, *340*

hospitals: Baltimore medical institutions, 310; Bethesda Naval Medical Center, 255; Clifton T. Perkins State Hospital, 281; Eastern Shore hospitals, 306–7; Peninsula General, 191; Peninsula Regional Medical Center, 306–7; Provident Hospital, 184; staff integration, 286; University of Maryland, 310; US army, Civil War, 160, *160*; Walter Reed, 220; Western Maryland Hospital, 191; Western Maryland State Hospital, 281. *See also* Johns Hopkins Hospital
housing: alley housing, 182; colonial, 33, 37–40, *38*, *39*; company housing, 111, 170, 196, 228; discrimination in, 122, 176, 182, 211, 231, 287, 288, 290; laws and standards, 263, 264, 322; New Deal programs, 240, 241, 242; overcrowded conditions, 179, 181, 231, 246, 263, 284–85, 290; post–World War II, 260, 261, 262, 265; public housing projects, 260, 263, 268; row houses, 182, 241, 268; rural, 237; slums, 205; suburban growth, 226, 250, 325; urban renewal, 266, 267, 268; wartime housing units, 254
Houston, Charles, 249, *249*, 287
Howard County, 101, 264, 278, 281, 303, 317, 319. *See also* Columbia; Ellicott City
Hughes, Harry, 283, 284
Hughesville, 274
hurricanes, 271, 329, *329*
Hyattsville, 230, 337

immigration: colonial period, 12, 20–21, 32; late 18th and early 19th centuries, 98, 102, 122–23; late 19th and early 20th centuries, 169, 175–79, 182–84, 195, 198, 201, 229; late 20th and early 21st centuries, 301, 317–20; post–World War II, 262. *See also specific nationalities*
indentured servants. *See* servants, indentured and convict
Independence, War of: Boston Tea Party, 53; burning of the *Peggy Stewart*, 54–55, *55*; Fee Proclamation, 51–52, 58; First Continental Congress, 53; independence, 57–61; and Maryland, 47–49, 51–53, 61–65, 71–77; nonimportation, 50–51; opposition to independence, 56–57; revolutionary governments, 53–57;

Stamp Act (1765), 44–47, 52, 60; Sugar Act (1764), 44; Tea Act (1773), 52–53, 68; Townshend Acts (1767), 49–50, 52; Virginia Resolution (1776), 57
Industrial Revolution, 101, 259, 278
industry and industrialization: colonial period, 30, 31, 32; early 19th century, 100, 101, 103, 111, 121; effects of, 172–82, 292–93; information technology, shift to, 278–79; late 20th and early 21st centuries, 302–3, 315; mid-19th century, 135–36; post–Civil War period, 169–71; post–World War I period, 227–28; during War of Independence, 62; during World War II, 250–52. *See also* aircraft industry; defense industries; ironworks; labor unions; lumber industry; mills; progressives; seafood; shipbuilding; shipping; steel industry; textile industry
Information Revolution, 259, 273, 278
infrastructure, 226, 266, 306, 311–12, 325. *See also* canals; Chesapeake Bay Bridge; rail transportation; roads
Ingle's Rebellion, 15, 17
Inner Harbor, Baltimore, 267, 267, 268, 309, 341
internal improvements: antebellum period, 108–112. *See also* canals; rail transportation; roads
Irish immigrants, 31, 86, 122, 129, 134, 167, 179, 182–83; Hibernian Free School, 183; industrial workers, 86, 134, 135; poverty and discrimination, 122, 183
ironworks, 28, 30, 30, 32, 111
Italian immigrants, 183, 198, 229

J. S. Farrand Packing Company, 179
Jackson, Andrew, 121, 123–24
Jackson, Lillie May Carroll, 247, 281, 286, 286, 287
James I, King (England), 4
James II, King (England), 23
Japan, 250, 259, 260, 274
Jazz Age, 231–33, 232
Jefferson, Thomas, 81, 82, 86, 88, 89
Jenifer, Daniel of St. Thomas, 80
Jewish immigrants, 183–84. *See also* Polish immigrants; Russian immigrants

Jews, 138, 183–84, 335; discrimination against, 68, 118, 182, 228, 231; and evening school, 184; Ku Klux Klan and, 230; rejection of Poe amendment, 206; voting rights, 68, 118–19, 123; and World War I, 217
John Brown's raid, 145
Johns Hopkins Applied Physics Laboratory (APL), Laurel, 279, 304, 311
Johns Hopkins Hospital, Baltimore, 209, 219, 220, 303, 310
Johns Hopkins School of Medicine, Baltimore, 190, 209, 254–55
Johns Hopkins University, Baltimore, 224, 239, 303–4
Johnson, Thomas, 53, 57, 81
Jones Falls, 32, 101, 136, 137, 138, 237
Jones Town, 32. *See also* Baltimore
Joppa, 30–31
journeymen, 105–6

Kelly-Springfield Tire Company, 227, 227, 229, 276, 302, 326
Kennecott Refining Company, 276
Kennedy, John Pendleton, 121, 133, 147, 150
Kennedy, Thomas, 118
Kent County, 16, 149, 195, 202, 317–18. *See also* Betterton; Chestertown; Tolchester Beach
Kent Island, 7, 11, 15
Key, Francis Scott, 93, 95, 96
King, Martin Luther, Jr., 263, 290
King William's School, Annapolis, 23
King William's War, 24
Knights of Labor, 185, 196
Know-Nothing Party, 128–32, 160, 161, 202
Korean War, 260–61, 280, 281, 299
Ku Klux Klan, 228, 229–30, 230, 231

La Plata, 243, 336
labor. *See* workers
labor unions, 185–86, 228–29, 240, 245–46, 335
Lafayette, Marquis de, 70
land preservation programs, 327
Lane, William Preston, Jr., 270, 270, 279
Latino immigrants, 262, 301, 317–20, 320, 321
Latrobe, Benjamin Henry, 122
Laurel, 112, 311

Lee, Robert E., 157–59
Leopard (ship), 90
Lewis, David J., 209, 210, 210
Liberia, 114, 120, 144, 318
life expectancy, 137
Lincoln, Abraham, 147–52, 154, 155, 157, 159, 160–62
Lingan, James, 104–5
literacy tests, 201
livestock: colonial period, 7, 14, 17, 19, 21, 29, 39–41; 19th century, 111; 20th century, 274
Lloyd Street Synagogue, Baltimore, 119, 119
Loch Raven reservoir, Baltimore County, 209, 216
Locust Point, Baltimore, 175, 216, 224
Loudon Cemetery, Baltimore, 167
Louise (steamboat), 225, 225
Lowndes, Lloyd, 205, 208
Loyalists, 65, 75
lumber industry, 29, 133, 172
Lundy, Benjamin, 113
Lutherans, 31, 122, 138, 139, 217
lynching, 207, 230, 231, 246–47

Maddox, Etta Haynie, 185, 212
Madison, James, 89, 90–91, 104
Mamout, Yarrow, 20, 20
Mandel, Marvin, 283, 283–84
manufacturing. *See* industry
MARC Train service, 312, 312
Married Woman's Property Act (1882), 137, 211
Marshall, Thurgood, 249, 249, 273, 287, 287
Marshall Plan, 274
Martin, Luther, 80, 81
Martin-Marietta Aircraft, 276
Maryland Arts Council (1967), 296
Maryland Commission on Interracial Problems and Relations, 286
Maryland Constitution of 1776, 65–69, 74, 89, 98, 117
Maryland Constitution of 1851, 125, 128
Maryland Constitution of 1864, 86, 127, 128, 162, 188
Maryland Constitution of 1867, 128, 154, 166
Maryland Day, 11
Maryland Federation of Women's Clubs, 185, 211

Maryland Gazette, 34, 44, 46, 47, 48, 77
Maryland General Assembly: balance of power, 67; establishment of, 13. *See also* Maryland House of Delegates; Maryland Senate
Maryland House of Delegates, 67, 78, 125, 212, 223, 224, 290, 320, 331
Maryland in Liberia, 114, 144. *See also* Liberia
Maryland Institute College of Art, Baltimore (MICA), 338
Maryland-National Capital Park and Planning Commission, 266–67
Maryland Port Authority, 275, 281
Maryland Senate, 66–67, 78–79, 89, 125, 212, 224, 290, 331
Maryland State Fair, 167, 297
Mason-Dixon line, 110, 142, 249, 281, 282
Massachusetts, 49, 52–53. *See also* Boston
McCarthy, Joseph, 280–81
McClellan, George B., 157, 161
McCormick and Co., 228
McHenry, James, 80, 81, 88
McKeldin, Theodore R., 281, 282, 288; Baltimore Inner Harbor redevelopment, 267, 268; Chesapeake Bay Bridge opening, 261, 262; civil rights support, 286
McLane, Robert, 180
medicine, 138, 209, 262, 278, 303. *See also* health and health care
Memorial Stadium, Baltimore, 339, 341
Mencken, H. L., 178, 181, 222, 232, 233
Mercer, John Francis, 80
Merriweather Post Pavilion, Columbia, 296, *296*, 336
Merryman, John, 153
Methodists, 76, 99, 113–15, 118, 120, 138, 139, 164, 189
Meyerhoff Symphony Hall, Baltimore, 296, 336
Mifflin, Thomas, 71, 72, 73
Mikulski, Barbara, 332
Miller, Thomas V. "Mike," 331
mills, 29, 32, 101, 102, 103, 137, 170, 172
Mitchell, Clarence, Jr., 289, *289*
Mitchell, Juanita Jackson, 286
Mitchell, Parren, 290, *290*
Mitchell, R. Clayton, 331
Modell, Art, *340*
Monocacy River and Valley, 31, 33, 158

Montgomery County: arts and culture, 297, 337; Asian immigrants, 319; creation of (1776), 67–68; farms, 194, 195; federal agencies, 279, 304; federal workers, 254, 278; free black community, 115; high-tech firms, 279, 303; household income, 317; Latino population, 317, 319; minimum wage, 316; politics, 68, 90, 203–4, 330–32; population growth, 226, 254, 264; racial diversity, 264, 318; roads, 312; Sandy Spring, 115; school desegregation, 288; streetcar lines, 193; suburban development, 263, 264. *See also* Bethesda; Gaithersburg; Rockville
Morgan State University, Baltimore, 164, 189, 248, 249
Morris Mechanic Theatre, Baltimore, 296
Mount Vernon, VA, 73, 79
Mount Vernon (VA) Conference, 79
Mount Vernon Place, Baltimore, *201*
Murphy, Carl, 286, 287
Murphy, John, *164*
Murray, Donald, 249, *249*
Murray, John, Lord Dunmore, 63–64
museums, 336–38; African American Museum and Cultural Center, 338; American Visionary Arts Museum, 337; Banneker-Douglass Museum, *118*, 338; Chesapeake Bay Maritime Museum, 338; Jewish Museum of Maryland, *119*, 338; National Great Blacks in Wax Museum, 337; Peale Museum, *122*, 296; Ratner Museum, 338; Reginald F. Lewis Museum of African American History and Culture, 338; Washington County Museum of Fine Arts, 296
music: Baltimore Symphony Orchestra, 296, 336; "Maryland, My Maryland," 154; national anthem, 93, 96; slave songs, 146. *See also* concert halls and theaters
musicians, 336; Manuel Barrueco, 336; Toni Braxton, 336; Cabell "Cab" Calloway, 232; Leon Fleisher, 336; Good Charlotte, 336; Hilary Hahn, 336

Nanticoke, 10, 21, 40–41
Nat Turner rebellion (1831), 106, 116

National Association for the Advancement of Colored People (NAACP), 231, 286, 287, 289, 310
National Institutes of Health (NIH), Bethesda, 264, 279, *310*, 311
National Road, 109, 226
National Urban League, 246
Native Americans, 5, 7–12, 31, 33, 40–41, 101; artifacts, *10*; challenges of European settlement, 21; Choptank, 10, 21, 40–41; dwellings, 3, 9, *10*; Eastern Shore, 11, 16, 41; French and Indian War, 33, 34; as indentured servants, 18; Nanticoke, 40–41; Piscataway, 11; religious beliefs, 9; Susquehannock warrior, *11*; trade networks, 10; Yaocomaco, 10, 11
natural resources, 30, 133, 173, 208, 212, 284, 305, 341; bituminous coal, 277; Civilian Conservation Corps projects, 242; Eastern Shore, 306; natural gas, 294, 327, 328
Natural Resources, Maryland Department of, 283, 292, 327
New Deal, 239–42, *241*, 244–47, 250, 265, 278, 279
New Orleans: slave market, 97; War of 1812, 95–96
New York, 49, 61–62, 108
New York City: airmail service, 228; Cotton Club, 232; foreign trade, 223; as former national capital, 86; railroads, 133, 195; Revolutionary War era, 61–62, 74, 103; September 11 attacks (2001), 333; settlement houses, 184; typhoid (1924), 235
New York Stock Exchange: 1929 crash, 234
newspapers and periodicals, 99, 121, 273; abolitionist, 113; advocacy by, 204–5; *Baltimore Correspondent*, 183; *Baltimore Evening News*, 204; *Baltimore South*, 154; *Der Deutsche Correspondent*, 183; *Evening Sun*, 215; *Federal Republican*, 90; *Freie Presse*, 217; *Genius of Universal Emancipation*, 113; German-language, 102, 122, 183, 217; *Kent Conservator*, 149; *Maryland Journal and Baltimore Advertiser*, 48; *Niles' Weekly Register*, 121; *Port Tobacco Times*, 162. *See also Baltimore Afro-American*; *Baltimore Sun*; *Maryland Gazette*

Nice, Harry W., 245
Nicholson, Francis, 23–24
nuclear power, 294, 295, 327–28

Ober Law, 280
Ocean City, 192, 193, 222, 225, 271, 307; environmental concerns, 271, 307; hurricanes, 271, 329; rapid growth, 271, 272, 307; tourism, 271, 306, 307; wind turbine controversy, 330
Ocean Pines, 307
Ohio River Valley, 34, 81, 101, 108, 110
O'Malley, Martin, 331, 332, 333, 334, 336
orchards, 18, 32, 41, 195, 234, 315
organic farming, 314, *314*
Oriole Park at Camden Yards, 308, *308*, 341
Orioles. *See* Baltimore Orioles
Oxford, 30–31, 99, 162
oyster processing plants, 170, 172, 179
Oyster Navy, 198; during World War II, 216
Oyster Wars, 198
oysters, 8, 323; conservation of, 208–9; decline and threats to, early 20th century, 234–35; new markets for, pre–Civil War, 99; 19th century, post–Civil War, 198–99; post–World War II, 276–77, 294; uses by Native Americans, 10

Paca, William, 58, 66; as delegate to Continental Congress, 53, 57, 58, 60; as governor, 71; political leadership, 47, 52, 81; pronunciation of surname, 66
Parks, Henry, *286*
Parliament (British), 37; and English Civil War, 15; and Glorious Revolution, 23; Revolutionary War era, 43–45, 47, 49–53, 60
Patapsco River and Valley, 83; Baltimore Iron Works, 30; Ellicott's Mills, 110–11; War of 1812, 94; water power, 32, 82, 101, 135, 137
patronage, political, 123, 128, 131, 202
Patterson Park, Baltimore, 94, 209
Patuxent Institution, Jessup, 281
Patuxent Naval Air Station, 255, 330
Patuxent River, 94; "government farms," post–Civil War, 164; riverkeeper, 324; War of 1812, 93
Peabody, George, 124, 189
Peabody Institute, Baltimore, 124, 189

Peggy Stewart (brigantine), 54–55, *55*
Pennsylvania: canal building, 110, 111; coal miners, 196; efforts to save Bay, 293, 324; fugitive slaves, 131, 144, 145; fur traders, 34; German areas, 102; grain trade with, 29, 32, 103; nuclear power plants, 328; roads, 108–9; Underground Railroad, 142, 143; Whiskey Rebellion (1794), 87. *See also* Philadelphia
Pennsylvania Avenue, Baltimore, 231, 247, 248
Pennsylvania Railroad, 186, 224, 228
Pennsylvania Steel Company, 170
Perryville, 151, 312, 334
Philadelphia, PA: canals and waterways, 103, 110, 224; demand for produce and seafood, 99, 195, 306; railroads, 133, 198; Revolutionary War era, 53, 57, 60, 71, 74, 80–81; Underground Railroad, 143, 144; and wheat, 29, 103
philanthropy and philanthropists, 107, 189–91; Wiley Bates, 189; Mary Elizabeth Garrett, 190, *190*; John and Mary Goucher, 189; Rebecca Alban Hoffberger, 337; Johns Hopkins, 190, *190*; William H. Jackson, 191; Reginald F. Lewis, 338; Elmer and Joanna Martin, 338; Joseph Meyerhoff, 296; Benjamin F. Newcomer, 191; George Peabody, 124; Enoch Pratt, 189; Philip and Dennis Ratner, 338; Mary Lemist Titcomb, 191
Phillips Packing Company, 245, 246, *246*
Pickersgill, Mary Young, 94, *96*
Piedmont plateau, 8, 29, 30, 31
Piscataway, 10, 11, 21
planters: gentry, 39–40; merchant-planters, 19; "middling," 25, 29, 38, 39, 40; small, 19, 29, 37–40; wives of, 25
Plater, George, 66, 81
Plessy v. Ferguson, 163, 211
Plug Uglies, *130*
Pocomoke City, 181, 314
Pocomoke State Forest, 242
Poe, Edgar Allan, 121, *121*
Poe Amendment, 206, 208
Point Lookout, 156, 163
Polish immigrants, 176, 183, 229
politics: colonial period, 26–28, 47–49, 51–56; corruption, 129, 148, 200, 203, 279, 282–84; in the 1850s, 128–32; late

19th century, 199–203, 210–11; in the 1930s, 244–49; political machines, 199–200, 203; post–Civil War, 165–66; post–Revolutionary period, 81, 86–89, 91, 123–25; post–World War II, 279–84; turn of 21st century, 330–36
poll tax, 24, 68
pollution. *See* air pollution; water pollution
Popular Party, 47–48, 51–54, 56, 58, 60, 66. *See also* Country Party
population: Africans and African Americans, 21, 25; Baltimore, 32, 74, 107, 134; colonial period, 12, 19, 21, 35; by color and condition (1860), *141*; demography of, mid-18th century, 40; early 19th century, 97–98; Native Americans, 21, 40–41; native-born majority, 21; outmigration, post–War of Independence, 75; post–World War II, 261–62; pre-colonial, 8–10
Port of Baltimore, 274–75, 313, *313*
Potomac River, 7, 11, 31, 33, 79, 81, 101, 102; canal building, 110–11; and Civil War, 157, 158; effluents, 324; as source of drinking water, 181
poverty: among African Americans, 181, 290; economic inequities and, 315–16; during Great Depression, 237–38; among immigrants, 176, 183, 318; philanthropy and, 107; rates, 316, 317; rural, 317; turn of 20th century, 182, 183; urban, 107, 169, 263, 268, 317
Pratt, Enoch, 189
Pratt, Thomas, 124, *124*
Preakness, 299, *340*
Presbyterians, 21, 22, 23, 105, 118, 121
preservation, historic, 24, 30, 244, 268–69
Pride of Baltimore (ship), 275, *275*
Prince George's County: arts and culture, 338; colonial period, 30; and constitution of 1851, 125; farms, 133, 194, 195; federal agencies and workers, 254, 278, 304; football stadium, 309, 341; high-tech firms, 303; manufacturing, antebellum period, 112; minimum wage, 316; NAACP chapter, 247; politics, 203–4, 330, 331–32; school desegregation, 288; streetcar lines, 193; suburbs, 226, 264. *See also* Bladensburg; College Park; Greenbelt; Upper Marlboro

Princess Anne, 246, 248, 295, 307
Principio Iron Works, 30, *30*
Priority Places, 326–27
prisoner-of-war camps: Civil War, 156, *163*; World War II, 255
prisons, 281, 305–6
privateers, 24, 94; Revolutionary Era, 62, 104; War of 1812, 91, *91*, 93
Program Open Space (POS), 327
progressives, 203–5, 208–13, 221, 279
prohibition, 221–22, 232, 239, 244–45
Public Works Administration (PWA), 240, 243
Puritans, 15–16, 17

Quakers. *See* Society of Friends
Queen Anne's County, 58, 225, 233. *See also* Kent Island
Queen Anne's War, 24

rail transportation: advantages of, 133; Light Rail (Baltimore, 1992), 309, 312; MARC Train service, 312, *312*; Metro (Baltimore, 1983), 265, 312; Metro (DC, 1976), 265, 309, 312; railroads, 110, *111*, 111–12, 112, 133, 172, 192–93, *193*, 195; routes, *109*, *172*, *312*. *See also* Baltimore and Ohio (B&O) Railroad; Pennsylvania Railroad
Randall, James Ryder, 154
Rasin, Isaac Freeman, 202, 203, *203*, 204, 208
Ravens. *See* Baltimore Ravens
Reconstruction, 106, 163–66, 200
recreation, 192, 225, 297, 304–5; colonial period, 34–35; Gwynn Oak Amusement Park, Baltimore, 288
referenda, 211; Civil Marriage Protection Act, 335–36; constitution of 1864, 162; education funding, 119; gambling, 334; In-State Tuition Act, 335; manumission ban, 147; Poe amendment to disenfranchise African Americans, 206–8
Reform Act (1837), 124
Reform League, 204, 206
Regional Planning Council, 282
regionalism: antebellum period, 98–102; colonial period, 29, 31–32, 35–36; economic, 29–31; internal improvements, 111, 112; and slavery, 97–98; in state constitutions, 69, 125, 166

religion: colonial period, 15–16; discrimination based on, 5–7, 26, 118, 122, 182; disestablishment, 68, 116–117; established church, 24, 47–49; freedom of, 16, 68; German Lutheran and Reformed congregations, 31; Islam, 20, 21; mid-19th century, 138–39; Native American religious beliefs, 9; religious diversity, 20–21, 116–19; and slavery, 76, 99. *See also specific religions and denominations*
Republican Party: African American voters, 201, 247; Civil War period, 128, 131, 147–48, 160, 165; early 19th century, 86–90, 96; late 19th to early 20th century, 200–208; late 20th to early 21st century, 281–82, 301–2, 330–32. *See also* Democratic-Republican Party
resorts, 181, 191–92, 225; Deer Park Hotel, 191–92; Rocky Gap Lodge and Golf Resort, 304; Wisp Resort, 304. *See also* Ocean City
Revolution of 1689, 22–23
Revolutionary War. *See* Independence, War of
Ridout, Mary Ogle, 75
riots, 78, 90, 150–51, *151*, 289–90
Risteau, Mary W., 223, 224, *224*
Ritchie, Albert C., 222–24, 229, 239, 246; and New Deal, 238–39, 243, 245
roads: colonial network, 32; during New Deal, 240, 243; early 19th century, 108–10; early 20th century, 225–26; Harbor Tunnel Expressway System, 281; labor for, 122; post–World War II, 272, 311–12. *See also* Smart Growth
Rockville, 143, 187, 264, 311, 337
Rogers, John, 57, 60
Roman Catholics, 117–18, 138, 229, 291, 335; colonial period, 5–7, 20, 52, 58; discrimination against, 7, 117, 129, 161, 230
Roosevelt, Franklin D., 237; desegregation efforts, World War II, 252, 255; end of prohibition, 244; New Deal, 239–42, 244–47, 250, 265, 278, 279
Ross, Major General Robert, 94, 95
Rouse, James, 265, 266
Rural Legacy Program, 327
Russia: anti-Jewish pogroms, 176; Communist revolution (1917), 230; end of World War II, 260, 280

Russian immigrants, 176, 183–84, 206, 229–30, 318

Salisbury, 235, 297; airport, 273; blue-collar workers, 276; impact of Bay bridges, 272; higher education, 295, 308; hospitals, 191, 286, 306–7; industries, 172; lynching (1931), 246; rural-urban migration, 262; tourism, 265; utility services, 187
same-sex marriage, 332, 335–36
Savage River State Forest, 323
Schaefer, William Donald, 268, *268*, 275, 302, 308, 331
school desegregation, 287–88
schools. *See* education
Scots-Irish immigrants, 102, 105
Scott, Dred, 145
Scottish immigrants, 20, 31
seafood, 170–71, 192, 306, 323. *See also* clams; crabs; fish; oysters
secession, 148–52
segregation, 181–84, 207, 248–49, 255, 284, 287–88
servants, indentured and convict, 7, 14, 18, 19, 27, 37, 64
Severn River, 16, 253
Severna Park, 192–93
Sharp Street Methodist Church, Baltimore, 114
Sharpe, Horatio, 34, 43, 44, 46, 48, 49–50
Sharpsburg, 157, *159*. *See also* Antietam National Battlefield
Shaw, John, 71
shipbuilding, 129, 134, 229, 276; colonial period, 30; Revolutionary era, 65, 103; World War I, 216; World War II, 251, 253, 260
shipping, 62, 74, 103, 171, 211, 216, 223, 292, 313
shopping centers, 261, 264–66, 306, 308, 325
Shriver family, 88, 127
6th Massachusetts Regiment, 131, 150, *151*
slavery: end of, in Maryland, 162, 166; family life, 36; Fugitive Slave Act (1850), 86, 143, 144, 162; impact of War of 1812, 96–97; impact of War of Independence, 63–64, 67, 69, 77; importation from Africa, 35–36, 85–86, 112–13; internal slave trade, 97, 113; religion and, 76, 99; runaway slaves, 97, 131, 142–47, *146*; slave

songs, 146; Underground Railroad, 142–44; "Vox Africanorum," 77. *See also* abolitionists

slavery, Maryland laws: colonial, 19–20, 36; 19th century, 116, 140, 147, 162; post–War of Independence, 75

Smart Growth, 325–27

Smith, John, 3, 10–11

Smith, Samuel, 87, 88, *89*, 91, 93, 97

Smith Island, 273, 329

smuggling, 222, 232

Social Darwinism, 182

Social Security, 240, 278, 305

social work, 184–85, 237, 238

Society of Friends: colonial period, 21, 22–23, 24; education and schools, 83, 115, 139; opposition to slavery, 76, 99, 113, 142, 143, 144; Revolutionary War era, 56, 68; social welfare outreach, 138–39; voting rights, 69

Somers Cove. *See* Crisfield

Somerset County, 16, 29, 30, 160, 317; Almodington, *39*; during Great Depression, 236; proposed wind farm, 330. *See also* Princess Anne

Sons of Liberty, 53

Southern Maryland, 100–101, 123, 262, 333; African American population, 100, 134, 167; baseball, 309, *309*; and Civil War, 153, 156; farmers, 133, 315; politics, 87, 124, 131, 162, 166, 245, 330–31; railroad benefits, 112; slavery, 64, 100, 162; tobacco, 100, 112, 315; urban-rural conflict, 108. *See also* Calvert County; Charles County; St. Mary's County

Southern Maryland, College of, 321

Soviet Union, 280, 295, 318

Space Telescope Science Institute, 304

Spanish-American War, 204, 205

Sparrows Point, 170, 216, 228, 250, 260, 303

sports, 233–34, 297–99, 339–41; jousting, 167, 299. *See also* baseball; football; horse racing

St. Clement's Island, 11

St. John's College, Annapolis, 69, 120, 139, 220; Civil War hospital, 160

St. Mary's City, 10, 11–12, 12, 13, 14, 15, 17, 23, 110

St. Mary's County, 125, 327; "government farms," 164; slave quarters, 112. *See also* Patuxent Naval Air Station; Point Lookout; St. Mary's City

St. Michaels, 99, 106, 227, 265, *338*

Stamp Act (1765), 44–47, 52, 60

standard of living: amenities, 186–94, 215, 231, 235, 263, 295; colonial period, 14, 25, 37–40; during Great Depression, 237; late 19th century, 178; and lower-paying jobs, 303; of miners, late 19th century, 196; post–World War II, 279; sanitation, 162, 187–88, 235, 263, 284–85; turn of 20th century, 172–73, 186–88. *See also* housing

"The Star-Spangled Banner," 93, 96

State House, Annapolis, 65, 71, 72, 73, 75, 80, 82

State House, St. Mary's City, 12, 13

states' rights, 147, 150, 223

steamships, 151, 191, 192, *192*, 195, 225

steel industry: manufacturing centers, 19th century, 172; during World War II, 250–51; post–World War II, 260, 276. *See also* Sparrows Point

Stewart, Anthony, 50, 54–55

stock market, 234, 236

Stone, Thomas, 57, *59*, 60

strikes, 136, 185, 196, 210, 219, 228–29, 244–46; B&O Railroad (1877), 186, *186*; Phillips Packing Company (1937), 245, 246, *246*

suburbs: growth of, post–World War I, 225–27; growth of, post–World War II, 264–66; rural-urban-suburban transition, 262–66; suburban living, 191–94; suburban sprawl, 325, 327; Washington, DC, suburbs, 193, 215, 235, 264, 310–11

Sugar Act (1764), 44

Susquehanna River, NY-PA-MD, 8, 31, 102, 103, 133, 151; canal building, 110, 111; effluents, 324

Susquehannock, 10, 11, *11*, 16

Swann, Thomas, *165*, 165–66

Szold, Henrietta, 184, *184*

Talbot County, 16, 40, 106, 107, 133, 195. *See also* Easton; St. Michaels; Tunis Mills

Taney, Roger B., 91, 102, 145, 153

Tawes, J. Millard, *270*, 281–82, 292, 295

taxation: colonial period, 17, 24, 44, 45, 47–51, 60, 117; income tax, 160; property taxes, 139, 238; suburbs vs. cities, 264, 265; on trade and commerce, 79, 85; as voting issue, 281, 284, 332

Tea Act (1773), 52–53, 68

television, 273, 339

tenant farmers, 37, 75, 234

terrorism, 301, 333

textile industry, 102, 135, 136, 137, 172, 245

theater, 34, 233, 296, 336. *See also* concert halls and theaters

Tidewater region: description of, 8; economy, early 19th century, 132; economy, 18th century, 18; economy, post–Civil War, 164; elite culture, 39; health and sanitation issues, 137, 236

Tilghman, Matthew, 53, 57, 66

tobacco: auctions, 274; cultivation of, 18, 35, 100; as currency, 28–29; decline of, 98–99, 315; environmental damage from, 21; houses, 18, 32, 37; and Native Americans, 9, 10; and slavery, 29; tobacco-based economy, 18–21, 24–26, 29, 98–99; trade, 18, 19; vs. wheat, 29, 103

Tobacco Buyout program, 315

Tobacco Inspection Acts, 28, 50, 51, 52

Tolchester Beach, 192, 225

Tom Thumb (steam engine), 110, 111

tourism, 267, 268, 339; beaches, 271, 307; Eastern Shore, 265, 269, 306; historic towns, 306; service-sector jobs, 309; Western Maryland, 304–5

towns: colonial development of, 11–12, 30–31, 32, 34; urban-rural contrast, mid-18th century, 34–35. *See also* company towns

Townshend Acts (1767), 49–50, 52

Towson, 134, 149, 167, 181, 195, 224; as county seat, 125, 181, 282; farmers market, *314*; manufacturing companies, 228, 260

trade: with Caribbean and West Indies, 19, 29; colonial period, 4, 5, 19, 24–25, 28–31, 39, 44; early and mid-19th century, 89, 90, 113, 134, 135; in enslaved labor, 19, 20; internal slave trade, 97; late 18th century, 85, 86, 90, 103–4; late 19th and early 20th centuries, 171, 216, 223, 227; late 20th and early 21st centuries, 274, 275, 303, 311, 313; Revolutionary War era, 49–50, 52–54, 62, 65, 74, 78–80. *See also* internal improvements

transportation: early 20th century, 223–25; late 20th and early 21st centuries, 265, 270–73, 311–12; post–Civil War period, 191–94; water, early advantages of, 103. *See also* air travel; automobiles; canals; rail transportation; roads; shipping
Treaty of Paris (1783), 72, 73–74, 75, 82
Trimper family, 192, 271
Truman, Harry S., 255, 259, 273
tuberculosis, 137, 181, 209, 246
Tubman, Harriet, 99, 142, 143, *143*
Tunis Mills: one-room school, *188*
Turner, Nat, 116
Tydings, Millard, 280–81
typhoid fever, 137, 138, 181, 234–35

Unconditional Unionists, 162
Underground Railroad, 142–44
unemployment, 124, 246, 247, 251, 252, 268, 269, 290; early 21st-century recession, 302, 316; Great Depression, 236–39, 240, 241, 242, 245; post–World War II, 260
Union Manufacturing Company, 101
Unionist Party, 127, 152, 153, 154, 160, 165
United Food and Commercial Workers, 335
United Mine Workers, 196, 229
United Railways, 220
United States in Congress Assembled. *See* Continental Congress
University of Baltimore, 295
University of Maryland: antiwar protests, 291; biotechnology park, 303–4, 310; established (1784), 69; integration expanded, 286, 290
University of Maryland Eastern Shore, Princess Anne, 307–8
University of Maryland Hospital, Baltimore, 310
University of Maryland Law School, Baltimore, 249
University of Maryland Medical School, Baltimore, 254–55
Upper Marlboro, 93, 274
urban development: early 19th century, 86, 99, 103–8; "edge cities," 308–9; infrastructure and, 171–72, 271–72; mid-nineteenth century, 134–35; planned cities, 241, 265; post–World War I, 223; pre–Civil War, 134–35;

Revolutionary War era, 65; urban renaissance, 268–69. *See also* company towns; suburbs; towns
urban renewal, 263–69
urban-rural conflict, 108. *See also* regionalism
US Constitution, 80–81, 83, 85, 86, 88, 201; Bill of Rights, 81, 113; Fourteenth Amendment, 127; Fifteenth Amendment, 127, 165, 167, 199, 201, 208; Eighteenth Amendment, 221–22; Nineteenth Amendment, 201, 212, 224; Twenty-First Amendment, 222, 244
US House of Representatives, 59, 290, 330
US Naval Academy, Annapolis, 114, 204, 205, 220; Civil War hospital, 160
US Senate, 59, 202, 205
US Supreme Court: *Brown v. Board of Education of Topeka*, 189, 287–88; *Dred Scott v. Sandford*, 145; housing segregation laws and, 182, 207; local African American disenfranchisement, 207–8; *Plessy v. Ferguson*, 163, 211
utility services, 186, 187, 194, 196, 204, 226, 284, 294–95

Vietnam War, 264, 290, 291, 299
Virginia: and Civil War, 154–57, 159, 160; colonial period, 4, 6–8, 11, 14–16, 19–21, 24, 28, 34–36; efforts to save Bay, 293, 324; Nat Turner rebellion (1831), 106, 116; Oyster Wars, 198; Revolutionary War era, 57, 69–70, 73, 79; rivalries with Maryland, 198, 277; Yorktown, 69–71. *See also* Alexandria, VA
Volstead Act, 222. *See also* prohibition
voters and voting: colonial period, 7, 13–14, 24, 35; early 19th century, 89, 116, 123; post–Civil War period, 127, 167, 169, 200–202; Revolutionary War era, 67, 68, 69; turn of 20th century, 200–202, 203, 207–8. *See also* women's suffrage
Voting Rights Act (1965), 289
"Vox Africanorum," 77

Waldorf, 274, *309*
War of 1812, 89–97, 121; Baltimore mobs, 90, 91, 104–5; bombardment of Fort McHenry, 94, *97*; burning of Washington, DC, 82; privateers, 91–93

War of Independence. *See* Independence, War of
Washington, DC: African American residents, 263; arts and culture, 296; building of, 81–82; efforts to save Bay, 293, 324; federal workers, 239, 279; freedom for enslaved, 140, 162; railroads, 111, 312; suburbs, 193, 215, 264, 310–11; typhoid (1924), 235; War of 1812, 82, 92–93, 94
Washington, George, 34, 61, 69–75, *70*, *74*, 81, 86–88, *87*, 122
Washington College, Chestertown, 69, 120, 139, *139*
Washington County, 67–68, 102, 191, 312, 315; Boonsboro, 242. *See also* Hagerstown; Sharpsburg
Washington Monument State Park, 242
Washington Nationals, 339, 341
Washington Redskins, 309, 341
water pollution, 181, 187–88, 271, 292–94, 322–25; Chesapeake Bay, 199, 235, 276, 292–94, 315, 324, 325; ground water, 328; rivers, 133, 325; streams, 196, 226, 323, 325
Waterloo Inn, Howard County, *109*
watermen, 67, 99, 198–99, 234–35, *276*, 276–77, 306, 324
Watkins, Levi, 303
Watkins, William, 121, 122, 140, 144
Welch, William Henry, 189, 209
West Indies, 7, 20, 28, 29, 44, 104, 196
West Virginia, 196, 253, 305, 312
Western Maryland, 67–68, 101–2, 196–97, 304–6, *305*; blue-collar workers, 276; Civil War, 156, 157, 158, 159; coal mining, 128, 129, 185, 196–97, 215; farming, 102, 215; foreign-born immigrants, 56, 68, 105, 122–23; French and Indian War, 34; German-language newspapers, 102, 183; and Great Depression, 234; John Brown's raid, 145; mine workers' strike (1922), 229; native-born whites, 319; politics, 88, 125, 200; poverty, 302; roads, 102, 244, 311; rural-urban migration, 262; urban-rural conflict, 108; wheat, 32, 102; WPA workers, 244. *See also* Allegany County; Garrett County; Washington County
Western Maryland Health System, 305
Western Maryland Railroad, 224, 229
Westminster, 87, 187

wheat, 29, 31, 32, 78, 98–99, 102, 103
Wheaton, 264
Whig Party, 123–25, 128–29, 131, 132
Whiskey Rebellion (1794), 87, *87*
White, Andrew, S.J., 7
White, William Pinkney, 202
Wicomico County: airport, 273; farm products, 195; poverty rates, 317; railroad station, Mardela Springs, *193*. *See also* Salisbury
William and Mary, College of, Williamsburg, VA, 23
William of Orange, King (England), 23
Williams, Matthew, 246
Williams, Otho H., 88
Wills Creek, PA-MD 33, *33*
Wilson, Woodrow, 203, 216, 222
wind power, 330
Winder, Levin, 93
Winder, William, 93
women: and Civil War, 161; clubs and organizations, 185, 211, 212, 219, 231; colonial period, 14, 18, 25, 40; daily life, mid-19th century, 137; education, 76, 122, 178, 190, 212; employment, during wartime, 94, 219, 219–20, 252–54, *252*, *253*; employment, late 19th century, 177, 177–79, *179*, 209–10; employment, since World War II, 278, 314; end of 19th century, 185; Native American life, 9, 10; Revolutionary War era, 76; roles in World War I, 219, *219*; World War II work, 252, 252–53. *See also* women's suffrage
Women's Cooperative Civic League, 185, 231
Women's Medical School Fund, 190
women's suffrage, 106, 122, 190, 200–201, 207, 211–12, 223, 239
Worcester County, 14, 29, 195, 244, 334. *See also* Ocean City; Ocean Pines; Pocomoke City
work relief programs (Great Depression), 240–43
workers: artisan system, 105; company housing, 170, 196, 228; federal, 305, 310; immigrants, treatment of, 198; labor unions, 185–86, 240, 245; late 18th-century Baltimore, 105–7; minimum wage, 316, 335; under New Deal programs, 240–44, *242*; 19th-century Baltimore, 107, 135–36; in services, 277–78, 303, 316; during wartime, 252, 252–54, *253*; white-collar, 277–78. *See also* child labor; strikes; women: employment
workers, blue collar: antebellum, 105–6; during wartime, 219–20, 228–29, 252–53, *252*; early 20th century, 209–10; late 19th century, 177, 177–79, *179*; post–World War II, 276, 302–3, 315–17
Works Progress Administration (WPA), 243–44
World War I, 215–21, 225–26, 229, 230, 252, 254, 255; home front contributions, 219–20; scarcity of resources, 218, 219; victory parade (1919), *221*; women's work, 219–20
World War II, 228, 239, 250–57, 261, 305
Wright brothers, 228
writers, 121, 297, 339; Mary Chase Barney, 121; John Barth, 297; Taylor Branch, 339; Gilbert Byron, 297; Lucille Clifton, 263, 297; Ta-Nehisi Coates, 339; Frank DeFord, 339; David Anthony Durham, 339; Daniel Epstein, 339; F. Scott Fitzgerald, 232, 233; Josephine Jacobsen, 297; Laura Lippman, 339; Edgar Allan Poe, 121, *121*; Jared Sparks, 121; Christopher Tilghman, 339; Anne Tyler, 297, 339. *See also* Harper, Frances Ellen Watkins; Kennedy, John Pendleton

Yaocomaco (Yaocomicos), 10, 11
Youghiogheny River, WV-MD-PA, 305
Yorktown, VA, 69–71